New Directions in the Effective Enforcement of EU Law and Policy

New Directions in the Effective Enforcement of EU Law and Policy

Edited by

Sara Drake

Lecturer, Cardiff School of Law and Politics, Cardiff University, UK

Melanie Smith

Reader, Cardiff School of Law and Politics, Cardiff University, UK

EE Edward Elgar PUBLISHING

Cheltenham, UK • Northampton, MA, USA

Source for Figure 10.2: Anthony E Bottoms, 'Morality, Crime, Compliance and Public Policy' in Anthony E Bottoms and Michael Tonry (eds), *Ideology, Crime and Criminal Justice: A Symposium in Honour of Sir Leon Radzinowicz* (Willan 2002), 30.

Published by
Edward Elgar Publishing Limited
The Lypiatts
15 Lansdown Road
Cheltenham
Glos GL50 2JA
UK

Edward Elgar Publishing, Inc.
William Pratt House
9 Dewey Court
Northampton
Massachusetts 01060
USA

A catalogue record for this book
is available from the British Library

Library of Congress Control Number: 2015957859

This book is available electronically in the **Elgar**online
Law subject collection
DOI 10.4337/9781784718695

FSC www.fsc.org MIX Paper from responsible sources FSC® C013604

ISBN 978 1 78471 868 8 (cased)
ISBN 978 1 78471 869 5 (eBook)

Typeset by Servis Filmsetting Ltd, Stockport, Cheshire
Printed and bound by CPI Group (UK) Ltd, Croydon, CR0 4YY

Contents

Figures

Tables

Contributors

Estella Baker, Professor of European Criminal Law and Justice, De Montfort University

Pablo Cortés, Senior Lecturer, University of Leicester

Sara Drake, Lecturer in Law, Cardiff University

Mariolina Eliantonio, Associate Professor in European Administrative Law, Maastricht University

Mogens Hobolth, Danish Immigration Service and external lecturer at the Department of Political Science, University of Copenhagen

Micaela Lottini, Lecturer in Administrative Law, University of Rome III

Dorte Sindbjerg Martinsen, Professor at the Department of Political Science, University of Copenhagen

Ryan Murphy, Lecturer in Law, Aston University

Carlo Petrucci, Research Associate, Cardiff University

Josine Polak, Researcher, Maastricht University

Melanie Smith, Reader in Law, Cardiff University

Jeroen van der Heijden, Senior Research Fellow, Australian National University and Associate Professor of Environmental Governance, University of Amsterdam

Esther Versluis, Professor of European Regulatory Governance, Maastricht University

Preface

This collection originated from discussions held at a Jean Monnet workshop in September 2014 at Cardiff University's Centre for European Law and Governance (CELAG), a Jean Monnet Centre of Excellence funded by the European Commission. The purpose of the workshop, organized by the editors of this collection, was to bring together a number of leading European Union (EU) legal, political science and regulatory scholars working at national and international level on different aspects of enforcement of EU law and policy. The papers delivered at the workshop, and the subsequent discussions between the contributors, form the basis of the chapters for the edited collection.

This collection aims to provide a foundation to bridge the gaps that have emerged between these distinct disciplinary discourses, and by doing so, engage with and develop new approaches to the enforcement of EU law and policy. The collection explores new developments in the effective enforcement of EU law and examines potential synergies that may arise from these sometimes dissonant and distinct areas of research and practice. In this sense, this collection makes an original and innovative contribution to the literature on enforcement of EU law and policy.

The collection would not have come to fruition without the support of Professor Stijn Smismans, Director of the Centre for European Law and Governance at Cardiff University, the financial support of the European Commission to fund the workshop, and Cardiff University courtesy of its Research Leave Fellowship Scheme. We are extremely grateful to all of the participants at the workshop including Mr Alvydas Stancikas, European Commission, who brought useful institutional insights into enforcement from the Directorate General for Internal Market and Services (DG MARKT), and Professor Paul Furlong, Cardiff School of Law and Politics, for chairing. We would also like to thank all of the contributors for their valiant efforts in responding to our editorial requests and for engaging with scholars from neighbouring disciplines in good spirits. Without this cross-disciplinary dialogue, the collection would not have fulfilled its intended goals. A special word of thanks goes to Antoinette Samuel, whose organizational capabilities meant that the workshop ran smoothly, and to Stephanie Theophanidou and Charell van Rooy for their efficient research assistance.

Finally, special thanks goes to the authors' families, friends and many colleagues for their endless patience and unwavering support which has allowed this project to be completed in a relatively smooth fashion. Sara Drake would like to dedicate this collection to Rod, Isabelle and Phoebe. Melanie Smith would like to dedicate the collection to Vincent.

Sara Drake
Melanie Smith
July 2015

Abbreviations

ADR	Alternative dispute resolution
AFSJ	Area of Freedom, Security and Justice
ANCI	National Association of Italian Municipalities
ASM	Asmodee II database
BAT	Best available techniques
BE	Bespoke Enforcement
BEUC	Bureau Européen des Unions de Consommateurs
BREF	Best Available Techniques Reference Document
CADR/CDR	Consumer Alternative Dispute Resolution
CC	Conformity Checking
CHAP	Centralized database managed by the Secretariat General
CIS	Common Implementation Strategy
CJEU	Court of Justice of the European Union
CLJ	Cambridge Law Journal
CLR	Columbia Law Review
CMLRev	Common Market Law Review
Comp Pol Stud	Comparative Political Studies
CPC Network	Consumer Protection Cooperation Network
CSN	Consumer Safety Network
CT	Correlation Tables
CYELP	Croatian Yearbook of European Law and Policy
DEA	Department of European Affairs
DG	Directorate General
DG COMP	Directorate General Competition
DG ENER	Directorate General for Energy
DG MARKT	Directorate General for Internal Market and Services
DG SANCO	Directorate General for Health and Consumers
DWP	Department of Work and Pensions
EASA	European Aviation Safety Agency
EASA-alliance	European Advertising Standards Alliance

EBA	European Banking Authority
EC	European Community
ECB	European Central Bank
ECC	European Consumer Centre
ECC-Net	European Consumer Centres Network
ECHR	European Convention on Human Rights
ECJ	European Court of Justice
ECrtHR	European Court of Human Rights
EDP	Excessive Deficit Procedure
EEA	European Economic Area
EEC	European Economic Community
EEELR	European Energy and Environmental Law Review
EELR	European Environmental Law Review
EFTA	European Free Trade Association
EIOPA	European Insurance and Occupational Pensions Authority
ELJ	European Law Journal
ELRev	European Law Review
ENO	European Network of Ombudsmen
Env Pol	Environmental Politics
EO	European Ombudsmen
ESAs	European Supervisory Authorities
ESCP	European Small Claims Procedure
ESMA	European Securities and Markets Agency
ESSG	European SAFA Steering Group
EU	European Union
EUCFR	Charter of Fundamental Rights of the European Union
EURES	European Employment Services
EV	Evaluation
FC	Fitness Check
FL	Formal Letter
FTC	US Federal Trade Commission
GAP	General and persistent
GPS	General Product Safety
HC	Home Centre
HL	House of Lords
ICPEN	International Consumer Protection and Enforcement Network
IED	Industrial Emissions Directive
II	Investigations and Inspections

IMF	International Monetary Fund
IMI	Internal Market Information System
IMPEL	European Union Network for the Implementation and Enforcement of Environmental Law
Int J Sociology of Law	International Journal of the Sociology of Law
IO	International Organization
IPE	Investor Protection Europe
IPPC	Integrated Pollution Prevention and Control
ISO	International Standards Organization
J Com Mar St	Journal of Common Market Studies
J Europ Integration	Journal of European Integration
JCMS	Journal of Common Market Studies
JEL	Journal of Environmental Law
JEPP	Journal of European Public Policy
JHA	Justice and Home Affairs
JIBLR	Journal of International Banking Law and Regulation
JPART	Journal of Public Administration Research and Theory
JPP	Journal of Public Policy
JURI	European Parliament's Legal Affairs Committee
Law & Pol	Law & Policy
Law & Soc Rev	Law & Society Review
LC	Lead Centre
LIEI	Legal Issues of Economic Integration
LTI	Late Transposition Instruments
MIP	Macro-Economic Imbalance Procedure
MJ	Maastricht Journal of European and Comparative Law
MTO	Medium-Term Budgetary Objective
NCA	National competition authority
NDA	National data protection authority
NGO	Non-governmental organization
NIF	Neighbourhood Investment Facility
Nw.U.L.Rev	Northwestern University Law Review
ODR	Online dispute resolution
OECD	Organisation for Economic Cooperation and Development
PL	Public Law
PM	Package Meetings

Proc Nat Ac Sc USA	Proceedings of the National Academy of Sciences of the United States of America
QMV	Qualified majority voting
REER	Real effective exchange rates
REFIT	Regulatory Fitness and Performance Programme
Regul Gov	Regulation & Governance
RJE	Revue Juridique de L'Environnement
RO	Reasoned Opinion
rQMV	Reverse qualified majority voting
SAFA	Safety Assessment of Foreign Aircraft
SGP	Stability and Growth Pact
SLRev	Statute Law Review
SPS	Scandinavian Political Studies
SSPAL	High level School of Local Public Administration, Italy
SUP	Stanford University Press
TEU	Treaty on European Union
TFEU	Treaty on the Functioning of the European Union
TGN	Transgovernmental Network
TIPS	Transposition and Implementation Plans
TSCG	Treaty on Stability, Coordination and Governance in the Economic and Monetary Union
TWG	Technical Working Group
UNCITRAL	United Nations Commission for International Trade Law
UNECE	United Nations Economic Commission for Europe
WEP	West European Politics
WFD	Water Framework Directive
WTO	World Trade Organization
YEEL	Yearbook of European Environmental Law
YEL	Yearbook of European Law
YUP	Yale University Press

Table of cases

EUROPEAN UNION COURT OF JUSTICE (NUMERICAL)

GENERAL COURT (NUMERICAL)

DECISIONS OF THE BOARD OF APPEAL OF THE EUROPEAN SUPERVISORY AUTHORITIES

NATIONAL CASES

Finland

France

Germany

Slovak Republic

United Kingdom

Table of treaties and legislation

EU LEGISLATION

Regulations

place within these fields. We then opted to engage with the concept of networked enforcement, from its roots in regulatory scholarship to its metamorphosis in EU governance as 'network enforcement', a mode of policy steering and enforcement. We deliberately follow this model of enforcement from the regulatory, political science and legal perspectives, and juxtapose two studies of SOLVIT, an emanation of network enforcement, from both a legal and political science viewpoint.

In terms of policy areas, those selected have very different enforcement challenges, from the diffuse rights associated with environmental law to the economic complexities of competition law. It was also important to draw out new and emerging methods of enforcement in more traditional policy areas, such as consumer law where alternative dispute resolution (ADR) and particularly online dispute resolution (ODR), buttressed by networks and backed up by hard law, are being explored. Finally we selected some new or expanding policy areas, in this case the area of freedom, security and justice and economic and monetary governance, in order to see if new or expanding areas of competence brought with them new ideas, or whether the same problems of enforcement were repeated time and time again.

II. CROSSING THE RUBICON: ENGAGING DIFFERENT DISCIPLINES IN THE STUDY OF EFFECTIVE ENFORCEMENT

In order to cross the disciplinary divide between lawyers, political scientists and regulatory scholars in the study of effective enforcement of EU law and policy, all of the authors were invited to address a common set of issues, namely, what does effective enforcement mean to their particular area of study? What theoretical or normative lens is used? For example, is 'effective enforcement' explored from the perspective of better regulation, efficient problem solving, improving decision-making, better governance, or upholding the rule of law? How is the effectiveness of the enforcement instruments measured or assessed? What are the new trends or approaches that have emerged or are emerging, and what are the implications of these changes for effective enforcement? Crossing the disciplinary divide proved to be no easy feat. Whilst it may be assumed that EU scholars speak one common language, what clearly emerged from collating these chapters is that the various disciplines attribute different meanings to the same terms and interpret the enforcement mechanisms in different ways. This collection marks an important step in addressing this 'Babylonian' confusion of tongues.

Despite the challenges faced in establishing a true interdisciplinary debate on the topic of effective enforcement of EU law and policy, common themes and cross-over concepts emerge from the chapters and play an important role in ensuring that future research agendas give a fuller picture of the EU's enforcement regime and that, in turn, policy development can be more effective. The starting point in this volume is the acceptance that in terms of regulatory implementation of EU policies, particularly the internal market and its flanking policies of competition, environment and consumer policy, there is an 'unknown universe of compliance'. This makes assessing the effectiveness of any enforcement regime particularly troublesome. The institutional structure of the EU requires that regulatory implementation takes place at national level, but in practice once transposition has occurred, it is at the state, regional and local administrative level that application of EU law takes place. So once the substantive rules have been enacted, a variety of actors besides the Member States are involved in implementation and application. The Commission cannot be aware of all breaches of EU law. Moreover, there are limits to what the law can achieve in terms of public or private enforcement. It is clear that reliance on deterrence alone with the fear of sanctions or remedies is insufficient to ensure full compliance with EU law, but that other forms of enforcement can be effective when they operate in this 'shadow of hierarchy'.

The question of what is considered to be 'effective enforcement' was something which each author was asked to focus upon, and this proved to be a difficult term to unpick across the disciplines. Political scientists[2] and regulatory scholars[3] tend to perceive the enforcement of EU law as effective. Compliance levels of EU law compared with those of other international law regimes are relatively high and on a par with those attributed to national law.[4] Legal scholars tend to fixate on notions of effectiveness of judicial enforcement found in the case law of the European Union's Court of Justice (CJEU). This collection makes an important contribution in seeking to unravel the assumptions made by the different disciplines in terms of what is being measured when we use this nebulous term of 'effective enforcement' and why, and attempts are made to make them more explicit. All of the authors in this collection start their analyses from

---

2 For an account of the political science research on EU compliance, see Lisa Conant, 'Compliance and What the EU Member States Make of It' in Marise Cremona (ed.), *Compliance and the Enforcement of EU Law* (OUP, 2012), pp. 1–30.

3 Bronwen Morgan and Karen Yeung, *An Introduction to Law and Regulation: Text and Materials* (CUP 2007), p. 327.

4 Conant, noted at 2, p. 1.

different points on the spectrum of regulatory implementation, which spans from institutional design through to standard setting, monitoring and enforcement.[5] Whilst legal scholars focus on enforcement in terms of the legal avenues open to individual litigants once the law has actually been infringed, political scientists and regulatory scholars adopt a much broader approach focusing on securing compliance at earlier stages of the regulatory cycle. Their research also focuses on a wider range of actors and considers the impact of different compliance techniques. It is important to recall that the standpoint chosen can determine what is understood by effective enforcement from the outset.

Looking at this question from an institutional perspective, the European Commission has characterized the notion of effectiveness as an element of output legitimacy, that is, effectiveness is defined with reference to policy outputs, meaning good policy management techniques which result in effective implementation and achieving the maximum results from each policy initiative.[6] On the other hand, the Court has referred to the notion of effectiveness in its case law on private enforcement in a myriad of ways giving the term a fluid character whose meaning can vary according to the values the Court is seeking to promote in a particular context, taking into account the interests of the different, and often competing, actors.[7] This gives rise to confusion at a doctrinal level and is arguably holding back the creation of a visible, accessible and coherent avenue for judicial enforcement.

The contributors to this collection adopt a variety of approaches to defining 'effective enforcement', which range from using proxies such as 'problem solving capacity and timeliness' (Martinsen and Hobolth),

---

[5] Karen Yeung, *Securing Compliance: A Principled Approach* (Hart, 2011), p. 12. Regulatory implementation takes place once the overall regulatory goals of a particular course of action are determined.

[6] European Commission, European Governance: A White Paper COM (2001) 428, pp. 10, 13, 18.

[7] See further Michael Dougan, *National Remedies Before the Court of Justice: Issues of Harmonisation and Differentiation* (Hart, 2004), p. 27 who identifies four different manifestations of the notion of effectiveness in the Court's case law: In terms of ensuring the realization of a substantive policy or concept in a practical way before the national courts, the Court refers to (i) the effectiveness of subjective rights when enforced against Member States or private parties and (ii) the effectiveness of provisions safeguarding the general interest as enforced against national authorities and individuals. With regard to the judicial architecture, the Court has referred to (iii) the effectiveness of the preliminary ruling procedure and (iv) the effectiveness of the ability of individuals to challenge the legality of EU acts indirectly before the national courts as an alternative to Article 263(4) TFEU (a claim which is widely disputed).

to those which considered objective and non-political mechanisms to be essential to the meaning of effectiveness (Murphy). Certainly many questions arose as to the choice between conceptualizing effective enforcement in terms of quantity (eg, achieving legal transposition) and/or quality, for example, implementation and application of EU law and the realization of EU law rights by citizens, either individually or collectively. Indeed for some legal scholars (Eliantonio and Cortés) 'effective enforcement' ranges from the availability and accessibility for individuals and non-governmental organizations (NGOs) to invoke and secure the benefits of EU rights in a timely fashion before courts, to exploring 'softer' means of realizing EU rights through ADR or networked enforcement.

Another common approach across the collection is the acknowledgement that there ought to be a careful balance between the quest for more effective enforcement (however defined) and the realization, promotion and protection of overarching constitutional values: not everything should be sacrificed on the altar of effectiveness.[8] Both Murphy and Smith acknowledge that there might be tensions between achieving effectiveness within a regime, and enabling transparent and accountable systems of enforcement. Similarly, Drake's model comprising regulatory goals and constitutional values demonstrates the inherent tensions in constructing and operating a multi-level enforcement regime. How should the conflict be resolved between the principle of legal certainty and the need for regulatory flexibility? Should legal certainty, effective judicial protection and equality be prioritized over legality and legitimacy in the name of 'effective enforcement'? For some, the need for legitimacy emerges as fundamental in the establishment of an effective enforcement regime. In a Union based on the rule of law, compliance will only be secured if it is accepted by the actors whose behaviour EU norms are seeking to change. This has been a source of strife at different levels where the Court has been seeking to create a private enforcement regime through its case law (Drake) and through EU hard law measures (Petrucci). The contribution by Baker which draws on compliance theory in the field of criminology provides important theoretical insights into how compliance could be achieved in a multi-level enforcement regime. Any disconnect between the top-down approach based on hard law and the 'street level' actors required to comply with the law jeopardizes effectiveness.

---

[8] This term is taken from Mariolina Eliantonio, 'Judicial Review and the New Modes of Governance: The Case of Standardization – Sacrificing the Rule of Law on the Altar of Effectiveness', paper presented at the 22nd International Conference of Europeanists, Sciences Po, Paris, 10th July 2015.

Viewed holistically, this collection draws out common themes and problems that may be identified across the wide variety of enforcement approaches, and at times, also demonstrates some clear contradictions. Broadly speaking, the majority of chapters essentially accept that there is no 'one size fits all' approach to achieving effective enforcement, and that whilst hard law has its limits, total disregard of hard instruments is not recommended either. One discernible trend from the contributions is that a 'mix and match' approach to enforcement is considered the best way to achieve effectiveness, so that both soft and hard forms of governance need to work in harmony in order to achieve the optimum level of enforcement. The first task of course is to be able to identify the relative strengths and weakness of each type of enforcement technique before going on to plug any enforcement gaps that emerge, and this task in and of itself proves difficult due to existing and contradicting gaps in the literature and the lack of empirical data.

The majority of contributions include some element of hard law as the basis of the enforcement regime, although that overarching legal framework may or may not provide the means by which the policy area is enforced. Chapter 2 (Smith) on centralized enforcement of EU law has little to say about the governing legal regime since most of the enforcement work takes place behind the veil of diplomacy. The same can be said of the chapters by Cortés, Petrucci, and Murphy whose particular areas of study begin with legal frameworks that ultimately rely on much softer forms of enforcement, from online dispute resolution in consumer law, to soft law principles in competition law, and largely political will in the area of economic and monetary governance despite the plethora of legal instruments.

In those chapters not primarily concerned with law, other concerns emerge. The proliferation of network enforcement, not as a way of ensuring accountability through interdependence as originally envisaged and encapsulated in Chapter 3 on networked enforcement, but as a way of implementing policy without any apparent concerns of accountability, (input) legitimacy or transparency is in evidence. Where network enforcement is considered, it is clear we have travelled far from any pretence of relying solely on command and control approaches. Such regimes are set up under soft governance mechanisms (SOLVIT) and even those that have some legal architecture (Polak and Versluis), it is the perception of that network as a forum for cooperation and problem solving that remains paramount to its effectiveness rather than the overarching regime from which it flows. It is what happens outside of the law, in practice by those who participate in such regimes as well as the 'end user', that is of interest in considering the notion of effective enforcement.

By presenting a variety of approaches which analyse effective enforcement through different lenses, gaps and challenges in the current enforcement framework are exposed and this illustrates how important it is for actors to be more explicit about the choices that they are making between different (competing) goals and values when enforcing EU law at multiple levels and in multiple arenas. Adopting a specific perspective clearly shapes our research questions and answers. It is only by being up front and more transparent about these matters, that new innovations, whether legal or policy based, can effectively achieve their intended goals.

III. ORGANIZATION OF THE COLLECTION

The collection is divided loosely into three sections. The first two chapters of the collection explore the EU's 'dual vigilance' framework of centralized and decentralized enforcement, but seek to go beyond the traditional legal (doctrinal) accounts which rarely assess effectiveness in the operational sense and adopt a more holistic, schematic account. Both draw on regulatory scholarship in order to conceptualize the enforcement regimes as more than a set of legal rules, but as regulatory schemes in themselves which reflect policy choices on how EU regulation is to be enforced. In Chapter 1, Drake assesses the effectiveness of key doctrinal and institutional features of the EU's private enforcement regime including new constitutional provisions introduced by the Treaty of Lisbon and the EU's Charter of Fundamental Rights. By viewing the private enforcement system as a regulatory scheme aimed at achieving the collective regulatory goal of effective compliance of EU law, and mapping the scheme (legal doctrine and institutional design) against carefully chosen regulatory goals and constitutional values, Drake is able to identify where and how the system can align regulatory goals and constitutional values to improve the effectiveness of the private enforcement regime. In Chapter 2, Smith addresses the effectiveness of the classic, public enforcement system set out in Article 258 TFEU in which the European Commission is the chief enforcer of EU law and policy. Smith presents us with a new, layered model of centralized enforcement and laments the inability of scholars across the disciplinary divide to fully assess the effectiveness of the infringement mechanism due to misplaced assumptions created by a lack of transparency at the very core of the infringement process. A more complex, fragmented process of enforcement is revealed, populated by a multitude of actors that are not subject to public scrutiny. What is apparent from these first two chapters is that the simplistic way in which the 'dual track' of enforcement is often portrayed in the literature is far from accurate. These 'gaps' in understanding provide the basis for new research agendas.

The second part of the collection explores the shift in regulatory enforcement from deterrence-based (command and control) strategies to more management focused compliance strategies. There is a particular focus on network(ed) enforcement, with both political scientists, regulatory scholars and lawyers contributing theoretical and empirical chapters. In Chapter 3, van der Heijden, makes a fundamental contribution to the collection which serves as an important platform for future dialogue between the different disciplines and between EU scholars and regulatory scholars in general. The chapter charts the evolution of the regulatory theory of enforcement since the 1980s and evaluates its expansion from relying solely on the traditional deterrence-based strategies to compliance-based strategies. This chapter provides the theoretical framework against which the subsequent empirical chapters on network enforcement can be juxtaposed. It also plays an important role in reminding legal scholars that a full assessment of the effective enforcement of EU law and policy can only be achieved by looking beyond the traditional command and control model from a singular perspective, namely that of the individual litigant. Moreover, it provides a useful reference point against which developments in EU regulatory strategies and, in particular, the proliferation of EU networks can be compared with classic regulatory models.

Chapters 4, 5 and 6 go on to examine instances of networked enforcement within the EU. In Chapter 4, Polak and Versluis provide an empirical study of network cooperation in the EU context. Their qualitative study of the implementation of EU directives on product safety, air safety, and pollution prevention draws out the factors that promote effective cooperation within the networks and identifies the importance of informality and mutual trust and learning. In Chapter 5, Lottini explores a specific example of network enforcement, namely the SOLVIT network, which is a network based in the Member States (but managed by the Commission) whose original design was premised as a 'dispute resolution service' which has morphed into a network that allows citizens and businesses to benefit from EU rights 'on the ground'. Lottini examines this network from a lawyer's perspective and considers the possibilities for effective enforcement at three distinct levels: the individual, the administrative and the regulatory level of governance. Chapter 6 by Martinsen and Hobolth focuses on the same network but this time from a political science perspective, examining SOLVIT as an example of a trans-governmental network enforcement. This qualitative study focuses on assessing the effectiveness of the SOLVIT network itself in managing the practical application of EU law. It uses the network's problem-solving capacity and resolution speed as proxies for assessing its effectiveness. The study makes an important contribution to the effective enforcement of EU law since it aims to identify whether the claims in the literature on network enforcement (that it is indeed an effective method of enforcement) can be empirically proven with an empirical study of the network in operation, in particular, whether such networks work to 'plug the gap' between top-down centralized enforcement which focuses predominantly on transposition problems by the Member States, and the misapplication of EU law in practice by national agencies, which obstruct the enjoyment of EU rights by EU citizens.

The third and final part of the collection analyses new innovations in enforcement in traditional policy sectors such as environmental policy, consumer policy, competition law, and in newly expanded fields, policy sectors such the area of freedom, security and justice and economic and monetary governance. By analysing the different enforcement mechanisms in a specific policy context, we are presented with a much starker picture of the limitations of the traditional 'dual' enforcement mechanisms and how new innovations are being developed to address its inadequacies. Chapter 7 by Eliantonio demonstrates unequivocally how the nature of environmental law presents real challenges for the EU's enforcement regime. Where the law is designed to protect the public interest and does not create individual rights, a private enforcement system predicated on individuals litigating to protect their rights presents severe shortcomings. Moreover, environmental damage cannot always be undone. For this reason, there is an important focus on compliance strategies in this policy area. Yet, Eliantonio argues that the lack of empirical research on whether the use of soft law does achieve greater levels of compliance needs to be addressed. Furthermore, the use of network enforcement can play an important role and should be promoted further. In Chapter 8, Cortés explores the three pillars of enforcement adopted by the EU in the context of consumer policy. This chapter first considers the emergence of network(ed) enforcement in this field before exploring the limitations of private enforcement for obtaining redress where the cost of litigation is likely to outweigh the value of the claim. The author then turns to explore the potential offered by innovations in extra-judicial redress through consumer ADR and ODR mechanisms. For Cortés, only a holistic approach where all three pillars work in conjunction with each other will optimal enforcement in this sector be achieved. Chapter 9 turns to the field of EU competition law. Traditionally, an area where centralized enforcement by the Commission has dominated, and private enforcement has been underused, Petrucci explores EU attempts to change the legal regime to promote collective redress. Petrucci evaluates the effectiveness of this strategy by assessing the Commission's policy process through the lens of input and output legitimacy derived from political theory. This interdisciplinary analysis reveals clear tensions between the 'top down' quest for a more effective private enforcement regime and legitimacy at 'street level' from the actors ultimately responsible for ensuring that the regime works. Petrucci advances the debate on input/output legitimacy by providing new insights into the relationship between legitimacy and effectiveness.

The final two chapters of the book explore two contemporary EU policy areas, the establishment of an area of freedom, security and justice and economic and monetary governance. Both reveal new paradigms in the quest for compliance and enforcement. In Chapter 10, Baker makes an original and groundbreaking cross-disciplinary contribution drawing on compliance literature within the field of criminology and applying it within the context of the new Article 83(2) TFEU which codifies EU competence to introduce criminal sanctions in order to achieve 'effective implementation' of existing EU harmonizing policies. She predicts the emergence of a multi-levelled approach to enforcement embracing a range of actors within a staged process which she terms 'nested enforcement'. The chapter unpacks the challenge to EU policy-makers in using this new legal base to adopt not only new criminal measures but as another step in the construct of the EU's constitutional framework. Baker warns against adopting a top-down technocratic approach which fails to take into account the moral realm. The chapter also presents an important typology of compliance which may have applicability in other policy sectors. In Chapter 11, Murphy critically assesses the effectiveness of the new and revised system of enforcement of the rules on economic and financial governance in the EU post-economic crisis. This chapter reveals the complexity and range of the new mechanisms and instruments being swiftly adopted in the aftermath of the financial meltdown. The tensions and contradictions examined in previous chapters are highlighted here in sharp relief as Murphy explores the problématique between seeking effective enforcement of EU law and the limitations imposed on an enforcement regime as a result of realpolitik.

The collection marks an important step in expanding the boundaries on current legal approaches to enforcement and lays down bridges for future scholarly engagement with neighbouring disciplines in this fundamental area of EU law and policy.

1. More effective private enforcement of EU law post-Lisbon: aligning regulatory goals and constitutional values

Sara Drake*

INTRODUCTION

Enforcement of European Union (EU) law through litigation by private parties before national courts[1] plays a critical role in securing the effective compliance of EU law. This so-called private enforcement complements the public enforcement mechanism set out in Article 258 TFEU.[2] Together, they constitute the 'dual enforcement' system upon which the judicial enforcement of EU law has been traditionally based. This chapter evaluates the effectiveness of the EU's system of private judicial enforcement which has been developed predominantly by the Court of Justice of the European Union (CJEU) through its case law[3] by a process of adjudication.[4] The case law centres around two overlapping and inter-

* I am grateful to Melanie Smith for comments on an earlier version of this chapter and to Stephanie Theophanidou for her research assistance. The usual disclaimer applies.

[1] This is distinct from the rules governing the ability of private parties to judicially review EU law directly before the Union Courts by virtue of Article 263 TFEU. This provision was originally set out in the European Economic Community (EEC) Treaty, but revised by the Treaty of Lisbon to improve 'access to justice'.

[2] The centralized public enforcement mechanism set out in Article 258 TFEU is discussed in Ch 2 of this volume.

[3] For a comprehensive account of the Court's case law, see Angela Ward, *Judicial Review of and the Rights of Private Parties in EU Law* (2nd edition, OUP, 2007).

[4] Francis Snyder, 'The Effectiveness of European Community Law: Institutions, Processes, Tools and Techniques' in Terence Daintith (ed), *Implementing EC Law in the United Kingdom: Structures for Indirect Rule* (Wiley, 1995) at pp 51–87.

linked stages of the litigation process. First, whether and how individuals can enforce rights conferred on them by EU law directly before their national courts. Second, as a corollary, and in the absence of EU harmonizing measures, which procedural rules apply and what legal remedies are available. The legal framework is complex, opaque and has been based (controversially) on a range of legal bases. The Court's policy has fluctuated in scope stemming from the complex interplay of competing zones of competence in the absence of a clear legal base in the Treaties, the different interests of the various actors, and friction between the kaleidoscope of constitutional values and regulatory goals which it seeks to pursue. The Treaty of Lisbon would have been an ideal opportunity to address the so-called 'enforcement deficit'[5] and to explicitly place the judge-made system of judicial enforcement on a sound, legal basis within the Treaty framework. Regrettably, this did not materialize. It follows that post-Lisbon the private enforcement system created by the Court is here to stay. That said, there are changes afoot, both constitutional and regulatory, which can improve the effectiveness of private enforcement in this post-Lisbon era and which need to be assessed.

The legal literature contains extensive accounts of the Court's jurisprudence which focus on the effectiveness of the key legal doctrines from the perspective of the individual litigant. In other words, to what extent can EU rights be enforced before national courts by private litigants?[6] More interdisciplinary accounts explore the contribution of the doctrines to the constitutionalization process as well as the role of the Court and its relationship with national courts.[7] Few scholars have yet to assess the private enforcement system in a holistic and systematic manner. This chapter will adopt an innovative, interdisciplinary approach to an assessment of the effectiveness of the private enforcement regime by drawing on regulatory scholarship. Based on the premise that the Court has constructed a regulatory scheme with effective compliance of EU law as its overarching goal, it will draw on the regulatory scholarship of Yeung[8] and map the key principles and institutional design of the EU's private enforcement system against selected regulatory goals and constitutional values.

---

5 For a comprehensive analysis of the 'enforcement deficit', see Michael Dougan, *National Remedies before the Court of Justice: Issues of Harmonisation and Differentiation* (Hart, 2004).

6 See Ward, n 3.

7 Alec Stone Sweet, *The Judicial Construction of Europe* (OUP, 2004).

8 Karen Yeung, *Securing Compliance: A Principled Approach* (Hart, 2004). Yeung uses this framework in a similar way but in a different context, namely the public enforcement of competition law in Australia.

This chapter's contribution to the literature is threefold. First, the chapter will go beyond traditional doctrinal accounts by analysing afresh the effectiveness of the private enforcement model from a broader, more contextual perspective.[9] Second, within this analysis, the chapter will consider the impact of two legal innovations in the Treaty of Lisbon: the new Article 19(1), second subparagraph Treaty on European Union (hereinafter Article 19(1) TEU) which states that 'Member States shall provide remedies sufficient to ensure effective legal protection in the fields covered by Union law', and Article 47 of the now legally binding Charter of Fundamental Rights which explicitly refers to the right to an effective remedy. Third, by mapping the regulatory goals and constitutional values against the legal principles around which the regime is structured as well as its institutional features, it is possible to expose the inadequacies of the private enforcement system which jeopardize its effectiveness in a more systematic and objective manner. More importantly, it is argued that where the regulatory goals and constitutional values are most aligned, the system is operating most effectively.

This chapter will first set out the normative framework of analysis drawn from the regulatory scholarship and identify the regulatory goals and constitutional values chosen for the analysis (Section 1). This framework of analysis will be applied to the key foundational legal doctrines upon which the system is based, namely direct effect and indirect effect, and procedural rules and remedies including state liability (Section 2) as well as the new post-Lisbon innovations, namely Article 19(1) TEU and Article 47 of the Charter of Fundamental Rights (Section 3). The final section will go beyond the legal doctrines and map the framework against key institutional features of the private enforcement system (Section 4). The chapter will conclude by identifying the EU *acquis* where the regulatory goals and constitutional values work in harmony. This allows us to present a normative legal framework which promotes the private enforcement of EU law most effectively and pave the way for future research and policy development.

9 For an earlier attempt, see Snyder, n 4.

1. THE EFFECTIVENESS OF THE PRIVATE ENFORCEMENT OF EU LAW: A NEW FRAMEWORK OF ANALYSIS

It is argued by regulatory scholars like Yeung[10] that enforcement through litigation brought by private actors can be an effective policy choice for a number of reasons, particularly where the regulatory framework is designed to incentivize damages actions. Claims for damages actions can be instrumentally valuable as a deterrent and allow private actions to be aligned with public objectives.[11] Damages actions can also be intrinsically valuable by providing compensation for those who have suffered loss resulting from a breach of the law and by (financially) punishing the infringer. Private actions can also play an important role in engaging citizens with the public interest goals served by regulation. As part of this regulatory strategy, the enforcement role of the Member State and/or EU is to provide the judicial framework for it to operate successfully and effectively, namely the court structure and procedural rules which govern legal proceedings.[12]

For the purpose of this chapter, Yeung's original framework has been transposed (with alterations) to a supranational context and to a private, decentralized system of enforcement created by a supranational court through its jurisprudence. The regulatory goals and constitutional values chosen represent the fundamental characteristics that a system of enforcement of EU rights should embody in a Union based on the rule of law whether public or private. They reflect the *sui generis* nature of the Union legal order, particularly the distinct role of the Court and the decentralized nature of private enforcement. The constitutional values do not replicate the values of the EU set out in Article 2 TEU in full, but some of these are included. Adherence to them need not be absolute (except for the constitutional value of legality[13]), but a question of degree.[14] Using this framework is advantageous as it allows us to move forward the debate on effectiveness

---

[10] See Karen Yeung, 'Privatising Competition Regulation' (1998) 18 OJLS 581–615. Whilst these arguments have been made in the context of the private enforcement of competition law at national level, they apply equally to the advantages of private enforcement in the EU across the full breadth of policy areas.

[11] See further Ch 9 in this volume.

[12] Bronwen Morgan and Karen Yeung, *An Introduction to Law and Regulation: Text and Materials* (CUP, 2007) at p 216.

[13] Since this is identified by Yeung as a legal doctrine resting on respect for the rule of law and democratic governance, n 8 at p 45.

[14] Yeung refers to this as 'thin legality', n 8 at p 44.

of the EU's private model by bringing together an assessment of the foundational legal (doctrinal) concepts set out by the Court in relation to the law on rights, remedies and procedural rules, *in combination* with the institutional design of this regulatory scheme operating in its social and political context. Viewing these aspects of the private enforcement system together reveals a more complete picture of its effectiveness, and identifies when it operates most effectively. It also allows new innovations, both constitutional and regulatory, to be assessed and to illuminate pathways for future research and policy development.

1.1. Regulatory Goals

The EU's private enforcement system is categorized as a regulatory scheme and the single, overarching collective goal of this regulatory scheme (as distinct from the substantive EU law that may need to be enforced) is deemed to be the effective compliance of EU law. It is argued that in *Van Gend en Loos*, the Court set out this paradigm when it stated that, 'The vigilance of the individuals concerned to protect their rights amounts to an *effective* supervision in addition to the supervision entrusted by Articles [258] and [259] to the diligence of the Commission and of the Member States.'[15]

In order to achieve the overall regulatory goal, there are a number of more specific regulatory goals which taken together present the essential characteristics which a regulatory scheme of private enforcement should possess. The first[16] regulatory goal is that of *clarity and visibility*. In the context of the EU's private enforcement model, this refers to the clarity of the legal rules espoused by the Court and the extent to which their content and application is understood by national courts, Member States, EU institutions, and individuals. Regulatory scholars consider that the most effective frameworks of regulation are those comprised of precise rules which are stable, consistently applied, not frequently altered, visible by those for whom they have been devised and not unduly complex or opaque.[17] The second regulatory goal is that of *predictability*. This is an important goal of a legal framework because

---

[15] Case 26/62 *Van Gend en Loos* [1963] ECR 1 at p 13. Emphasis added.

[16] Yeung's first regulatory goal is that of efficiency, which requires an assessment of the desired outcome of the regulatory scheme with the lowest cost. This is outside the scope of this chapter. Suffice to say that such arguments have been raised in the context of private enforcement of competition law.

[17] Yeung, n 8 at p 33 citing Joseph Raz, 'The Rule of Law and its Virtue' (1977) 93 LQR 195 and CS Diver 'The Optimal Precision of Administrative Rules' in Robert Baldwin, Colin Scott and Christopher Hood (eds), *A Reader on Regulation* (OUP, 1998).

it allows actors to act in a rational way in their self-interest.[18] The third regulatory goal is that of *flexibility*. This goal may seem to conflict with those of clarity and predictability, but it has been argued by Yeung that flexibility is also required in a regulatory system in order to facilitate effectiveness.[19] This goal concerns both the nature and content of the rules and in how they are interpreted and applied. A too formal adherence to legal rules can undermine their ability to achieve their objective. Flexibility on the other hand can facilitate their effectiveness since it can allow a more purposive approach to be applied to the interpretation and application of rules 'in order to give effect to their underlying purpose or "spirit."'[20] Such a teleological approach is a distinct feature of the CJEU's approach to its interpretation of EU law. Yeung also argues that regulatory schemes should aim to be responsive in the sense of being able to adapt and adjust within the environment in which they are operating. Hence, *responsiveness* is the final regulatory goal to be applied.[21] If a scheme is unable to adapt, it can become ineffective and fail to fulfil its collective goal(s).[22] This regulatory goal is particularly important in the regulatory context of the EU, which is dynamic and multi-level in nature, and in which changes to a regulatory regime at a transnational level can take a long time to agree and implement.

1.2. Constitutional Values

The constitutional values chosen act as constraints on the pursuit of the collective goal by the EU and its institutions. The first constitutional value to be applied is the need for the system to be *authorized by law (legality)*. This requirement stems from adherence to the rule of law[23] which in turn implies compliance with democratic legitimacy.[24] In the context of the EU, Article 2 TEU now explicitly states that the Union is founded on the rule of law.[25] The second value, which is closely connected to the first, is *legiti-*

---

[18] Ibid, citing Max Weber's work and his analysis of law and social action in *Law in Economy and Society* (Harvard University Press, 1954).

[19] Ibid at p 34.

[20] Ibid.

[21] This is distinct from the theory of responsive regulation developed by Ayres and Braithwaite discussed in Ch 3.

[22] Ibid at p 35.

[23] Ibid at p 37 citing Raz, n 17. See also Paul Craig, 'Formal and Substantive Conceptions of the Rule of Law: An Analytical Framework' (1997) PL 467.

[24] Ibid at p 37 citing Giandomenico Majone *Regulating Europe* (Routledge, 1996) 291–3.

[25] It was the Court which first held in its *Les Verts* judgment that the now Union is based on the rule of law: Case 294/83 [1986] ECR 1339 at para 23. The

macy.[26] In this analysis, the focus will be on *judicial legitimacy* given the fundamental role played by the Court in the development of the private enforcement system through its case law. It refers to the Court's respect of the limits of its interpretative duties and powers in fulfilling its role set out in Article 19(1) TEU.[27] The third constitutional value is that of *certainty and stability*. This requirement also stems from the rule of law and requires the law to be clear and certain in advance for those who will be subject to it, and not change too frequently.[28] This is deemed to be particularly important where civil and criminal sanctions are imposed.[29] The fourth constitutional value is the *fair administration of justice*.[30] In the context of private enforcement, this represents a cluster of fundamental values based on fairness which must govern the judicial proceedings. In building the EU's private enforcement system, the Court has paid particular attention to determining the values it should protect and translating these values into legal rules upon which private litigants can depend. The principle of effective judicial protection has played a significant role and underpins many of the Court's judgments in which it has introduced rights for individuals such as the right of access to a court and the right to an effective remedy. The final constitutional value chosen is that of *equality*[31] which requires substantive fairness, and which has particular significance in the EU context with rights conferred on individuals which may need to be enforced in the event of a breach in 28 Member States.

1.3. Relationship between Regulatory Goals and Constitutional Values

Yeung claims that it is possible for the regulatory goals and constitutional values to 'co-exist in harmony' as set out in Figure 1.1.[32] However, there is undoubtedly scope for conflict, both between the different regulatory goals *or* constitutional values, as well as between the regulatory goals *and* constitutional values. How should such conflict be resolved? Yeung's theoretical framework provides a useful method for dealing with such

---

rule of law was inserted into the Treaty on European Union by the Treaty of Maastricht.

26 Note that this replaces Yeung's third constitutional value of accountability and transparency.

27 Formerly, in substance, Article 220 European Community (EC) Treaty.

28 Yeung, n 8 at p 38.

29 Ibid.

30 This is inspired by but broader than Yeung's fourth constitutional value of procedural fairness or due process.

31 For the purpose of this analysis, uniformity is incorporated within equality.

32 Yeung, n 8 at p 49.

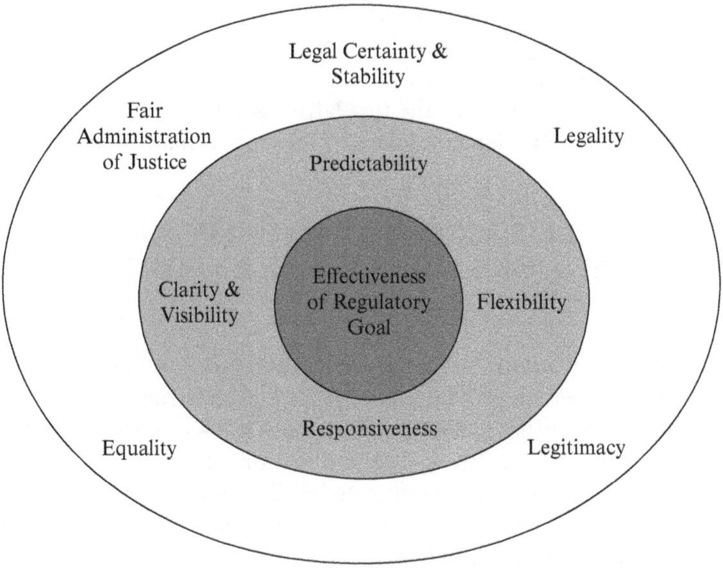

Figure 1.1 Regulatory goals and constitutional values

conflicts. First, where there is a conflict between regulatory goals the conflict should be resolved according to the particular context as well as to the overarching collective goal. Preference should be given to the goal which leads to long term substantive compliance. If any policy trade-offs are made these should be clearly explained (in this context by the CJEU).[33] Second, where there is a conflict between constitutional values the conflict should be resolved in favour of the constitutional value which is most important (this may depend on the context).[34] Third, where there is a conflict between constitutional values, the value which reflects a fundamental right should prevail.[35] Fourth, should there be a clash between two fundamental rights, it may be a question of degree as to which one takes priority.[36] Fifth, should a conflict arise between regulatory goals and constitutional values, Yeung argues against prioritizing the regulatory goals over constitutional values simply to achieve the overarching collective goal. In a liberal democratic society, regulatory goals may be promoted by public powers on condition that the constitutional values are also

[33] Ibid at p 36.
[34] Ibid at p 45.
[35] Ibid at p 49.
[36] Ibid.

respected. Adherence to these values to the requisite degree ensures that the pursuit of the regulatory goals by society is legitimate.[37] Should the constitutional value provide the foundation for rights, once again the level of protection is one of degree; the regulatory goal(s) may be promoted on the ground that the fundamental core of the right is maintained.[38]

2. THE EFFECTIVENESS OF THE LEGAL FRAMEWORK FOR PRIVATE ENFORCEMENT OF EU LAW

The normative framework will be applied only to the foundational parts of the Union *acquis* which provides us with the key constructs of the Union's private system of enforcement: the doctrines of direct effect and indirect effect, the principles governing the application of procedural rules and remedies including the doctrine of state liability, and the initial principles constructed by the Court to ensure that its system of private enforcement complies with fundamental rights.

2.1. Effective Enforcement and the Doctrine of Direct Effect

The doctrine of direct effect is the foundational tenet upon which the system of private enforcement is based since it provides individual litigants with the ability to bring legal proceedings to protect their EU rights directly before a national court in the event of a breach. There is no doubt that direct effect plays an important role in achieving the overall collective regulatory goal of effective compliance of EU law as well as the effectiveness or *effet utile* of substantive provisions. Nevertheless, it is a view commonly held that the full potential of the doctrine to promote effective compliance with EU law is undermined by the Court's long-standing position that directives cannot have direct effect in horizontal situations.[39] This can and does have a dramatic effect on the ability of some individuals to effectively enforce their EU rights and creates inequality between different private litigants. The classic example is the inability of an employee working in the private sector to enforce their directly effective rights against their employer, compared to an employee working in the public

---

[37] Ibid at p 50.

[38] Ibid at p 50.

[39] In other words, directly effective provisions can only be enforced in actions between an individual and the state or an emanation of the state (vertical direct effect) and not in an action between two private parties (horizontal direct effect).

sector who would be able to so. Paradoxically, in policy areas designed to protect individuals such as employment policy and consumer protection, the enactment of EU rights tends to be in the form of directives, rather than regulations. This long-held stance has been qualified somewhat by the Court's (controversial) 2005 ruling in *Mangold*, in which a Directive which gave expression to a specific general principle of EU law, namely the principle of non-discrimination on grounds of age, could be relied upon in an action between private parties.[40]

The Court's initial refusal to grant directives horizontal direct effect was arguably in response to criticisms of the Court's introduction of direct effect by adopting a teleological interpretation of the Treaty and basing it only minimally on the text of the Treaty. This raised questions about the legality and legitimacy of the Court's rulings by the Member States and their national courts,[41] particularly in view of the role of direct effect in constitutionalizing the Treaties, as well as issues of legal certainty. Deeply aware that first and foremost the overall success of the private enforcement system relies on the acceptance of its ruling by the Member States and their national courts rather than adherence to those values which confer greater protection on the individual litigant, the Court responded by prioritizing legality, legitimacy and legal certainty over effective judicial protection and equality. Notwithstanding its ruling in *Mangold*,[42] the Court has maintained its prohibition on the horizontal direct effect of directives in later cases. From a regulatory perspective, the constraints placed on the development of the doctrine of direct effect

---

[40] C-144/04 *Mangold* [2005] ECR I-9981. The Court's approach was confirmed and clarified post-Lisbon in C-555/07 *Kücükdeveci* [2010] ECR I-365 which also referred to the principle of age discrimination as set out in Article 21(1) of the Charter. The *Mangold* judgment attracted a great deal of criticism from both judicial and political quarters and was subject to a constitutional review by the German Federal Constitutional Court: *Honeywell Re*, BVerfG, 2 BvR 2661/06 [2011] 1 CMLR 33. In light of this, it is unsurprising that its reach has been curtailed in subsequent case law: see in particular, C-282/10 *Dominguez* [2012] EU:C:2012:33 which concerned the right to paid annual leave, which also appears in Article 31(2) of the Charter. See further, Mirjam de Mol, '*Dominguez*: A Deafening Silence (Case Comment)' (2012) 8(2) *European Constitutional Law Review* 280–303.

[41] The French and German courts refused to recognize the direct effect of directives: *Ministre de l'Intèrieur v Daniel Cohn-Bendit* [1980] 1 CMLR 543; *Re Value Added Tax Directives* (Case V B 51/80) [1982] 1 CMLR 527.

[42] It is noteworthy that the Court has been required to retreat from applying its *Mangold* decision more broadly for similar reasons. Whilst the judgment clearly prioritizes the constitutional values of equality and effective judicial protection, it undermines legal certainty as well as the legitimacy and legality of the Court's jurisprudence.

by the differing constitutional values have led to a lack of visibility, clarity and predictability. Yet, this seems to be of a degree currently acceptable.

It is suggested that codification of the doctrine in the Treaty framework would be a clear way of improving the effectiveness of direct effect as a means of achieving effective compliance of EU law and allow for greater alignment of the regulatory goals and constitutional values. However, this would be difficult given the uncertainty amongst legal scholars in the different Member States as to its exact meaning[43] as well as previous hostility shown by the Member States to the doctrine.[44] The time may come for the EU institutions and the Member States to show a greater commitment to the private enforcement regime and agree to explicitly state whether a provision has direct effect when it is being enacted and recognize the horizontal direct effect of directives.

2.2. Effective Enforcement and the Doctrine of Indirect Effect

The scope of the doctrine of direct effect as a means of ensuring effective compliance of EU law has been limited as a result of the Court's strict adherence to its interpretation of legality and the rule of law, trumping the constitutional values of effective judicial protection and equality based on fairness. Nevertheless, the Court has acted responsively and flexibly in developing alternative legal avenues for individuals to enforce their EU rights before national courts.[45] The most significant and now well-entrenched doctrine developed by the Court is that of 'indirect effect', also referred to as the principle of consistent interpretation.[46] In *Von Colson*,[47] the Court held that a national court is under a duty to interpret national law to comply with EU law. This allows individuals to secure their EU rights indirectly by virtue of national law, and independently of direct effect. Indeed, an empirical study, dating back to 1998, demonstrated

---

[43] Paul Craig and Gráinne de Búrca, *EU Law: Text, Cases and Materials* (3rd edition, OUP, 2003) pp 178–82.

[44] Article 34 TEU (M) expressly states that framework decisions, similar instruments to directives, do not have direct effect. This provision was repealed by the Treaty of Lisbon 2009.

[45] Unfortunately, there is insufficient space to map the framework onto the principles emanating from the Court's judgments in Case C-194/94 *CIA* [1996] ECR I-2201 ('incidental' horizontal direct effect).

[46] See further Sara Drake, 'Twenty Years after "*Von Colson*": The Impact of "Indirect Effect" on the Protection of the Individual's Community Rights' (2005) 30 ELRev 329.

[47] Case 14/83 *Von Colson* [1984] ECR 1891.

that whilst in theory the principle of direct effect is regarded as the starting point for an individual seeking to enforce their EU rights because it guarantees full compliance with a right, in practice, it is the principle of indirect effect that is the main legal mechanism for enforcing EU rights before British courts.[48] The doctrine has been further strengthened in subsequent case law.[49]

The principle of indirect effect addresses the inequality in the enforcement of rights depending on the status of the defendant and secures the constitutional value of effective judicial protection to a large degree. However, once again, tensions arise as to the doctrine's compliance with legality. This teleological interpretative approach of the Court has created tension regarding the legitimacy of its rulings. The doctrine can also create legal uncertainty for both the claimant and the defendant since the outcome is dependent on the interpretation of the national judge. In terms of regulatory goals, this can affect clarity and predictability. In subsequent case law, the Court sought to enhance the legality and legitimacy of the doctrine by ruling that the duty imposed on national courts is 'inherent in the system of the [TFEU]'.[50] The Court has acted responsively and flexibly in developing this doctrine in order to secure effective compliance with EU law and has prioritized the constitutional values of effective judicial protection and equality over strict compliance with legality, legitimacy and legal certainty.

2.3. Effective Enforcement and Procedural Rules and Remedies

One of the most contentious areas in the construction of the EU's private enforcement system has been the determination of the procedural and remedial laws that should apply.[51] In the absence of EU secondary legislation regulating such matters, the Court's approach veers somewhere between the two different approaches set out below. First, its default position has been to respect the national procedural and remedial autonomy of the Member States subject to EU minimum standards. This means that national procedural rules and remedies apply provided they do not treat actions based on EU law less favourably than similar actions based on domestic law (principle of equivalence) and the national rules must not make it practically impossible or excessively difficult to bring a claim

---

48 Damian Chalmers, 'The Positioning of EU Judicial Politics within the United Kingdom' (2000) 23 WEP 169, 190.

49 Joined Cases C-397–403/01 *Pfeiffer* [2004] ECR I-8835.

50 Ibid.

51 For a comprehensive account of this area of EU law, see Dougan, n 5.

based in EU law (principle of effectiveness[52]). The national court makes this assessment:

> by reference to the role of that provision in the procedure, its progress and its special features, viewed as a whole, before the various national instances. In light of that analysis the basic principles of the domestic judicial system, such as the protection of rights of the defence, the principle of legal certainty and the proper conduct of proceedings must, where appropriate, be taken into consideration.[53]

This initial approach of the Court is based on the principle of loyal or sincere co-operation set out in Article 4(3) TEU which applies to all institutions of the Member States including the judiciary. By taking national procedural autonomy as its starting point, the legitimacy of this approach has not been challenged by the Member States or their courts. The formula allows national courts some discretion provided that the overall goal of effective enforcement of EU law is not jeopardized. In this sense, the principles of equivalence and effectiveness play an important role in delineating the zones of competence between the EU and Member State which could be argued to be in compliance with the principle of subsidiarity and proportionality. Under this first approach, the constitutional values and regulatory goals work in harmony to a large degree. The principles of effectiveness and equivalence are in themselves clear and predictable and given the level of discretion granted to the national courts can be applied in a responsive and flexible manner. The main downside of this approach is that it can cause inequality between individual litigants across the Member States who will be subject to different rules which can affect their ability to effectively enforce their EU rights. This can cause a degree of legal uncertainty for litigants and may obscure an individual's ability to assess the likely success of a claim.

A second, more interventionist approach emerged in the mid-1980s based on a teleological interpretation of the law. The Court's request for EU secondary legislation to be enacted on a general scale was not forthcoming.[54] The jurisprudence from this period has given rise to an important body of legal principles setting out uniform remedies[55] and

---

52 Note the multiple uses of the term 'effectiveness' with different meanings in this area of EU law.

53 Cases C-430–431/93 *Van Schijndel* [1995] ECR I-4705 at para 19. See also Case C-312/93 *Peterbroeck* [1995] ECR I-4599.

54 See, for example, Case 130/79 *Express Dairy Foods* [1980] ECR 1887 para 12.

55 This includes the right to repayment of unlawful levies and the right to interim relief: Case 199/82 *San Giorgio* [1983] ECR 3595; Case C-213/89 *Factortame (No 1)* [1990] ECR I-2433.

common procedural rules derived from EU law rather than national law. This phase of the Court's case law culminated in the Court's *Francovich*[56] decision in which it introduced the EU remedy of state liability, which grants individuals an EU right to bring an action for damages against a Member State.

The main advantage of this second approach is that it promotes the effective enforcement of EU law by granting private litigants greater legal certainty, equality and effective judicial protection through uniform remedies derived from EU law. This removes the vagaries of the national legal systems and promotes clarity and predictability. There is also scope for flexibility and responsiveness in that whilst the *existence* of the remedy is derived from EU law, it is *exercised* in accordance with national rules subject to the principles of effectiveness and equivalence.

The Court's *Francovich* ruling represents the zenith of its expansionist case law in creating a private system of enforcement in pursuit of the collective goal of effective enforcement of EU law. By examining state liability through the two normative lenses, it can be seen that the constitutional values and regulatory goals are in harmony, achieving high levels of effective judicial protection for individual actors, and yet maintaining some scope for flexibility and responsiveness. Notwithstanding these benefits, the *Francovich* ruling is well known amongst legal scholars and political scientists for the controversy it raised in terms of legitimacy. It provoked strong political reactions from the Member States[57] which accused the Court of having insufficient legal authority to create this new remedy.[58]

In response to the challenges to the legitimacy of its rulings which follow this second approach, the Court is considered to have embarked on a limited retreat, entering a period which has been termed 'selective deference'[59] or 'judicial restraint'.[60] In other words, the Court's standard approach now is to allow national rules to be applied subject to the

---

56 Joined Cases C-6/90 and 9/90 *Francovich* [1991] ECR I-5357.

57 At the IGC 1996, the UK proposed inter alia that the *Francovich* and Case C-208/90 *Emmott v Minister for Social Welfare* [1991] ECR I-4269 rulings be curbed: Jonas Tallberg 'Supranational Influence in EU Enforcement: The ECJ and the Principle of State Liability' (2000) 7 *Journal of European Public Policy* 104.

58 Empirical research suggests that the remedy has had limited success: Tobias Lock 'Is Private Enforcement of EU Law through State Liability a Myth? An Assessment 20 Years after *Francovich*' (2012) CMLR 1675.

59 Takis Tridimas, 'Enforcing Community Rights in National Courts: Some Recent Developments' in Claire Kilpatrick, Tonia Novitz and Paul Skidmore, *The Future of Remedies in Europe* (Hart Publishing, 2000) 35 at p 49.

60 Anthony Arnull, 'The Principle of Effective Judicial Protection in EU Law: An Unruly Horse?' (2011) 36 ELR 51–70.

principles of effectiveness and equivalence, and only occasionally intruding on the national procedural autonomy of the Member States to develop or refine its existing framework of EU remedies.[61] The main problem with this current approach in terms of meeting its regulatory goals is its lack of clarity and predictability and the corresponding constitutional value of legal certainty. In any given case, it is not clear which approach the Court will adopt. The application of our two normative lenses reveals that the current approach of 'selective deference' seems to be the least appropriate in order to achieve effectiveness.

2.4. Effective Enforcement and Fundamental Rights

The EU's system of private enforcement is bolstered by a strand of sometimes overlapping case law which sets out the fundamental right to an effective remedy, including the right of access to a court.[62] This would fall within our constitutional value of fair administration of justice. It is this aspect of the Court's jurisprudence on private enforcement in which the constitutional values and regulatory goals set in our normative framework are the most aligned. The legitimacy of this strand of the case law on private enforcement is far stronger given that the Court sought to derive its legality from the national constitutional traditions of the Member States and fundamental rights reflecting fair administration of justice set out in the European Convention of Human Rights (ECHR).[63] More recently, the Court ruled in its *Unibet* judgment that the (broader) principle of effective judicial protection incorporating the right to an effective remedy including access to a court is a general principle of EU law.[64] This provides legal certainty, greater equality, and common standards of fundamental rights in the Member States. This is an example of the constitutional values working in harmony. In terms of regulatory goals, the rules are for the most part clear and predictable. However, from a doctrinal perspective, there are deep concerns about the lack of clarity over the Court's use of

[61] See, for example, Case C-224/01 *Köbler* [2003] ECR I-10239 and Case C-453/99 *Courage* [2001] ECR I-6297.

[62] Case 222/84 *Johnston* [1986] ECR 1651; Case 222/87 *Heylens* [1987] ECR 4097; Case C-185/97 *Coote* [1998] I-5199.

[63] Article 6 ECHR confers on everyone the right to a fair and public hearing before an independent and impartial tribunal established by law and within a reasonable time when determining civil rights and obligations or any criminal charge brought against them; Article 13 states that everyone whose rights and freedoms set out in the ECHR which have been violated has a right to an effective remedy before a national authority.

[64] See Case C-432/05 *Unibet* [2007] ECR I-2271 at para 37.

the terms 'effective judicial protection' and 'effective remedy' and how these relate to its extensive body of case law on remedies (discussed above) for their meanings vary in different contexts. It is important to recall that not all aspects of private enforcement raise issues of fundamental rights, but they can entail the protection of (lesser) constitutional values, for example, recovery of sums levied by Member States in breach of EU law and national time limits.[65]

3. THE IMPACT OF POST-LISBON INNOVATIONS ON THE EFFECTIVENESS OF THE PRIVATE ENFORCEMENT MODEL

The aim of the Treaty Establishing a Constitution for Europe 2004 (also known as the Constitutional Treaty) which morphed into the Treaty of Lisbon was to provide the framework for the functioning of the EU for the next 50 years. Yet, what is astonishing from a private enforcement perspective is that given its crucial role in the enforcement of EU law, there is a remarkable absence of discussion or proposals to increase its visibility and codify its key characteristics such as direct effect,[66] state liability and the principles of effectiveness and equivalence. Moreover, there were no references to the key role played by the national courts in enforcing EU law.[67] Nevertheless, the Treaty of Lisbon contains two new constitutional provisions which could play a significant role in improving the effectiveness of the private enforcement system, particularly remedies and procedural rules – Article 19(1) TEU and Article 47 of the Charter of Fundamental Rights. The application of these innovations by the Court will be explored in this section and analysed in light of our two strands of normative standards. The analysis reveals that post-Lisbon we have

---

[65] See, for example, the case law in relation to national time limits in which the CJEU has tried to strike the balance between the sound administration of the national legal orders and legal certainty and the effective protection of individuals' directly effective EU rights: see discussion in Anthony Arnull, *The European Union and its Court of Justice* (2nd edition, OUP, 2006) at pp 300–304.

[66] It could be argued that the attempt to insert the primacy provision into the Constitutional Treaty was an attempt to recognize its important role in the constitutionalization of the Treaty, but there is no equivalent attempt relating to its twin principle of direct effect. For discussion against incorporating direct effect into the Constitutional Treaty and the difficulties this would raise, see Monica Claes, *The National Courts' Mandate in the European Constitution* (Hart Publishing, 2006) at p 679.

[67] Ibid at pp 680–83.

moved into a new phase in the Court's case law on remedies and procedural rules before national courts which have important ramifications for the effectiveness of the private model of enforcement. However, the Court has not yet harnessed the full potential of these provisions to improve the effectiveness of the private model overall.

3.1. Article 19(1) TEU: The Missing Legal Base or More?

The new Article 19(1) TEU states that 'Member States shall provide remedies sufficient to ensure effective legal protection in the fields covered by Union law.'[68] It is clear from the discussions on the Court of Justice within the Convention on the Future of Europe which led to the signing of the Constitutional Treaty[69] that this addition was introduced in order to complement the broadening of access for individuals under Article 263(4) TFEU and reinforce the Court's controversial claim in *UPA* that the Treaties created a 'complete system of legal remedies and procedures designed to ensure judicial review of the legality of acts of the institutions, and has entrusted such review to the [Union] Courts',[70] rather than to address the legality and legitimacy deficit of the Court's judge-made remedies system before national courts. This narrow view has been confirmed by the Court post-Lisbon in its *Inuit* judgment.[71] This is in line with the principle of effective judicial protection which the national courts are under a duty to respect in accordance with Article 4(3) TEU.[72] Nevertheless, it is clear that the provision is broad enough to cover not only judicial review actions and the fundamental right of access to effective judicial review before a national court, but all litigation where national courts are involved in the enforcement of Union law.[73] Most importantly, it has the potential to provide the CJEU at the very least with a more legitimate legal basis for its existing system of remedies which would in turn grant the national courts a stronger mandate for engaging in their enforcement role.

---

[68] This provision survived the Constitutional Treaty: Article I-29.

[69] See the Discussion Circle on the Court of Justice: Final Report of 25 March 2003 at p 6.

[70] Case C-50/00P *UPA* [2002] ECR I-6677 at para 40. It should be noted that this is contrary to the views of a swathe of academic commentators and Advocates General, the most prominent critic being Advocate General Jacobs: see his Opinion in *UPA*.

[71] Case C-583/11P *Inuit* EU:C:2013:625 at para 90.

[72] Case C-50/00P at paras 41–2.

[73] Claes, n 66 at p 683.

A survey of the case law post-Lisbon illustrates that this is indeed the approach being adopted by some of the Advocates General, particularly in litigation involving the recovery of sums from the Member States that have been unlawfully levied. In *Banca*, Advocate General Mazák claims that Article 19(1) TEU imposes on Member States and their national courts the same obligations that have arisen pre-Lisbon under the principles of effectiveness and equivalence.[74] Admittedly, hidden away in a footnote, in *Macinský*, Advocate General Wahl referred to Article 19(1) TEU as 'enshrining' aspects of the principle of effectiveness originally set out in *Rewe* and *Comet*.[75] For some, Article 19(1) TEU provides an additional guarantee of effective remedies giving rise to its own obligations. For example, in *Test Claimants (No. 3)*, Advocate General Wathelet argues that Article 19(1) TEU formalized the obligation on Member States to provide effective remedies that had already been set out in *UPA* (in the context of judicial review).[76] He then goes on to apply it in the context of an action for recovery of sums unlawfully levied as a supplement to the principles of effectiveness and equivalence.[77] In *Donau Chemie*, Advocate General Jääskinen goes further and argues that the standard of effective judicial protection that should be provided by national courts should be reconsidered in light of the new Article 19(1) TEU. He held that in light of this 'supplementary guarantee' found in the Treaty, '. . .the standard of effective judicial protection for EU based rights seems to be more demanding than the classical formula referring to practical impossibility or excessive difficulty. In my opinion this means that national remedies must be accessible, prompt, and reasonably cost effective.'[78]

The Court's approach to Article 19(1) TEU has been more tentative than that of some of the Advocates General. In many cases on remedies, there is no mention of the provision at all. The Court has referred to it several times in combination with Article 47 of the Charter of Fundamental Rights stating that its role is to ensure that Article 47

---

[74] Opinion of Advocate General Mazák in Case C-427/10 *Banca* [2011] ECR I-13377 at para 16.

[75] See Opinion of Advocate General Wahl in Case C-482/12 *Macinský* EU:C:2013:765 at footnote 26.

[76] Opinion of Advocate General Wathelet in Case C-362/12 *Test Claimants in the Franked Investment Income Group Litigation (No 3)* EU:C:2013:834 at para 34.

[77] He argued that in accordance with Article 19(1) TEU a remedy is not 'effective' if the conditions in which it can be invoked successfully are not known in advance. Ibid, at paras 46–7.

[78] Opinion of Advocate General Jääskinen in Case C-536/11 *Donau Chemie* EU:C:2013:366 at para 47 and reiterated in Case C-61/14 *Orizzonte Salute* EU:C:2015:307 at footnote 23.

is respected by the Member States.[79] The Court has also referred to Article 19(1) TEU as an additional and more specific obligation to the principle of sincere co-operation set out in Article 4(3) TEU and the duty imposed on Member States to ensure judicial protection of an individual's rights under EU law.[80] It is strongly argued that the effectiveness of the EU's private enforcement system would be improved if the Court explicitly based the principles of effectiveness and equivalence on Article 19(1) TEU. It would strengthen the legality and legitimacy of this key feature of its private system of enforcement and promote legal certainty. From a regulatory perspective, a clearer legal base would improve clarity and predictability, whilst there is sufficient discretion granted to Member States to maintain flexibility and responsiveness. Whether the qualitative standard of effective legal protection would be enhanced depends on whether the Court follows the approach suggested by Advocate General Jääskinen in *Donau Chemie* and uses Article 19(1) TEU as the basis of higher standards, but which intrude further on the national procedural autonomy of the Member States in a non-fundamental rights context.

3.2. Article 47 of the Charter on Fundamental Rights: Moving Closer to Aligning Regulatory Goals and Constitutional Values

The Treaty of Lisbon marks a new era in the protection of fundamental rights under EU law. Article 6(1) TEU finally grants the Charter of Fundamental Rights of the European Union (EUCFR) equal legal status with the Treaties.[81] It is now legally binding on the EU institutions and Member States, but only 'when implementing EU law'[82] and is subject

---

[79] See, for example, Case C-418/11 *Texdata* EU:C:2013:588 at para 78; Case C-562/12 *Liivimaa Lihaveis MTÜ* EU:C:2014:2229 at para 68.

[80] Case C-404/13 *ClientEarth* EU:C:2014:2382 at para 52 citing Case C-432/05 *Unibet* [2007] ECR I-2271 at para 38.

[81] The Charter was 'solemnly proclaimed' in 2000: [2000] OJ C364/1. An adapted version became legally binding on 1 December 2009 along with the Treaty of Lisbon: [2012] OJ C326/02. During this interim period, the Charter still had influence on the Court's rulings: see further Sara Iglesias Sánchez, 'The Court and the Charter: The Impact of the Entry into Force of the Lisbon Treaty on the ECJ's Approach to Fundamental Rights' (2012) 49 CMLR 1565, 1569–73.

[82] Article 51(1) EUCFR. It should be noted that the Court has adopted a very broad interpretation of this phrase in Case C-617/10 *Fransson* EU:C:2013:105 to the extent that it is difficult to consider an area of EU law which is not now subject to the Charter.

to important limitations and exceptions.[83] The importance of this development for the EU's private enforcement model lies in Article 47 of the Charter of Fundamental Rights which is found under Title VI entitled Justice and explicitly refers to the right to an effective remedy and to a fair trial. It states that:

> Everyone whose rights and freedoms guaranteed by the law of the Union are violated has the *right to an effective remedy* before a tribunal in compliance with the conditions laid down in this Article.
>
> Everyone is entitled to a fair trial and public hearing within a reasonable time by an independent and impartial tribunal previously established by law. Everyone shall have the possibility of being advised, defended and represented.
>
> Legal aid shall be made available to those who lack sufficient resources in so far as such aid is necessary to ensure effective access to justice.

The Charter is accompanied by Explanations which act as an interpretative aid to its provisions.[84] The Explanations confirm that Article 47 is based on Articles 6(1) and 13 of the ECHR and emphasize that the right to an effective remedy set out in Article 13 ECHR has already been established as a general principle of EU law by the CJEU, which was based in part on these provisions of the ECHR as well as the constitutional traditions of the Member States.[85]

The principal advantage for individual litigants is that they have been granted a new source of (primary) law to challenge the legality of EU law and national law which is 'implementing EU law' in relation to, inter alia, their right to an effective remedy. There is no question that individuals (and their lawyers) are seizing on the Charter as a 'sword' with a large number of preliminary rulings being made to the CJEU concerning the interpretation and scope of Article 47. Although the language of direct effect has

---

[83] Articles 52–54 EUCFR set out limits to its scope and the interpretation of rights and principles. See also Protocol No. 30 on the application of the Charter of Fundamental Rights of the European Union to Poland and the United Kingdom. Note that in Joined Cases C-411/10 and C-493/10 *N.S.* [2011] ECR I-13905, a reference from the Court of Appeal of England and Wales, the CJEU held that Protocol 30 does not generally disapply the Charter in the UK.

[84] See Article 52(7) EUCFR which requires the Union courts and the national courts to take the explanations into account when interpreting the Charter.

[85] The Explanations also confirm that Article 47 is wider in scope than both Articles 6(1) and 13 of the ECHR. Unlike Article 13 ECHR, Article 47 refers to the right to an effective remedy before a court and not just before a national authority. Article 47 is also broader than Article 6(1) ECHR in that it is not restricted to disputes relating to civil law rights and obligations since the EU is a Community (now Union) based on the rule of law.

not been used,[86] individuals have successfully relied on Article 47 vertically to strike down conflicting EU and national legislation.[87] In so doing, this litigation is forcing the Court to consider the contours of Article 47 and its relationship with its existing case law on remedies discussed above. Whilst a comprehensive exploration of the case law is outside the scope of this chapter, it is possible to discern a number of trends emerging in the Court's case law in which Article 47 EUCFR has been invoked. What will become clear is that this constitutional innovation is fast emerging as a new foundational pillar around which the law on procedural rules and remedies is starting to orbit. Undoubtedly, it has huge potential to improve the effectiveness of the EU's private enforcement system since it provides an opportunity for a more complete alignment of the regulatory goals and constitutional values.[88]

Article 47 as a new source of fundamental rights

One of the most interesting new trends to emerge is where the Charter has been drawn upon by the CJEU as the main source of EU law in accordance with which national courts should interpret national procedural law and remedies when implementing EU law. In its *DEB* judgment,[89] the Court seized the opportunity to reformulate the question referred by the German court from one concerning the principle of effectiveness and whether it was being infringed by the German provision to one relating to the interpretation of Article 47 and placing this provision centre stage. Admittedly, the Court may have been influenced by the fact that it was being given the opportunity for the first time to rule on the interpretation of EU law in relation to national provisions on legal aid contained in Article 47, third paragraph, where there is no existing EU case law on this issue. The Court drew quite significantly on the existing case law of the European Court of Human Rights (ECrtHR) on legal aid promoting an alignment of the different sources of fundamental rights law on

---

[86] Paul Craig and Gráinne de Búrca, *EU Law: Text, Cases and Materials* (6th edition, OUP, 2015) p 196.

[87] The CJEU has yet to declare that provisions of the Charter have horizontal direct effect. Nevertheless, in *Benkharbouche v Sudan* and *Janah v Libya*, the Court of Appeal (England and Wales) (Civil Division) held that since Article 47 EUCFR reflects a general principle of EU law and following the approach of the CJEU pre-Lisbon in Case C-144/04 *Mangold* [2005] ECR I-9981 and post-Lisbon in Case C-555/07 *Kücükdeveci* [2010] ECR I-365 and Case C-176/12 *AMS* EU:C:2014:2, it has horizontal direct effect: [2015] EWCA Civ 33 at paras 69–81.

[88] This argument applies equally to the procedures which apply before the EU institutions, but this issue is outside the scope of this chapter.

[89] Case C-279/09 *DEB* [2010] ECR I-13849.

this issue.[90] Thus, the *DEB* judgment not only promotes more effective judicial protection for individuals asserting their EU rights grounded in fundamental rights, but also ensures greater clarity and predictability in the case law.

Article 47 and the right to an effective remedy as a general principle of law

Whilst such an approach on the part of the Court is unsurprising in relation to the new provisions of Article 47 on legal aid, the Court's approach has been more mixed in relation to the first paragraph of Article 47, which refers to the right to an effective remedy. In many of the post-Lisbon cases, the Court has ruled that Article 47 is simply an affirmation of the well-established right to an effective remedy. It is therefore recognized as a supplementary source of fundamental rights.[91] It could be argued that this approach is understandable given the incremental and chronological development of fundamental rights protection in EU law as well as the limitations on the scope of the Charter's application. Yet, an interesting development has arisen in some later cases where the Court has referred to Article 47 first in its reasoning followed by the right to an effective remedy as a general principle of EU law. For example, in *Liivimaa Lihaveis MTÜ*,[92] the Court drew on Article 47 as its main source for its ruling, and its traditional case law as an additional source of fundamental rights.

Is there any significance that should be given to this subtle reordering of the different sources of fundamental rights protection? On the one hand in both types of cases, the Court's recognition of different sources denotes a pluralistic approach which is consistent with some views of the Charter[93] and arguably implicit in Article 53 EUCFR.[94] Yet, it could also be argued that in cases like *Liivimaa Lihaveis MTÜ*, by starting its reasoning with the Charter, the Court is placing it at the apex of the sources of fundamental rights protection and recognizing it as the pre-eminent source of fundamental rights in EU law. This would suggest that the Court is trying to create a more hierarchical, but coherent and consistent body of case law

---

90 This is in compliance with Article 52(3) EUCFR.

91 See Joined Cases C-317–320/08 *Alassini* [2010] ECR I-02213; Case C-93/12 *ET Agrokonsulting* EU:C:2013:432.

92 Case C-562/12 *Liivimaa Lihaveis MTÜ* EU:C:2014:2229.

93 See Advocate General Bot in Case C-399/11 *Melloni* EU:C:2013:107.

94 Article 53 EUCHR complements Articles 51 and 52 and states that '[n]othing in this Convention shall be construed as limiting or derogating from any of the human rights and fundamental freedoms which may be ensured under the laws of any High Contracting Party or under any other agreement to which it is a Party'.

which complies with its own vision of the EU legal order[95] and a system of remedies grounded in fundamental rights.

Article 47 and the principles of effectiveness and equivalence

This brings us on to the relationship between Article 47 and the principles of effectiveness and equivalence, which is far from clear and a number of different approaches are emerging. In *DEB*, the Court refused to adopt its classic approach and base its ruling on the principle of national procedural autonomy subject to the principles of effectiveness and equivalence, but used Article 47 as its main source of law together with the case law of the ECrtHR. In *Alassini*,[96] an earlier case concerning the implementation by Italy of elements of the Universal Services Directive dealing with consumer disputes, the CJEU first applied the principle of national procedural autonomy subject to the principles of equivalence and effectiveness as set out in its traditional case, and then secondly, and as a separate part of the adjudication, made an assessment on the basis of fundamental rights. It referred to 'the principle of effective judicial protection as a general principle of EU law stemming from the constitutional traditions common to the Member States, which has been enshrined in Articles 6 and 13 of the ECHR and which has also been reaffirmed by Article 47 of the Charter of Fundamental Rights'.[97] Recalling both its own case law and that of the ECrtHR, the Court ruled that fundamental rights are not absolute and may be curtailed by restrictions which are in the general interest, proportionate and do not amount to an 'intolerable interference which infringes upon the very substance of the rights guaranteed'.[98] Thus, the Court adopted a pluralist approach and conducted its adjudication using two juridically distinct strands of case law.[99] The dividing line is not always clear and can be difficult to draw. There have been calls by Advocates General Bot and Jääskinen to consider the principles of effectiveness and equivalence as falling under the umbrella of Article 47.[100] Whilst this proposal sounds laudable, it

---

[95] Advocate General Bot in C-399/11 *Melloni*, n 93 and Damian Chalmers, Gareth Davies and Giorgio Monti, *European Union Law* (3rd edition, CUP, 2014) pp 259–75.

[96] Joined Cases C-317–320/08 *Alassini*, n 91 at paras 61–3.

[97] Ibid para 61.

[98] Ibid para 63.

[99] For discussion of the separate nature of these two 'tests' to be conducted at court, see Advocate General Jääskinen in Case C-61/14 *Orizzonte Salute* EU:C:2015:307 at paras 33–7.

[100] See Opinion of Advocate General Jääskinen in Case C-562/12 *Liivimaa Lihaveis MTÜ* EU:C:2014:2229 at para 47; Case C-61/14 *Orizzonte Salute*

does require clarification about the interrelationship between the two strands of law.

In a third category of cases, the Court has referred to Article 47 *in conjunction* with the principles of effectiveness and equivalence. In *Unitrading Ltd*,[101] the Court ruled on the interpretation and scope of Article 47 with regard to the rights of the defence. In the absence of EU law governing further aspects of the national customs procedure at issue such as the concept of evidence, the Court applied the principles of effectiveness and equivalence. In this respect, it held that Article 47 had not been infringed provided that the national procedural law in question complied with the principles of effectiveness and equivalence. So whilst Article 47 and the principles of effectiveness and equivalence were applied separately in its adjudication by the Court, they are closely connected to the extent that the Court held that compliance with Article 47 requires the principles of effectiveness and equivalence to be satisfied when a Member State applies its own national procedural rules.

In a fourth category of cases, the Court has not mentioned the Charter at all. In *Nicula*,[102] a Grand Chamber judgment concerning the repayment of unlawful taxes, the Court relied on its well-established case law. This is understandable given that repayment of unlawful taxes is not usually a fundamental rights issue. More broadly, it is argued that it illustrates that the Court is keen to maintain a distinction between the different strands of its remedies case law.

Aligning regulatory goals and constitutional values

Article 47 EUCFR presents a more visible and highly legitimate legal basis upon which the Court can develop its standards of fundamental rights protection in relation to the right to an effective remedy. A clear advantage to this approach is that Article 47 of the Charter grants national courts more confidence to strike down national law and impose EU standards.[103] Article 47 also provides the Court with the opportunity to qualitatively increase national standards[104] relating to the fair administration of justice.

EU:C:2015:307 at para 24; Opinion of Advocate General Bot in Case C-93/12 *ET Agrokonsulting* EU:C:2013:432 at para 30.

[101] Case C-437/13 *Unitrading* EU:C:2014:2318.

[102] Case C-331/13 *Nicula* EU:C:2014:2285.

[103] See judgment of the Court of Appeal (England and Wales) (Civil Division) in *Benkharbouche v Sudan* and *Janah v Libya*, n 87.

[104] Although note that this may not always be the case. In *Melloni*, a higher standard of fundamental rights protection was provided by the Spanish Constitution as interpreted in the case law and was in conflict with the European

Indeed, the jurisprudence on EU asylum procedural law is developing at some pace in this respect.[105] Legitimacy and equality are important constitutional values to uphold when ruling against national standards and take on particular significance in the area of freedom, security and justice. Article 47 EUCFR adheres to the regulatory goals of clarity and predictability. Furthermore, the open-textured nature of Article 47 enables the Court to be flexible and responsive in how it is interpreted and applied.[106]

Nevertheless, the diverse patterns that are emerging in the Court's case law could prove detrimental to the effectiveness of this area of EU law and the private model of enforcement. The improved visibility of the fundamental rights in the Charter has given rise to a huge proliferation of cases in which Article 47 is being invoked by litigants, sometimes in a spurious manner, in all areas of EU law and policy. The delegation of cases to the different Chambers of the Court is resulting in a multiplicity of different approaches being adopted. Indeed, at times, it is difficult to find a common thread to the Court's approach. This lack of consistency in the Court's judgments is causing legal uncertainty and a lack of clarity and predictability in the law. This in turn may undermine the effectiveness of the EU's reliance on private litigation before national courts to ensure compliance with EU law. This suggests that there are tensions being played out on a number of different planes. A number of observations can be made. First, as Chalmers correctly predicted, and as noted by Advocate General Bot in *Melloni*,[107] there are tensions arising from the adoption of different lenses to interpret fundamental rights. In some cases such as *Alassini*, the Court is adopting a formalistic, pluralist approach in which it determines the standard of fundamental rights to be protected in reference not only to the Charter, but sources external to it such as the Explanations, international treaties such as the ECHR and national constitutional provisions. It recognizes and respects a range of sources of fundamental rights and is sensitive to the interplay between them. In other cases such as *Liivimaa Lihaveis MTÜ*, the Court is adopting a bolder, more 'Unionist' approach which accords to a particular vision of the EU

Arrest Warrant. The Court held that national standards of fundamental rights protection could only apply in accordance with Article 53 of the Charter if the level of protection provided in the Charter and the primacy, unity and effectiveness of EU law would not be comprised. In this case, EU law should prevail: Case C-399/11 *Melloni* EU:C:2013:107 at para 60.

[105] See, for example, Marcelle Reneman, *EU Asylum Procedures and the Right to an Effective Remedy* (Hart Publishing, 2014).

[106] Chalmers et al, n 95 at p 254.

[107] Ibid p 261.

legal order and making assessments which relate to the social, historical and cultural context of the legal order in question.[108]

Whilst an approach which reflects a singular EU view of remedies under the umbrella of Article 47 EUCFR may be more coherent, it is argued that there is merit in maintaining a pluralistic approach to remedies since the various sources of law differ in scope and have a range of functions. Article 47 will apply where the Member State is 'implementing EU law' only and is subject to the limitations and exceptions set out in Articles 52–54 EUCFR. Further, not all private litigation raises issues of fundamental rights. There are other procedural and remedial provisions which are a matter of policy choices and these may have evolved over many years and reflect cultural, political and budgetary choices. They may not infringe fundamental rights, but may affect the assertion of an EU right effectively and need to be challenged. And so, such sources need to be kept separate and autonomous as they may not always apply in a given scenario. There may also be mixed cases like *Unitrading* where the Court is unwilling to develop EU standards through its case law and prefers to leave such matters to the national legal orders.

It may take some time before the familiar tussles between the interests of the Member States seeking to preserve the integrity of their national legal order (subject to the minimum standards imposed by the principles of effectiveness and equivalence) and those seeking to rely on higher standards of judicial protection provided by EU law when asserting EU law rights now bolstered by the Charter have been teased out. These tensions previously existed in the case law. We are in an evolutionary period which will take time to settle down. The effectiveness of this arm of the EU's system of private enforcement may depend on the level of intrusion into their national legal orders that the Member States and their national courts deem legitimate and are prepared to accept.

4. THE EFFECTIVENESS OF THE INSTITUTIONAL DESIGN OF THE PRIVATE ENFORCEMENT SYSTEM

A full analysis of the EU's system of private enforcement can only be complete by moving beyond an analysis of the legal doctrines and viewing its institutional and operational features through the lens of our regulatory goals and constitutional values. First, we consider the impact of relying on

---

[108] Advocate General Bot, n 93 at para 109.

the case law as the key instrument in the building of the legal framework of this regulatory scheme. Second, we examine the effectiveness of the process by which the case law evolves in the EU context, namely through the preliminary ruling procedure.

4.1. The Effectiveness of a Judge-Made System of Law

For the most part, the laws governing the EU's private enforcement system continue to be developed and refined by the CJEU in a piecemeal manner. This poses a considerable challenge to achieving legal certainty and stability as well as clarity and predictability. There are certain characteristics of CJEU judgments which can exacerbate this tendency. First, the Court is prone to delivering opaque and ambiguous judgments. A lack of clarity in a judgment or in the meaning of EU law can give rise to further requests for preliminary rulings and the cycle of confusion and complexity continues. Indeed, as we are seeing post-Lisbon, it can take some time before the law on a particular issue is clearly established.[109] As the workload of the Court increases, the delegation of cases to the different Chambers can result in divergent approaches emerging. These uncertainties can also stem from the collegiate nature of the judgments which reflect the majority view of the relevant Chamber of the Court.[110] There are no dissenting judgments to shed light on any alternative interpretations that were considered. The judgment will be translated from the working language of the Court, which is French, into the other 24 official languages of the EU. Accuracy in translation can be an issue as different terms may have different meanings in the Member States. This too can lead to different interpretations and applications of the law emerging in the different Member States.

Is there a case for legislation?

A logical question would be to ask whether secondary legislation would improve the effectiveness of the legal framework from both regulatory and

---

[109] For example, in Case C-453/99 *Courage v Crehan* [2001] ECR I-6297, the Court failed to clearly confirm whether or not it had created a right in EU law allowing individuals to sue other individuals for damages arising from losses sustained for breach of the EU competition rules and its scope. This gave rise to different applications of the judgments in the Member States. See further Assimakis Komninos, 'New Prospects for Private Enforcement of EC Competition Law: *Courage v. Crehan* and the Community Right to Damages' (2002) 39 *Common Market Law Review* 447.

[110] See Lord Bingham's Foreword in Anthony Arnull, Piet Eeckhout and Takis Tridimas (eds), *Continuity and Change in EU Law: Essays in Honour of Sir Francis Jacobs* (OUP, 2008) at p vi.

constitutional perspectives? Would it improve the individual's awareness of their rights by stating clearly whether or not a measure grants a directly effective right? Would an action be more swiftly resolved if secondary legislation clearly indicated the procedural rules and remedies which should apply? In theory, secondary legislation would allow greater compliance with the regulatory goals and constitutional values. However, introducing legislation is not a quick fix solution. Given the nature of EU law-making, the enactment of legislation raises complex legal and political questions.

In the context of private enforcement, the most fundamental issue is meeting the constitutional value of legality which relates to the need for legal competence. The principle of conferral requires a legal basis in the Treaty framework before the Commission can initiate legislation. The original European Economic Community (EEC) Treaty contained no *specific* legal base for introducing *general* legislation on procedural rules or remedies.[111] Calls by the Commission,[112] the Court[113] and academics[114] have not, in the past, led to this deficit being remedied on a general scale.[115] The focus of the legislator has been on rule-setting rather than rule-enforcement.[116] This does not mean in any way that no EU legislation exists which contains provisions relating to remedies or procedural rules. Yet, the overall pattern for many years has been one of sector specific measures. Whilst some policy areas have a high degree of harmonization,[117] the most common approach has been to adopt measures which are fairly small scale in nature.[118] It is argued that this traditional pattern is starting to shift, particularly where the EU has been given explicit competence to establish an Area of Freedom, Security and

---

[111] For discussion of the creation of a new legal base, see Ch 10 in this volume.

[112] Contribution by the Commission to the Intergovernmental Conference (1991) (Document drawn up on the basis of COM (90) 600 and SEC (91) 500) published in 'Intergovernmental Conferences: Contributions by the Commission' (1991) *EC Bulletin*, Supplement 2/91, pp 151–4.

[113] Discussed above at n 54.

[114] Marcel Storme (ed), *Report on the 'Approximation of Judiciary Law in the European Union'* (Dordrecht: Martinus Nijhoff, 1994).

[115] Chris Himsworth, 'Things Fall Apart: The Harmonisation of Community Judicial Procedural Protection Revisited' (1997) 22 E.L.Rev. 291, Dougan, n 5 at pp 97–9.

[116] Stephen Weatherill, 'Addressing Problems of International Implementation in EC Law' in Claire Kilpatrick, Tonia Novitz and Paul Skidmore, n 59 at 91.

[117] The most harmonized field is that of public procurement.

[118] Some measures represent a codification of the Court's case law on remedies: Article 11 of Council Directive 2000/78/EC of 27 November 2000 establishing a general framework for equal treatment in employment and occupation [2000] OJ L303/16 is the codification of the Court's judgment in *Coote*, n 62.

Justice[119] or where the Commission sees private enforcement as a key part of its regulatory enforcement strategy, for example, EU anti-trust law.[120] Once competence has been established, the Commission also has to comply with the principle of subsidiarity and proportionality.[121] There is a strong argument for the governance of procedural rules and remedies to remain at national level on grounds of subsidiarity. There has to be a clear-cut case for it to be more effective to legislate at EU level. Moreover, such initiatives are now subject to the scrutiny of national parliaments. With regard to proportionality, the Commission will need to decide which instrument to adopt. Whilst regulations are best suited to achieving uniformity and arguably effectiveness, there are often arguments that directives are a more proportionate response to the objective to be achieved. Once these legislative and political hurdles have been overcome, it should not be forgotten that any legislation will have to be implemented by the Member States, applied by the national authorities and, in the event of a dispute, interpreted and applied by the national courts. All open up the possibility for the effectiveness to be undermined.[122]

4.2. The Effectiveness of the Preliminary Ruling Procedure

The way in which the Court and the preliminary ruling procedure function under Article 267 TFEU can undermine the development of the legal framework for private enforcement law in a manner which conflicts with the need for legal certainty and stability, and clarity and predictability. The process is dependent on the Court receiving an appropriate case in which it can extend or refine its regulatory scheme. Referral rates from the Member States can differ. The attitude of the national judges can be a significant factor. It is known that the length of proceedings can deter judges from referring in some Member States, and their propensity to refer may also depend on their knowledge and acceptance of EU law. Sanctions for failing to refer in accordance with

---

[119] See Ch 10 in this volume.

[120] See Ch 9 in this volume.

[121] Article 5 TEU.

[122] Consider the difficulties facing passengers seeking to enforce their right to compensation under Regulation (EC) No 261/2004 of the European Parliament and of the Council of 11 February 2004 establishing common rules on compensation and assistance to passengers in the event of denied boarding and of cancellation or long delay of flights, and repealing Regulation (EEC) No 295/91 [2004] OJ L46/1.

Article 267 TFEU exist in the national law in some Member States, but not in all. At EU level, the sanction is arguably underdeveloped and lacks bite. In *Köbler*[123] and *Traghetti*,[124] the CJEU failed to rule that on the facts, a failure to refer by a national court of last resort under Article 267 (3) TFEU in these cases amounted to a sufficiently serious breach giving rise to state liability.[125]

There are also practical considerations. Not only does the 'right' question have to be referred to the Court, but the referral also needs to be allocated to the 'right' Advocate General and judges who will have to appreciate its significance for the development of EU law in the field of private enforcement. For that matter, if it is not clearly articulated by the national judge, an opportunity may indeed be missed to develop the legal framework further. Having said that, the Court may spot an opportunity and exploit it, reformulating the question referred as it did in the *DEB* case. As we have seen in the post-Lisbon case law, it is clear that variations in interpretations occur, particularly on new areas of law pending a Grand Chamber judgment. This may depend on whether there is agreement between the judges as to the guidance to be given to a national court to resolve the matter before it. This may not simply depend on the EU judges, but on the amount of information the Court has been given by the national court on the facts of the case. It may be that the issue is deemed 'sensitive' and that the Court does not want to be seen to 'interfere' in certain areas of law and policy. Indeed, this has been a key issue for the Court in the area of private enforcement which has led to inconsistency in its judgments. Furthermore, despite the elaboration of principles at Union-wide level, their effective application often depends on the attitude of the national courts. In general, there has been widespread acceptance of the Court's judgments by the national courts, but at times, it can be less than satisfactory and can lead to diversity in the level of protection available.[126] The EU's current judicial architecture presents real challenges to developing a body of law which is visible, clear and coherent, and as a consequence, there is a lack of legal certainty and predictability for all parties involved in the proceedings.

---

[123] Case C-224/01 *Köbler* [2003] ECR I-10239.

[124] Case C-173/03 *Traghetti* [2006] ECR I-5177.

[125] Sara Drake, 'State Liability for Judicial Error: All Bark and No Bite? The Consequences of National Courts' Failure to Refer' in Adam Cygan and Lorenzo Spadacini (eds), *Constitutional Implications of the Traghetti Judgment: Italian and European Perspectives* (Bibliofabbrica, 2010) pp 49–79.

[126] See Komninos, n 109.

CONCLUDING REMARKS

This chapter adopts an innovative analytical approach drawn from regulatory scholarship to evaluate the effectiveness of the EU's private enforcement model. It brings a fresh perspective to the debate on effective enforcement by making a broader, more contextual assessment of the EU *acquis* including post-Lisbon developments as well as the judicial architecture and processes. Starting from the premise that the EU's private enforcement system is a regulatory scheme seeking to achieve the collective regulatory goal of effective compliance of EU law, a normative framework of carefully selected regulatory goals and constitutional values was constructed. This theoretical framework was then mapped first against the key legal doctrines governing rights, remedies and procedural rules which underpin the private enforcement regime before moving on to assess two constitutional innovations set out in the Treaty of Lisbon. Finally, for a more complete and holistic assessment, the method of constructing a regulatory scheme through case law and the preliminary ruling procedure was also assessed. This systematic approach enables us to identify the strengths and weaknesses of each aspect of the private enforcement system and enriches our understanding of the Court's policy in pursuit of the overall regulatory goal of effective compliance with EU law.

The analysis reveals that there is a persistent tension in the legal doctrines upon which the EU's system of private enforcement is based. The Court's policy sways between prioritizing the constitutional values of legality and legitimacy on the one hand and those of effective judicial protection and equality on the other. It is also evident from the case law that there have been shifts in policy which have led to an expansion or limitation of the legal doctrine in response to the reactions of Member States and their national courts. When asserting EU rights, the Court's persistent refusal to recognize the horizontal direct effect of directives demonstrates that it has prioritized legality, legitimacy and legal certainty over equality and the effective judicial protection of individuals' EU rights. It has sought to compensate for the inequality this creates in a responsive manner by developing alternative methods for individuals to enforce their rights such as the doctrine of indirect effect. Yet, this creates new tensions with the legality and legitimacy of its rulings. From a regulatory perspective, whilst the Court's actions have led to a system which is responsive and flexible, it lacks clarity and predictability and is arguably overly complex.

When determining the applicable procedural and remedial rules, the Court's two approaches both satisfy our normative framework to a large degree. The application of the principles of effectiveness and equivalence are considered to have a high degree of legitimacy, but can cause inequality, uncertainty and a lack of predictability. The more interventionist approach which has resulted in the introduction of the doctrine of state liability achieves high levels of effective judicial protection for individual actors, and slightly more equality, yet its legitimacy has been rigorously questioned. What is certain is that the current approach of 'selective deference' seems to be the least appropriate in order to achieve effectiveness creating higher levels of uncertainty.

The Treaty of Lisbon was a missed opportunity to address the deficiencies in the EU's private enforcement system and to provide a clear legal and legitimate Treaty base for the Court's jurisprudence. What is clear is that post-Lisbon, we have moved into a new phase in the development of the Court's jurisprudence on private enforcement and specifically on remedies. The Treaty of Lisbon has given the Court the constitutional tools required to align to a greater extent the regulatory goals and constitutional values upon which this regulatory scheme is based, and improve its effectiveness in the field of remedies. The Court has seized the opportunity presented by Article 47 of the EUCFR to increase the legality and legitimacy of its previous case law and, for the most part, to insert higher standards of judicial protection into the legal orders through the national courts. Yet, the lack of clarity in relation to definitions of key concepts, their scope and interrelationship with existing case law are proving to complicate matters further. There is serious potential for the complexity to increase and a danger that the system becomes unworkable. In contrast, the Court has yet to embrace the full potential of Article 19(1) TEU, second subparagraph, to strengthen not only the legality and legitimacy of its existing remedies case law, but also to qualitatively increase the standards of remedies in a non-fundamental rights context. This would promote an alignment of the regulatory goals and constitutional values and improve the effectiveness of important aspects of the private enforcement system.

The chapter also considers how the institutional design of the model of private enforcement can impinge on its effectiveness. It is clear that the construction of a private enforcement system through case law can present challenges to the constitutional values of legal certainty and stability and the corresponding regulatory goals of clarity and predictability. Whilst it is acknowledged that these pressures are not confined to EU law, they are exacerbated in the EU context by the nature of the Court's judgments and its heavy workload. The enactment of EU secondary legislation may appear to be the solution, but this possibility raises further challenges, particularly in relation to legality and legitimacy. An analysis of the functioning of preliminary ruling procedure reveals that the Court has put in place legal principles to enhance legal certainty and stability as well clarity and predictability. Yet, the effectiveness of the procedure is also contingent on the broader context in which it operates including socio-legal factors and judicial politics, undoubtedly fertile ground for further research.

2. The visible, the invisible and the impenetrable: innovations or rebranding in centralized enforcement of EU law?

Melanie Smith

plus ça change, plus c'est la même chose

INTRODUCTION

The centralized mechanism of enforcement in the EU law system of governance is known as the 'infringement proceedings' and has its legal basis in Article 258 TFEU.[1] The Commission has the power to ensure Member States fulfil their obligations under EU law and is considered the 'guardian of the treaties'. As part and parcel of this guardian role, the Commission undertakes a wide variety of tasks and has developed a plethora of compliance strategies to aid it in its mission to ensure the full application of EU law. Whilst the 'headline' legal procedure based on Article 258 TFEU is well known by lawyers and the data derived from it is often used by political scientists, only a small part (around 20 per cent) of the known enforcement work is carried out at this stage. Instead the majority of the Commission's enforcement work remains hidden, and there are multiple layers of enforcement behaviour[2] beneath the visible legal architecture. Despite this apparent imbalance there is little research undertaken into the

[1] The Commission finds its power as guardian of the treaties in Article 17 TEU; the Member State is obliged to cooperate with the Commission's investigation under the fidelity duty in Article 4(3) TEU.

[2] The term 'enforcement behaviour' is used here to denote enforcement practices of the Commission, rather than to describe certain regulatory styles (facilitative, rigid, and so on) or enforcement strategies writ large (eg, command and control, responsive regulation, and so on). It always refers to the Commission as this is the only actor under consideration in this chapter.

majority of the Commission's activity: indeed in order to appreciate the relevance and effectiveness of the 20 per cent it is crucial to understand the enforcement behaviour that precedes it.

Legal (doctrinal) scholarship on centralized enforcement has considered the nature of Commission discretion,[3] the inefficiency of the execution of proceedings,[4] the use of sanctions,[5] as well as examining centralized enforcement as just one of a plethora of tools and techniques of integration and governance in the EU.[6] More interdisciplinary work in this field has charted the increasing difficulties faced by the Commission in trying to hold onto a mechanism of enforcement that was born and raised in a different political, economic, legal and institutional setting to the one the EU faces today. Such works investigate the constitutionalization of the EU and the resultant changing nature of the institutional relationships involved,[7] expanding the reach of infringement proceedings from something of a closed process of diplomacy to a space of interaction that is much more nuanced and complex, involving multiple actors, all of whom have their own interests in the centralized mechanism of enforcement. This space of interaction has become ever more crowded: first the European citizen waded in, demanding to be treated better than information fodder; next the European Ombudsman made the case for the principles of good administration to be applied to this administrative behemoth;[8] finally

---

[3] AC Evans, 'The Enforcement Procedure of Article 169 EEC: Commission Discretion' (1979) *European Law Review* 442, Alan Dashwood and Robin White, 'Enforcement Actions under Articles 169 and 170 EEC' (1989) 14 *European Law Review* 388, Ann Bonnie, 'Commission Discretion under Article 171(2) EC' (1998) 23 *European Law Review* 537.

[4] Ann Bonnie, 'The Evolving Role of the European Commission in the Enforcement of Community Law: From Negotiating Compliance to Prosecuting Member States?' (2006) 1 *Journal of Contemporary European Research* 39.

[5] Steve Peers, 'Sanctions for Infringements of EU Law after the Treaty of Lisbon' (2012) 18 *European Public Law* 33, Ian Kilbey, 'Financial Penalties under Article 228(2) EC: Excessive Complexity?' (2007) 44 *Common Market Law Review* 743, Melanie Smith, 'Inter-institutional Dialogue and the Establishment of Enforcement Norms: A Decade of Financial Penalties under Article 228 EC (now 260 TFEU)' (2010) 16 *European Public Law* 547.

[6] Francis Snyder, 'The Effectiveness of European Community Law: Institutions, Processes, Tools and Techniques' (1993) 56 *Modern Law Review* 19.

[7] Melanie Smith, *Centralised Enforcement, Legitimacy and Good Governance in the EU* (Routledge 2009), Melanie Smith, 'Enforcement, Monitoring, Verification, Outsourcing: The Decline and Decline of the Infringement Process' (2008) 33 *European Law Review* 777.

[8] Richard Rawlings, 'Engaged Elites: Citizen Action and Institutional Attitudes in Commission Enforcement' (2000) 6 *European Law Journal* 4.

the European Parliament began to take a sustained and critical interest in the Commission's use of its guardian power, attempting to instil some accountability as the Court had, metaphorically, left the building.[9]

In exploring these tensions studies have chartered the various obstacles encountered in attempting to change the status quo, either from the perspective of greater transparency, accountability and legitimacy or from the perspective of increasing the effectiveness of a notoriously slow and cumbersome mechanism of enforcement. Yet other works have scrutinized the operation of the infringement process from the perspective of an emerging and increasingly significant body of EU administrative law principles which challenge the settled legal wisdom which cossets the Commission from judicial (or other) scrutiny of its exercise of executive power.[10] Taken together these studies form a picture of centralized enforcement that is increasingly complex. However, none of the existing scholarship pays sufficient attention to the Commission's enforcement role in its entirety.

The novel contribution to the scholarship on centralized enforcement in this chapter is the analysis of the whole of the Commission's activity in its centralized enforcement role, positing it as a layered enforcement model. The chapter will firstly analyse the centralized enforcement mechanism through the lens of regulatory scholarship in an attempt to understand the prevailing norms or phases which have led to its present incarnation. Secondly, the chapter will examine the relatively unknown elements of the enforcement model that comprise the Commission's compliance promoting toolkit,[11] questioning whether these tools are recent innovations in the Commission's arsenal of compliance or merely rebranding of old ideas in regulatory terminology. In doing so this chapter seeks to unpack the messy, apparently ad hoc approach to enforcement and present a more

---

[9] Melanie Smith, 'Accountability in Issue: The Commission, the European Parliament and Enforcement of EU Obligations' (forthcoming).

[10] Smith, *Centralised Enforcement*, supra n 7, Alexandros Tsadiras 'Unravelling Ariadne's Thread: The European Ombudsman's Investigation Powers' (2008) 45 *Common Market Law Review* 757, Maria Mendrinou, 'Non-compliance and the European Commission's Role in Integration' (1996) 3 *Journal of European Public Policy* 1, Roberto Mastroianni, 'The Enforcement Procedure under Article 169 of the EC Treaty and the Powers of the European Commission: Quis Custodiet Custodes?' (1995) 1 *European Public Law* 535, Päivi Leino, 'The Wind Is in the North. The First European Ombudsman (1995–2003)' (2004) 10 *European Public Law* 333, Carol Harlow and Richard Rawlings, 'Accountability and Law Enforcement: The Centralised EU Infringement Procedure' (2006) 31 *European Law Review* 447.

[11] These are the range of regulatory tools and techniques that the Commission employs in order to ensure compliance with EU law as part of its guardian role.

systematic model. Finally the chapter will consider whether we can really evaluate the effectiveness of this model of enforcement when seen in its entirety (ie, horizontally across policy sectors and vertically in the enforcement model), whether the quest for greater effectiveness is the apparent driver behind the changes in the enforcement model, and questions what effective enforcement might mean for centralized enforcement of EU law.

Section 1 of this chapter presents the Commission's model of enforcement as a layered and complex set of enforcement behaviours. Section 2 then maps out the very patchy legal rules and principles (layer one) that govern the centralized mechanism of enforcement, contrasting this sparse legal picture with the assumptions present in certain political science approaches to centralized enforcement. Section 3 provides a more detailed overview of what occurs in the second (invisible) and third (impenetrable) layers of the enforcement process (the administrative operation and executive choices) where the majority of enforcement occurs, in order to elucidate the somewhat shadowy processes that drive the enforcement activity of the Commission. It unpacks the least visible enforcement activity of the Commission with respect to its smart regulation agenda – the compliance promoting toolkit – and considers whether these elements of the model represent innovations in enforcement techniques or merely rebranding of old practices in new regulatory terminology.

1. THE COMMISSION'S LAYERED MODEL OF ENFORCEMENT

The model below is essentially a diagrammatic representation of the whole of the centralized enforcement process. The triangle format merely represents the decreasing volume of actual compliance work undertaken by the Commission by stages, where the tip of the enforcement regime represents the smallest amount of actual enforcement work undertaken.[12] The tip of the enforcement triangle is the part of the enforcement behaviour discussed below in this section – that is, the legal process of the infringement procedure, producer of beloved data sets.[13] It is on this (very limited)

[12] It does not attempt to mirror Ayres and Braithwaite's responsive regulation model (see van der Heijden in Ch 3) which advises regulators to begin at the bottom and move upwards through increasingly severe sanctions. Ian Ayers and John Braithwaite, *Responsive Regulation* (OUP 1995).

[13] For the purposes of this model, the complex inter-institutional interactions that take place within this element of the procedure have not been included as they are not germane to this analysis.

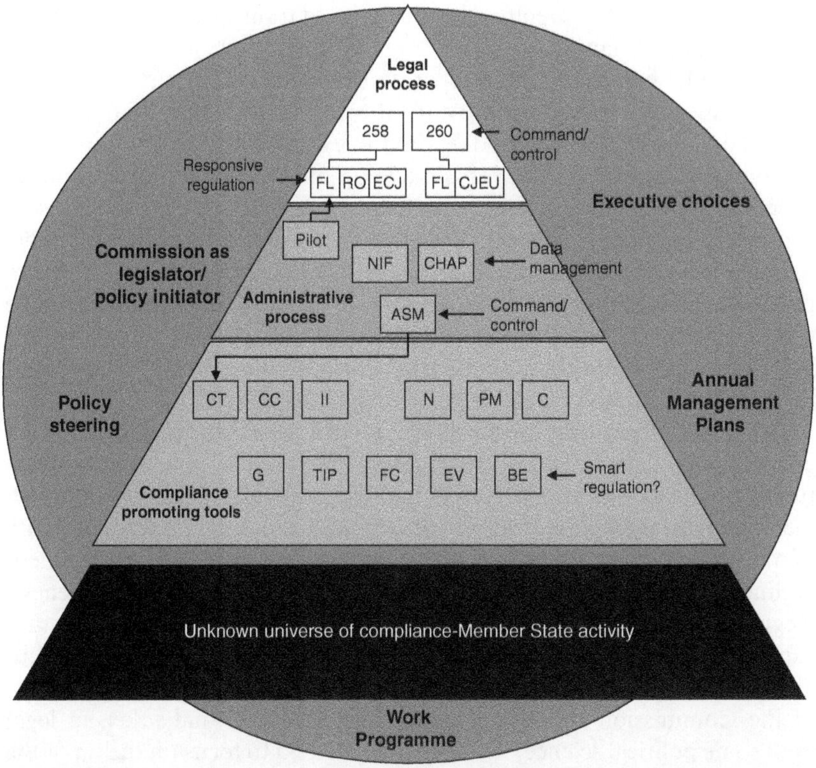

Note: CT (Correlation Tables), CC (Conformity Checking), II (Investigations and Inspections), N (Networks), PM (Package Meetings), C (Committees), G (Guidelines), TIP (Transpositions and Implementation Plans), FC (Fitness Check), EV (Evaluation), BE (Bespoke Enforcement).

Figure 2.1 The Commission's enforcement model

aspect of centralized enforcement that both legal literature and political science scholars focus. When viewed through the analytical lens of the model, it is argued that this is a rather limited vision of what centralized enforcement really encompasses.

In order to understand and evaluate the effectiveness of the centralized enforcement mechanism we must first attempt to bring coherence to enforcement practices. Figure 2.1 attempts to bring a systematic approach to discussion of the centralized enforcement by presenting the Commission's enforcement practices as constituent parts of a cohesive model, connected to, but not necessarily driven by, the unknown universe of compliance (ie, the Member State activity in transposing, implementing and applying EU law).

The model comprises three separate but interrelated parts: the tip of the enforcement triangle represents the formal (visible) legal process; the second layer consists of the (invisible) administrative enforcement behaviours; and the third layer is made up of the (impenetrable) compliance promoting toolkit, which is part administrative and part executive in character. Floating below this but slightly disconnected is the unknown universe of compliance. Finally this enforcement model sits within a policy and legislative sphere made up of multiple factors that shape the Commission's enforcement strategies and behaviours, including the prioritization of its political agenda which influences the selection of instruments for enforcement as part of its guardian role.

Regulatory theory can provide an analytical lens through which we can conceptualize how enforcement regimes that exist in governance structures (ie, outside traditional 'top down' hierarchical government arrangements) might operate in order to preserve a certain level of accountability of the actors found in traditional command and control enforcement regimes, whilst at the same time attempting to optimize its effectiveness. Regulatory scholarship is particularly adept at providing heuristics that can encapsulate multiple actors, multiple strategies and a range of available sanctions in any given enforcement regime. This moves the analysis of the Commission's model of enforcement beyond that taken in legal (and some political science) literature, which tend to focus on the tip of the enforcement model and understand it as a simple command and control regime: a rule is breached and the Commission prosecutes. Analysing the Commission's model of enforcement through the lens of regulatory scholarship moves this discussion forward since it enables us to unpack what actually occurs in the enforcement practices of the regulator (the Commission).

Even when we use the explanatory tools available in regulatory scholarship, analysis of the Commission's enforcement model still proves challenging, either at the micro (individual) or macro (holistic) level, as not all of the Commission's enforcement practices conform to pre-established regulatory techniques. There are aspects of Ayres and Braithwaite's heuristic of responsive regulation[14] present in the legal process: as the Commission moves through each stage of the process the Member State incurs increasingly serious sanctions. The formal letter (FL) and reasoned opinion (RO) stages are publicized and are part of the Commission's

---

[14] See Ch 3 of this book for a detailed explanation of this model, n 12.

'name and shame' sanctioning of Member State behaviour. Proceeding to the CJEU increases this level of naming and shaming, with the possibility of: (a) declaring that Member States have broken the law, and (b) for non-communication of transposition measures, a possible financial sanction. As the legal process moves on to Article 260 TFEU, the sanctions become ever more severe, with the Member State facing much larger financial sanctions in the form of a lump sum and/or penalty payment to reflect the original infraction and the breach of the rule of law.[15]

Moving downwards through the enforcement triangle to the second layer, the administrative process itself contains a mix of regulatory styles. Although certain elements in the administrative process relate to simple data management (NIF database and CHAP),[16] the Asmodee II database (ASM) which tracks Member States' efforts at transposition (including notification measures) acts more like a command and control type mechanism since breach here is more or less automatically pursued as an infringement.[17] In contrast the EU Pilot[18] (Pilot) is a forum for negotiation and communication between the Member State and the Commission, where the Commission makes multiple attempts to come to a solution with the Member State before moving the file onwards to the formal legal process. It is unlikely that this could be considered as part of the command and control or responsive regulation approach as there are no (increasingly serious) sanctions throughout this process: it is completely confidential so there is no element of naming and shaming present.

The third layer of the model reveals the Commission's largely unexplored compliance promoting toolkit (analysed in detail in Section 3 of this chapter). These various enforcement tools are a mix of identification measures aimed at discovery (and prevention) of infringements, meetings and consultations between Member States, networks, interested parties

---

[15] See Paul Craig and Gráinne de Búrca, *EU Law: Text, Cases and Materials* (6th edn, OUP 2015) ch 12.

[16] NIF is the database that the Commission uses to manage infringement files once the formal legal process begins. It is from this database that the infringement 'fiche' is constructed and presented to the College of Commissioners. CHAP is a database that is used to register complaints and inquiries to the Commission regarding potential infractions of EU law by Member States.

[17] See Commission Communication 'Better Monitoring of the Application of Community Law' COM (2002) 725 final, Commission Communication 'A Europe of Results: Applying Community Law' COM (2007) 502 final.

[18] For a more detailed analysis of this method of infringement case handling, see Melanie Smith, 'The Evolution of the Infringement and Sanction Procedures: Of Pilots, Diversions, Collisions and Circling' in Anthony Arnull and Damian Chalmers (eds), *The Oxford Handbook of EU Law* (OUP 2015).

and the Commission (a type of regulation through consensus building?) and policy management tools.[19] The Commission itself has branded many of these tools as a form of smart regulation.[20] Finally all of these enforcement techniques are situated within a much bigger picture that determines the choices made by Commission staff in pursuing infringement cases. The Commission's Work Programme sets out the Commission's political vision and strategic priorities which feed into each Directorate General's (DG) Annual Management Plan that in turn contain specific enforcement goals for that DG set in advance of (and not as a reaction to) what is happening in the unknown universe of compliance. Besides these formal management structures, the Commission is both the initiator and drafter of legislation and this policy-steering role also influences its choices when it comes to its enforcement strategy.

Regulatory theory can provide tools to understand and better describe certain practices of the Commission when it acts as regulator, but as yet, it cannot (nor does it seek to) provide an explanatory tool for the Commission model as a whole. It is perhaps easier to understand the development of this model by referring to regulatory theory, and additionally, evaluating it through the various phases of (general) policy development over the last 15 years or so. Many aspects of the enforcement regime pre-dated any turn to good governance techniques or new regulatory fashions. Certainly the legal regime at the tip of the enforcement model has remained largely unchanged since inception;[21] large parts of the

---

[19] It probably does not conform to standards of collaborative governance since the Commission only recognizes the Member State as an actor it proactively cooperates with.

[20] Communication from the Commission to the European Parliament, the Council, the European Economic and Social Committee and the Committee of the Regions 'Strengthening the Foundations of Smart Regulation: Improving Evaluation' COM (2013) 686 final, Communication from the Commission to the European Parliament, the Council, the European Economic and Social Committee and the Committee of the Regions 'Regulatory Fitness and Performance (REFIT): Results and Next Steps' COM (2013) 685. Although this is the Commission's version of smart regulation rather than that found in academic literature, see van der Heijden, Ch 3.

[21] Article 258 TFEU, the focus of this chapter, has not changed at all since 1957. However, changes have been made to the associated financial sanctions which have evolved from a mere second declaration (see the original Article 171 EEC) to the inclusion of a financial sanction under the Treaty of Maastricht (see Article 228 EC), the evolution in CJEU jurisprudence to include the possibility of a double sanction of daily penalties and lump sum, to finally the Lisbon amendments of including a sanction in Article 258 TFEU by way of Article 260(3) TFEU and removing the requirement of a reasoned opinion in Article 260(2) TFEU.

administrative phase have evolved with the greater use of IT platforms but have been around in some form or another for some time, preceding, for example, the Commission's focus on good governance in the early 2000s.[22] The most recent addition to layer two, the administrative layer of enforcement, is the EU Pilot which may be framed as a part of the Commission's good governance programme, although all it really achieved was a formalization of previously existing informal processes of negotiation that were a long-standing part of the Commission's enforcement behaviour before it engaged the legal process.[23]

Regulatory trends evolved into better regulation initiatives that had political and economic resonance in an EU that was increasingly unpopular and seen to be overburdening small and medium sized enterprises through excessive red tape.[24] One current iteration of this, smart regulation, has so far focused on developing evidence-based legislation in the form of impact assessments,[25] streamlining regulatory programmes through Fitness Checks[26] and the REFIT[27] initiative, and latterly through focusing on *ex post* evaluations of interventions in order, amongst other things, to enhance the effectiveness of the policy cycle.[28] These policy phases have enabled the Commission to retrospectively re-label some of

---

22 Commission Communication 'European Governance: A White Paper' COM (2001) 428 final.

23 There were multiple reasons for the development of the EU Pilot, for example, the enlargement of the Union and the need to streamline and make more efficient complaint handling systems as well as the Commission taking more interest in standardizing DG's enforcement behaviour and to enable a better quality of internal monitoring to take place by the Secretariat General.

24 This is not the sequence of evolution of regulatory theory, see van der Heijden, Ch 3, and the Commission has recently started using the term 'better regulation' again, see the 2015 Commission Work Programme: Communication from the Commission to the European Parliament, the Council, the European Economic and Social Committee and the Committee of the Regions 'Commission Work Programme 2015' COM (2014) 910 final.

25 See <http://ec.europa.eu/smart-regulation/impact/index_en.htm> accessed 10 March 2015 for more details.

26 Labelled FC in the model. See <http://ec.europa.eu/smart-regulation/evaluation/docs/fitness_checks_2012_en.pdf> accessed 10 March 2015.

27 REFIT is the European Commission's Regulatory Fitness and Performance programme. It focuses on making EU law simpler and to reducing regulatory costs 'thus contributing to a clear, stable and predictable regulatory framework supporting growth and jobs', <http://ec.europa.eu/smart-regulation/refit/index_en.htm> accessed 10 March 2015.

28 Labelled EV in the model. See <http://ec.europa.eu/smart-regulation/evaluation/index_en.htm> accessed 10 March 2015 for more details on the Evaluation programme.

its existing enforcement behaviour and have led to a few new enforcement techniques being developed, largely in layer three of the model.

The ad hoc development of centralized enforcement has led to a complex mix of regulatory techniques at the micro and macro level. The multiple layers of enforcement have visible vertical links, for instance moving upwards through the model, there are obvious connections between elements of the Commission's compliance promoting toolkit located in layer three (Correlation Tables and Conformity Checking) which clearly relate to, and flow from, the Commission's Asmodee II database which tracks transposition of directives. There is also a link between the EU Pilot (layer two) and the formal letter stage of the formal legal process (layer one). It is not the case, however, that each potential infraction proceeds smoothly upwards through the triangle of measures, nor that each stage can be cleanly disentangled from the next. The Commission demonstrates a decidedly 'pick and mix' approach to its enforcement model and potential infractions are not all treated in the same way. Some begin immediately in the legal process whilst others are left to languish amongst the compliance promoting toolkit.

Analysing the Commission's enforcement behaviour in this way raises some difficult questions about judging the effectiveness of centralized enforcement of EU law (at the micro or macro level). Since the model is both complex and interrelated it is indefensible to try to take one level to stand for all: one cannot simply point to enforcement data and conclude it is/is not effective. Is it possible (and practical) to have multiple measures of effectiveness at each level of the model, with the overall effectiveness being judged as a composite of all of these? On what normative basis should we assess effectiveness? Is it to be judged on assessing how many EU norms have been translated (exactly) into Member State laws, or is it about how many EU norms are being applied and facilitated correctly? Is it about uniformity of treatment (of measures, policy sectors and Member States) or is it about efficient and effective targeting of resources to 'problem' areas which have the greatest effect on EU values transmuted into political priorities (Energy Union, Digital Union, migration, and so on)? Should we measure total compliance or the best available given limited resources? Is it about assessing the efficiency and effectiveness of the Commission, questioning its use of resources and rendering its actions both transparent and accountable to the European Parliament, the Member States and the citizen? And when judging effectiveness, from whose perspective should we assess it? From the Commission's perspective or that of the end user of EU law (the individual who is trying to realize their EU rights) or the public interest? And whom is to be judged in this question of effectiveness? The Commission as the responsible institution for ensuring the application of EU law or the Member State as the actor largely responsible for implementing it? Is it a complex triangulation of all of the above?

Different studies tend to focus on only one of these elements when judging the effectiveness of the infringement procedure, and in much of political science, the focus is on implementation within the Member State rather than Commission behaviour as guardian or regulator. However, when judging the effectiveness of the centralized mechanism of enforcement it is arguable that we should limit our focus to judging the Commission's performance as guardian of the treaties: it is the Commission that controls and designs this process of enforcement and it is the Member State who is the subject of it. Herein lies the rub: we have only the Commission's own assessment and data to tell us how effective the Commission is as guardian of the treaties, and much of this information is incomplete.[29]

2. THE LEGAL FRAMEWORK: THE VISIBLE LAYER OF COMMISSION ENFORCEMENT

Article 258 TFEU, and the Commission's concomitant duty as guardian of the treaties, has been analysed extensively in legal literature. Doctrinally, very little has changed since the CJEU set the rules of the game very early on in the 1960s and so, besides the odd interesting case which might deal with something of particular political significance, there appears to be little or nothing new under the sun. The legal framework tells us that if a Member State does not 'fulfil' their obligations under EU law the Commission has the power to refer them to Court. The infringement process is characterized by the Court as a closed diplomatic process of negotiation between the Member State and the Commission which first attempts to negotiate a solution to the potential infringement and, if this negotiation phase fails, then the case *may* (but not must) progress to the legal process[30] outlined in the treaty text: sending a letter of formal notice, a reasoned opinion, referral to Court and CJEU judgment. If the Member State continues to infract, the case *may* again (after a formal notice) be

[29] Although in assessing Member State performance, we may be able to show a difference between the Commission's assessment of a Member State's performance and the Member State's actual or own assessment of its performance, these questions do not elaborate the Commission's enforcement behaviour in detail.

[30] The use of the term 'may' denotes the legal encapsulation of the Commission's discretion. It may do whatever it wants at each of these stages. It is in the 'black hole' of this discretion that most of the Commission's model of enforcement has evolved.

Table 2.1 Snapshot of the visible layer: Commission activity in prosecuting infringements (2013)

Stage of the Procedure	Number	Top Three Sectors	Member State
FL	761	Environment, Transport, Health	Italy, France, Spain
RO	217	Environment, Energy, Tax	Italy, Romania, Belgium
CJEU Article 258	52	Taxation, Transport, Environment	France, Poland, Spain
Ref (Article 260(3) LTI referrals)	14	Energy	Belgium, Bulgaria, Estonia, Romania, UK
CJEU Article 260(3) LTI referrals)	12 pending*	Energy	*UK complied, proceedings withdrawn
CJEU Article 260 (2)	5	Environment, Transport, Tax	Belgium, Czech Republic, Luxembourg

Note: LTI – Late Transposition Infractions

referred under Article 260 TFEU for a financial penalty. Since Lisbon, the Commission *may* request a financial penalty under Article 260(3) TFEU for failure to notify measures in relation to the transposition of directives in the course of Article 258 proceedings.[31]

Table 2.1 provides a snapshot of the Commission's activity in the legal process in 2013. Transport and Energy, Internal Market and Tax have consistently been in the top four sectors pursued by the Commission for some time.[32] The internal market is not as prominent as it once was in these latest statistics, perhaps in part due to the fact that there are now well-established alternative mechanisms to pursue problems in this area (eg, SOLVIT).[33] Environment, however, continues to dominate the (visible) enforcement activity of the Commission. Environmental compliance is relatively challenging for well-rehearsed reasons – the difficulty

[31] Article 260(3) TFEU. Although Article 260 is a corollary provision to Article 258 it will not be extensively analysed in this chapter.

[32] See Smith, *Centralised Enforcement*, supra n 7 ch 5, which analyses Commission behaviour between 1998–2008.

[33] See Chs 4, 5 and 6 in this volume.

in compliance (social, political, and financial cost) and the complexity of achieving compliance.[34] In addition to this, environmental problems tend to occur over a long period of time, persisting for decades and therefore suit the machinations of a convoluted and lengthy enforcement process. The Energy sector has also been part of the top three or four sectors for several years[35] and now has the distinction of being the sector that the Commission is using to trailblaze its new enforcement powers in relation to non-notification of measures for transposing directives. There are in fact fewer cases of non-compliance pursued by the Commission in the Energy sector present in the earlier stages of the administrative procedure (see Table 2.2), however, in the legal stages DG ENER (Directorate General for Energy) is pursuing the remaining cases with some ambition and against Member States that are traditionally considered as 'good' performers in Commission annual reports. The Member States that consistently appear to be the laggards at the earlier stages of the legal process (Italy, Spain, France) are the same states that historically always feature highly in the Commission statistics. The Commission's success rate before the CJEU has historically been very high (in 2012, for example, 91 per cent of cases were decided in the Commission's favour)[36] but for 2013 the success rate was down to 51 per cent.[37] There is no explanation provided by the Commission for this sudden decrease in its effectiveness before the CJEU and it is not connected to an increase in 'case traffic' since fewer cases were taken this year than last.

The basic legal architecture has seen very little change in jurisprudence and no secondary legislation. This lack of legal development perpetuates a rather limited view of the infringement process and has been subject to criticism in legal literature. To begin with the 'exclusive nature' of the legal process is seen as outdated and lacking procedural legitimacy. Third parties (such as complainants, NGOs and others) have no access to this process nor can they assert any rights in a court of law in connection with infringement proceedings. Even if they are the originator of the investigation, they cannot force the Commission to take the Member State to Court to protect their EU rights, or force the Commission to take a deci-

---

[34] On this see Ch 7 in this volume.

[35] Historically it was merged with Transport for the purpose of the Commission's annual reports, and now the Energy Union is a stated political priority of the Juncker Commission.

[36] Report from the Commission '30th Annual Report on Monitoring the Application of EU Law (2012)' COM (2013) 726.

[37] Report from the Commission '31st Annual Report on Monitoring the Application of EU Law (2013)' COM (2014) 612.

sion on a potential infraction, or to provide reasons for their decisions (or lack of) to pursue or not pursue a Member State; nor can they command access to any information that the Commission may have uncovered in the course of its investigation in order to assist in a private action.[38] All information on infringements is considered confidential and is not accessible under the usual public access rules.[39] Even when the subject of the potential infringement has passed into historical fact, documents may still be protected (although in certain circumstances these may be released after the court has given a judgment on the case).[40] In contrast Member States have been granted limited rights of defence that have been protected by the Court.[41]

In respect of centralized enforcement of EU law the Commission's power is total and (save the Member States' limited rights) totally unregulated by the Court. It is at the Commission's discretion as to whether it starts an investigation (or closes it) or refers the Member State through each stage outlined in the treaties. There is nothing inevitable about a case being referred to the Court once the Commission has discovered an infraction: quite the opposite in fact, the Commission will generally try to avoid this at all costs.[42] Even if the Commission fails to resolve the infraction,

---

[38] Case 48/65 *Lütticke v Commission* [1966] ECR 19, Case 247/87 *Star Fruit v Commission* [1989] ECR 291.

[39] Regulation (EC) No 1049/2001 of the European Parliament and of the Council of 30 May 2001 regarding public access to European Parliament, Council and Commission documents OJ L 145/43.

[40] Case T-105/95 *WWF UK v Commission* [1997] ECR II-313, Case T-309/97 *Bavarian Lager Company v Commission* [1999] ECR II-3217, Case T-191/99 *Petrie and Others v Commission* [2001] ECRII-3677. In Case T-194/04 *Bavarian Lager v Commission* [2007] ECR II-4523 the Court confirmed that documents relating to a case that had been closed 6 years previously could be released in certain circumstances and in Joined Cases C-514/07 P, C-528/07 P and C-532/07 P *Sweden and Others v API and Commission* [2010] ECR I-8533 that documents would not be protected once the CJEU had handed down a judgment on that case.

[41] These relate to ensuring that the Commission sets out its legal case in the reasoned opinion, Case C-371/04 *Commission v Italy* [2006] ECR I-10257, Case C-494/01 *Commission v Ireland* [2005] ECR I-3331, Case C-11/95 *Commission v Belgium* [1996] ECR I-4115, and does not take 'excessive time' to bring a case (although no time limit is set), Case C-350/02 *Commission v Netherlands* [2004] ECR I-6213.

[42] Although the Commission has the power to see through a case even once the infraction has been remedied. See Bonnie, 'The Evolving Role of the European Commission in the Enforcement of Community Law', supra n 4, and Commission Communication 'Better Monitoring of the Application of Community Law' COM (2002) 725 final, Commission Communication 'A Europe of Results: Applying Community Law' COM (2007) 502 final.

there is nothing to suggest it *must* refer the case to Court. Although the process is characterized as 'objective' in nature, this should not be confused with a portrayal of the Commission as a somehow objective actor who pursues every infringement with equal vigour. An 'objective procedure' simply means that cases proceed before the CJEU on the basis of findings of fact (the Member State has or has not fulfilled its obligations) not on the basis of whether they intended to infract or infracted with an omission by reason of malice or negligence.[43]

This brief overview of the legal framework representing the pinnacle of the Commission's enforcement model establishes that the legal rules in this area: (a) do not dictate that the Commission pursues all infringements, (b) that the Commission is not neutral or objective nor is it required to be in law, (c) does not dictate how the Commission carries out its enforcement work as part of the infringement process or before the Commission instigates that process, and (d) that the Commission is completely protected from outside interference of how it executes its duty as guardian of the treaties. The rights and wrongs of this position have been debated extensively elsewhere and need not detain us here.[44] It would be easy for non-lawyers to assume this is a highly regulated area of institutional conduct since it is so critical to EU integration, respect for the rule of law, and central to the Commission's institutional duties but in fact the converse is true. The legal rules and principles tell us next to nothing about how the Commission centrally enforces EU law: it is only in the study of the Commission's enforcement behaviour as a whole that things become clearer. Not understanding this leads to dangerous assumptions.

2.1 Janus-Faced: Focusing on the Tip of the (Visible) Layer of Enforcement Data

Whereas lawyers tend to look in one direction in the study of centralized enforcement (the legal rules), political science work often looks in the opposite direction (Member State implementation) with little acknowledgement or connection made between the research findings. There is a rich and extensive literature in political science that uses the

---

43 There is case law on this precise point: Case C-71/97 *Commission v Spain* [1998] ECR I-5991, see also Roland Beiber and Francesco Maiani, 'Enhancing Centralized Enforcement of EU Law: Pandora's Toolbox?' (2014) 51 *Common Market Law Review* 1057.

44 Damian Chalmers, Gareth Davies and Giorgio Monti, *European Union Law: Text and Materials* (3rd ed, CUP 2014), Smith, *Centralised Enforcement*, supra n 7, Rawlings, 'Engaged Elites', supra n 8.

data generated by Article 258 TFEU both theoretically and empirically. Infringement data provide beloved data sets on which assumptions can be built and tested, and hypotheses proved or disproved. Enforcement data has been used predominantly in compliance theory and in international relations work.[45] There are numerous studies on the compliance with particular aspects of EU law, such as compliance within or across Member States with particular directives, or a group of directives. Compliance studies can focus on simple transposition data (who transposed x number of directives on time), or through case studies that look into barriers to compliance, or specific transposition measures and implementation of directives in one or more Member States.[46] Studies may take a cross-section of Member States and a cross-section of directives. Drawing from these empirical observations, political scientists construct hypotheses or theories regarding worlds of compliance,[47] or good states versus bad states[48] and so on.[49]

When studying compliance with EU law, empirical and statistical work essentially faces two choices: scholars can either source data individually or through collaboration across states (time-consuming, expensive and linguistically difficult) or they can use Commission data which is (relatively) accessible through the Commission's annual reports.[50] However, both of these approaches to sourcing data have serious problems with respect to positing generalizations about EU-wide Member

---

[45] For example, Tanja A Börzel, 'Non-Compliance in the European Union: Pathology or Statistical Artefact' (2001) 8 *Journal of European Public Policy* 803, Jonas Tallberg, *European Governance and Supranational Institutions: Making States Comply* (Routledge 2003).

[46] Markus Haverland, Bernard Steunenberg and Frans van Waarden, 'Sectors at Different Speeds: Analysing Transposition Deficits in the European Union' (2011) 49 *Journal of Common Market Studies* 265 is a study of over 1,000 instruments across 8 policy sectors and 5 Member States.

[47] Gerda Faulkner, Oliver Treib, Mirian Hartlapp and Simone Leiber, *Complying with Europe: EU Harmonization and Soft Law in the Member States* (CUP 2005).

[48] Tanja A Börzel, 'Pace-Setting, Foot-Dragging and Fence-Sitting: Member State Responses to Europeanization' 40 *Journal of Common Market Studies* 193.

[49] Chs 4 and 6 both provide a state of the art literature review in political science approaches to enforcement of EU law.

[50] Relatively because unfortunately the Commission has redesigned its annual reports over the last six years or so on a fairly regular basis, and so it no longer presents the same information that it did ten years previously, and there can be 18 months' delay in publication. This makes historical comparison of trends, for instance, particularly difficult. Some researchers have had limited access to the Commission's NIF database although this is rare.

State behaviour. The sample size of EU legislation (including treaty principles and case law) amounts to thousands of instruments translated across 28 Member States. It is simply too large for any one study to be able to collect and analyse: as such drawing generalizations from partial data sets will always be compromised.[51] When it comes to research using Commission data things become especially problematic: these may be used as a 'good enough' dataset considered representative of true compliance across the Union. This false premise leads to fundamental misunderstandings of how the infringement process works (including its governing legal framework).

A recent study by two political scientists, Börzel and Knoll,[52] illustrates the difficulties faced by some scholars working in isolation within their discipline. Börzel and Knoll compiled a database comprised of statistics from the Commission as part of its (legal) infringement work and from this data analyse how many reasoned opinions are issued, the time taken per prosecution, number of infringement proceedings per state, variance across EU states and so on. However, the purpose of the study is to quantify non-compliance across the EU, not to report Commission data on legal proceedings, and so they make a number of conceptual leaps in order to bridge the gap. They readily admit that Commission data does not represent a complete picture of compliance but nevertheless assert that the cases represented at the legal stage are 'a fair representation of the universe of non-compliance'.[53] According to this line of argument the Commission has a 'clear legal mandate' to prosecute infringements (true, but as explained above this does not equate to it being 'mandated' to do so – it is at the Commission's absolute discretion). They also point to the 'unequivocal' formulation of Article 258: again Article 258 clearly gives the Commission discretion to do whatever it wants and has never been interpreted by the CJEU to mean that the Commission must prosecute all matters of non-compliance, rather, quite the opposite. There are then repeated invocations in the study that the Commission is 'bound to

---

[51] We may accept individually sourced Member State data as a true reflection of what has been studied. It is possible to say with certainty that directive x was (or was not) implemented across x Member States, for example, if this work is done by studying the legislation in a Member State rather than Commission data. When we know this, we might be able to say with certainty that, say, a directive on dealing with environmental waste is more problematic in one Member State and not in another.

[52] Tanja A Börzel and Moritz Knoll, 'Quantifying Non-Compliance in the EU: A Database in EU Infringement Proceedings' *Berlin Working Paper on European Integration* 15 (November 2012).

[53] Börzel, ibid 7.

prosecute'[54] when the converse is true: there is a clear and fundamental misunderstanding of *both the law and practice* here.

Following on from this, Börzel and Knoll state that if the Commission 'selected' cases it would undermine its own legitimacy and credibility, therefore to do so is counter-intuitive (though the Commission itself readily admits to selecting cases[55]); furthermore the Commission is bound by a powerful 'logic of appropriateness' which ensures that it will not act inappropriately in case selection (the argument here concerns demonstrating obvious bias between Member States).[56] Many studies into the Commission as an organization contradict this position as they characterize the Commission as a multifunctional body full of motivations and agendas depending on which function it is executing,[57] and furthermore studies into the infringement mechanism show the Commission can lack legitimacy on precisely these grounds.[58] Moreover the selection of one specific type of bias (of favouring one State over another) skews the analysis further since there are many different types of potential bias in play, for example, as between instruments, policy sectors, DGs, individual Commissioner's political preference, ease of prosecution and so on, that to premise the hypothesis on one type of bias (own country preference) is very misleading. A thorough understanding of actual practice in selecting cases for prosecution instantly rebuts this premise.[59]

Börzel and Knoll also point to the clear supranational character (here they mean neutral) of the Commission which prevents Commission officials demonstrating bias in favour of their own country, and that in any case decisions to prosecute and escalate prosecutions are taken by the (political) College of Commissioners. This in itself appears contradictory – on the one hand suggesting that prosecutions are automatic, non-political

---

[54] Börzel, ibid 8.

[55] See the Commission Communication on Better Monitoring, supra n 17.

[56] Applying a theory by James G March and Johan P Olsen, 'The Institutional Dynamics of International Political Orders' (1998) 52 *International Organization* 943. In reality it is these kinds of practices (not being entirely transparent in its choices) that have led to the extensive criticism of the Commission by academics, the European Parliament and the European Ombudsman.

[57] Michelle Cini, *The European Commission: Leadership, Organisation, and Culture in the EU Administration* (Manchester University Press 1996), Michele Chang and Jörg Monar (eds), *The European Commission in the Post-Lisbon Era of Crisis* (PIE Peter Lang 2013).

[58] A lack of regulation and review of the exercise of executive discretion inevitably leads to problems of administrative legitimacy, see Smith, *Centralised Enforcement*, supra n 7 ch 4, 5.

[59] Ibid ch 4, 5, 6.

and mandatory, whilst on the other acknowledging the important role played by the political body of the Commission, which is ever consumed with politics. Even if it is true that there is no prosecuting bias from Commission officials with regard to their country of origin (which may well be correct and probably is), it is certainly not true that there is no prosecuting bias as regards particular pieces of legislation or policy areas: in fact again the converse is true. The Commission is the instigator and evaluator of most Union legislation and has a particular interest in prioritizing some areas over others – it freely admits this in its own publications. Börzel and Knoll fail to mention in any case that Commissioners do not discover infringements: they may only take a decision once this has been presented to them by the staff of the DG, and by the Commission's own reckoning 80 per cent of the infringement work is managed out of the official process and never makes it to this formal stage. There is a set of 'pre-College' decisions that determine both policy and practice of infringement prosecutions.

The authors go on to make a second argument about why the sample of data is a fair representation of the universe of compliance: that although one could argue there might be a 'detection bias' (since the Commission lacks resources to pursue every possible infringement), this argument is invalid because the detection of non-compliance does not rely on the Commission alone as there are various other actors involved. It is true that complainants make up 49 per cent of detection,[60] however, only the Commission decides which of these 'detections' are investigated, negotiated, pursued or dropped as an infringement investigation. Regardless of who detects potential infraction, it is the Commission that moves the case forward, so a lack of detection bias is irrelevant: bias can occur after detection in case selection.

The data produced by Börzel and Knoll is both interesting and important and could be used to answer interesting research questions, but those questions are different to the ones being asked. What is certain is that the Commission top-line statistics tell us something about the *Commission*, but almost nothing about the Member States. To study Member State behaviour, one must study Member State data derived from the actual legal picture in each Member State on each instrument, and indeed this is precisely the work that many political scientists

[60] Excluding those picked up by the Asmodee II database. Börzel and Moritz also point to the Asmodee II database which records notifications of transposition of measures from Member States although this is a Commission database so technically is also a Commission 'detection' for monitoring compliance.

pursue. To study Commission behaviour, however, we must look to Commission statistics. These tell us about Commission choices and strategies and can inform us about how the Commission's enforcement activities interweave with its wider policy positions and interventions, however, as posited in Figure 2.1, they do not describe (or even reflect) the universe of non-compliance.

3. UNPACKING THE ENFORCEMENT MODEL: THE (INVISIBLE) ADMINISTRATIVE LAYER AND THE (IMPENETRABLE) COMPLIANCE PROMOTING TOOLKIT

The second and third layers of the Commission's enforcement model encapsulate the majority of Commission enforcement activity. According to Commission figures, it deals with 80 per cent of the files opened as potential infractions in the format of the EU Pilot located in layer two (excluding detection of non-notification of measures through the Asmodee II database). How much of its enforcement work is then dealt with in the third layer of the model is a complete mystery to anyone outside of the Commission (and Member State representatives) as the Commission's activity here, and what it achieves in terms of quantification of concrete results, is not documented. The following sections unpack what occurs in these layers of enforcement. Once we can identify what occurs and begin to understand these processes, it becomes apparent just how difficult it is to assess the effectiveness of the centralized mechanism of enforcement.

3.1 Layer Two of the Model: The Administrative Procedure, Detection and Processing

The administrative stages of the infringement process are as follows. First an infraction is detected, either by a direct complaint to the Commission via individuals, legal entities, NGOs or petitions forwarded by the European Parliament; or by the Commission on its own initiative through officials auditing national practices; through standard investigating processes triggered by a review process contained in legislation; through cooperation with national agencies; through direct inspection by EU staff; or through the Commission's database which tracks the notification of measures by Member States that indicate they have transposed a directive. Once a potential infraction is notified to the Commission by a complainant it is registered in a centralized database managed by the Secretariat

General known as CHAP.[61] This begins a notional timeline for action on behalf of the Commission which has two weeks to initially respond to the complainant, an additional one month to open a file in EU Pilot and 12 months to take a decision to move the case forward or close it.

If the Commission decides to pursue the potential infringement, or the Commission discovers a potential infraction through an own initiative investigation, a file is opened in EU Pilot. This online platform enables direct communication between the Commission and Member State for the purpose of resolving potential infractions. Again non-binding time limits for actions are proposed by the Commission with a back-and-forth communication between itself and the Member State aiming to take just 20 weeks. If the Commission cannot resolve the file to its satisfaction, it will communicate this to the complainant and the Member State and *may* decide[62] to launch the formal legal process by sending a letter of formal notice, at which point the file is first put before the College of Commissioners for approval and entered into the NIF database. If the DG decides to close the case (resolved or unresolved), the DG does this on its own recognizance and does not take this to the College.

The College may decide in its monthly meeting to pursue or drop the case through each of the formal legal steps (formal letter, reasoned opinion and referral to CJEU) if it is presented with the opportunity to do so by the DG staff. These meetings are confidential and when a case is progressed or dropped no reasons are publically supplied. If the College approves further action, the DG continues to try and negotiate a solution at each stage and there is no time limit for action here – cases can and do stretch on for years, hence the well-rehearsed critique of the infringement process as slow and cumbersome. Should the case be referred to the CJEU the Commission can still decide to drop the case (at the DG level) if they choose to do so before a judgment is given.

The above description shows that there are multiple opportunities to either resolve or drop the infringement file which are not open to public scrutiny or reported in any format. If 80 per cent of the 'universe

---

[61] This database enables the Commission to keep track of its communications with citizens and its creation was necessitated by repeated complaints to the European Ombudsman regarding maladministration particularly in respect of acknowledging receipt of complaints.

[62] This decision is not the job of one desk officer. A case file has many hurdles to overcome as it must be approved by the supervisor, the Unit Head, the Director of the DG, the Commissioner via his *chef de cabinet* of the Commissioner for that DG before it is placed before a meeting of the College. At any point this file may be dropped.

of compliance' is dealt with at this stage, then clearly the remaining 20 per cent are not a 'fair representation' of the picture. This is because the reasons for not proceeding with a case can be complex, resource driven, strategy driven, administrative, and often relate to the particular culture of each DG (and each Commissioner) and the surrounding political circumstances. Such decisions can be as prosaic as how many people are dedicated to enforcement in a particular unit (it varies significantly) to how much emphasis a Director or Commissioner places on *ex post* enforcement as opposed to drafting new legislation.[63] It can be much more complex: the type of enforcement practice written into legislation may encourage other forms of direct and decentralized enforcement by business and citizens which enables the Commission to turn away from these types of interventions when prioritizing its own enforcement strategies.[64] The variables at play are, if not infinite, many and complex.

Within this second layer of the model, the 'innovations' in enforcement are not real innovations at all, but are all based on technological advancement i.e. the construction of multiple databases. Management of compliance by database is clearly resource efficient and institutionally there is a preference for this. There is an advantage in pursuing Asmodee II database infractions first – these are the easy cases, in both factual terms (it is a binary question – you have or have not notified measures which the database checks automatically) and in terms of Commission resources (its automated).[65] Certainly the NIF database which tracks the formal legal process and contains the infringement 'fiche' presented to Commissioners has been around for many, many decades and the practice of presenting infringement cases in this format dates back to the beginning of the Community.[66] The same can be said of the transposition database. The relatively new additions to the administrative layer, CHAP and EU Pilot are mere formalizations in database form of what always happened in the 'administrative letter' phase of the enforcement process, albeit less efficiently and with little management oversight.[67] This has not prevented

---

63 Smith, *Centralised Enforcement*, supra n 7, ch 4, 5, 6.

64 Melanie Smith, 'Evaluations and the Salience of Infringement Data' (2015) 6 *Journal of European Risk Regulation* 90–100.

65 The Commission's new powers in Article 260(3) TFEU are focused on exactly this problem, although LTIs were already the Commission's priority before these powers were introduced. Indeed this is precisely why the Commission agitated for them in the treaty revision process.

66 In 2008 the Commission started to present these cases monthly as opposed to quarterly to increase efficiency in processing infringement files.

67 HAH Audretsch, *Supervision in European Community Law* (2nd ed, Elsevier 1986), and Smith, *Centralised Enforcement*, supra n 7 ch 2, 4.

Table 2.2 Snapshot of the invisible layer two: Commission's administrative activity (2013)

Commission Action	Number	Top Three Sectors	Member State
Commission Own Initiative cases	1023	Transport, Environment, Justice	Italy, Greece, Spain
Complaints (overall)	3505	Justice, Environment, Internal Market	Italy, Spain, Germany
LTI (Asmodee II)	478	Environment, Health and Consumers, Internal Market	Cyprus, Slovenia, Italy
EU Pilot (total new files)	1502		
EU Pilot (complainant)	479	Environment, Tax, Internal Market	Italy, France, Spain
EU Pilot (Commission)	1023	Transport, Environment, Justice	Italy, Greece, Spain
EU Pilot (pending)	1462	Environment, Justice, Transport	Italy, France, Spain

Note: LTI – Late Transposition Infractions.

the Commission from presenting the Pilot as part of its good governance agenda,[68] and then as part of its smart regulation measures (ie, the Commission here conflates layers two and three).[69]

Commission data on the second administrative layer is relatively sparse. All it can tell us (and only to a limited extent) is *what the Commission is saying it is doing* in its administrative layer of the enforcement model.[70]

These figures paint a very familiar picture to anyone engaged in longitudinal studies of Commission enforcement practices. The number of complaints received have increased this year compared to previous years but despite this the Commission has closed more cases than ever before in a single reporting period. However, there are still more cases open at the end of the year than in the previous year. These statistics may indicate that the Commission has indeed increased its efficiency (effectiveness?)

[68] Communication from the Commission of 25 July 2001 'European Governance: A White Paper' COM (2001) 428 final, and Communication on Better Monitoring, supra n 17.

[69] Report from the Commission '30th Annual Report on Monitoring the Application of EU Law (2012)' COM (2013) 726.

[70] Commission Annual Report, 2013 (2014), supra n 37.

through the use of EU Pilot with the result that there has been an increase in 'complaint traffic'. The Commission's own assessment of EU Pilot is that it has increased both its efficiency and effectiveness through the creation of a more structured dialogue between Commission officials and Member State representatives.[71]

The Commission made an initial assessment of EU Pilot (2008–11) where a total of 2,121 files had been submitted. Of these 1,410 completed the process (defined as obtaining Member State responses and analysis by the Commission). Of these 80 per cent were deemed 'successful' (effective?), that is, after an answer from the Member State, the Commission closed the file. The average time taken by Member States to respond to the Commission is 67 days, which is in line with the putative 10 week deadline.[72] From the Commission's perspective this is a huge improvement on what was an indeterminate amount of time under the pre-EU Pilot 'administrative letter' procedure. However, less encouraging is the practice of the Commission itself where the average time taken to respond to Member States is 102 days, significantly exceeding its own 10 week deadline. From the complainants perspective this might not be perceived as quite the success story since the system encourages the Member State and Commission to negotiate a solution that might not be consistent with the complainant's understanding of the law. The ultimate result of this is that the legal position is never tested before the CJEU. Overall the Commission judges the success of this second enforcement layer on the basis of how many cases it concludes before it finally has to launch formal infringement proceedings. If we look back 10 years to compare the figures for 2003 to those from 2013, we can see that despite the fact that there are now 12 additional Member States to supervise and significantly more legislative instruments, the Commission now launches significantly fewer cases. In 2003 there were 1,552 formal letters, 533 reasoned opinions, 215 cases before the CJEU and 69 cases under Article 260(2). The figures for 2013, as highlighted in Table 2.1 were (FL) 761, (RO) 217, (CJEU) 52 and (260) 5.[73]

The Commission's enforcement policy continues to focus on late transposition cases recorded by the Asmodee II database, that is, cases of late transposition of directives (non-notification of measures by Member States)

---

[71] Report from the Commission 'EU Pilot Evaluation Report' (2010) COM 70 final, Report from the Commission 'Second Evaluation Report of EU Pilot' SEC (2011) 1629/2.

[72] Second Evaluation Report, ibid 5.

[73] If we look back to post accession in 2005, there is the same significant difference in figures: 1,632 (FL), 737 (RO) 215 (CJEU) and 100 (260).

despite the fact that these account for a small proportion (only 30 per cent) of all open infringements by the end of 2013: incorrect transposition and bad application of EU laws amounts to a whopping 70 per cent of cases.[74] One may ask then why this is such a strategic priority (and the subject of increased powers in the Lisbon Treaty in the form of Article 260(3)) given the generally high state of compliance with transposing directives?[75] It might be argued that the Commission is relatively effective at handling compliance with (legal) transposition but less effective at managing compliance 'on the ground' and that enforcement strategies should be aimed at tackling this type of non-compliance as a priority. Indeed it may be that the third layer of the Commission's enforcement model is dedicated to these types of infractions but we do not know for certain.

Table 2.2 shows that only 13.7 per cent of all complaints received make it into the EU Pilot, as opposed to 100 per cent of the Commission's own initiative investigations. This means that 68 per cent of cases in the EU Pilot are Commission cases (with 32 per cent complainant cases chosen by the Commission as worthy to proceed), reinforcing the point made earlier that a wide variety of detection sources is irrelevant to sculpting the universe of compliance. The concerns of the 'successful' complainants and the Commission (unsurprisingly) overlap when it comes to which sectors receive the most enforcement attention (reinforcing the statistical bias), although internal market issues are raised by the complainant more than the Commission, whereas the Commission seems to focus on transport. In terms of Member States, Italy, Greece, Spain and France receive the most attention from the Commission at the administrative stage, with the complainant mirroring this activity along with Germany. The exception to this (long term) trend is that of late transposition cases where Cyprus, Slovenia and Italy are the worst performers. Although these states figure highly in the administrative stage, they disappear from the statistics (come into compliance?) as sanctions become increasingly severe.

Assessing the effectiveness of this second administrative layer is fraught with difficulties even on the Commission's own terms. It would require access to all of the databases and access to the reasons for file closure in each of these databases in order to begin to assess efficiency of decision

---

[74] That is, 1,300 open cases of which only 390 were late transposition infringements.

[75] The EU average is 0.7 per cent transposition deficit, meaning 99.3 per cent of transposition has occurred, see http://ec.europa.eu/internal_market/scoreboard/performance_by_governance_tool/transposition/index_en.htm, accessed 10 March 2015 for a detailed transposition analysis by the Commission.

taking and to be able to discern which cases were closed because they were compatible with EU law and which were closed because (a) the best solution had been reached between the Commission and Member State or (b) because the file was not a strategic priority. Even using efficiency as a proxy for effectiveness requires information that is not accessible. This kind of research, however, is crucial if we are to understand the relevance of the remaining cases that persist through to the pinnacle of the enforcement model.

3.2 The Impenetrable Third Layer: The Compliance Toolkit

The final layer of the Commission's enforcement model comprises the 'compliance promoting tools'.[76] Lawyers and political scientists who are very familiar with the infringement process, and its administrative stages, might look upon this list with surprise, having heard little or nothing about this 'toolkit'. Is this because these practices are new innovations in the Commission's enforcement arsenal? Or are these merely long-standing methods of unofficial diplomacy renamed in an era of 'smart regulation' as something else? The answer is a little of both: rebranding and some innovations have taken place. However, since this toolkit is little researched and unreported it is difficult to evaluate its effectiveness since it is unknown how many (or which) cases are 'solved' through these mechanisms. A rigorous testing of the effectiveness of centralized enforcement, and a comprehensive assessment of the universe of compliance, requires full transparency of which measures, and which Member States, are invited to resolve non-compliance at this level of the enforcement model.

Table 2.3 lists these 'compliance tools' and identifies the rough timescale for when each tool is deployed throughout the life of an instrument and the particular aspect of non-compliance that the Commission hopes to combat by the use of each tool. The different processes outlined in Table 2.3 can be loosely grouped into three distinct types of enforcement behaviour: (a) the 'identification tools', (b) the 'elite actor meeting' tools, and (c) the 'policy' tools.

The identification tools comprise correlation tables, conformity checking and inspections and investigations. Correlation tables require Member States to communicate transposition of measures using a table which cor-

[76] This toolkit refers to practices that are associated with the infringement process rather than the plethora of other enforcement mechanisms and techniques that are highlighted in other chapters of this volume.

Table 2.3 The compliance toolkit

Type of Mechanism[77]	When it Occurs	Focus of Compliance
Correlation Tables (CT)	Ex post	Transposition
Conformity Checking (CC)	Ex post	Transposition
Inspections/Investigations (II)	Ex post	Implementation/Application
Networks (N)	Ex ante/ex post	Transposition/Implementation/Application
Package Meetings (PM)	Ex ante/ex post	Transposition/Implementation/Application
Committees (C)	Ex ante/ex post	Transposition/Implementation/Application
Guidelines (G)	Ex ante	Implementation
Transposition and Implementation plans (TIPS)	Ex ante	Transposition/Implementation
Bespoke Enforcement (BE)	Ex ante/ex post	Implementation and application
Fitness Checks (FC)	Ex post	Strategic (Steering)
Evaluations (EV)	Ex post/ex ante	Strategic (Steering)

relates provisions in the EU measure to provisions of national law. This facilitates the Commission's checking of conformity. These tables are a source of inter-institutional wrangling with the Commission agitating for such tables to be a legally binding requirement on Member States, preferably contained within each directive, or alternatively, in an instrument such as a regulation or decision (making it a horizontal legal requirement across the board) with the consequence that failure to include these tables would in itself be an infraction subject to infringement proceedings. So far the Commission has failed to achieve either of these positions since the Council oppose these tables at every opportunity. The current position is that the Council, Parliament and Commission have committed to 'including information' in transposition measures as part of a political inter-institutional agreement.[78] Conformity checking studies on the other hand are deployed where easy reconciliation is not possible: these are mainly outsourced to third party contractors and to a large degree remain

[77] The abbreviations are cross references to the model outlined in Section 1.

[78] Framework Agreement on relations between the European Parliament and the European Commission [2010] OJ L304/47 s 44. A new inter-institutional agreement is promised as part of the Commission's new Work Programme in 2015.

private documents not accessible by the public (although some are now being made available on DG websites in archival form as part of the smart regulation redesign[79]). Finally there are inspections by the EU level (and national) bodies which check implementation on the ground in certain fields, notably fisheries and agriculture. The identification tools are not innovations, rather they are long-standing methods that have been used by the Commission to aid and manage compliance as part of its guardian duty and pre-date the turn to good governance or smart regulation.

'Elite actor meeting' tools comprise package meetings, Committees and networks. Package meetings involve the Commission officials meeting with individual Member States to discuss numerous enforcement issues across a variety of instruments and policy sectors, whereas Committees are formally constructed meetings according to a specific legal instrument that involve numerous Member States and address one particular issue. Networks are more informal meetings with stakeholders to assist the Commission in identifying and solving potential enforcement problems usually relating to implementation and application of the law since as non-government actors they would have little direct control over transposition itself. The elite actor tools are the most established and long-standing mechanism of centralized enforcement (albeit one now extended to non-governmental actors) due to the diplomatic heritage of the infringement process: secret, closed negotiations with Member State representatives would always have been de rigueur in the Commission's enforcement work.[80]

The final set of compliance tools are labelled 'policy' tools and comprise guidelines, implementation plans, bespoke enforcement, fitness checks and evaluations. Guidelines are a form of 'soft law' setting out the Commission's interpretation of a particular measure that may help Member States to avoid conflict with the Commission later on in infringement proceedings.[81] They are a long-standing instrument of the Commission and are used across the board of EU sectors, but for the purposes of enforcement significantly in environmental law. Transposition and Implementation Plans (TIPS) on the other hand are more recent innovations: they are drawn up by the Commission with the aim of identifying the main risks in

[79] See the archives now available on some DG websites, http://ec.europa.eu/environment/archives/law/conformity_2008.htm accessed 10 March 2015.

[80] These appear to have been in place for at least 40 years, see Audretsch, supra n 67.

[81] Such instruments have no formal legal effect but can lead to instruments or decisions that do have formal effect. There is an extensive literature on 'soft law' including guidelines and their effects in law and political science.

transposition and implementation of a directive, alongside suggestions to counteract those risks.[82] They are anticipatory in nature and may include checklists, guidelines and scoreboards. In various policy documents the Commission has begun to emphasize the importance of designing bespoke enforcement arrangements for each legislative intervention. This focus on inserting decentralized enforcement provisions could begin to shape the Commission's *ex post* duty of enforcement by steering other actors to become the main enforcers of particular interventions, as opposed to relying on the Commission's centralized mechanism. Finally fitness checks and evaluations are much broader mechanisms that have a strategic policy-steering element to them: they are a nexus between the Commission's other roles (as policy initiator, initial drafter and implementer of legislation) and its role as guardian of the treaties. Fitness checks and evaluations are the newest additions to the Commission's smart regulation policy. Fitness checks involve the Commission assessing the framework of measures covering a policy sector, identifying excessive administrative burdens and obsolete measures. They aim to enhance compliance through, amongst other things, simplification of the regulatory measures. Evaluations are currently at a nascent stage of development. In relation to enforcement, evaluations offer the possibility of both complementing and driving the Commission's role as guardian of the treaties by considering enforcement practices at the time of drafting interventions and creating substantial linkages between compliance behaviour and the drafting of new legislation.[83]

3.3 Effectiveness of the Toolkit: The Black Box of Compliance?

The compliance toolkit is the black box of enforcement measures: although we may view the inputs (instruments/mechanisms) and outputs (statistics relating to compliance overall) in a rather general way, scholars have absolutely no idea of what goes on inside this box. Besides the Commission, none of the other actors have a complete picture of what occurs at this level of enforcement either since they will only know about the individual isolated activities that they are invited to take part in. The identification tools and the elite actor tools are processes of enforcement that are all secret; they are unrecorded in the annual reports or any official documentation on enforcement. There is no information on which tool is deployed

---

[82] The Commission has included these in some of its latest proposals, eg, 'The Reduction of National Emissions for Certain Atmospheric Pollutants' COM (2013) 920.

[83] Smith, 'Evaluation and the Salience of Infringement Data', supra n 64.

for which instrument (and why), or whether instruments are subject to one or various tools, or if there is a hierarchy in deploying these measures. The use of Committees is legally required so will clearly be mentioned in the relevant legal instrument, but there is no exhaustive catalogue of where and when (and why) Committees are chosen as the appropriate compliance tool. Conformity checking studies for the most part remain confidential to the Commission, and furthermore it is not clear why some instruments are chosen for conformity studies and others are not. The more recent innovations such as TIPS, fitness checks and evaluations are still being developed. There is no catalogue for instruments which have TIPS attached to them. The areas which are to have fitness checks and evaluations are recorded for public scrutiny but it is difficult to assess at this early stage what effect this will have in relation to compliance. Without access to this very basic information it is impossible to judge the effectiveness of each tool overall or in relation to a specific instrument. Until very recently no research had been done in this area at all, and the research that has been done is limited in scope and utility precisely because of some of the issues outlined in the legal literature, that is, a lack of transparency leading to questions of legitimacy in enforcement behaviour.

In order to ameliorate these problems the European Parliament commissioned a study to detail the Commission's compliance tools, the infringement process and the EU Pilot.[84] The purpose of the study was to assess the effectiveness of the tools and techniques of ensuring the application of EU law. The authors of the study were to come up against the very same issues common to researchers in this area: the Commission denied them access to the various databases and datasets on compliance, and prevented DG staff from speaking freely to researchers about their own experiences.[85] The results were then based on interviews with 32 Member State representatives (from 16 Member States) about their *perceptions of the effectiveness* of these various compliance tools, rather than measuring their actual effectiveness.[86] The study found that in general

---

[84] See the study performed by the European Parliament which challenges the Commission's definition of 'successful', European Parliament Study: Directorate General for Internal Policies, Policy Department C: Citizens' Rights and Constitutional Affairs 'Tools for Ensuring Implementation and Application of EU Law and Evaluation of their Effectiveness' PE 493.014.

[85] Only 7 DG staff were permitted to take part, and no Commission staff were able to speak about the EU Pilot.

[86] The study does not include fitness checks and evaluations, and it includes scoreboards and checklists which are omitted from Table 2.3 as I have chosen to concentrate on the most substantive aspects in the toolkit.

the Commission thought their tools were effective, with the Member States finding the same tools less effective (although there was not a great deal of difference between the two positions). The exception to this was the 'Committee' tool which Member States rated more highly than the Commission. This tool, according to the study, is the one mechanism by which the Member States are able to exert power over the Commission to collectively defend their interests whereas the other tools are Commission-controlled initiatives. Whilst such studies are an important starting point in gathering information on the type of activities undertaken they are clearly not sufficient to evaluate the effectiveness of the toolkit.

Many important research questions thus remain unanswered in relation to the compliance promoting toolkit. From an administrative law perspective, these mechanisms pose numerous questions in terms of transparency and the legitimacy of hidden enforcement work. Questions arise regarding which elite actors are invited by the Commission to take part in networks (social partners, NGOs, professional networks?) and which are excluded and on what basis. Do transposition and implementations plans, like guidelines, have the status of 'soft law' (since they have no legal basis in the treaties) and, if so, should Member States fail to abide by such plans does this lead to an enforcement action? What status could these have before the CJEU in evidential terms? Moreover all these instruments are aimed at avoiding the CJEU, decreasing legal scrutiny of Member State actions but also increasing Commission power to essentially interpret the law since it becomes the final arbiter. Paradoxically this is a position endorsed by the CJEU, generally not known for undermining its own interpretative authority in any other area of EU law.

CONCLUSIONS

The centralized enforcement mechanism can be conceptualized as a multi-layered process far removed from the simplistic linear model framed by the visible legal architecture. Inside the cavernous legal framework there has been a lot of room to manoeuvre for the Commission and accordingly a multiplicity of approaches to enforcement have developed under the banner of its guardian duty. The development of the Commission's practices has not progressed in a systematic fashion that fits neat regulatory models and as a result attempts to measure its effectiveness are, at this point, necessarily limited. If the primary function of the centralized enforcement mechanism is as a lever of accountability wielded by the Commission against the Member States, how do we ensure that the Commission is performing this role to the best of its ability? Certainly not by measuring Member State activity as judged from Commission statistics. This leads to questions about why and how the model of enforcement has developed in the fashion that it has: is the evolution of this model due to the Commission striving for greater efficiency (as a proxy of effectiveness) or, as is argued here, have these developments mainly been rebranding of old ideas in the current policy lexicon whilst keeping the *status quo* intact (essentially a diplomatic relationship between itself and the Member State)?

The tendency of lawyers and political scientists (in general) to conceptualize centralized enforcement as the tip of the enforcement model depicted in this chapter – a neat if simplistic view of the Commission's role in enforcement in legal terms – propagates a somewhat one-dimensional characterization of the data it generates alongside a limited set of research questions. This fracture between the understanding and the reality of centralized enforcement must heal if there is to be innovative research in this area. This can only be done when scholars collaborate in order to really understand that what happens in centralized enforcement is not mandated by a few legal principles, but rather it is the absence of legal regulation that has enabled layers of enforcement practices to develop. In this vacuum there is neither traditional administrative (legal accountability) nor political accountability. It is in the lack of transparency at the second and third layers that we can most clearly show the tensions perceived in the legal literature where the lack of judicial review, leading to a lack of administrative transparency and legitimacy, creates a vacuum of information. Preservation of this vacuum for the purposes of perpetuating internal flexibility (a synonym for no accountability) to deal with enforcement as the Commission sees fit is presented as a requirement for effectiveness of the enforcement model, whilst paradoxically (or intentionally), it ensures the conditions which resist any attempts to measure that effectiveness.

Unpacking Commission regulatory behaviour can assist in taking research agendas forward, by firstly serving to highlight the fissures between political science scholars and legal research on basic concepts such as the visible legal layer of Article 258 and furthermore bringing attention to the 'known unknowns' within the Commission's overall approach to ensuring the application of EU law. Future research has much to tell us about the actual effectiveness of much of the compliance tools being utilized in the so far impenetrable third layer of the model, through providing a systematic evaluation of the actual, rather than perceived, effectiveness of the multiple enforcement tools used by the Commission as guardian of the treaties.

3. The long, but promising, road from deterrence to networked enforcement

Jeroen van der Heijden*

Je n'ai fait celle-ci plus longue que parce que je n'ai pas eu le loisir de la faire plus courte[1]

INTRODUCTION

This chapter reviews the rich regulatory enforcement literature, seeking a better understanding of the evolution of enforcement models as discussed in political science and legal scholarship. It is not an easy task to bring together both areas of scholarship on this topic. Political science and legal scholarship have different research traditions, use different terminology, and build on different ontologies. It is not often that political scientists and legal scholars work together on joint interdisciplinary research projects such as that of the current book.[2] More troublingly, legal scholars

* With many thanks to Melanie Smith and Sara Drake for their helpful comments, and for their willingness to discuss much of the Babylonian confusion that the author of the current chapter, a regulatory scholar, experienced when trying to understand the traditions, terminology and preferences of legal scholarship. All usual disclaimers apply.

[1] Words of the French mathematician and philosopher Blaise Pascal in 1657. See further: Fred Shapiro, *The Yale Book of Quotations* (YUP 2006). It translates as: I would have written a shorter [chapter], but I did not have the leisure for doing so.

[2] For good examples of interdisciplinary work in political science and legal scholarship, see, among others: Frank Cross, 'Political Science and the Legal Realism: A Case of Unfortunate Interdisciplinary Ignorance' (1997) 92 Nw.U.L.Rev 251; Theodore Ruger, Pauline Kim, Andrew Martin and Kevin Quinn, 'The Supreme Court Forecasting Project: Legal and Political Science Approaches to Predicting Supreme Court Decision-making' (2004) 104 CLR 1150; Melanie Smith, *Centralised Enforcement, Legitimacy and Good Governance in the EU* (Routledge 2010).

and political scientists often have a completely different view on the world, which complicates collaborative projects.[3]

Taking the world views to extremes, legal scholars start with black letter rules and judge a person's behaviour according to whether or not it is in compliance with these rules. If a violation is found, a regulatee[4] should be judged and disciplined accordingly. If the circumstances explain this violation then a precedent for a decision may be found in earlier cases. Reasoned judgment, precedent, statute, and treating like cases alike, are key.

Political scientists start with a person's behaviour and look at her or his capacity to comply with a particular black letter rule. To them, personal, economic or institutional constraints may not only explain, but also justify, non-compliance – and could even point out that there is something inherently wrong with that black letter rule. Political scientists, more so than legal scholars, also look at the role of street-level bureaucrats, such as police officers and judges, in making decisions about compliant and non-compliant behaviour. By carefully unpacking the choices made by an individual (regulatee), the constraints faced by that individual, her or his interaction with a street-level bureaucrat, and that specific bureaucrat's decision, it often turns out that there are no 'like cases'. People do not respond similarly to regulatory requirements, enforcement and disciplinary actions; and street-level bureaucrats do not respond similarly to comparable situations.[5] Legal scholarship is often oblivious to the ever-growing insights into these matters from the political sciences (and other areas); yet, at the same time, political scientists are sometimes wholly unaware of the legal model of the real world examples they study.[6] For as

---

[3] James Taranto and Leonard Leo, in Appendix 1 to their book, present a somewhat similar argument: James Taranto and Leonard Leo, *Presidential Leadership* (Free Press 2004).

[4] The use of the term regulatee to refer to those subject to law and regulation is the first striking difference between scholars of various disciplines. The term is widely accepted in political science, regulation and governance scholarship.

[5] Research from the behavioural sciences has shown that judges are more lenient just after lunch, and give harsher penalties later in the day, even when presented with 'like cases'. See further: Shai Danziger, Jonathan Levav and Liora Avnaim-Pesso, 'Extraneous Factors in Judicial Decisions' (2011) 108 Proc Nat Ac Sc USA (17) 6889.

[6] Speaking of Babylonian confusion between legal scholars and political scientists, to a legal scholar the word 'case' refers to a court case. It is as simple as that. To a political scientist the word 'case' refers to anything that can be studied empirically: a judge can be a case in a study on the impact of food breaks on judges' decisions, a legal system can be a case in a study that compares the legal system of the USA with that of India, and even a court case can be a case in a study

long as scholars from the two disciplines do not acknowledge (and accept) each other's vantage points, terminology and differences in world view, it will be impossible to pursue a fruitful research agenda that allows a better understanding of important topics and gives answers to relevant questions that are of interest to both disciplines.

Whilst it is beyond the scope of this chapter to discuss all the differences (and similarities) between political science and legal scholarship, it is important to keep these two pictures in mind when reviewing the different enforcement models that have been developed by scholars from the two disciplines. In going through the evolution of these models, it becomes clear that, over the years, they have moved from models that are fairly technocratic and are built on a fear of the consequences of non-compliance to models that are responsive to individual regulatees and seek to incentivize compliance through support and facilitation. It is not difficult to place the former approach as being more closely related to (traditional) legal scholarship, and the latter approach as being more related to political science scholarship. The current chapter begins by discussing the traditional command-and-control approach that builds heavily on deterrence (as opposed to cooperation) that was in vogue until the late 1980s.[7] The chapter subsequently discusses compliance-based and other types of strategies in regulatory enforcement that have developed since then, including self-regulation and enforced self-regulation; responsive regulation; smart regulation; and finally networked enforcement, which may be considered the current state of the art in this literature. It links, to the extent possible in a brief contribution, these ideas to regulation and enforcement in the EU.

A contribution such as the current chapter of course brings to the fore the question of what is effective and efficient enforcement. Whilst easy to pose, it turns out that this is a difficult question to answer, and again here the differences in world view between political scientists and legal scholars might be important. For political scientists in particular it is incredibly complicated to evaluate the performance of law and policy, including regulatory enforcement. This is not because they lack the methods and analytical techniques to crunch data on law and policy outcomes. For political scientists the 'problem' is, particularly, that effectiveness is such a vague concept – and that achieving effectiveness often comes at the cost of

---

on motivations for non-compliance. This chapter aims to use the word 'case' only to refer to court cases, and the word 'example' to refer to empirical examples.

[7] Robert Baldwin, Martin Cave and Martin Lodge, *Understanding Regulation: Theory, Strategy and Practice* (2nd edn, OUP 2011).

not or only partly achieving efficiency, accountability or transparency.[8] Is enforcement effective when it achieves the greatest compliance possible, if not full compliance? This is a rather utilitarian understanding of enforcement, which puts the ambition of achieving (almost) full compliance above all other consequences, costs and constraints of enforcement – and which might result in very costly, and thus inefficient, enforcement models. Alternatively, is enforcement effective at the point when an additional unit of enforcement effort no longer results in an additional unit of compliance? Such a cost–benefit understanding of enforcement seeks to achieve the highest amount of compliance against the lowest cost of enforcement (i.e., cost-effectiveness) – but might let considerable violations go unpunished when the costs of taking action do not outweigh the (immediate) costs of the violations.[9] Or is enforcement effective when regulatees comply with regulatory or legal requirements without experiencing (adverse) enforcement activities from authorities, for instance because they get tailored support from street-level bureaucrats? This understanding of effective enforcement indeed fits well with recent compliance models, but might result in accountability and transparency problems if the relationship between regulatee and street-level bureaucrat becomes too close. In addition, it is very complicated to carry out enforcement effectiveness studies. Ideally one would set up an experiment in which one or more groups of regulatees are made subject to a specific enforcement model, and a control group is not. Ethical considerations make such experimenting impossible.[10]

This chapter reflects on such questions for the various models discussed. From these reflections it becomes clear that none of the models discussed is 'perfect'. Each model comes with its own opportunities and constraints. The model that currently appears most useful for achieving compliance in a cost-effective, low-interventionist, accountable and transparent way is the 'networked enforcement model'. This model can be understood as a mix and match of various characteristics of earlier enforcement models.

---

8 An excellent primer on these issues is Deborah Stone, *Policy Paradox* (Norton 2002).

9 The typical example would be the build-up of environmental harm over time. On an individual basis the costs of inspecting paper mills may not outweigh the benefit, as most paper mills are likely to comply with environmental regulations. However, if one mill breaches the regulatory requirements by dumping chemicals into a river the results may be detrimental, and the costs of solving the resulting environmental problem may be substantial. This example is roughly based on: Neil Gunningham, Robert Kagan and Dorothy Thornton, *Shades of Green* (SUP 2003).

10 Luckily, the author wishes to add.

It has, however, not seen a large-scale uptake in real world settings. The chapter therefore concludes by discussing at some length the opportunities and constraints of this particular model, as well as a set of questions that might be a starting point (for political scientists and legal scholars alike) for studying real world examples of regulatory enforcement and might further advance our understanding of regulatory enforcement.

1. THE EVOLUTION OF REGULATION

1.1 Deterrence- and Compliance-Based Strategies

For a long time scholars and practitioners have been trying to answer the question of why people (and organizations) obey the law. After all, if we have a better understanding of what drives compliance, we will be better able to develop effective and efficient regulatory enforcement strategies.

Until the 1980s it was assumed that compliance results from a fear of the consequences of being found in violation.[11] The then popular *deterrence-based enforcement strategy* was aimed at deterring non-compliance prior to the law being broken,[12] or at sanctioning non-compliance after the law had been broken.[13] A central hypothesis within this strategy is the notion that the greater the chance of getting caught breaking the law and/or the higher the sanctions if the law is broken, the less willing people are to break it.[14] Sanctions are then often a (financial) penalty or imprisonment. This model has a strong top-down and highly technocratic understanding of compliance. Whilst the thinking about enforcement has moved on, this model is still likely to be what many legal scholars think about when discussing enforcement and compliance. The model is also still dominant in real world regulatory enforcement. Deterrence is, for instance, key in many regulated activities such as driving a car (you are likely to get a fine if you are caught speeding), constructing a building (you are likely to

---

[11] Anthony Ogus, *Comparing Regulatory Systems: Institutions, Processes and Legal Forms in Industrialized Countries* (Centre on Regulations and Competition 2002).

[12] Albert Reiss, 'Selecting Strategies of Social Control over Organizational Life' in Keith Hawkins and John M Thomas (eds), *Enforcing Regulation* (Kluwer-Nijhoff 1984).

[13] Keith Hawkins, *Environment and Enforcement Regulation and the Social Definition of Pollution* (OUP 1984).

[14] Chris Coolsma and Mark Wiering, *Handhaving in stukken beschouwingen over theorie en praktijk van de handhaving van recht* [Regulatory enforcement: theory and practice] (SISWO/Instituut voor Maatschappijwetenschappen 1999).

have to pay the costs of demolishing a structure that you build illegally if the construction authorities decide to take it down), or interacting with your colleagues (you are likely to lose your job if you bully or sexually harass your colleague). Whilst the deterrence strategy has been and still is very popular as an approach to regulatory enforcement, the critics of this strategy state that it is ineffective and expensive, leads to problems with enforcement and concentrates too much on end-of-the-line solutions.[15] The strategy is also said to be prone to what is termed 'regulatory capture', when too close a relationship between regulator and regulatees comes into being.[16]

An alternative approach to regulatory enforcement, which was introduced in the 1980s, was *compliance-based enforcement strategy*. This approach considers that it is not negative incentives such as fines and imprisonment that will result in compliance, but that positive incentives such as grants and subsidies,[17] or education and support can be expected to have a better result.[18] Grants and subsidies may help take away the barriers met by regulatees when complying with the law. The proponents of this strategy consider that grants and subsidies give more freedom to regulatees about how they wish to comply, and that these freedoms incentivize regulatees to reduce harm to zero, if possible, rather than to a prescribed level. One could, however, question whether this is an enforcement model per se, or an alternative approach to governing societal problems.[19] As such, this model is left outside the scope of the current chapter. The focus on education and support, as alternative enforcement strategies, is of interest. These activities allow a regulator to explain to regulatees the rationale behind the law, and to provide advice on how a regulatee can best comply with it. This focus clearly steps away from a traditional technocratic understanding of the law – that is, that the law will affect all regulatees (more or less) similarly and is interpreted univocally by those implementing it. The model takes a more bottom-up approach and questions why regulatees do (not) comply with laws and regulations. Do they lack the financial or physical capacity to do so? Do they not understand the rules? Do they perhaps not know of the rules? The proponents of this particular model consider that intensive interaction between regulatee

---

[15] Robyn Fairman and Charlotte Yapp, 'Enforced Self-regulation, Prescription, and Conceptions of Compliance within Small Businesses: The Impact of Enforcement' (2005) 27 Law & Pol 4.

[16] Baldwin, Cave and Lodge n 7.

[17] Ibid.

[18] Bridget Hutter, *Compliance: Regulation and Environment* (OUP 1997).

[19] Baldwin, Cave and Lodge n 7.

and regulator may result in valuable information flows between the two. However, this approach is found to introduce its own complications as well: regulations based on positive incentives are often complicated; they only work indirectly and may therefore respond too late; and the general public may question why some undesired behaviour is nevertheless being accepted under a compliance-based strategy. Questions have also been raised about whether or not close interactions between regulator and regulatee will result in undesired regulatory capture.[20]

Of course, the deterrence- and compliance-based approaches are two very stylized models, and real world enforcement situations are unlikely to fit these perfectly. The policeman who catches a speeding car is likely to assist with getting the car to the hospital if it has on board a woman in labour; and even if this policeman is primed to explain first how a regulatee can become compliant, before turning to more interventionist action, he is not likely to think twice before taking a drunk driver off the road. Nevertheless, the two somewhat overly stylized models are of interest exactly because they flesh out the differences in how legal scholars and political science scholars look at regulation and enforcement. In analysing the rich enforcement literature for this chapter no research was found that contrasts the effectiveness of the two models.

1.2 Beyond Command-and-Control Regulation and Enforcement

Whilst we can still see many of the origins of these two strategies in current enforcement practice and theory, for instance in the enforcement of the implementation of EU law,[21] more contemporary regulatory enforcement practice and thinking differs from traditional deterrence- and compliance-based enforcement strategies in at least three respects. It is important to unpack these first before focusing more closely on the evolution of the regulation and enforcement literature.

First, the traditional structure of regulation and enforcement following deterrence- or compliance-based strategies is often described as a *command-and-control* regime.[22] In such a regime, the government develops and introduces regulation and brings enforcement actions – that is, it commands through regulation and controls through enforcement. Whilst such regimes may seem attractive from a governmental point of view, they

---

20 Ibid.

21 See Ch 2 of the current book.

22 Robert Kagan, 'On Regulatory Inspectorates and Police' in Keith Hawkins and John M Thomas (eds), *Enforcing Regulation* (Kluwer-Nijhoff 1984).

come with considerable complications. Governments are often unable to understand fully what is going on in a regulated sector. Input from this sector in the development of regulation and enforcement may result in more effective and efficient regulatory regimes than regimes that are developed and implemented solely by governments.[23] Over recent decades governments have become more open to including non-governmental actors in the development of regulation and enforcement strategies. Collaborative governance processes in which governments, citizens and firms develop rules and strategies for the enforcement of regulations in a consensus-based process are no longer an exception.[24] For instance, the European Water Framework Directive (WFD),[25] introduced in 2000, requires the Member States to ensure the involvement of citizens and other stakeholders in the implementation of the Directive. The goal of the WFD is to ensure a particular water quality throughout Europe by 2015, and to see this quality improving over time. This is the first Directive in which Member States faced mandatory public participation processes.[26] When the WFD was introduced, the idea of public participation in policymaking was (and still is) expected to be an answer to an oft-experienced lack of public support for governmental interventions. By involving the general public in the implementation process of the WFD in the various Member States, it was expected that citizens would give more support to the policies and regulatory requirements that would follow from this implementation, and be more willing to comply with these because they had been involved in their development.

Second, contemporary regulation and enforcement strategies are often characterized by a mixture of deterrence- and compliance-based incentives. It is considered that a single focus on either penalties or rewards is unlikely to provide an adequate enforcement mechanism for the wide variety of regulatees and regulatory situations faced by regulators. Also, contemporary enforcement strategies focus not only on black letter rules but also on how regulators can best interact with regulatees in implementing and enforcing such rules. Lipsky's studies on street-level bureaucrats (regula-

---

[23] Beth Noveck, 'The Single Point of Failure' in Simone Van der Hof and Marga M Groothuis (eds), *Innovating Government* (Asserr Press 2011).

[24] Vasudha Chhotray and Gerry Stoker, *Governance Theory and Practice* (Palgrave 2010).

[25] Directive 2000/60/EC of the European Parliament and of the Council of 23 October 2000 establishing a framework for Community action in the field of water policy [2000] OJ L327/1.

[26] Jeroen van der Heijden and Ernst ten Heuvelhof, 'The Mechanics of Virtue' (2012) 22 *Environmental Policy & Governance* (3) 177.

tors who interact directly with regulatees) have, in particular, highlighted the fact that different forms of interaction may yield different compliance responses.[27] Building on Lipsky's work, scholars have identified different enforcement styles for inspectors that sit on a sliding scale defined by a consultative, facilitative approach at one end and a rigid, legalistic approach at the other. It is thought that a facilitative style fosters compliance by encouraging affirmative motivations to comply, whilst a legalistic style may detract from motivations of this type. A typical example here is the enforcement of building codes in various European Member States.[28] In the EU, building codes are often laid down by a national government and implemented and enforced by local building control authorities. These authorities normally have significant enforcement powers, and can fine builders for non-compliance, or issue stop-working orders when non-compliance is observed. In the area of environmental regulation in particular, these authorities report that a lack of awareness of particular building codes is the main reason for non-compliance, and they consider that a facilitative enforcement strategy of explaining why a particular rule is in place is more just than a strict punitive approach in such situations.[29] The current literature is, however, inconclusive as to whether different enforcement styles are indeed operating and obtaining results as predicted by the theory in various regulatory settings.[30]

Third, more and more non-governmental actors are involved in regulation and enforcement. This is the case not only in the collaborative development processes discussed above, but also in the actual implementation of regulation and enforcement. Since the 1990s, under an ongoing neoliberal agenda, governments have privatized, delegated and outsourced regulatory and enforcement roles to non-governmental actors.[31] There seems to be no sector where non-governmental actors are not, in one way or another, involved in the development of standards or the auditing and certification of goods and services on behalf of governments. A well-known

---

[27] Michael Lipsky, *Street-level Bureaucracy: Dilemmas of the Individual in Public Services* (Russell Sage Foundation 1980).

[28] Jeroen van der Heijden and Ellen van Bueren, 'Regulating Sustainable Construction in Europe: An Inquiry into the European Commission's Harmonization Attempts' (2013) 5 *International Journal of Law and Built Environment* (1) 5.

[29] Ibid.

[30] Vibeke Lehmann Nielsen, 'Are Regulators Responsive?' (2006) 28 Law & Pol (3) 395, Peter May and Robert S Wood, 'At the Regulatory Front Lines' (2003) 13 JPART (2) 117.

[31] Graeme Hodge, *Privatization: An International Review of Performance* (Westview Press 2000).

organization in this field is the International Standards Organization, the ISO;[32] and a well-known European initiative that brings together public authorities, citizens and businesses is SOLVIT – a European Commission programme that supports citizens and businesses when a public authority is not doing what it is required to do under EU law.[33] At the same time, non-governmental actors are getting more and more involved in drafting and implementing regulations for areas of society in which they feel that governments are too slow in introducing regulatory requirements.[34] This trend of voluntary regulation appears particularly dominant in the area of environmental sustainability and consumer products, and has been studied and discussed at great length in the literature.[35] Typical examples are the more than 900 voluntary food labelling schemes that are in place across Europe.[36] These voluntary schemes show striking similarities with mandatory food labelling, an area that is heavily regulated by law in Europe. They allow producers of food products to make visible specific aspects of such products. Often these are not required by statutory regulation or other legislation, but are requested and appreciated by consumers. Basically these schemes seek to tap into a market of consumers who are willing to pay more for food products if they meet specific requirements that are not (yet) required by statutory regulation. These schemes set specific requirements for food producers to meet, they assess, in one way or another, whether products meet these requirements, and they allow food producers to use a food label that showcases the specific credentials of the product. Food labelling often provides consumers with information on the geographic origin of a food product or whether it is organically produced, has health benefits, or has been produced in accordance with additional requirements relating to animal welfare.[37] Such labelling schemes fit a wider trend of voluntary programmes that generally resemble traditional direct regulatory interventions: a set of rules specifies the criteria a food product has to meet, these rules are enforced, and a label is awarded when

---

[32] ISO, *ISO & Construction* (International Organization for Standardization 2012); Michael Power, 'Auditing and the Production of Legitimacy' (2003) 28 *Accounting, Organizations and Society* (4) 185.

[33] <http://ec.europa.eu/solvit/index_en.htm> accessed 2 February 2015.

[34] David Levi-Faur and Shana Starobin, *Transnational Politics and Policy: From Two-way to Three-way Interactions* (Hebrew University of Jerusalem 2014).

[35] Axel Marx and Jan Wouters, *Competition and Cooperation in the Market of Voluntary Sustainability Standards* (KU Leuven 2014).

[36] IPSOS and LEC, *Consumer Market Study on the Functioning of Voluntary Food Labelling Schemes for Consumers in the European Union EAHC/FWC/2012 86 04* (Ipsos and London Economics Consortium 2013).

[37] Ibid.

a food product complies with the rules.[38] The schemes differ from traditional direct regulatory interventions in that they are not mandatory, and producers are free to decide whether or not to join them. Similar labelling schemes have been introduced to make visible the environmental credentials of buildings, forest products and corporate management practices, among others.[39]

1.3 Self-Regulation and Enforced Self-Regulation

By the end of the 1980s traditional direct regulatory interventions, and particularly command-and-control regulations, were considered too costly an approach for steering society.[40] It is particularly the ideas of Reagan in the United States and Thatcher in the United Kingdom on how to steer society that are at the base of a neo-liberal, deregulatory and privatization agenda that has been in force in many countries around the world for at least two decades now – in other words, the cost-effectiveness of government in general and regulatory enforcement in particular became important evaluation criteria. It was no longer governments but regulated firms that were considered to be in the right position to monitor and enforce behaviour and compliance. Governments, so the argument goes,[41] often lack the means to carry out adequate monitoring and enforcement tasks. They have a limited amount of resources, which they have to allocate to inspect a large number of regulatees. As a result regulatees are, at best, periodically subject to regulatory enforcement by government inspectors. Regulatory enforcement by governments also lacks inspectorial depth. If a government inspector inspects regulatees on a periodic or ad hoc basis she or he is likely to have difficulty in capturing the full regulated process. Self-regulation is considered a (partial) solution to this issue.

---

[38] Matthew Potoski and Aseem Prakash, *Voluntary Programs: A Club Theory Perspective* (MIT Press 2009).

[39] Voluntary regulation may sound like a contradiction in terms to legal scholars, but to scholars in political science, regulation and governance they are the order of the day. Moreover, it is widely assumed that many pressing societal problems are too complicated to be resolved by more and more top-down statutory regulation, but may be overcome by various combinations of voluntary programmes. This holds particularly for environmental problems, including the overabstraction of resources, the loss of biodiversity and climate change. See further: Jeroen van der Heijden, 'Voluntary Environmental Governance Arrangements' (2012) 21 Env Pol (3) 486.

[40] Ian Ayres and John Braithwaite, *Responsive Regulation* (OUP 1992).

[41] John Braithwaite, 'Enforced Self-Regulation: A New Strategy for Corporate Crime Control' (1982) 80 *Michigan Law Review* (7) 1466.

Self-regulation refers to a situation in which a regulatee or a group of regulatees monitors and enforces its own behaviour or that of the group.[42] Self-regulating firms are expected to have higher levels of expertise than government regulators. They are highly aware of their own processes and will therefore know better than a government inspector where to look, when to look, and what to look for. It is also argued that self-regulating firms are more capable of freeing up resources to carry out enforcement tasks when needed. Besides, self-regulating firms are a lighter burden for society since the firms, and not the ordinary taxpayer, pay the costs related to inspections. A typical area of self-regulation in Europe is advertisement.[43] The advertising industry, led by the European Advertising Standards Alliance (EASA-alliance), has set up codes of practice to ensure that advertising is responsible. The code of practice is enforced locally by self-regulatory organizations within the European Member States.[44] The advertising industry has a clear interest in self-regulation:

> . . . advertising must enjoy a high level of consumer trust and confidence; it must be legal, decent, honest and truthful. If consumers are misled by advertising, they will not buy again; if it offends them, they will not buy in the first place. Bad advertising, even though it may account for only a small percentage of the whole, will gradually undermine consumer confidence and all advertising will suffer. So it is in the interests of the advertising industry to ensure that advertising is properly regulated.[45]

This advertising self-regulation sits in a larger European framework of advertisement legislation, including the EU Directive on Misleading and Comparative Advertisement,[46] which seeks to harmonize the rules of the various EU Member States on comparative advertising. Whilst the EASA-alliance spells out the typical advantages of self-regulation (rules are thought to be quicker to amend; the system does not burden the taxpayer; and complaints can be dealt with quickly),[47] self-regulation is no panacea for failing governmental enforcement. Self-regulating firms

---

[42] Baldwin, Cave and Lodge n 7.

[43] EASA, *The Blue Book* (European Advertising Standards Alliance 2010).

[44] The EASA-alliance codes of practice are also followed in other countries, such as Australia, India and Brazil.

[45] <http://www.easa-alliance.org/About-us/page.aspx/165> accessed 2 February 2015.

[46] Directive 2006/114/EC of the European Parliament and of the Council of 12 December 2006 concerning misleading and comparative advertising (Office for Official Publications of the European Communities 2006).

[47] <http://www.nss-bg.org/files/d3d7bd389a2cc1a79b6e3024746cee11.pdf> accessed 2 February 2015.

are often reported to have a poor record of choosing the public interest over the private interest in their activities.[48] Without some form of governmental involvement, self-regulation may lack accountability and the right incentives for self-regulating actors to ensure they comply with the regulations.[49]

This, then, is how and why *enforced self-regulation* entered the scene.[50] Enforced self-regulation refers to a regulatory strategy under which regulatees are required to assess, monitor and control the risks they create. The requirements for such assessment, monitoring and control are set by governments. Critical to this approach to enforcement is that a regulatee develops an internal control system, documents the results of its self-monitoring activities, and reports these to the relevant regulatory authority.[51] Enforced self-regulation often operates against the backdrop of more direct regulatory interventions, and violations of agreed self-regulatory rules are punishable by law. Enforced self-regulation is considered to have the same advantages as traditional self-regulation, but may overcome some of its weaknesses. In particular, the accountability problems related to pure self-regulation may be overcome because regulatees have to come to an agreement with the regulator on how to assess, monitor and report compliance. An additional advantage of enforced self-regulation is that governments and regulatees can tailor an enforcement strategy that best suits a particular situation.[52]

However, enforced self-regulation comes with its own constraints.[53] Firm size appears to be related to the success of this strategy. Small and medium-sized firms are often found to lack the capacity to implement enforced self-regulation successfully. Enforced self-regulation also requires that regulatees see advantages for themselves in the strategy. For instance, they may make enforcement a part of their ongoing production process, instead of having to halt production until a governmental inspector is available. Let us take again the inspection of advertising: for an advertiser, it may be more efficient to check its own advertisement campaign against the EASA-alliance's code of practice, instead of having to wait for a government inspector to do so. After all, advertising can be a rather ad hoc process

48 Ian Bartle and Peter Vass, 'Self-regulation within the Regulatory State' (2007) 85 *Public Administration* 885.

49 Baldwin, Cave and Lodge n 7.

50 Braithwaite n 41, Fairman and Yapp n 15.

51 Ayres and Braithwaite n 40.

52 Fairman and Yapp n 15.

53 Baldwin, Cave and Lodge n 7, Bridget Hutter, 'Is Enforced Self-regulation a Form of Risk Taking?' (2001) 29 Int J Sociology of Law 379.

with a lot of time pressure, and may not fit well with the long waiting times of governmental enforcement processes. Finally, without sufficient governmental monitoring and oversight (i.e., enforcement of the enforcement process) this approach may result in too little compliance, whilst too much governmental monitoring and enforcement is likely to undo efficiency gains for both the government and the regulatees involved.[54] One could, of course, question how much enforced self-regulation and self-regulation truly differ from more traditional approaches to regulatory enforcement. The delegation of assessment, monitoring and control tasks from government to regulatees is a shift in *who* carries out enforcement rather than in *how* enforcement is carried out.

1.4 Responsive Regulation

A significant change in regulatory scholars' thinking about how enforcement is (best) carried out began with the well-known book *Responsive Regulation*.[55] In this book Ayres and Braithwaite argue for a staged approach to enforcement in which deterrence- and compliance-based strategies are combined.

The responsive regulation approach considers that punishment as a first choice is unaffordable, unworkable and counterproductive. Governments generally have limited enforcement capacity, and not all who are subject to regulation need a similar level of enforcement to ensure their compliance. In other words, to make regulatory enforcement more cost-effective governments can perfectly safely assume that with a moderate level of enforcement a large part of the population will still show compliant behaviour. Yet completely rejecting punitive incentives is considered naïve as well, as had become clear from negative experiences with self-regulation. The trick in regulatory enforcement, according to the responsive regulation philosophy, is to combine the stick and the carrot. Instead of applying a one-size-fits-all enforcement strategy, it is of more avail to ask where regulatees can be supported in achieving compliance. How can they be persuaded to comply with regulation? What is the ultimate enforcement measure that induces enough fear, even when regulators do not have to use it very often?

The responsive regulation philosophy has introduced a second innovation in regulatory enforcement: it considers not only the role of black letter rules but also the day-to-day interactions between regulatees and regulators to be important in achieving compliance (through a mixture of

---

54 Hutter n 53.

55 Ayres and Braithwaite n 40.

deterrence- and compliance-based strategies). Building on Braithwaite's years of research on health and safety regulation in the Australian mining industry, the authors of *Responsive Regulation* argue that regulators can and do use different enforcement styles. These styles roughly range from a facilitative attitude of the regulator to a formalistic attitude. A facilitative regulator is willing to explain why the regulatee should be in compliance and how the regulatee can best achieve compliance, and may even accept a violation today as long as the violation will be remedied by a set date. A formalistic regulator, on the other hand, sticks closely to the letter of the law and takes disciplinary measures as soon as a violation is found. This combination of strategies and styles is the core of the philosophy's *responsiveness*: regulators can choose between different responses in their interactions with regulatees. This gives the regulator an advantage over the regulatee, since the latter does not know what the response to its behaviour will be.[56]

The book introduces the now oft-cited concept of enforcement pyramids, a heuristic for how regulatory enforcement can be organized. Figure 3.1 gives a schematic of that heuristic. Such pyramids mostly illustrate a staged regulatory and enforcement process with moderate interventions (such as consultation and self-regulation) at the base and more severe interventions (such as fines and imprisonment) at the top. The pyramid illustrates the idea that, to achieve compliance, moderate interventions are often enough for a large number of regulatees, and that only a small number of regulatees need to be incentivized through more severe steps. The authors of *Responsive Regulation* strongly support the idea that regulators start with moderate interventions and work their way to the top when a regulatee does not respond to these interventions.

Scholars of regulation often stress (and support) the normative and intellectual appeal of responsive regulation, but they have also begun to question whether responsive regulation indeed improves compliance. It is of interest that responsive regulation is widely applied, and often referred to in policy documents as an ideal type of model to follow,[57] but that hardly any empirical research has been carried out on its actual performance. Lehmann Nielsen and Parker are among the few scholars who have empirically tested the underlying premises of the philosophy. Building on self-reported survey data from 141 Australian businesses,

---

[56] John Braithwaite, *Restorative Justice and Responsive Regulation* (OUP 2002).

[57] Mary Ivec and Valerie Braithwaite, *Application of Responsive Regulatory Theory in Australia and Overseas* (Regulatory Institutions Network 2010).

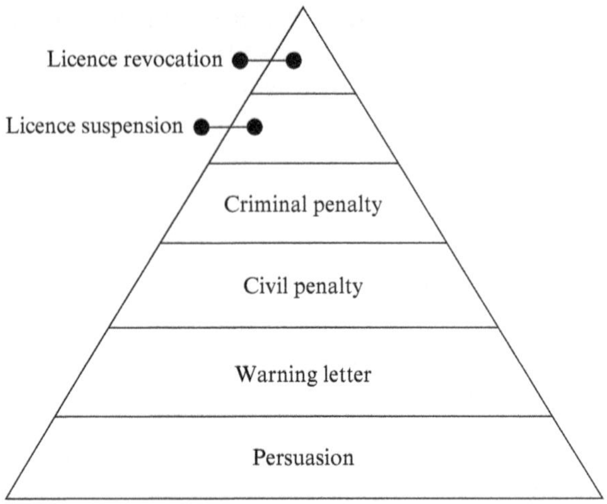

Example of an enforcement pyramid. The proportion of space at each layer represents the proportion of enforcement activity at that level

Source: Reproduced from Ian Ayres and John Braithwaite's work (see footnote 40), with permission from John Braithwaite.

Figure 3.1 Schematic representation of the responsive regulation philosophy

they find limited evidence that responsive regulation does indeed result in improved behaviour.[58] In an earlier study Parker also identified a 'compliance trap' in responsive regulation: when facing non-compliance by large and well-organized firms, regulators opt for avoiding conflict by taking the relatively easy option of enforcing regulation through facilitative and collaborative approaches rather than through strict and coercive ones.[59] In other words, Ayres and Braithwaite consider that the strength of responsive regulation is that regulators have a big stick (i.e., fines or penalties) but do not often have to use it to achieve compliance. Parker, however, finds that when given the option not to use the stick in complex enforcement situations, regulators prefer to take that option. In another study on the enforcement of rules on building homes in the United States, May found that too much switching between enforcement styles is experienced

[58] Vibeke Lehman Nielsen and Christine Parker, 'Testing Regulation in Regulatory Enforcement' (2009) 3 *Regulation & Governance* 376.
[59] Christine Parker, 'The "Compliance" Trap' (2006) 40 Law & Soc Rev 3.

as negative by regulatees, and may even make them less willing to comply.[60] Responsive regulation is in need of further empirical investigation if we wish to understand its true value, and if we are to be successful in improving the philosophy.

1.5 Smart Regulation

An aspect that is not addressed by the responsive regulation theory introduced by Ayres and Braithwaite is the possibility of bringing third parties into the regulatory process. Such third parties could be independent auditors, registered certifiers or even citizens.

This is exactly the idea that underpins another well-known book, *Smart Regulation*,[61] which has taken another significant step in how regulatory scholars think about regulatory enforcement. In this book Gunningham and Grabosky study the regulatory and enforcement process by considering parties, roles and interactions. The focus on the possibility of there being different parties in the process has, in particular, been a move away from the traditional ideas of regulatory regimes that considered the regulatory process to be too much of 'a dance between two participants – government and business'.[62] The key to the smart regulation philosophy is to involve in the regulatory process those actors who are best fitted to enforce regulation. This may sometimes be through traditional government agencies; sometimes through self-regulatory or co-regulatory initiatives in which private sector actors enforce rules against members of their own bodies; and sometimes through third parties, such as consumer interest groups or insurance companies, which act as 'surrogate regulators'.

Gunningham and Grabosky ascribe most value to surrogate regulators when large companies are involved and when non-compliance is easy to identify. A well-known example of success by surrogate regulators is Greenpeace's 1999 campaign against Home Depot, the then largest supplier of do-it-yourself products in the United States. Through their campaign Greenpeace sought to ensure that do-it-yourself suppliers in the United States moved away from supplying old growth wood and had all their wooden products certified under the voluntary Forest Stewardship Council certification regime for timber products. By carefully targeting the largest supplier, Home Depot, first and by seeking media attention

---

[60] Peter May, 'Compliance Motivations: Perspectives of Farmers, Homebuilders and Marine Facilities' (2005) 27 Law & Pol 317.

[61] Neil Gunningham and Peter Grabosky, *Smart Regulation: Designing Environmental Policy* (OUP 1998).

[62] Ibid 93.

for this campaign, Greenpeace could convince other suppliers of do-it-yourself products to participate in the Forest Stewardship Council's certification scheme with a mere phone call.[63]

But introducing surrogate regulators and third parties does not always bring such success. In particular, research on 'whistle-blowers' who report misconduct in their own firm or sector shows the shortfalls of surrogate regulation. The chance of being stigmatized in the future may lead surrogate regulators to withhold insights from the regulator, or the impact of the regulator's response may dissuade them from reporting at all. After all, why would someone report her or his own firm, knowing that this could affect, for instance, the firm's licence to operate and thus her or his own job?[64] In other words, whilst surrogate regulators may add to the effectiveness of regulatory enforcement, regulators should not depend on them to gain insight into their regulatees' behaviour.

Introducing third parties into regulatory enforcement may come with its own complications. A study on the role of third party regulators in the enforcement of construction regulation in Australia and Canada highlights some of these.[65] In both countries, regulatees have the choice of involving either a government or a private sector inspector in the monitoring and enforcement of their compliance with regulations. The research indicates that involving private sector inspectors in certain monitoring tasks makes the regulatory enforcement process more effective and efficient as a result of specialization, but that too much private sector involvement comes with accountability problems. Once private sector actors operate at great distance from governments, shirking and cutting corners was found to be a considerable risk. That is, without sufficient governmental oversight of the enforcement tasks of these private sector inspectors, the latter may bend to the wishes of their clients – which implies that they may certify construction work as being compliant with regulatory requirements and issue building and occupancy permits where standards have not been met.

From an EU perspective, it is interesting that the European Commission

---

[63] Joseph Domask, 'From Boycotts to Global Partnerships' in Jonathan P Doh and Hildy Teegen (eds), *Globalisation and NGOs* (Praeger Publishers 2003).

[64] Yuval Feldman and Orly Lobel, 'Decentralized Enforcement in Organizations' (2008) 2 *Regulation & Governance* 165, Joyce Rothschild and Terance Miethe, 'Whistle-blower Disclosures and Management Retaliation' (1999) 26 *Work and Occupations* 107.

[65] Jeroen van der Heijden. 'Friends, Enemies or Strangers? On Relationships between Public and Private Sector Service Providers in Hybrid Forms of Governance' (2011) 33 Law & Pol 367.

has used smart regulation terminology since roughly 2010. Nevertheless, the Commission's understanding of smart regulation differs significantly from that in Gunningham and Grabosky's work. To the Commission, smart regulation implies:

> To ensure that EU action is effective, the Commission assesses the impact of policies, legislation, trade agreements and other measures at every stage – from planning to implementation and review.[66]

Key to the Commission's smart regulation philosophy is the so-called Regulatory Fitness and Performance Programme, or REFIT. Through this programme, the Commission seeks to identify opportunities to reduce the regulatory burden and to simplify existing laws. Simplification and burden reduction has been achieved in areas such as chemicals legislation, public procurement and patents.[67] The Commission's smart regulation philosophy is dealt with in more detail in Chapter 2.

---

66 <http://ec.europa.eu/smart-regulation/> accessed 2 February 2015.

67 <http://ec.europa.eu/smart-regulation/refit/index_en.htm/> accessed 2 February 2015. It is somewhat striking to see that a single term, smart regulation, can imply different things. Smart regulation has a very specific meaning in the regulatory literature (the ideas discussed in Gunningham and Grabosky's book), and this is very different to the meaning of the term when used by the European Commission. Of course, there is nothing inherently wrong with this (the word 'smart' is often used as an addition), but it may result in situations where different people in a single conversation talk about wholly dissimilar things. This example only reminds us to check with our interlocutors whether we indeed mean the same thing with the terms we use. A short anecdote is relevant here. On 10 and 11 March 2011, the international Regulatory Reform Conference was held in Amsterdam, the Netherlands. One of the panels brought together Professor Neil Gunningham and Robert Scharrenborg from the European Commission in a panel to discuss 'What is smart about Smart Regulation?'. Prof Gunningham discussed regulatory pyramids, policy mixes and surrogate enforcers, while Mr Scharrenborg was talking about the need to keep end-users in mind, the need to have smart regulation embedded in all aspects of policy making, the need to learn from best practice, and the need for the various EU institutions to work together in the development and design of policy. It goes without saying that the Babylonian confusion around the term 'Smart Regulation' did not result in a coherent answer to the question that drove this panel, with some members of the public even suggesting to Prof Gunningham that he might want to change his conceptualization of Smart Regulation as it is not fully in line with that of the European Commission.

2. CURRENT TRENDS: NETWORKED ENFORCEMENT

2.1 The Theory of Networked Enforcement: Different Approaches

In the previous sections, the development of the regulation and enforcement literature until roughly the late 1990s has been discussed. This section discusses what may be considered the current state of the art in regulatory scholars' thinking on regulatory enforcement: *networked enforcement*.[68] Networked enforcement seeks to overcome the critical characteristic of all enforcement models discussed so far: a dual desire (or need) for governments to steer away from allocating limited resources to regulatory enforcement and at the same time to keep sufficient insight into whether regulatees comply with regulatory requirements – and whether those responsible for monitoring and enforcement perform as desired. Networked enforcement seeks to bring together the various understandings of effective enforcement discussed in the introduction. It aims for as much compliance as possible, but at an acceptable cost and in such a way that regulatory enforcement is not considered an adverse intervention in the daily lives of regulatees. It should again be noted that we see a fairly different use of terminology here between the current chapter's conceptualization of a 'network' and, for instance, Dorte Martinsen's or Esther Versluis and Josine Polak's use of the term in this book (Chapters 6 and 4).

The idea underlying networked enforcement is that the various stages in the responsive regulation strategy are carried out by those actors who are best suited to them. The key is for the government to find these actors and include them in the development of direct regulatory interventions and in their enforcement practice. Networked enforcement seeks to combine the best of the responsive regulation, smart regulation and collaborative governance approaches. In other words, the model is expected to be cost-effective, as enforcement tasks are delegated, to the extent possible, to those who are in the best position to carry them out. If industry

---

[68] Robert Baldwin and Julia Black, 'Really Responsive Regulation' (2008) 71 *Michigan Law Review* 59; John Braithwaite, 'Methods of Power for Development' (2004) 26 *Michigan Journal of International Law* 297, Peter Drahos, 'Securing the Future of Intellectual Property' (2004) 36 *Case Western Reserve Journal of International Law* 53; Peter Drahos, 'Rethinking the Role of the Patent Office from the Perspective of Responsive Regulation' in Frederick Abbott, Carlos Correa and Peter Drahos (eds), *Emerging Markets and the World Patent Order* (Edward Elgar 2013); Peter Grabosky, 'Beyond Responsive Regulation' (2013) 7 *Regulation & Governance* 114.

self-regulation is expected to be a better option than government-led enforcement, self-regulation will be chosen. If private sector actors are expected to be more specialized than public sector bureaucrats, then monitoring and enforcement tasks might be privatized. Yet the model seeks to overcome the transparency and accountability shortfalls highlighted in the other models by keeping governments closely involved in the oversight of the actors who are tasked with monitoring and enforcement, as well as by building in additional accountability relationships.

The key difference with more traditional approaches to regulatory enforcement (responsive regulation and smart regulation included) is that networked enforcement does not put the responsibility for enforcement and the disciplinary power in the hands of only one actor. This is truly a key innovation. After all, if this actor, intentionally or not, carries out inadequate monitoring, or does not respond adequately to violations, by taking no or limited disciplinary action, then violations may go unnoticed. Under a networked enforcement approach, a regulatee is accountable to a range of actors, and all of these have specific responsibilities and powers to monitor, enforce and take disciplinary action.

2.2 The Practice: An Example of a Functioning Model of Networked Enforcement

What does networked enforcement look like in practice? Drawing on research conducted, once again, in the construction sector, the example below gives us an illustration, and Figure 3.2 gives a schematic.

Figure 3.2 is a schematic illustration of a promising example of networked enforcement from a study on the enforcement of construction regulation by certified private sector actors in Vancouver, Canada. The study sought to understand how the privatizing of regulatory enforcement plays out in real world settings. It studied ten slightly different forms of privatized enforcement of construction regulation in Australia, Canada and the Netherlands, building on a series of 150 interviews with experts such as policymakers, street-level bureaucrats, developers, contractors, architects and engineers.[69]

Private sector actors (also referred to as certified professionals) were introduced in the enforcement of construction regulation in the greater Vancouver region in the early 1980s. In order to become a certified professional an individual needs to be acknowledged and registered by the City of Vancouver. The requirements for registration are related

---

[69] van der Heijden n 65.

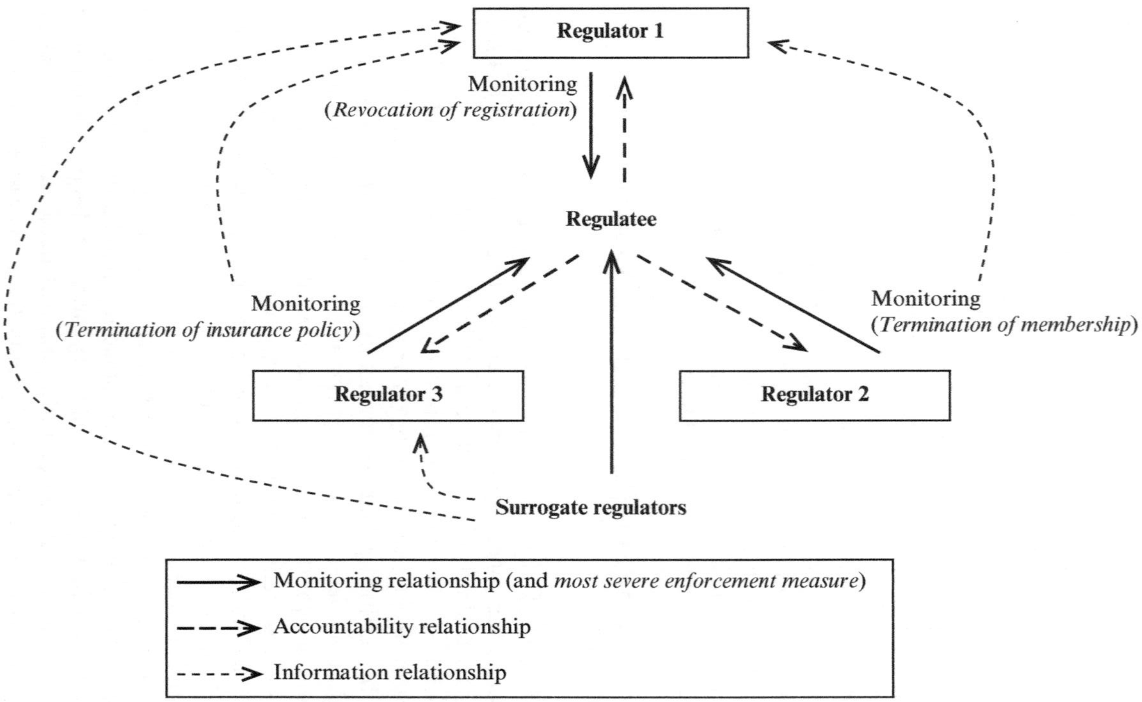

Source: Adapted from Jeroen van der Heijden, *Governance for Urban Sustainability and Resilience* (Edward Elgar 2014).

Figure 3.2 Schematic representation of a networked regulatory enforcement regime

to the (prospective) certified professional's level of education, working experience and ongoing professional development. In addition, the (prospective) certified professional needs to hold a particular level of professional indemnity insurance, and needs to be a member of the architects' association or the engineers' association. Once registered, the certified professional is accountable to three separate organizations (government, trade associations, insurance companies), which have their own disciplinary measures to incentivize compliance, as well as to other certified professionals, as described below. In addition, a specific 'surrogate regulator' plays an important role in this networked enforcement regime. In sum:

- *Regulator 1, government*: The government of the City of Vancouver randomly inspects the work of certified professionals. If violations are found it can, ultimately, withdraw a certified professional's registration, which puts the professional out of work. The City normally applies a responsive regulatory strategy and seeks compliance first through less intrusive means.
- *Regulator 2, the certified professional's trade association*: Trade associations play a strong role as well. They can terminate a private professional's membership if it becomes clear that the professional is not abiding by the association's code of conduct. The associations have, for instance, a system in place to investigate consumer complaints made about certified professionals. If they decide to terminate a certified professional's membership then the certified professional also loses the necessary registration with the City. These associations have a strong incentive to ensure compliant members. After all, one rogue member may change the general public's view of the association for the worse.
- *Regulator 3, the certified professional's insurance company*: Insurance providers play another strong role in the regime. They can decide that they will no longer provide a certified professional with a professional indemnity insurance policy. This can, for instance, be done if the insurance company has to pay out too often for work in which the certified professional was involved. Again, this de facto puts the certified professional out of business because without the necessary insurance the certified professional cannot be registered with the municipality. It goes without saying that insurance companies have a strong financial incentive to terminate the insurance policies of rogue certified professionals.
- *Other certified professionals as surrogate regulators:* Finally, the role of other certified professionals appears key in this regime. The group of certified professionals is relatively small in Vancouver, and

the professionals know about each other's work. They have a very strong incentive to ensure that their peers stick to the regulatory requirements. After all, the City of Vancouver may decide to terminate the role of certified professionals altogether if it considers that the system does not work as desired. Similarly, insurance companies may decide to increase all insurance premiums when they have to pay out on too many claims related to certified professionals.

In short, in this example a variety of direct regulators, third party regulators and surrogate regulators are involved in the assessment, monitoring, controlling and disciplining of private certified professionals. The municipality, the associations and the insurers all have 'big sticks' (i.e., the power to withdraw registration, to terminate membership, and to end an insurance policy) that they not only threaten to use, but can use with relative ease.[70] They also all have considerable interest in using the sticks when necessary. The role of the self-interested certified professionals as 'surrogate regulators' adds to the overall performance of this networked enforcement regime.

Whilst this model is a stellar example of how regulatory enforcement could be organized in an almost perfect manner (i.e., in a way that is cost-effective, results in a high level of compliance, and is not too adverse) it has to be noted that it is (almost) textbook perfect. The author of the current chapter has studied regulatory enforcement for over a decade and has not encountered many other examples that are as textbook perfect as this one. Some other inspirational examples are provided by Scott, who has studied accountability structures in the provision of telecom services in the United Kingdom.[71] Scott's work indeed supports the notion that multiple enforcement and accountability relationships between actors create interdependencies and redundancies (overlapping accountability relationships) that take away the centrality of more traditional enforcement models. The idea of redundancy, particularly, helps to strengthen enforcement models because a second (or third, etc.) enforcement relationship might pick up on problems that the first relationship misses – and it might even be that the mere existence of a second (or third, etc.) enforcement relationship keeps the actors in the first enforcement relationship sharp. However, critics might argue that such redundancy is superfluous and therefore too costly.

---

[70] Braithwaite n 68.

[71] Colin Scott, 'Accountability in the Regulatory State' (2000) 27 *Journal of Law & Society* 36.

CONCLUSION

In this chapter, some of the major steps taken on the road from deterrence-based enforcement strategies to networked enforcement regimes have been addressed. The opportunities and constraints of a variety of enforcement strategies have been identified. What binds these together is that much is expected of a retreat of governmental actors from the assessment, monitoring and controlling of regulatees' behaviour (i.e., through specialization, availability and in-depth knowledge of the regulated group or sector), but that governments at the same time need to think carefully about how to maintain sufficient oversight of the way others carry out these tasks. In addition, whilst the move from deterrence-based strategies, with intrusive disciplinary actions to incentivize compliance, to compliance-based approaches based on facilitation have normative appeal, they hold a risk that those responsible for monitoring, enforcement and disciplining steer away from using 'big sticks'. Whilst easier to implement, soft enforcement responses (i.e., consultation, advice or agreements) may not always provide sufficient incentives to regulatees to ensure they behave in the desired way.

What has become clear in discussing the various enforcement models is that they all have different underlying assumptions. The deterrence-based approach considers that fear of the consequences of breaking the law will stimulate compliance. The somewhat technocratic solution to achieving compliance would then be to ratchet up disciplinary measures. The compliance-based approach takes a different point of departure and considers that regulatees are likely to comply when they are supported in doing so. It is not fear of disciplinary measures this model seeks to achieve but an internal, normative acceptance of law and regulation by regulatees. Both approaches do, however, require considerable enforcement capacity on the regulator's side, and this is what the new models introduced in the 1980s strove to avoid. Self-regulation and enforced self-regulation argued that previous models were too time- and cost-intensive for both regulator and society. These models argue that governments are often unable to gain the same depth of knowledge of a regulated sector or organization as representatives from that sector or organization. Those in favour of self-regulation and enforced self-regulation challenged governments to delegate their monitoring and enforcement powers to the regulatees, or to contract out or privatize enforcement tasks. A key driver for government in doing this was to become more cost-effective in delivering public services. The next set of models discussed, responsive regulation and smart regulation, took yet again a different point of departure. Responsive regulation has a strong focus on the regulatee and questions why she or he is (not) willing to comply. It argues that most regulatees are in fact willing to comply, and that a regulatee violating the law can often be incentivized to comply through an intervention that is not very intrusive, such as a letter explaining that the regulatee is in violation of the law, giving advice on how to solve the breach, and setting a time limit after which the regulatee is expected to be in compliance. Smart regulation agrees with this regulatee-oriented focus, but adds that a wide range of actors can be involved in monitoring and enforcement tasks: governments, representatives from the regulated sector or organization, or even members of the general public in the role of 'surrogate regulators'.

These different underlying assumptions make it difficult, if not impossible, to compare the 'enforcement effectiveness' of the various models presented. A deterrence-based approach may ensure quite a high level of compliance (think of speeding regulations), yet it is costly to enforce this type of regulation (it works well for road safety, for example, where much enforcement is carried out using speed cameras that do not need live monitoring, but it would require ongoing and therefore costly monitoring in most other aspects of life). A self-regulation or enforced self-regulation approach may be cost-effective for the regulator, but it remains a question whether it results in a sufficient level of compliance (self-regulation by banks is often considered one of the key causes of the 2008 financial crisis) and whether regulators (still) have enough understanding of the regulated sector when things go wrong and they have to intervene after all.[72] Responsive regulation and smart regulation have a great deal of normative appeal as they, among other approaches, seek to avoid adverse interventions; they do, however, challenge key legal principles of equality and fairness as they argue that like cases should not be treated in like manner but that the regulator should respond to specific local circumstances to bring a regulatee into compliance.

Seeking to build on the strength of these models and overcome their weaknesses, the networked enforcement strategy can be understood as a mix-and-match approach using these earlier models. In this chapter it was introduced as the current state-of-the-art thinking in regulatory enforcement by regulatory scholars. Its strengths lie in its flexibility and non-centrality: a variety of enforcement actors, a variety of enforcement strategies and a variety of enforcement styles are brought together. But it is not only the mixing and matching that makes networked enforcement different from the other strategies discussed. An important difference

---

[72] Renée Birgit Adams, 'Governance and the Financial Crisis' (2012) 12 *International Review of Finance* 7.

compared to the other strategies is that it builds on the clear self-interest of regulators and surrogate regulators. There are, however, some considerations that may stand in the way of implementing the model at all levels of the EU and its Member States – two major ones are addressed. First is the question of scale. The model appears to work well in the greater Vancouver area, but this is a fairly small geographical jurisdiction and, compared to most European cities, fairly isolated from other cities. In other words, the construction community in Vancouver is tight and there is little flow of 'outsiders' through the system. Most contractors, developers and building inspectors know each other. This does not hold for most European cities (or even countries) where industry sectors are much more open, with many more individuals and organizations working in various jurisdictions (cities, regions, Member States, and so on). Second is the question of how the model would perform in another industry sector. The construction industry is a complicated industry with a wide variety of trades, organizations and product suppliers involved, but for regulatory enforcement it has one big advantage: buildings are static. Building inspectors know where a building is and can inspect it when they want (theoretically); this does not hold true for many other production processes, and certainly not for products that move around a lot (most consumer goods such as household appliances, food, legal drugs, and so on are difficult to track once they have left the shop). The model seems even less applicable when enforcement is aimed at assessing not the quality of a good or service, but the specific behaviour of regulatees. Take again speeding as an example: what would be the relevant network of actors who should be involved in the enforcement process? Who would be the relevant surrogate regulators? What are the checks and balances (besides fines) that could incentivize regulatees not to speed, and what are the checks and balances that would ensure that the various regulators carry out sound monitoring and enforcement tasks?

In conclusion, regulation and enforcement literature has come a long way, from deterrence-based enforcement strategies to networked enforcement. Yet, it has also become clear that designing and implementing an 'effective enforcement' strategy is not an easy task. Different regulatory contexts (differences between EU Member States, differences between regulated sectors, even differences at different levels of scale) require a careful analysis before 'just any' enforcement model can be implemented – or something that works elsewhere is copied. Some important questions to ask are: which actors are involved in the regulatory enforcement process, and what are their interests and motivations for sound enforcement? What type of regulatee is involved and what incentives (deterrence-based? compliance-based? a mix?) are likely to result in her or him complying?

Which network actors and surrogate regulators are available in the regulated context, what type of monitoring tasks can they take up, and what disciplinary power do they have? How much interdependency and redundancy is needed to strengthen the model, and at what point will this hamper the model? Also, more empirical research is vital if we wish to understand better why a particular enforcement model achieves the desired outcomes in one context but not in another. The EU as an institution provides an intriguing context for such studies, but it also provides a set of Member States. The EU is fairly exceptional in that the various Member States have implemented a series of EU Directives, but all have taken different approaches to the implementation of the Directives, including the monitoring and enforcement of compliance. This provides scholars with the unique opportunity to study a variety of enforcement models that seek to obtain similar outcomes but through different strategies.

Between the lines, it has also become clear from this chapter that scholars in regulation and political science use a slightly different terminology from the terminology of scholars of law. This may result in some Babylonian confusion when scholars (and policymakers) do not give examples of what they mean by particular terms, as the example of smart regulation highlighted (see footnote 67). This chapter by no means wishes to force the terminology of regulatory scholars and political scientists onto those interested in the making and implementation of law in the EU, but it hopes to have provided a range of insights from the regulation and enforcement literature that may also be applicable (whether similar or different terminology is used) in other fields as well.

4. The virtues of interdependence and informality: an analysis of the role of transnational networks in the implementation of EU directives

Josine Polak and Esther Versluis

INTRODUCTION

A lot has been written about transnational networks as governance instruments.[1] This should not come as a surprise; the ubiquitous networked character of public administration in this 'new, networky world'[2] is something that can hardly be disregarded. Governance networks may broadly be conceptualized as structures of interdependence involving horizontal cooperation of multiple, operationally autonomous actors pursuing common public goals.[3] They are governed by reciprocal, preferential, and mutually supportive actions.[4] The adjective 'transnational' implies that these networks constitute a vehicle for officials of national authorities to act directly with their counterparts in other countries.[5]

While a phenomenon in governance contexts across the globe, it is in

---

[1] See also Chapter 5 of this volume.

[2] Bruno Latour, 'Networks, Societies, Spheres: Reflections of an Actor-network Theorist' (International Seminar on Network Theory: Network Multidimensionality in the Digital Age, Annenberg School for Communication and Journalism, Los Angeles, 19 February 2010).

[3] Tanja A Börzel and Karen Heard-Lauréote, 'Networks in EU Multi-level Governance: Concepts and Contributions' (2009) 29 *Journal of Public Policy* 135; Eva Sørensen and Jacob Torfing, *Theories of Democratic Network Governance* (Palgrave Macmillian 2007); Laurence J O'Toole Jr, 'The Ties That Bind? Networks, Public Administration, and Political Science' (2010) 43 *Ps-Political Science & Politics* 7.

[4] Walter W Powell, 'Neither Market nor Hierarchy: Network Forms of Organization' (1990) 12 *Research in Organizational Behaviour* 295.

[5] Note that transnational is not the same as transgovernmental; the latter term is not exactly appropriate in this context, since the participants in the networks

particular in the EU that a whole literature arose regarding 'networked governance',[6] or 'regulation by networks'.[7] This literature has been triggered in particular by the increased reliance of the European Commission on networked governance as an independent mode of steering rather than as a mere element of the traditional governance structure.[8] The emergence of transnational networks as governance instruments must generally be seen as a response to the 'governance dilemma' faced by the EU.[9] This dilemma entails an acknowledgement of the need for more government at the supranational level on the one hand, and an aversion to greater centralization and coercive authority on the other hand.[10] More centralization is needed in view of the desire to ensure greater consistency in the implementation of EU law. More centralization is, however, politically impossible and probably undesirable.[11] One reason for this undesirability lies in the notion that according to the principle of subsidiarity, it is national authorities that should be primarily responsible for the administration of EU law. Regulation by networks has been seen as an apt way to meet the need for increased uniformity while preserving the decentralized nature of the implementation system in the EU.[12]

It has been suggested that the usefulness of networks should be evaluated at three levels: the community level, the network level, and the participant level.[13] On the community level, the strength of networks is that

under consideration here are empathically not government officials (but officials from national administrations instead).

[6] Adriaan Schout and Andrew Jordan, 'Coordinated European Governance: Self-organizing or Centrally Steered?' (2005) 83 *Public Administration* 201.

[7] Renaud Dehousse, 'Regulation by Networks in the European Community: The Role of European Agencies' (1997) 4 *Journal of European Public Policy* 246.

[8] Dehousse (n 7); David Coen and Mark Thatcher, 'Network Governance and Multi-level Delegation: European Networks of Regulatory Agencies' (2008) 28 *Journal of Public Policy* 49; Burkhard Eberlein and Abraham L Newman, 'Escaping the International Governance Dilemma? Incorporated Transgovernmental Networks in the European Union' (2008) 21 *Governance: An International Journal of Policy Administration, and Institutions* 25; Mark Thatcher and David Coen, 'Reshaping European Regulatory Space: An Evolutionary Analysis' (2008) 31 *West European Politics* 806.

[9] Schout and Jordan (n 6). Term coined by Robert O Keohane, 'Governance in a Partially Globalized World: Presidential Address, American Political Science Association, 2000' (2001) 95 *American Political Science Review* 1.

[10] See A Slaughter, *A New World Order* (Princeton University Press 2004) 8.

[11] Dehousse n 7.

[12] Dehousse n 7.

[13] Keith G Provan and H Brinton Milward, 'Do Networks Really Work? A Framework for Evaluating Public-sector Organizational Networks' (2001) *61 Public Administration Review* 414.

since they 'softly harmonize Member State regulatory activities'[14] they lead to more uniform law administration practices.[15] The beneficiaries of more consistent implementation practices are notably EU citizens and businesses operating in the single market. On a micro level, networks may bring several concrete and direct benefits for the participants involved in cooperation. The participants that are of interest in the context of this chapter are those involved in the practical implementation of EU law on the ground, rather than 'metagoverners'[16] (politicians and public managers; think of the European Commission) or other actors (think of business actors or civil society organizations) that may be involved in networks (and whose interests may differ from those of national officials).

This chapter focuses on what those network participants who are involved in the implementation of EU law on the ground actually think of the functioning of networks and of the extent to which the concrete theoretical benefits that networks are associated with (see further below) materialize in practice. The perceptions that network participants hold of these issues co-determine the eventual effectiveness of such networks as policy instruments in practice. If the actors who actually have to implement EU legislation do not see the added value of cooperation for supporting implementation practices, networks are unlikely to have a positive impact on the implementation of EU rules. Note that while officials' perceptions do not necessarily reflect actual behaviour, perceptions are likely to influence behaviour by serving as 'cognitive and normative frames for action'.[17] This makes them relevant tools through which to understand phenomena. The aim of this chapter is to shed light on the usefulness of networks for supporting national officials in the implementation of EU law. This analysis does not allow us to say anything about the effectiveness of implementation – that is, about Member State compliance with EU law – or to measure the effect of the networks

---

[14] Burkhard Eberlein and Edgar Grande, 'Beyond Delegation: Transnational Regulatory Regimes and the EU Regulatory State' (2005) 12 *Journal of European Public Policy* 89, 100.

[15] Karin Van Boetzelaer and Sebastiaan Princen, 'The Quest for Co-ordination in European Regulatory Networks' (2012) 50 *Journal of Common Market Studies* 819.

[16] The term 'metagoverners' is taken from Eva Sørensen and Jacob Torfing, 'Making Governance Networks Effective and Democratic through Metagovernance' (2009) 87 *Public Administration* 234. For benefits for such actors, see Emilia Korkea-aho, 'Watering Down the Court of Justice? The Dynamics between Network Implementation and Article 258 TFEU Litigation' (2014) 20 *European Law Journal* 649.

[17] Morten Egeberg and Jarle Trondal, 'EU-level Agencies: New Executive Centre Formation or Vehicles for National Control?' (2011) 18 *Journal of European Public Policy* 868, 874.

under examination on actual implementation. The latter is a sheer impossibility, not in the least since the effect of much of what is going on inside networks – notably knowledge and experience sharing – is not quantifiable and impossible to objectify. What this analysis does allow us to say something about is the 'internal effectiveness' of networks, that is, about the extent to which network participants themselves benefit from the theoretical virtues that networked cooperation is associated with, and under which conditions these theoretical benefits materialize in practice.

This chapter first outlines the literature on networked governance. It provides some theoretical reflections on the question why networks are expected to contribute to effective implementation. Moving on to the empirical material from the case studies, we demonstrate how the perception of officials that authorities are interdependent in ensuring effective implementation motivates multilateral cooperation, and how the perception of such cooperation as informal magnifies its benefits. While we do recognize that informal cooperation has its limits when it comes to improving the implementation of EU legislation, the chapter concludes that it must nevertheless be seen as an important part of the solution for achieving compliance with international norms on the ground. In view of the tendency of international organizations to rely on networks in a variety of policy domains[18] – and the implicit assumption that cooperation leads to more uniform levels of implementation – indeed the results of this study may have a wider relevance in practice, beyond the scope of implementation in the European Union (EU).

1. SCOPE OF STUDY

This chapter examines the perceived effectiveness of implementation networks in the context of three EU directives, and for officials from three Member States. The Member States selected for study are the Netherlands, Poland, and Portugal, which are understood to face very different obstacles in the process of implementing EU legislation.[19] Officials from those countries may therefore be expected to demonstrate different perceptions on the usefulness of networks for improving the implementation of EU legislation.

---

[18] O'Toole n 3.

[19] Gerda Falkner and Oliver Treib, 'Three Worlds of Compliance or Four? The EU-15 Compared to New Member States' (2008) 46 *Journal of Common Market Studies* 293; Simone Leiber, 'Transposition of EU Social Policy in Poland: Are there Different "Worlds of Compliance" in East and West?' (2007) 17 *Journal of European Social Policy* 349.

The directives that have been selected for study are the EU General Product Safety Directive (GPS Directive),[20] the Directive on Integrated Pollution Prevention and Control (IPPC Directive),[21] and the Directive on Safety Assessment of Foreign Aircraft (SAFA Directive).[22] The networks existing in the context of these directives are, amongst others, intended to support national competent authorities in carrying out market surveillance for non-food consumer products (Consumer Safety Network and Prosafe; GPS); help national administrations in the determination of environmental permits for large industrial installations (European Union Network for the Implementation and Enforcement of Environmental Law (IMPEL); IPPC); and support civil aviation authorities in carrying out ramp inspections for third-country aircraft landing on airports in the Member States (European SAFA Steering Group; SAFA).

What all these networks have in common is that they gather (street-level) officials involved in the implementation of the directives in practice; what differentiates them from one another is, importantly, their degree of formality. On the one side of the formality scale we find the Consumer Safety Network (CSN), which is a consultative experts group made up mainly of representatives of the Member States and chaired by the Commission. The CSN is an example of a legally formal network; it is encapsulated in the EU institutional framework by codification in legislation and subject to regular, publicly sanctioned exchanges.[23] Legally informal but materially formal is the European SAFA Steering Group (ESSG).[24] The ESSG, a technical advisory group composed of, amongst others, the SAFA National Coordinators of the EU Member

---

[20] Directive 2001/95/EC of the European Parliament and of the Council on general product safety [2001] OJ L11/4.

[21] Council Directive 96/61/EC concerning integrated pollution prevention and control [1996] OJ L257/26; Directive 2008/1/EC of the European Parliament and of the Council of 15 January 2008 concerning integrated pollution prevention and control (codified version) [2008] OJ L24/8. This Directive has been replaced by Directive 2010/75/EU of the European Parliament and of the Council on industrial emissions [2010] OJ L334/17.

[22] Directive 2004/36/EC of the European Parliament and of the Council on the safety of third-country aircraft using Community airports [2004] OJ L143/76. This Directive has been repealed and replaced by implementing rules, which acquired general applicability in autumn 2014.

[23] Thomas Christiansen, Andreas Follesdal and Simona Piattoni, 'Informal Governance in the European Union: An Introduction' in Thomas Christiansen and Simona Piattoni (eds), *Informal Governance in the European Union* (Edward Elgar 2003).

[24] The name of the Group is set to change into 'Ramp Inspection Coordination and Standardisation'.

Table 4.1 Networks in the context of the GPS, IPPC and SAFA directives

	Legally formal	Materially formal	Informal
GPS	Consumer Safety Network (CSN)		Prosafe
IPPC			IMPEL
SAFA		European SAFA Steering Group (ESSG)	

States, is materially embedded in the EU framework and characterized by a strong presence of the European Commission, the European Aviation Safety Agency (EASA), and Eurocontrol. As purely informal networks, Prosafe and IMPEL, both of which were founded by authorities from a number of countries in Europe, find themselves at the other extreme of the scale of formality. While Prosafe comprises market surveillance officers from over 30 European countries (plus Hong Kong), IMPEL consists of environmental authorities from more than 20 countries throughout Europe. Table 4.1 which classifies these networks according to their degree of formality and the directive to which they belong.

The analysis in this chapter is partly based on literature review and document analysis. Given our interest in the perceptions of those involved in the networks under consideration, the analysis is, however, mainly based on 28 in-depth interviews with national officials involved in Prosafe and/or the Consumer Safety Network (ten interviews), in IMPEL (seven), and in the ESSG (three); and with officials from Prosafe (four), the European Commission (three), and EASA (one).

2. WHY NETWORKS?

The conceptualization of networks outlined in the introduction to this chapter sets networks apart from the two other primary modes of governance, states and markets.[25] The state mode is characterized by a reliance on hierarchy and 'legitimate' authority as the means to regulate relationships between actors; the market mode relies on 'price signals and formalized, legal con-

[25] Powell n 4.

tractual relations to bring dispersed suppliers and purchasers together'.[26] Many governments in west European countries have long resorted to a mix of state and market-based governance in the provision of public services.[27] States and markets do, however, have certain weaknesses in this regard. States can fail to solve public policy problems because of a weak centralization of resources that are needed for the effective resolution of public policy problems.[28] Markets can fail amongst others because they are unable to control, and to compensate for, the production of negative externalities, leading to an inefficient allocation of resources in society and an overall loss of welfare. Both problems associated with the two traditional modes of governance have led governments to shift their focus away from states and markets towards networks as a third mode of steering.[29]

What exactly is it that implementation networks are expected to bring to the table? Section 1 of this chapter has suggested that the answer to this question depends on the level of analysis, of which there are three: the community level, the network level, and the participant level.[30] Given the interest of this chapter in the effectiveness of networks for network participants, the focus of the following subsections will be on the benefits that these actors may derive from cooperation.

2.1 Actor-Centred Institutionalism: Resource Sharing and Mutual Trust

In the vein of actor-centred institutionalism, networks are institutions that are capable, first of all, of lowering information and transaction costs for national authorities by drawing together knowledge and expertise that single actors may not possess.[31] This function is particularly important in view of the complexity of contemporary policy problems,[32] and in a situation in which the implementation of common policies is decentralized and the availability of resources greatly differs across jurisdictions.[33] In such a situation, resource sharing can support individual authorities to implement the law more efficiently and more effectively.

---

[26] Robyn L Keast, Myrna Mandell and Kerry A Brown, 'Mixing State, Market and Network Governance Modes: The Role of Government in "Crowded" Policy Domains' (2006) 9 *International Journal of Organization Theory and Behavior* 27.

[27] Keast, Mandell and Brown n 26.

[28] Börzel and Heard-Lauréote n 3, 141.

[29] Keast, Mandell and Brown n 26.

[30] Provan and Milward n 13.

[31] Eva Sørensen and Jacob Torfing, 'The Democratic Anchorage of Governance Networks' (2005) 28 *Scandinavian Political Studies* 195, 198–9.

[32] Börzel and Heard-Lauréote n 3.

[33] Giandomenico Majone, *Regulating Europe* (Routledge 1996) 277.

Secondly, networks are able to create mutual trust amongst network participants, reducing the risk of intentional deviation by reassuring actors that they are not being cheated upon.[34] In a situation of decentralized governance, cooperation between national administrations basically depends on their mutual trust and loyalty,[35] and that mutual trust is often lacking. The result may well be that Member States renege on their obligations under EU law, which may lead to a situation in which effective enforcement is compromised and other Member States see their suspicion of poor implementation confirmed.[36] Mistrust transforms into distrust, providing states with even stronger incentives to cheat. Cooperation may remedy defection by restoring mutual trust amongst authorities.

2.2 Learning Theories: Mutual Learning

Theories of policy learning generally hold that 'states can learn from their experience and that they can modify their present actions on the basis of their interpretation of how previous actions have fared in the past'.[37] Learning is important in a situation in which unequal expertise on the part of national authorities undermines the efficiency of the system of decentralized implementation in the EU.[38] In the vein of learning (inspired) theories, the diversity in the EU is a great asset for mutual learning, since it means that many different approaches will be tried out at the same time for similar policy problems. In such a context, the exchange of experiences and best practices amongst Member States may help them find new solutions to problems 'often thought to be unsolvable'.[39]

---

[34] Fritz Wilhelm Scharpf, 'Co-ordination in Hierarchies and Networks' in Fritz Wilhelm Scharpf (ed), *Games in Hierarchies and Networks: Analytical and Empirical Approaches to the Study of Governance Institutions* (Campus 1993).

[35] Xénophon A Yataganas, 'Delegation of Regulatory Authority in the European Union the Relevance of the American Model of Independent Agencies' (2001) 3/01 Jean Monnet Working Paper, 32.

[36] Maartje De Visser, *Network-based Governance in EC Law: The Example of EC Competition and EC Communications Law* (Hart Publishing 2009), 20, 238–40.

[37] Colin J Bennett and Michael Howlett, 'The Lessons of Learning: Reconciling Theories of Policy Learning and Policy Change' (1992) 25 *Policy Sciences* 275–276.

[38] Yataganas n 35.

[39] E.g. David M Trubek and Louise G Trubek, 'Hard and Soft Law in the Construction of Social Europe: The Role of the Open Method of Coordination' (2005) 11 *European Law Journal* 343, 358.

2.3 Constructivism: Socialization

For constructivists, networked cooperation is a principal tool for socialization. According to constructivists, socialization – 'which directs the individual away from the self to the socializing group'[40] – is the answer to compliance problems, since it has the effect of changing the preferences of individuals by internalizing them into the normative belief that a rule ought to be obeyed, that compliance is 'the right thing to do'. More concretely, socialization can persuade actors into widely shared causal beliefs about the operation of a policy issue and about the necessity of rules in order to promote valued policy objectives.[41] Operating through a logic of appropriateness, networked cooperation is thus expected to facilitate consensus and conflict resolution.[42] Material interests or coercion do not come into play as mediating factors in this regard; individuals are understood to develop preferences, because they are seen as 'natural, rightful, expected and legitimate',[43] not because they are the result of a rational calculation of material interests.

3. HOW USEFUL ARE NETWORKS FOR MAKING EU DIRECTIVES WORK?

The above section outlines several ways in which networks may be helpful to civil servants in the implementation of norms. What do the 'local units'[44] that participate in networks have to say about the effectiveness of networks in this regard? The current section aims at shedding light on this question by discussing the perceptions of Dutch, Polish, and Portuguese civil servants on the effectiveness of the networks that aim to support the implementation of the GPS, IPPC, and SAFA Directives. It suggests that perceptions differ across countries and across policy areas, not only when

---

[40] Liesbet Hooghe, *The European Commission and the Integration of Europe: Images of Governance* (Cambridge University Press 2001) 15.

[41] Peter M Haas, 'Compliance with EU Directives: Insights from International Relations and Comparative Politics' (1998) 5 *Journal of European Public Policy* 17, 32.

[42] James G March and Johan P Olsen, *Democratic Governance* (Free Press/McMillan 1995).

[43] James G March and Johan P Olsen, 'The Logic of Appropriateness' in Michael Moran, Martin Rein and Robert E Goodin (eds), *Oxford Handbook of Public Policy* (Oxford University Press 2006) 689.

[44] Charles F Sabel and Jonathan Zeitlin, *Experimentalist Governance in the European Union: Towards a New Architecture* (Oxford University Press 2010).

it comes to the question of what officials 'get out of cooperation', but also regarding the issue of what motivates them to engage in cooperation in the first place.

3.1 Perceived Interdependence: A Strong Impetus for Cooperation

When it comes to the extent to which officials attach significance to networks as implementation instruments, the interviews carried out for this study show an important demarcation line between directives. Officials involved in the implementation of the GPS Directive and the SAFA Directive unequivocally view networked cooperation as one of the most useful implementation instruments. In the case of the IPPC Directive, cooperation may be appreciated as supporting implementation, but its significance as an implementation instrument is less pronounced. Similar to Boetzelaer and Princen,[45] we argue that the notion of interdependence plays an important explanatory role in this regard.

In the cases of general product safety and safety assessment of foreign aircrafts, officials explicitly refer to interdependence as an important factor motivating cooperation with colleagues from other countries. The free movement of goods within the single European market makes product safety an issue of common concern for the market surveillance authorities of the Member States. In the words of an official from the informal product safety network 'Prosafe':

> Product safety is a topic of which you cannot think in national terms only. I spoke with a business operator that said: 'so my product is not admitted to the Antwerp port? I will take it to Hamburg and import it to Europe from there'. Then I answered: 'I will inform my colleagues from Hamburg that this product is coming to them'. My conversation partner didn't quite like that. This shows that it doesn't work to think nationally. We are in an internal European market, so we have to co-operate – otherwise products will enter our market after we have just sent them back because they are unsafe! (interview Prosafe1; similar Prosafe3)

Likewise, the international nature of air traffic makes air safety an issue of common concern for all civil aviation authorities. In the words of an official involved in the implementation of the SAFA Directive:

> It is impossible to impose national boundaries on aviation. Even if it is a foreign operator, the foreign operator is flying all over the world, and he may be taking some Portuguese citizens, even between Alaska and Mongolia. There is always

45 Van Boetzelaer and Princen n 15.

> a Portuguese guy traveling between Alaska and Mongolia. And I can say the same about Portuguese operators; there is always some Portuguese operator operating flights to Mecca during the pilgrimage period. So aviation, because it is international, is by nature a national issue. (interview PT17; similar NL29)

The functional argument outlined above does not seem to work in the case of the IPPC Directive. While pollution crosses borders just like products and airplanes do, the interdependency argument does generally not come to the fore as a motivational factor for cooperation, at least not in interviews carried out for this study. Even the suggestion that more lenient permit conditions for industrial installations in other Member States may provide a competitive edge to both those countries and the relevant economic operators does not particularly seem to be a factor motivating officials to cooperate. The relatively weak perceptions of interdependence in the case of the IPPC Directive, and the resulting relatively low value attached to cooperation, are underlined by the following quote:

> There is no committee for administrative cooperation in the IPPC Directive. This probably also depends on the topic: the cross-border element is not as strong as for example in the case of the General Product Safety Directive. There is not directly a reason to create something for the IPPC Directive. (interview NL23)

Relatively weak levels of interdependence in the case of the IPPC Directive may explain why officials demonstrate less of a preference for cross-border cooperation in this case than in the case of the other two directives subject to this study. The idea that cooperation through the IMPEL network does take place suggests that there are other factors that stimulate officials to engage in cooperation. It is here where the virtues of cooperation – other than those related to interdependence – come in as important.

3.2 The Virtues of Cooperation

Section 2 has suggested that the virtues that networks are associated with the notions of mutual learning, resource sharing, mutual trust, and conflict resolution. The importance that officials attach to these notions seems to depend on the nature of the policy domain and appears to vary across Member States, as the following subsections demonstrate.

Mutual learning: about students and teachers

Mutual learning seems to be appreciated as a product of cooperation mainly in the area of IPPC and in the domain of GPS. It seems to be less important in the area of SAFA. The focus in the current section will accordingly be on the perceptions of officials involved in the networks existing in the context of the IPPC and GPS Directives, and on inter-country differences that could be distinguished in this regard.

These inter-country differences basically express themselves in an appreciation of officials of networks as providing for *learning* opportunities on the one hand, and for *teaching* opportunities on the other hand. Although officials from all three countries included in this study seem to appreciate cooperation because it allows them to exchange experiences and best practices (e.g. interview NL5; PT6; PL2), it is Polish and Portuguese officials that refer most often to the fact that cooperation allows the participants to learn from one another. This is the case in both policy areas, as the following quotations illustrate:

> Cooperation [in the area of product safety] makes it possible to see how other Member States work, we find together a solution for issues, we help each other, and we learn with each other. We have to learn from each other. (interview PT6; similar PL2)

Moreover:

> In IMPEL, everyone has the chance to learn something, because we have different legal systems, different points of view, different solutions to solve the problems. It is very interesting. It gives us knowledge about how other countries solve the problems. (interview PL8; similar PT10)

The view that cooperation allows for *mutual* learning to take place, as expressed in the two above quotations, seems to resonate less with Dutch officials. This lack of resonance relates to the idea that whereas Polish and Portuguese officials may situate themselves as 'students' in the cooperation context, Dutch officials rather tend to position themselves towards the other side of the scale. There cannot be students without teachers, and it seems that it is, indeed, particularly the Dutch who conceive of their role in cooperation mainly as one of 'teaching others'. These officials feel that they are rightly placed to do so since it is, at least in their view, their authorities that are amongst those in the lead when it comes to the knowledge and expertise needed for adequate implementation (interviews NL5; NL10; NL11; NL12; NL13; NL22). These perceptions suggest that whereas cooperation may have a learning effect for all, it is appreciated most by authorities that position themselves as students in the cooperation context. For countries that – for whatever reason – do not in particular consider themselves to be in the position to learn, this learning effect is less pronounced.

Why, then, would the latter countries invest in cooperation? An important part of the answer to this question lies in the idea that in particular in situations of interdependence – as in the area of product safety – cooperation pays off where learning processes take the quality of implementation in 'laggard countries' to a higher level, rendering implementation practices more consistent across the board. Consistency lowers the implementation costs for well-performing countries and increases the effectiveness of their implementation efforts, as we have seen before.

Mutual trust: about leaders and laggards

The concept of mutual learning should not be conceived of in narrow terms only, as in involving the exchange of practical knowledge and experience about implementation in order to teach others how to do better or to learn how to improve one's performance. Where cooperation allows the participants to acquire insight into how colleagues from other Member States go about the administration of particular rules, it may shed light on the extent of compliance in other Member States as well. This 'learning in the broad sense' is important, since there seems to be a certain degree of mistrust amongst officials when it comes to compliance in other states than their own, and a reality check may well show this mistrust to be misplaced. Both notions are reflected in the assertion that 'cooperation is the most important thing. It creates awareness that the others aren't as bad as people may have thought. It's all about mutual trust'. (interview Prosafe4)

This is further elaborated in the following extracts:

> Often, the first thought is: why should we implement this here if other countries don't do it? Cooperation is used to hold a mirror to one's own performance. We may think that we are doing so well, but is this actually the case? And are they [Eastern-European countries] actually so bad over there? There is a lot of rabble-rousing. Images and noises come up very quickly. Sometimes they are the truth, but no one checks whether this is indeed the case. Because of cooperation, you see that things are done the same in other countries. IMPEL contributes to the strengthening of mutual trust. (interview NL18)

> Trust and cooperation are related: they reinforce each other. We all have the same aim. There are no competing interests. Safety is a basic principle, a basic value in the air safety domain. People that have a role to play here need to have the knowledge and expertise. And the question is whether these elements are always present. (interview NL29)

The notion that all the quotes above are taken from interviews with Dutch officials is not a matter of coincidence. It is these officials that express the most doubt about the adequacy of implementation in other countries, and it is those same officials that most connote cooperation with mutual trust. This need for reassurance is not surprising in view of the self-perception of the Dutch as being amongst those in the lead when it comes to the implementation of the three directives at issue in this study.

The negative effect of mistrust on cooperation does, however, go two ways. While countries that perceive of themselves as 'more advanced' or as 'better compliers' may feel a degree of frustration (why comply if others do not?), the same applies to countries that are subject to misgivings. For example, Polish and Portuguese officials involved in the area of IPPC indicate that they have felt a sense of misunderstanding from Member States that may or may not be more advanced (interview PL8; PT9). They indicate that cooperation has made officials understand each other better and that it has made them feel more accepted by their colleagues (ibid). The upshot of all of this is that cooperation is smoother not only because sceptical officials have gained trust, but also because those that were initially subject to misgivings may not anymore find themselves in the position of having to defend themselves. This side of the coin does not usually seem to surface in discussions regarding the importance of mutual trust for facilitating cooperation.

Resource sharing: the importance of money

The previous subsections address rather lofty concepts associated with transnational cooperation. When it comes to cooperation in the area of product safety legislation, however, both Polish and Portuguese officials underline a rather mundane benefit that participation in cooperation brings along for them: it reduces the financial burden of implementation. Consumer products covered by Prosafe joint projects are collected by inspectors from the participating market surveillance authorities, which forward them to one and the same laboratory for testing in order to ensure uniformity of test results. Both the labour and traveling costs of the persons involved from the partaking authorities and the costs of product testing are largely borne by Prosafe, which is awarded EU and European Free Trade Association (EFTA) funding for the management of joint projects. While this financial benefit pertains to all participating countries, it may be particularly helpful to authorities struggling with a lack of resources to undertake appropriate – that is, not just organoleptic but, where need be, laboratory – product tests on their own.

For Portuguese officials, this financial side appears to be a very important motivating factor to partake in cooperation projects:

> Well-functioning cooperation is the way. Just to show you how important cooperation is: you would not be able to perform so many product tests if you were not involved in a network. All these tests are very costly, and it would

be more useful if all Member States could get together and do more of this together. (interview PT5; also PT3)

What applies to the Portuguese authorities seems to apply even more so to the Polish authorities. The lack of financial resources for carrying out laboratory tests is a common theme running through all interviews with Polish inspectors and other officials. Prosafe actions are appreciated exactly because of the financial benefits that they bring along for the Polish authorities (interview PL2). However, Prosafe actions are just a drop in the ocean of needs: joint market surveillance actions have a rather narrow focus – they apply to a small section of consumer products only – and participation of the Polish authorities in such actions, while average compared to the participation rates of the other participating states, has nonetheless been limited.

Conflict resolution: 'bottom-up' coordination in the presence of interdependence

Section 3.1 has suggested that the participation of officials in cooperation in the areas of GPS and SAFA is driven by awareness that authorities in these fields depend on each other for making implementation work effectively for each of them individually. Officials indicate, more in particular, that they engage in cooperation because they find it crucial that authorities 'do the same thing in the same way'. While mutual learning may be an important mechanism to arrive at more consistent implementation, the potentiality of networked cooperation to facilitate the resolution of conflicts amongst Member States is just as important, officials say. The importance that officials attach to this particular virtue of cooperation is unsurprising not only in view of the idea that consistency serves the sheer self-interest of authorities, but also given the fact that a central arbitration mechanism in charge of arriving at common risk assessments in both areas is lacking. Were such a mechanism to exist, neither Prosafe nor the European SAFA Steering Group would have had (much of) a role to play as conflict resolution mechanisms.

The below citations suggest that while there is scepticism about the attainability of complete consistency in implementation outcomes, views on the usefulness of both networks for overcoming divergent opinions amongst Member States seem to be concurring:

> Sometimes it is difficult for all member states to arrive at similar risk assessment conclusions. When subjectivity is part of the problem, results can hardly be the same. Joint actions coordinated by Prosafe are helpful, since risk assessment is performed by member states all together, reaching a conclusion all together. (interview PT6)

> Whether harmonization is possible? Well, that's a political answer. On technical grounds, of course it is possible. Meetings of the European SAFA Steering Group are a very useful tool to achieve agreements on technical issues and so on. It is the only forum where we have the opportunity to express our different interpretations. I have to say that in 96–97% of the cases we reach an agreement, a very easy agreement. But there is always a margin of difficulty, you see. It is used like a political thing, because if a Member State runs out of all the technical arguments, the only way out is to say: 'it's a political thing and I have to stick with it'. (interview PT17)

This latter quotation supports the view that cooperation may be effective particularly for issues that are isolated from the political arena, since it is here where regulatory authorities are given most leeway to act independently. Since complete political isolation seems hardly imaginable – if politics plays a role in highly technical issues such as aviation, where then should it be absent? – one may expect the problem-solving potential of networks to be limited to some extent.

4. INFORMALITY: THE KEY TO MAKING COOPERATION WORK?

The finding that transnational cooperation may bring about the virtues discussed above broadly lends support to, and partly nuances, the postulations regarding the usefulness of cooperation set out in Section 2. Of course, cooperation needs to function well to deliver those benefits. The current section suggests that the perception amongst officials of cooperation as informal is a key facilitating factor in this regard. It underlines that the line between formality and informality is a fine one, though one which is not always easy to draw.

4.1 Informality: Key to Openness, Key to Mutual Trust

The importance of informality appears to be a common theme running through all interviews with officials engaged in the networks relevant in the context of this study. In particular, officials unequivocally refer to informality as the key to making cooperation work – and to formality as the most effective way to stifle meaningful cooperation. In the area of product safety, this unanimous perception basically translates into a preference of officials for informal cooperation through Prosafe over cooperation in the framework of the formal Consumer Safety Network. Cooperation within IMPEL is appreciated exactly because it functions outside the EU institutional order. And in the case of the European SAFA

Steering Group, the perceived informality of cooperation is referred to as a great strength, too.

What then are the benefits of informality? The answer is briefly summarized in the following words of a Portuguese official: 'Informality is why you have so much input from the participants' (interview PT10). In other words, informality translates into openness on the part of network participants. The dynamics that play a role here may be illustrated by the following citation:

> IMPEL started out as a network of the Member States. The European Commission wanted to join in; it saw IMPEL as some sort of a threat. The Commission got to co-chair meetings et cetera. But this practice was ended, since the Commission did not feel comfortable in this position. The interests and priorities of Member States on the one hand and of the Commission on the other hand diverged, and Member States did not really give any openness in the presence of the Commission. (interview NL18)

If the benefit of informality is openness about problems that authorities may struggle with, the benefit of openness, in its turn, is that it allows for cooperation to function as an effective learning, trust-building, and problem-solving instrument. In the words of an official from Prosafe:

> The solution to problems is found only if the reason for problems is explained. If the reason is not explained, we cannot find a solution that suits the problem. And there can only be trust when the information that comes in is honest. In Prosafe, we talk out freely. (interview Prosafe1)

The idea of informality as an important precondition for effective cooperation is commonplace not only amongst national officials; the case of product safety shows that also the European Commission sees the value of informality for making cooperation work (interview EC1). In this area, it is the CSN that is supposed to facilitate administrative cooperation between the market surveillance authorities of the Member States, as we have seen before. Established by the GPS Directive, this Network came into being following the Member States' dismissal of the proposal of the European Commission to make Prosafe fulfil this task. Prosafe had been founded a decade earlier following a shared awareness amongst market surveillance officers that, in a situation of interdependence, Member States should 'get together' for efficient and effective implementation to be ensured (interview Prosafe8).

The CSN did not, however, ever really get underway – at least not in the way envisaged by the GPS Directive. A comparison of what the CSN *aims* at doing and what it *actually* does suggests that the Network hardly does anything that it is formally supposed to do. What it aims to do is exchange information on market surveillance issues; establish and execute joint projects; exchange experiences and best practices; and improve supranational cooperation regarding the tracing, withdrawal, and recall of dangerous products. What it, according to interviewees, actually does is constitute a forum for reflection and discussion of topics related to consumer product and service safety. It also constitutes a database for knowledge work. As such, its operation clearly does not meet the objectives set in this regard in the GPS Directive.

Note that this does not mean that the CSN is useless; it only means that its potential usefulness must derive from somewhere else. In fact, certain national officials do appreciate cooperation through the Network because it complements the work undertaken within the framework of Prosafe, by providing room for discussions of a more political nature. It is indeed true that results of joint market surveillance actions may be discussed during meetings of the CSN, and that issues under discussion there may be taken further by the GPS committee for regulatory policymaking. In this sense, the CSN fulfils a function that Prosafe could never perform, which does seem to imbue it with a degree of added value in the implementation context. In view of the nature of the discussions and the dominance of policy officials rather than street-level actors in CSN meetings, the immediate added value of such discussions for street-level actors does, however, seem limited.

In contrast Prosafe has a history of organizing joint market surveillance actions. These actions address both horizontal issues (related to the development of best practices in market surveillance in general) and vertical, product-specific issues (food imitation, child appealing products, ladders, et cetera). Discussions of various issues of market surveillance take place during meetings of the General Assembly. A comparison between what the CSN does and is supposed to do, and what Prosafe actually does, can only lead one to the conclusion that:

> nothing of what happens in Prosafe, happens in the infamous Article-10 network. This network was an attempt to establish something like Prosafe, but it has been established several times, without any real success, even though one tried in different ways. (interview Prosafe1)

Also the Commission admits that whereas the CSN should have taken on the tasks stipulated in the GPS Directive, this has never really happened (interview EC2). In view of this observation, the Commission's proposition in its proposal for a Regulation on market surveillance of products to establish a European Market Surveillance Forum drawn up along the lines – though extending the tasks – of the CSN, seems neither logical nor advisable. What adds to the level of surprise of this proposal is a Commission official's view that the only reason why the CSN still exists is because 'it is, in the end, a formal body' (interview EC2), which officials feel obligated to make use of.

The perceptions of the usefulness of the CSN that are held by national officials appear to vary. Dutch officials appear to view the CSN as a mere redundancy, or of little use for stimulating practical cooperation at best (interview NL7; NL12; NL11). A Polish official indicates a clear preference for cooperation through Prosafe, relegating the CSN to a state of indifference (interview PL2). In the view of a Portuguese official frequenting meetings of both the CSN and Prosafe, the two networks complete each other (interview PT6) along the lines set out above.

Whether outwardly rejected or evaluated as useful in some way, one thing is clear: when it comes to actual administrative cooperation between the market surveillance authorities of the Member States, the CSN is no match for Prosafe (interviews with all relevant officials). The reason why the CSN has failed to constitute the type of forum that it purports to be – and now we return to the focal issue of the current section – is a simple one. In the words of a Commission official:

> If government officials come to Brussels to attend, they do so as representatives of the member states. The formal character of meetings does not quite foster cooperation on a practical level and can even act as a brake on cooperation. Prosafe works better, because it is informal. (interview EC2; also EC4)

4.2 What Really Matters: The Perception of Cooperation as Informal

The above section does not seem to leave any room for doubt regarding the crucial role that informality can play as a stimulus for effective cooperation. What exactly, however, do we mean by informality? Or, in other words, what makes cooperation informal? Interviews suggest that similar to the case for interdependence, it is the *perception* of cooperation as informal that determines the behaviour of officials in networks along the lines set out above. While legal informality – that is, the lack of codification in EU legislation – seems to be an absolute precondition in this regard, this is not the case for material informality – that is, the lack of involvement in the network by the European Commission or an EU agency – as we will see below.

The notion that even a network with a strong formal presence of the European Commission or an EU agency can provide a sense of informality is supported by the case of the European SAFA Steering Group

(ESSG). Legally speaking the Group is an informal platform for cooperation; it is not codified in EU legislation. Upon closer examination, however, it appears to be strictly tied to the EU institutional framework: it is chaired by the European Commission and attended by officials from the SAFA coordination team at EASA. Moreover, notes on meetings are produced by EASA, for example in the form of Training Bulletins that are distributed amongst SAFA Participating States (interview EASA1). In brief, even though one cannot speak of a 'legal formalization' of the network, the way in which it is managed – by EU bodies – make it from a material point of view very much look like a formal EU network.

Despite the formal outlook of meetings, officials nonetheless seem to experience ESSG meetings as rather informal events (interview PT17; PL15; NL29). This is not the case because of the legal informality of the network, at least not emphatically. The dynamics that do seem to play an important role here are illustrated by the following citation:

> I have to say that on this ESSG Committee, the European Commission acts as the chair of those meetings. So it is the EC representative who runs the show. But in 99% of the cases, the EC representative is very low profile, and it is a kind of a formal thing: he opens the meetings and thanks all the participants before closing the meeting and so on. But I don't feel watched by the EC, by no means. I am pretty sure that neither me nor my colleagues have ever felt constraints, say, because the EC representative is there. On the contrary. It is a technical discussion. The EC representative is not a technic; he's not an engineer or a pilot. So we can discuss freely between us, because the guy doesn't understand our language anyway, and that's very good. But if we, in this atmosphere amongst equals, amongst pilots and engineers, if we don't find an agreement, the last resort is to look at the EC representative, since the Commission is the owner of the forum, and say, 'look, please find us a way to deal with those issues'. (interview PT17)

Experiences seem to have been completely different in the case of IMPEL. During a certain period of its existence, IMPEL resembled the ESSG in the sense that it was closely tied to the EU institutional framework as well. At this point, however, perceptions start to diverge. Officials indicate that when the Commission started to formally participate in the network, Member States did not really provide openness. In fact, this is referred to as one of the reasons for the Commission to have quitted the network (interview NL17). Overall then, it seems that the participation of the Commission may trigger different reactions on the part of Member States. Informal networks embedded within the EU institutional framework may be experienced as informal, as in the case of the ESSG, but they may also be experienced as formal, as is the case for IMPEL. This seems to be rather paradoxical. How should this paradox be tackled?

It should be tackled first of all by letting go of the assumption that it is informality *stricto sensu* – meaning both legal and material informality – that is determinative for meaningful cooperation. Just as in the case of interdependence, it seems to be the *perception* of cooperation as informal that is crucial in this regard. The Commission's lack of specialist knowledge on the issues tabled for discussion, hinted at in the above quote from a SAFA National Coordinator, appears to be one factor making for such informality. Other factors are hinted at in the following excerpts from interviews with officials involved in cooperation through Prosafe:

> In contrast to the Consumer Safety Network, Prosafe is not an agent of the Commission. The Commission only finances Prosafe's work. And the Commission was never really present during Prosafe meetings. There was a representation at annual get-togethers, but it was very informal and they were not the main actors. (interview PL2)

> The strong point about Prosafe is that talking out freely is possible, since we can say anything without having to cover for ourselves in order to prevent losing face. We also talk freely to the Commission, when it is present at meetings. This works very, very well, as we know there is mutual confidentiality. We hear things from the Commission about how things are cooking inside the Commission that we never hear at any other platform. Newcomers find this strange, but in the end, things are being said. (interview Prosafe1)

Here, it is not a generally known lack of knowledge on the part of the Commission about the issues under consideration, but either the actually rather minor role of the Commission, or the principle of mutual confidentiality, that creates a sense of informality. If this seems to complicate the picture even further, the following citation adds another element to the equation:

> I recall that the Commission wanted to be closer to the people, and they organized some kind of get-together at the Berlaymont building with Commissioner Kuneva who was just cruising to the tables and then there were some unofficial meetings. But whenever these things take place in Brussels, it is too stiff. It is too strict, too formal, too Commission-centred. And whenever Prosafe meetings take place, because it is in different locations, everything changes. We had a Commission representative on one of our project meetings, and the meeting was on the same level of great cooperation because it was not in Brussels. It was in Warsaw and everybody felt very safe. Wherever the meeting takes place, because market surveillance authorities organizing the joint action host the meetings, it is always some kind of safe haven to be kind of talking normally about everything. (interview PL2)

In other words, location matters too. What all these very different elements – the Commission's perceived lack of knowledge, mutual confidentiality, meetings away from Brussels – seem to have in common is the facilitating role that they play in reducing the attention drawn by the Commission as a monitoring and enforcement body. Eventually, then, it seems that the following two things can be said: it is not informality *stricto sensu*, but the *perception* of cooperation as informal that smoothens such cooperation; and it is not necessarily the actual absence of the Commission, but rather the absence of the Commission as guardian of the treaties that makes for perceived informality.

5. CONCLUSION: THE IMPORTANCE OF INTERDEPENDENCE AND INFORMALITY FOR MAKING NETWORKS EFFECTIVE

In this chapter we explored how participants in transnational networks in the fields of product safety, air safety, and integrated pollution prevention and control perceive the effectiveness of such networks for contributing to the implementation of EU legislation. The analysis has shown that the extent to which officials attach value to cooperation varies depending on the characteristics of the policy issue at stake, more particularly on the degree to which authorities feel that they are interdependent in the administration of the relevant measures. Where authorities feel that their own successfulness in terms of law administration depends on the implementation performance of authorities in other Member States – as is the case in the areas of product and air safety – they are more likely to consider transnational cooperation to be a necessary implementation instrument. This does not mean that officials in policy fields characterized by a relatively low degree of interdependence are not motivated to cooperate; it only means that what motivates them to engage in cooperation must be something different.

It is in domains that do not feature particularly high degrees of interdependence that the virtues of networked cooperation – other than those related most directly to interdependence – enter the scene as prime motivational factors for cooperation. It is in particular officials in areas which are characterized by relatively high degrees of interdependence – product safety and air safety – who indicate that they attach much importance to cooperation for 'getting Member States on the same line' when it comes to safety assessments carried out in the implementation process. Officials in the field of integrated pollution prevention and control do not emphasize this function of cooperation.

In the latter field, and in the product safety domain in particular, cooperation is appreciated for the learning effect that it has. The benefits of learning do not seem to be unidirectional though. This is the case since the value of exchangeable resources – knowledge and expertise – differs across

Member States. Authorities that are lagging behind in the relevant policy field, or are otherwise unfamiliar with certain techniques or practices, benefit most directly since cooperation teaches them how to do things better. Authorities with a head start in the implementation process may take on a position as givers in networks and derive little benefit from cooperation in the short term, at least when it comes to learning processes that may occur. Where authorities on the receiving end implement the lessons back home, however, those that invest in cooperation as teachers benefit too, since the administration of the law is taken to a higher level overall.

Resource sharing in the mundane understanding of the word – money – seems to be relevant mainly for authorities struggling with a particular lack of financial resources in the implementation process. It is useful only in those fields that actually allow for the financial burden of implementation to be shared. For example, Prosafe may well allow consumer products to be tested for free, at least when their safety is assessed in the context of joint projects subject to external financing. Of course, something similar is not the case for airplanes and industrial installations. In the latter cases, financial resources may be saved because learning processes prevent officials from having to reinvent the wheel individually.

Finally in all three domains subject to this study, trust is referred to as an important product of cooperation, though particularly so by Dutch officials. These officials indicate that cooperation has reassured them that, to quote an official, 'other authorities are not as bad as they [these officials] thought they were'. There are indications that also the authorities initially subject to mistrust benefit from increasing levels of trust; relevant officials indicate that they have come to feel better understood and more accepted by their colleagues. Moreover, since mutual trust is a significant precondition for (effective) cooperation to take place, increasing levels of trust stimulate further (and more effective) cooperation. Cooperation and trust thus have a mutually reinforcing effect – at least where cooperation functions in such a way as to allow for trust building to take place indeed.

This chapter has suggested that informality is of particular importance in this regard. To be more specific, it appears that mutual trust materializes in particular in contexts in which officials perceive cooperation to be informal. The case studies investigated here suggest that while legally formal networks are sure to put a break on meaningful cooperation, this is not necessarily the case for networks that are formal in a material, but not in a legal, sense. The latter networks may nonetheless breed a sense of informality. Legally informal networks, on the other hand, may well breed a sense of formality where they act in the shadow of hierarchy. Given the essentialness of mutual trust for making networks work effectively, these findings seem to bear some importance.

Although considered to be indispensable implementation instruments, networks are, of course, not the magic bullet to solve the problems that implementation actors may be confronted with. This is the case not only because cooperation will not always be the right instrument to make countries comply, but also since cooperation may contain certain flaws that are difficult to repair. A major downside of (in particular informal) cooperation is, for example, that countries cannot be compelled to participate. Countries that, for whatever reason, refuse to partake in cooperation are unlikely to benefit from the virtues that cooperation may deliver. This limitation may be problematic more in cases where cooperation takes place completely outside the EU institutional framework than for cooperation that takes place in a (semi)formal context, since the pressure for the unwilling to 'get involved' may be greater in the latter case.

A second limitation relates to the idea that even where countries participate, the outreach of the virtues of cooperation in individual countries may be limited. This may be due to two reasons. First of all, the notion that officials may embrace cooperation for the lessons that it teaches them does not necessarily mean that these lessons are implemented back home. It is often not the officials participating in discussions and joint projects that are empowered to implement the necessary domestic changes, but their superiors who may have their own agenda. Issue salience may play a role here as well; where issues lack salience, chances that something will change may be low. Secondly, since cooperation involves a 'selective club' of officials, the thousands of actors involved in making EU legislation 'alive' in the 28 Member States, and who are not directly involved in the networks, are less likely to reap the fruits of cooperation. Lessons learned may be transferred, but the notion that this happens effectively is by no means certain. Moreover, the experience of increased trust in and/or by other Member States is even more difficult to transmit.

A final factor to be kept in mind as a potential limitation of networks for achieving better enforcement is the possibility of networks being captured by interests that they are not supposed to serve. While interest groups may be thought of as trying to influence the outcomes of networked cooperation, regulatory authorities themselves may also try to steer the network activities in such a way as to achieve their preferred outcomes. Capture seems possible in particular where the participation of national authorities within networks is unequal. On the one hand, a characteristic of networks is exactly the absence of quid pro quo behaviour;[46] something that is unavoidable because of the divergent resources that network participants have

---

[46] Powell n 4, 304.

at their disposal, and logical in view of the fact that it is exactly awareness of the existence of such divergences that may stimulate cooperation in the first place. On the other hand, where such inequality translates into hierarchy within a form of governance that is supposedly heterarchical, concerns about the network being captured by, and coming to benefit, some agencies do seem to arise. Legitimacy concerns – in terms of inclusiveness and in terms of the implementability of network outcomes – follow alongside.

Despite these (potential) limitations, the current chapter strongly suggests that it would be unwise to cast away informal cooperation as ineffective for ensuring better implementation of international norms. Where such cooperation works well, it may be a very effective complement to the infamous 'stick in the cupboard' that is needed to coerce unwilling countries into compliance indeed. This confirms the observation by van der Heijden in Chapter 3 of this book that the current state-of-the-art thinking about enforcement concentrates on mixing and matching a variety of enforcement strategies. Taking this into consideration, cooperation does certainly have a place in the toolbox of implementation instruments. The effect of cooperation may not always be predictable, but well-working cooperation certainly has effects that other implementation instruments cannot have.

5. The SOLVIT network and the effective enforcement of EU law: what is new?*

Micaela Lottini

INTRODUCTION

In September 2013, the European Commission adopted a 'Recommendation'[1] with the aim of rewriting and clarifying the principles governing the functioning of SOLVIT, after more than ten years since the adoption of the first policy documents on the network.[2] The 'Recommendation' takes into consideration the evolution of SOLVIT over the years and is based, in particular,[3] on the findings of an in-depth evaluation carried out by the Directorate General Internal Market and Services.[4] Altogether, while the 'Recommendation' does not require significant changes in relation to the procedure for the handling of cases, it

* This research has been undertaken as part of the PRIN Project 2012 (2012SAM3KM) on the Codification of EU Administrative Procedures financed by the Ministero dell'Istruzione, dell'Università e della Ricerca, Italy.

[1] Commission Recommendation, 'Principles for using SOLVIT – the internal market problem solving network' of 17 September 2013 (2013/461/EU).

[2] Commission Communication, 'Effective Problem Solving in the Internal Market ("SOLVIT")' COM(2001) 702 final; Commission Recommendation, 'Principles for using SOLVIT – the internal market problem solving network' of 7 December 2001 (2001/893/EC).

[3] The Recommendation also takes into consideration other relevant documents on SOLVIT, such as: the Commission Staff Working Document, 'Making the Single Market Deliver: Annual Governance Checkup 2011' SWD(2012) 25 final, 25, <http://ec.europa.eu/solvit> accessed 20 February 2015; DG Internal Market and Services, 'The Single Market Scoreboard, Performance by Governance Tool SOLVIT, Reporting Period: 03/2012–02/2013', ibid.; Commission Staff Working Document, 'Reinforcing Effective Problem-solving in the Single Market: Unlocking SOLVIT's Full Potential at the Occasion of its 10th Anniversary' SWD(2012) 33 final.

[4] European Commission, framework contract for projects relating to evaluation and impact assessment activities of Directorate General for Internal Market

does clarify the mandate of SOLVIT and give indications to improve the activity of the network.

Interestingly, it is well known that the primary aim of the SOLVIT network is not to increase compliance with EU law,[5] but rather to help citizens and businesses when they encounter 'internal market problems':[6] in other words, SOLVIT is not a service dedicated to the enforcement of EU law, but rather is a dispute resolution mechanism, its activity is focused on resolving the 'problems' faced by citizens and businesses that are prevented from materially exercising their European rights and liberties due to unlawful decisions of national authorities.[7] Despite all that, the 'Recommendation' emphasizes the importance of SOLVIT for the effective enforcement of EU law and for the integration of the internal market, as it is clearly stated by paragraph II, according to which: 'SOLVIT (. . .) contributes to a better functioning of the single market by fostering and promoting better compliance with Union law'.

In order to discuss the role that SOLVIT has been playing for the enforcement of EU law, it must be borne in mind that the concept of *enforcement*,[8] for our purposes, covers different aspects. On the one hand, Member States must fulfil their obligations under the Treaty and ensure that their national regulatory framework is in compliance with EU law.[9] On the other hand, EU law must be correctly applied by the

---

and Services, 'Evaluation of SOLVIT, Final Report', November 2011, <http://ec.europa.eu/solvit/> accessed 20 February 2015.

5 'Perfect compliance is not demanded: SOLVIT is aimed at solving problems – if a problem can be solved in a particular case, a Member State can still be in non-compliance with EU law'. Catharina Elisabeth Koops, 'Compliance Mechanisms Compared: An Analysis of the EU Infringement Procedures, SOLVIT, Pilot and IMS?', Paper presented at the Conference, Fostering Growth: Reinforcing the Internal Market, Madrid, 28 and 29 October 2013, 26.

6 In accordance with the Recommendation of September 2013, n 1: 'a problem an applicant in one Member State encounters involving a potential breach of EU law governing the internal market by a public authority in another Member State' (I B, 2).

7 In this respect, it is interesting to note that SOLVIT's intervention has also covered situations in which the 'internal market problem' was not caused by the misapplication of an internal market rule by a public authority, instead it was caused by the violation of the principles of good administration; by the same token, SOLVIT Centres have been helping citizens facing problems with their own national administrations.

8 On this topic, see, Melanie Smith, 'Enforcement, Monitoring, Verification, Outsourcing: The Decline and Decline of the Infringement Process' (2008) 33 *European Law Review* 777.

9 'The European Institutions and the Member States should continue to develop their work to ensure that Community law is correctly applied and

competent national authorities[10] to which citizens and businesses have to address themselves in case they want to take up their free movement opportunities,[11] namely they need to have their professional qualification recognized or to be issued an authorization to exercise an economic activity or to be granted permission to market a product, and so on and so forth. As is apparent, the exercise of the rights and liberties that the EU Treaties confer on individuals can in practice be impeded by the ill-founded decisions of those authorities. This is a major threat to the actual and effective enforcement of EU law, and ultimately is a major threat to the correct functioning of the internal market and to its integration. As the Commission pointed out:

> the single market will only deliver its full potential if barriers that remain – and, of course, any new ones that emerge – are removed. This may require legislative action to fill gaps in the single market framework, but it also calls for a significant change in national administrations' attitudes towards the single market.[12]

Moreover, 'the European Union's success in achieving its many goals as set out in the Treaties and in legislation depends on the effective application of Community law in the Member States'.[13] Also, it is apparent that in order to give a European norm full effect, citizens and businesses have to be provided with an effective and adequate redress mechanism where EU rules are misapplied by national authorities.

Bearing this in mind, it has to be stressed that over the years SOLVIT has been playing an important role in relation to the European integration

---

implemented and that citizens' enquiries and complaints are handled well'. Commission Communication, 'A Europe of Results: Applying Community Law' COM(2007)502 final, Introduction.

[10] Nikiforos Diamandouros, 'The European Ombudsman and the Application of EU Law by the Member States' (2008) 2 *Review of European Administrative Law* 5; Phedon Nicolaides, 'Enlargement of the EU and Effective Implementation of Community Rules: An Integration-based Approach', EIPA (1999), Working Paper 99/W/04, <http://www. eipa.nl/index.asp> accessed 20 March 2015.

[11] It must be born in mind, in this respect, that: 'obligation on the part of the Member States to ensure the full effectiveness of Community principles for which harmonization rules have not been laid down must be discharged, according to the case-law of the Court of Justice, in compliance with the principle of institutional autonomy, which means that the necessary measures for applying the Community rules must be taken, in the context of the national systems, by national institutions and in accordance with the procedures and powers inherent in those systems'. Opinion of Advocate General Léger in Case, C-66/95 *Sutton*, para 67.

[12] Commission Communication, 'Action Plan for the Single Market' of 4 June 1997 CSE(97) 1 final, 6.

[13] 'A Europe of Results', n 9.

process, by fostering the enforcement of EU law at three different levels. At an *individual* level, by providing citizens and businesses with an effective and adequate alternative to legal action; second, at an *administrative* level, by promoting a better application of EU law by national authorities and more importantly by promoting changes in national administrative practice and culture; third, at a *regulatory* level, by promoting amendments to the national regulatory framework in accordance with EU law. This chapter deals with all three of these aspects, by focusing in particular on the innovations that have been introduced by the 'Recommendation' adopted in September 2013, and by comparing them with what was provided in the previous policy documents on SOLVIT. In the final part of the chapter, some conclusions will be drawn in relation to the role that SOLVIT has been playing to secure an improved application of EU law at the national level, and possible future developments.

1. SOLVIT: PROTECTION OF THE INDIVIDUAL AND EFFECTIVE ENFORCEMENT OF EU LAW

The SOLVIT network was set up to provide a fast and informal mechanism to resolve disputes between individuals (citizens and businesses) and (foreign) national authorities, which have (allegedly) misapplied an internal market rule, and whose decisions in practice can prevent those individuals from freely moving and conducting their business throughout Europe. In other words, SOLVIT is aimed at fostering the proper enforcement of EU law by guaranteeing that the affected individual can promptly and effectively respond when his/her European rights are infringed by unlawful decisions of national authorities. As a matter of fact, a court action (especially a 'cross-border' court action) might not meet the needs of those affected by a wrongful decision of a national authority, especially in specific and sensitive areas of the internal market. In this sense, European institutions[14] and legal scholars[15] have long been stressing the importance

---

[14] Commission of the European Communities, 'White Paper on European Governance' COM(2001) 42 8 final.

[15] The European Ombudsman Annual Report 2005, 119 <http://www.ombudsman.europa.eu/> accessed 20 February 2015. M. Poiares Maduro, Advocate-General at the Court of Justice of the European Communities, was the keynote speaker in this session. In his view, Ombudsmen have two clear institutional advantages over Courts as far as the application of EU law is concerned: 'firstly, in an area such as free movement, judicial redress is not effective, because of the expense and the length of time involved. Ombudsmen are therefore particularly

of providing citizens and businesses with an alternative to a formal redress mechanism.[16] Ultimately in 2001, the European Commission adopted the Communication 'Effective Problem Solving in the Internal Market: SOLVIT'[17] to foster the setting up of an integrated system of national centres,[18] connected by an online database, with the aim of complementing the activity of the national courts and of aiding those citizens and businesses that otherwise would not have any legal protection due to the costs and lengths of a formal claim.

The procedure for handling a complaint in SOLVIT is as follows. The applicant, without having to meet any particular requirement as to standing, can submit the case to his Home Centre (HC) through the SOLVIT public interface. The Home Centre has to verify if the information provided by the applicant is sufficient or, alternatively, invite the applicant to submit the required documentation. Ultimately, the HC has to decide whether to take on the case; if it does so, it has to make a preliminary assessment. Otherwise, it has to provide reasons to the applicant explaining why the case did not meet the requirements and offer the applicant advice of another possible course of action. If the claim is well founded, the HC forwards the case to the Lead Centre (LC – i.e. the Centre of the Member State in which the cross-border problem occurred), which verifies whether there has actually been a breach of EU law. Its course of action can be twofold. On the one hand, it can dismiss the case and give reasons for the rejection. On the other hand, the LC can confirm acceptance of the case and it is then responsible for resolving the matter by *co-operating* with the public authority in question. To be more precise, the LC proposes a solution which is not binding on the authority or on the applicant. The problem is resolved only if the authority decides to comply with SOLVIT's proposed solution. SOLVIT Centres co-operate among themselves and with national public authorities. However, the Centres also work in strict interaction with the European Commission. In practice, the role of the Commission in relation to the system involves the management of the database and of the website. The Commission also provides

well placed to address citizens' concerns in this area; secondly, ombudsmen can perform a key role in educating public authorities about their obligations regarding the implementation of EU law. They have the moral authority to encourage the public administration to give full effect to EU law provisions'.

[16] For example, 'specific networks of Ombudsmen or mediators'. Commission of the European Communities, 'White Paper on European Governance', n 14, 25.

[17] Commission Communication, 'Effective Problem Solving in the Internal Market ("SOLVIT")' COM(2001) 702 final.

[18] In conformity with the 'Action Plan for the Single Market' n 12.

advice and assistance or any relevant information for the resolution of the problems that may arise. Moreover, the Commission is responsible for ensuring that all proposed solutions are in full conformity with EU law and for monitoring the quality and performance of the SOLVIT Centres.

All in all, SOLVIT is an informal, free of charge and non-binding mechanism aimed at resolving internal market problems by proposing a possible solution to the administration that allegedly breached EU law. SOLVIT's dispute resolution process rests on the principle of co-operation between national administrations. First, between the national Centres forming part of the network which have to carry out the legal analysis and propose a solution; second, between the Centres and the national administration in question which ultimately can accept SOLVIT's proposed solution and re-exercise its public powers in accordance with EU law. SOLVIT handles around 3000 cases per year. SOLVIT's action covers a wide range of policy areas, but its intervention is particularly significant in cases where a rapid and/or cost-effective solution is needed. Commission statistics show that 40 per cent of the cases handled by SOLVIT are social security cases, and 25 per cent involve residence permits and visas. In particular, several of these cases involve 'cross-border problems' related to the recognition of pension rights acquired in a Member State different from that of origin or involve the coverage of medical treatment outside the patient's home country. Other cases involve the recognition of professional qualifications (2 per cent), market access to products (2 per cent) or motor vehicle registration (2 per cent).

The effectiveness of the SOLVIT network as a mechanism for resolving individual disputes is unquestionable and the network has lived up to its expectations. In accordance with the SOLVIT evaluation documents,[19] the network as a whole is operating effectively. The percentage of cases that are actually resolved by the intervention of the network is very high – around 92 per cent. National authorities tend to follow the solutions proposed by SOLVIT despite the non-binding nature of its decisions. This is most likely due to the 'pressure' that the concerned public authorities receive from Centres that are part of the same national administrative structure and that are normally at a governmental level. In addition, most cases are handled within the 10-week deadline indicated in SOLVIT's governing guidelines.

Despite these positive conclusions, however, problems still remain.[20]

---

[19] See n 4 and the Resolution of the European Parliament, of 9 March 2010 on SOLVIT, 2009/2138 (INI).

[20] 'Evaluation of SOLVIT', ibid.

Half of the Centres are understaffed in relation to their caseload, the level of public awareness of SOLVIT's activities is relatively low[21] and co-operation between the Centres and between the Centres and the national authorities is not always effective.[22] Lastly it has been shown that the percentage of 'business cases' handled by SOLVIT remains low (about 15 per cent). This is probably due among other things[23] to the fact that due to the sums of money involved in the cases, businesses prefer to use formal channels of redress. As a matter of fact SOLVIT is an alternative to a formal court action, hence if a case is already the subject of legal proceedings it cannot be decided in SOLVIT; also if the applicant decides at any stage to initiate legal proceedings the case should be removed from the database. It remains confirmed of course that if the applicant is not satisfied with the proposed solution he/she can bring the case to court afterwards. In practice, however, this is not always feasible. The 11-week period that is necessary for a decision to be taken often exceeds the time limit laid down by national legislation to successfully submit a case to the competent courts (in Italy, for example, the deadline for starting proceedings before the Administrative Court is 60 days). Moreover, this deadline is not in any way affected by the case being entered into the SOLVIT database. Hence, the individual who chooses to refer a case to SOLVIT is de facto prevented from receiving court protection. In this respect it is interesting to note that a SOLVIT 'business case' ultimately ended up decided by a national court (after a preliminary ruling of the Court of Justice)[24] when the case was closed as unresolved because the Czech and the Slovak

---

[21] In this respect, it is worth noting that the European Commission acknowledges the fact that: 'if SOLVIT is expected to improve its quality of service delivery and respond to an increasing caseload then the issue of the current limited resources should be addressed', ibid. Moreover, the Commission also points out that the composition of the staff is relevant in relation to the effectiveness of SOLVIT. In particular, it points out that some Centres are managed by lawyers whilst others are composed of professionals without legal training.

[22] In this respect, it is interesting to note the specific case of the Belgian SOLVIT Centre. Co-operation between the Centre and the administration is channeled via a network of Euro-coordinators, which process the information relating to daily case management as well as data on any structural problems highlighted by SOLVIT. The tightening of relations between SOLVIT and the Euro-coordinators has greatly enhanced the success of the SOLVIT Centre in Belgium and enabled it to manage a high number of cases. Information available at <http://www.eutrio.be/> accessed 20 February 2015.

[23] In other words, SOLVIT is a network for settling cross-border disputes informally and for free, and these characteristics are more likely to attract citizens' and small businesses' cases.

[24] Case C-68/12 *Slovenská sporiteľňa* [2013] ECLI:EU:C:2013:71.

SOLVIT Centres could not agree on the interpretation of Article 101 TFEU, the key EU competition provision which prohibits restrictive practices. In particular, they could not agree on whether Article 101(1) TFEU should be interpreted as meaning that it is of legal relevance that a competitor adversely affected by an agreement between other competitors was allegedly operating illegally on the relevant market at the time when that agreement was concluded.

In response to the findings of the evaluation documents on SOLVIT, the new 'Recommendation' (2013) contains a series of provisions aimed at improving the operation of the network and at guaranteeing better protection of the individual, and ultimately better enforcement of EU law. In particular, the 'Recommendation' clarifies the level of service that individuals and businesses can expect from SOLVIT; the various procedural steps and deadlines that the Centres must respect when handling a SOLVIT case; together with the follow-up they need to give when a case cannot be resolved. Moreover, the 'Recommendation' indicates how applicants should be informed and what minimum assistance they should be offered. Furthermore, the 'Recommendation' sets out minimum standards that SOLVIT Centres should comply with in terms of organization, legal expertise, and relations with other networks.

In the evaluation documents, it was stressed that one of the major problems highlighted in relation to the SOLVIT network was the lack of clarity on its mandate.[25] In particular, the Commission made it clear that:

> in practice, SOLVIT's mandate has given rise to differences in interpretation and has evolved over time and in practice. This, in turn, has led to different approaches between Member States when it comes to deciding whether a case should be taken up by SOLVIT or not.[26]

For these reasons the 'Recommendation' tries to shed some light on SOLVIT's mandate. Firstly, it makes it clear that SOLVIT's intervention can cover not only situations wherein a public authority has incorrectly applied EU law, but also situations where a change in the national regulatory framework is needed. In other words, even if SOLVIT was set up as a mechanism for resolving individual disputes and to help individual citizens and businesses, practice has shown that SOLVIT can also help to prevent

---

[25] See Diana Urania Galetta, 'Informal Information Processing in Dispute Resolution Networks: Informality versus the Protection of Individual's Rights?' (2001) 1 *European Public Law* 71 on the protection of citizens and businesses and SOLVIT.

[26] 'Reinforcing Effective Problem-solving in the Single Market', n 3 p 7.

future problems by acting proactively to promote a better compliance with EU law at a national level.

Moreover, SOLVIT's mandate is extended to cover problems which are not *stricto sensu* cross-border, a change which goes to the heart of the original design of SOLVIT. In other words cases in which applicants confront not a foreign authority but a national one. The 'Recommendation' acknowledges the fact that SOLVIT Centres have been deciding these kinds of cases, acting in practice as national ombudsmen. To look at one example, the Italian SOLVIT Centre was able to resolve a problem involving a Sicilian municipality and an Italian citizen who had applied for a job in Germany. The authority in question had refused to certify a photocopy of the claimant's identity card because, under Italian legislation, citizens are entitled to self-certify their own legal status and despite the fact that the certificate in question had been requested by the future (German) employer of the claimant. SOLVIT was able to convince the authority to issue the certification by pointing out that self-certification is provided for by the Italian legislation as a service to its citizens, and that they are not bound to avail themselves of such a possibility.

The 'Recommendation' adopted in 2013 thus extends SOLVIT's mandate to include 'problems caused to applicants by their own public administrations, after having exercised their free movement rights or when trying to do so'.[27] In this respect, it should be noted that SOLVIT's intervention can be particularly significant in jurisdictions such as the Italian one with a weak tradition of non-judicial protection of citizens against public administrations. This is due to the idea that the administration is traditionally authoritative and the relations between the State and the citizens adhere to a top-down pattern.[28] The importance of SOLVIT in this context has also been indicated by the European Ombudsman (EO). In a presentation delivered at the joint session of the liaison officers of the European Network of Ombudsmen (ENO) and SOLVIT (June 2010), the former Ombudsman Diamandouros stressed the importance and the need to foster co-operation between the members of the ENO and the SOLVIT Centres to guarantee better protection of European citizens when confronting a public authority and foster a better enforcement of EU law.[29]

---

27 Recommendation 2013, n 1 at art 1, B, n 2.

28 See Mario Comba and Roberto Caranta, 'Administrative Appeals in the Italian Law: On the Brink of Extinction or Might they be Saved (and Are they Worth Saving?)', in Dacian Cosmin Dragos and Bogdana Neamtu (eds), *Alternative Dispute Resolution in European Administrative Law* (Springer 2014) 85.

29 Available at <http://www.ombudsman.europa.eu/activities/speech.faces/en/5467/html.bookmark> accessed 20 February 2015.

As a matter of fact, according to the EO Annual Reports, transferal of cases between the EO and SOLVIT has taken place when they have involved a cross-border dispute between a national authority and a European citizen or business. For example, one such case[30] concerned a French national who had complained against the German public authorities in relation to her pension. She claimed that the pension she received was not commensurate with the number of years she had worked, and that the German public authorities had failed to properly calculate the amount. The Ombudsman transferred the case to SOLVIT France, which later informed him of its intention to open an investigation and to contact the relevant German authorities to resolve the problem. In another case[31] a Spanish national complained against a decision of the Employment and Support Allowance Office at the Department of Work and Pensions (DWP) in the United Kingdom. She had moved from Spain to the United Kingdom and had worked part-time for two years before she was diagnosed with cancer. The DWP decided that she was not to be considered habitually resident in the country and thereby she was not entitled to employment and support allowance. The Ombudsman transferred the case to SOLVIT Spain.

To confirm the importance of the network within Member States it is worth noting that SOLVIT Italy is currently endorsing the pilot project 'SOLVIT nel Comune',[32] in co-operation with the Department for European Affairs, ANCI (National Association of Italian Municipalities) and SSPAL (High level School of the Local Public Administration). The aim of the project is to raise public awareness of SOLVIT at a local level and also to reduce the opening of formal infringement proceedings against Italy. Moreover, the project aims to establish a territorial network which can assist the work of SOLVIT Centres, namely a decentralized network, composed by a number of local contact points based in the main municipalities in Italy.

In line with the above, the 'Recommendation' of September 2013 reaffirms that in order to ensure that applicants get effective help, SOLVIT Centres have to co-operate with other European and national information and help networks (such as Your Europe, Europe Direct, Your Europe Advice, the Enterprise Europe Network, European Consumer Centres, EURES, Fin-net and European Network of Ombudsmen). Also, SOLVIT

---

30 Case 644/2012/MF.

31 Case 1944/2012/HK.

32 More information at <www.politicheeuropee.it/attivita/17699/solvit-in-comune> accessed 20 February 2015.

Centres have to establish good working relationships with the respective national members of the Administrative Commission for the Co-ordination of Social Security,[33] to enable the effective handling of social security cases. In this sense, the European Commission is committed to facilitating such co-operation by, inter alia, organizing joint networks events and establishing technical means of connection.

Lastly, it is interesting to note, at the end of this paragraph, that the 'Recommendation' does not take into consideration another de facto extension of SOLVIT's mandate, which should be clarified in the future. All in all, in numerous cases resolved by the intervention of SOLVIT, the internal market problem was not caused by an incorrect decision of a public authority on the merits, instead it was caused by the violation of the principles of good administration, in particular, by the delay or failure to act. Several scenarios could illustrate this point. Take the case of a Portuguese fisherman who was living near the border with Spain. He held a certificate allowing him to navigate certain types of fishing boats. However, in order to work for a Spanish fishing company, the fisherman needed to have his certificate recognized by the Spanish authorities. He submitted his application to the national authorities requesting the recognition of the certificate and waited for over six months without a response. This delay hindered his ability to work since he had to refuse various job offers in Spain due to not having a valid navigation certificate. SOLVIT intervened and was able to resolve the problem by successfully urging the national authority to recognize the fisherman's certificate.

---

[33] The Administrative Commission for the Co-ordination of Social Security Schemes is a specialized body composed of social security experts within national administrations. Its objective is to clarify EU regulations and administrative practices relating to social security issues, as well as clarify questions of interpretation. The Administrative Commission only deals with complaints received via the Commission, but citizens, workers, and businesses can contact SOLVIT Centres directly when they face cross-border problems related to social security issues. Experience has shown that, in some cases, the SOLVIT Centres do not have the necessary legal expertise to deal with such cases, in particular given the fact that, in the area of social security, EU law only coordinates national rules. On the other hand, individuals of the Administrative Commission often receive complaints about cross-border problems related to the application of social security rules, but they do not have effective tools for dealing with such complaints. Therefore, increasing the synergies and the co-operation between SOLVIT and the Administrative Commission could help to achieve more effective results when handling social security complaints.

2. SOLVIT AND THE CORRECT APPLICATION OF EU LAW BY NATIONAL PUBLIC AUTHORITIES

According to the European Commission,[34] 'benefits from a successful SOLVIT complaint will include both the immediate benefits to the applicant and also wider longer term benefits from changing procedures or rules that prevent similar problems in the future'. As a matter of fact SOLVIT Centres have been contributing 'to a "cultural change" in their own national civil service, inducing an overall improved compliance with EU law by national authorities'.[35] From this point of view SOLVIT has been promoting an effective enforcement of EU law by contributing to a change in patterns of administrative practice[36] that run counter to EU law,[37] and also by preventing its wrongful application by the national authorities[38] and, ultimately, by fostering the development of a common administrative culture.[39] This effect is due in particular to the shared database that allows SOLVIT Centres to record information on individual cases, the ability to exchange this information quickly among themselves, and to develop a common set of principles that are likely to affect the activity of national authorities.[40] In this context it is important to remember that in December 2003 the Centres and the Commission adopted a set

---

[34] 'Evaluation of SOLVIT, Final Report', n 4 p 59.

[35] 'Reinforcing Effective Problem-Solving in the Single Market', n 3, p 4.

[36] SOLVIT Centres have been contributing to change administrative practices commonly followed throughout the Member States (SOLVIT+ cases). In this sense, it has been pointed out that: 'SOLVIT may secure change in administrative practices. When customers of a Swedish company marketing in Denmark could not obtain a customary government rebate because the requisite registration number was available only to companies registered in Denmark, the Danish authorities announced after SOLVIT's intervention the number was no longer needed for the subsidy'. Carol Harlow and Richard Rawlings, *Process and Procedure in EU Administration* (Hart Publishing 2014) 85.

[37] 'Reinforcing Effective Problem-Solving in the Single Market', n 3 p 8.

[38] For example, following the intervention of SOLVIT a Portuguese local authority no longer requires a medical assistance card for British citizens residing in Portugal to be renewed on an annual basis.

[39] Sharing these conclusions, Anabela Correia de Brito, 'Modern Enforcement in the Single Market', Paper presented at the Conference, Fostering Growth: Reinforcing the Internal Market, Madrid, 28 and 29 October 2013.

[40] It is interesting to note, in this context, that the network, mainly through the annual reports, provides valuable information, in addition to that transmitted by other means (including the formal ones) about the difficulties faced by each state in the application of the internal market norms.

of common quality and performance standards[41] aimed at ensuring a high level of SOLVIT services consistently throughout the network, among which it is provided that the Lead Centre, 'when proposing the solution, has to check with the SOLVIT database to ascertain whether similar cases have already been solved satisfactorily and, if so, has to ensure that the applicant can benefit from the same treatment'.[42] It is interesting to note in this respect that SOLVIT is not just a co-operation mechanism between different national administrations; SOLVIT is a unified system connected by an online database managed by the Commission and the very essence of the system is this integrated approach. Hence, the rule in question has the scope of limiting the differences between national Centre's activities; these differences can in fact undermine the overall effectiveness of the system whose principal aim is to provide the same level of protection against national administrations' misapplication of EU law throughout Europe.

The importance of this role played by SOLVIT is bound to increase owing to the interaction between SOLVIT and the Internal Market Information System (IMI).[43] IMI is an online application (run by the Commission) that allows national, regional and local authorities to communicate quickly and easily with their counterparts abroad in order to facilitate administrative co-operation in specific areas of the internal market.[44] The Commission has recently rebuilt the SOLVIT online database as a stand-alone module in the Internal Market Information System.[45] The 'Recommendation' specifies that 'applicants should be able to submit their complaints to SOLVIT through a public interface linked to the Internal Market Information System, put at their disposal by the Commission'.[46]

One last point. As already mentioned, in the evaluation documents on SOLVIT the Commission stressed the importance of clarifying its

---

41 SOLVIT Annual Report, 2004, Annex I, <http://ec.europa.eu/solvit> accessed 20 February 2015.

42 Ibid., para II note 4.

43 All information available at <http://ec.europa.eu/internal_market/imi-net/index_en.html> accessed 25 January 2015.

44 For example, in relation to the Directive 2005/36/EC of the European Parliament and of the Council on 'The recognition of professional qualifications' [2005] OJ 255/22, as amended; in relation to Directive 2006/123/EC of the European Parliament and of the Council on 'Services in the internal market' [2006] OJ L376/36.

45 Council Regulation (EU) 1024/2012 on 'administrative cooperation through the Internal Market Information System and repealing Commission Decision 2008/49/EC ('the IMI Regulation')' [2012] OJ L316/1.

46 Recommendation 2013, n 1 para X note 1.

mandate and reaffirmed that the Centres can only handle cases where the breaches of EU law are caused by a public authority[47] and not by a private party, despite the fact that SOLVIT Centres have accepted cases where the entity which allegedly breached EU law could not be considered a 'public authority' in accordance with national law. For example, in the case where a French citizen complained to SOLVIT regarding the discriminatory entry fees for tourists to Romanian monasteries. The ticket price for non-Romanians was twice as high as that for Romanian citizens. Even though the church could not be considered a public authority, SOLVIT accepted the case and successfully persuaded the church authorities to establish non-discriminatory entry fees for the monasteries. Also, another case involved a Portuguese airline which applied different criteria for the minimum height of male and female employees. A male applicant who already worked for another airline could not apply because his height was inferior to the minimum indicated for men. After the intervention of SOLVIT, the airline company changed its rules to abandon the discriminatory provision and establish a minimum height criterion for both men and women.

In line with the view that the mandate of SOLVIT should be made as clear as possible the new 'Recommendation' offers a definition of 'public authority' as:

> (. . .) any part of the public administration of a Member State, at national, regional or local level, or any body, whatever its legal form, which has been made responsible, pursuant to a measure adopted by the State, for providing a public service under the control of the State and that has for that purpose special powers beyond those which result from the normal rules applicable in relations between individuals.[48]

It is interesting to note that the Commission is using a very extensive definition of public authority in order to extend SOLVIT's mandate. As a matter of fact, EU law does not provide for a general and fully fledged definition of public authority. The EU institutions and the EU courts

---

[47] In this respect, the Commission indicated that the concept of public authority should cover 'all levels of public administration (national, regional and local authorities), competent authorities (e.g., professional organizations in charge of recognizing professional qualifications) and bodies controlled by the state (e.g., universities)'. Commission Staff Working Document, of 24 February 2012, 'Reinforcing Effective Problem-solving in the Single Market: Unlocking SOLVIT's Full Potential at the Occasion of its 10th Anniversary' SWD(2012) 33 final, 9.

[48] Recommendation 2013, n 1 para B note 4.

on the contrary use a 'functional approach',[49] aimed at guaranteeing the widest and more effective application of the rule in question. More importantly, Member States cannot rely on their own national definition of public authority to avoid the application of EU rules both in positive and negative terms. For example, an entity which is a public authority in accordance with national law is considered as an undertaking if it exercises an economic activity and it is subject to free movement and competition rules.[50] At the same time, an undertaking (British Gas) is considered to be part of the 'State' in accordance with Article 288 TFEU[51] as the Court of Justice held in *Foster*[52] that: 'unconditional and sufficiently precise provisions of a Directive can be relied on against organizations or bodies which are subject to the authority or control of the State or have special powers beyond those which result from the normal rules applicable to relations between individuals'.

SOLVIT Centres have taken a proactive approach in trying to prevent the incorrect application of EU law by public authorities. For example, SOLVIT Sweden, having acknowledged that one of the main causes of misapplication was the lack of knowledge about EU law within governmental authorities, developed the Internal Market guide for public authorities (the IM-guide) in 2006. The guide contains general EU law principles, rules on free movement of goods, services, capital, persons and relevant case law – and explains how

---

[49] Mario Pilade Chiti, 'The EC Notion of Public Administration: The Case of the Bodies Governed by Public Law' (2002) 8 *European Public Law* 473.

[50] When the European Court of Justice is called upon to interpret the concept of public authority in relation to Article 51 TFEU, as an entity which exercises 'official authority' and to which consequently the rules on freedom of establishment and (in combination with Article 62 TFEU) the rules on free movement of services do not apply, it concludes, quite restrictively, that 'official authority' is that which arises from the sovereignty and majesty of the State; for him who exercises it, it implies the power of enjoying the prerogatives outside the general law, privileges of official power and powers of coercion over citizens. Opinion of Advocate General Mayras in Case C-2/74 *Reyners v Belgium* [1974] ECR 631. Moreover, an entity is considered a public authority only if its activities are, in themselves, directly and specifically connected with the exercise of official authority, Case C-438/08 *Commission v Portugal* [2009] ECR I-10219.

[51] (. . .) 'A directive shall be binding, as to the result to be achieved, upon each Member State to which it is addressed, but shall leave to the national authorities the choice of form and methods.' (. . .).

[52] C-188/89 *Foster and Others v British Gas plc* [1990] ECR I-3313. For a comment, see Nicolas Grief, 'Direct Effect of Directives and Organs of the State', (1991) *European Law Review* 136.

these should be interpreted by the authorities called upon to apply them.[53]

3. SOLVIT AND 'STRUCTURAL PROBLEMS': AMENDMENTS TO THE NATIONAL REGULATORY FRAMEWORK

In accordance with the SOLVIT policy documents adopted in 2001,[54] the network was set up to resolve individual problems caused by the misapplication of an internal market rule by a public authority, when the national regulatory framework did conform to EU law. The term misapplication was considered to imply that Centres could not deal with cases where national rules run counter to EU law. Nonetheless, it is well known that the Centres have developed a different practice, by dealing with and deciding cases where the 'internal market problem' was on the contrary caused by a national barrier raised either by a specific regulation or by an unlawful administrative practice.[55] In other words, the Centres

---

[53] Åsa Casula Vifell and Ebba Sjogren, 'Governing by Monitoring: The EU Commission's SOLVIT-Centers as Judicialized Internal Market Watchdogs – The Case of Sweden', *SSE/EFI Working Paper Series in Business Administration*, 2010, <http://swoba.hhs.se/hastba/papers/hastba2010_007.pdf> accessed 27 February 2015. Also, 'To facilitate the co-operation between Romania SOLVIT Centre and the national public administration authorities to efficiently solve SOLVIT cases was established, since December 2006, a net of "contact points" within the national authorities responsible for implementing the communal law on internal market domain, the contact persons helping to solve SOLVIT cases and to promote the center in the respective administrative structures.' Constanța Mătușescu, Cristian Mareș and Claudia Gilia, 'Consequently Governance through Cooperation: System and its Role in the Correct Implementation of the European Law by the National Public Administrations' (2011) 5 *International Scholarly and Scientific Research & Innovation* 51, 54.

[54] 'Principles for using SOLVIT', n 1, and 'Effective Problem Solving in the Internal Market', n 2.

[55] A regulatory obstacle can be raised even if the misapplication of an internal market rule is an 'administrative practice', commonly followed throughout the country. In accordance with the case law of the European Court of Justice (ECJ), when the misapplication of an internal market rule or principle (by national public authorities) is 'to some degree, of a consistent and general nature', the Member State concerned can be held responsible for failure to fulfil its obligations in accordance with Article 258 TFEU, even if the applicable national legislation complies with that rule or principle. For example, Italy failed to fulfil its obligations under the freedom of movement regulations, because state schools, when recruiting teaching staff, regularly did not take into account the professional experience

have been deciding cases where the breach of EU law was not simply the result of the misapplication of the rules applicable at the national level, but stemmed from bad transposition or lack of transposition of EU law. In cases such as these (so-called SOLVIT+ cases), SOLVIT Centres have resolved the individual problem by either getting the authority to disregard the unlawful regulation in question or to move away from the unlawful practice. Moreover, the Centres have reported the issue to the relevant national authorities to have the regulation in question amended, or to have the practice changed by the issuing of specific guidelines.[56] To look at one example, a company was trying to register in Poland a car which had previously been registered in Germany. The Polish authorities did not accept the harmonized German registration certificate but asked for a Polish translation. The problem could not be solved within the SOLVIT deadline, since it required an amendment to the Polish law in question. However, SOLVIT Poland convinced the authorities that the law needed to be amended. It is interesting to note that in SOLVIT+ cases the Centres are combining a twofold set of activities. On the one hand, they act as a dispute resolution mechanism; on the other hand, they act as a decentralized enforcement service. The two activities are, however, two faces of the same coin. All in all, the regulatory enforcement of EU law would be meaningless if in practice the correctly enforced rules could not be of use to the European citizens and businesses due to the unlawful activity of the national authorities.

The new 'Recommendation' of September 2013 acknowledges the

---

previously acquired by EU nationals in other Member States (Case C-278/03 *Commission* v *Italy* [2005] ECR I-3747). By the same token, the Federal Republic of Germany was held in breach of Article 34 TFEU due to the competent authorities' practice of classifying as 'medicinal products' preparations lawfully produced or marketed as food supplements in other Member States, because they exceed a specific daily amount of vitamins and minerals (Case C-441 /02 *Commission* v *Germany* [2006] ECR I-3449). Alicja Sikora, 'Administrative Practice as a Failure of a Member State to Fulfil its Obligations under Community Law' (2009) 1 *Review of European Administrative Law* 4.

56 It is interesting to note that, in some European countries, such as Italy or Romania, the national SOLVIT Centre is part of the Department for European Affairs (DEA) of the central government. Through its position in the Department, the SOLVIT Centre 'is thought to have additional valences from its perspective of identifying mechanism and deficiencies correcting of the transposition and implementation of the European legislation, as DEA, in consideration of its institutional competence, may request to the competent authority to promote some governmental decrees of modification, designed to ensure the compliance with the communal law on the mentioned issue'. Mătuşescu et al, 'Consequently Governance through Cooperation', n 53 p 54.

activity that the SOLVIT Centres have been carrying out with the SOLVIT+ cases and extends the mandate of the network to cover situations in which structural problems are detected. The 'Recommendation' makes it clear that:

> the SOLVIT network deals with cross-border problems caused by a potential breach[57]of Union law governing the internal market by a public authority, where and to the extent such problems are not subject to legal proceedings at either national or Union level. (. . .) the term 'breach' is used to specify that SOLVIT Centres take on as a SOLVIT case all situations where public authorities do not respect Union law governing the internal market, regardless of the root cause of the problem.[58]

As a matter of fact:

> (. . .) the overwhelming majority of cases handled by SOLVIT reflect situations wherein a public authority incorrectly applies Union law governing the internal market. However, SOLVIT Centres have also shown to be able to offer effective help where structural problems arise. Although structural cases present only a small part of SOLVIT's overall case load, the take-up of such cases by SOLVIT is important to ensure that such problems do not pass unnoticed. It offers the best guarantee that the structural problems are effectively tackled at the appropriate level.[59]

Overall, with SOLVIT+ cases the Centres have been playing (and will play in the future) an important role for the effective enforcement of EU law, and ultimately for the integration of the internal market, by helping to resolve structural problems and remove regulatory barriers. In practice, this role has been complementary to that of the Commission under Article 258 TFEU.

The new 'Recommendation' not only extends SOLVIT's mandate to include SOLVIT+ cases, but also gives specific indications to the Lead Centre, in order to speed up the process and facilitate the correct allocation of the cases. In particular:

> (. . .) where the problem submitted by the applicant to SOLVIT is a structural problem, the Lead Centre should assess as soon as possible whether the problem can be resolved through the SOLVIT procedure. If it considers that this is not possible, it should close the case as unresolved and inform the relevant national authorities responsible for the correct implementation of Union law in that

---

57 The previous Recommendation used the term 'misapplication'.

58 Recommendation 2013, n 1 para I.

59 Recommendation 2013, n 1 whereas number 10.

Member State, so as to secure that the breach of Union law is effectively put to an end. The Commission should also be informed through the database.[60]

The Commission has acknowledged the importance of the role that SOLVIT can play regarding the proper enforcement of EU law from a 'regulatory' point of view, but also from an opposite angle. In its Communication on 'Better Monitoring of the Application of Community Law' of 11 December 2002,[61] after having pointed out that recourse to infringement proceedings should be reduced, inter alia, by fostering the use of alternative problem-solving mechanisms and preventive measures, it identified SOLVIT as one such mechanism whose use should be increased when the case at issue does not qualify as a 'priority' one. In 2004, the Commission adopted a Staff Working Document[62] making it clear that it would work in strict co-operation with SOLVIT, by referring to it minor infringement cases.[63] In this respect, the 'Recommendation' reaffirms that, 'where appropriate, the Commission (more precisely the competent official) may refer complaints it has received to SOLVIT with a view to finding a rapid and informal solution, subject to the consent of the complainant'.[64] All in all, SOLVIT is helping to reduce and facilitate the activity of the Commission in relation to Article 258 TFEU, by dealing with non-priority cases that are referred to it either by the Commission or by the individual concerned. However, the Evaluation Report points out that only a small number of cases (approximately 1 per cent) are received by SOLVIT after an infringement complaint is lodged with the Commission.[65]

The Report also explains that the complaints addressed to the European Commission are entered into a central registry. When the cases concern individual problems of misapplication of internal market rules, in principle, they should be considered for submission to SOLVIT. However, the registry is not linked with SOLVIT and it is up to the Commission official handling the case to decide if the complaint should be dealt with directly

---

[60] Recommendation 2013, n 1 para. V, C, note 3.

[61] COM(2002)725 final.

[62] 'Setting Out the Approach for Assessing the Conformity of Solutions Proposed by the SOLVIT Network with Community Law', of 17 September 2004, SEC(2004) 11.

[63] 'For non-priority suspected infringements, the Commission services can decide to refer complaints it has received to SOLVIT with a view to finding a rapid and pragmatic solution on the condition that complainants have accepted beforehand that their identity will be divulged to the SOLVIT Centres involved'. Ibid 4.

[64] Recommendation 2013, n 1 para VI note 2.

[65] 'Evaluation Report', n 4 p 6.

by the Commission, or be sent to SOLVIT (subject to the complainant's approval). Cases can also be referred to the EU Pilot application in case more information is needed from the relevant Member State.[66] All in all, the Report acknowledges that in practice it is difficult to decide the best route for an individual case before the details and context of the case have been understood and assessed.[67] Hence, in order to reach a more efficient allocation of the cases, the Report suggests that co-operation should be fostered within the system. In this sense, the new 'Recommendation' on SOLVIT stresses the need for SOLVIT Centres to be in regular contact and to co-operate with their EU Pilot Contact Points. In this respect it is interesting to note that the Single Market score board (2013) specifies that: 'The working methods of EU Pilot will be adjusted to the new SOLVIT Recommendation'.[68]

In conclusion, contradictory as it may seem the intervention of SOLVIT can also favour the opening of infringement proceedings.[69] According to the 'Recommendation', the Commission has to assist and support the functioning of SOLVIT, inter alia, by:

> (. . .) monitoring the quality and performance of SOLVIT Centres and the cases they handle. In cases presenting a structural problem, the Commission will closely monitor the case and, where needed, lend advice and assistance to ensure that the structural problem is put to an end. The Commission will consider whether unresolved structural problems require further follow-up.[70]

Moreover the Commission will regularly report on the quality and performance of SOLVIT. It will also report on the type of problems SOLVIT has received and cases handled within SOLVIT, with a view to defining trends and identifying remaining problems in the internal market.

---

[66] The collaboration between the Commission and Member States is an opportunity for the Member State to eliminate non-compliance with EU law before the Commission possibly decides to open formal infringement procedures.

[67] See European Commission Staff Working Paper, 'Functioning of the System, Accompanying the Document Report from the Commission Second Evaluation Report on EU Pilot' SEC(2011) 1629/2.

[68] Available at <http://ec.europa.eu/> accessed 20 March 2015.

[69] Since the introduction of SOLVIT in 2002, the amount of infringement procedures based on complaints from individuals has gone down steadily, whereas the amount of cases based on own-initiative or non-communication has remained relatively stable or even gone up. Catharina Elisabeth Koops, 'Compliance Mechanisms Compared: An Analysis of the EU Infringement Procedures, SOLVIT, Pilot and IMS', Paper presented at the Conference, Fostering Growth: Reinforcing the Internal Market, Madrid, 28 and 29 October 2013, *passim*.

[70] Recommendation 2013, n 1 para VI (note 1 e).

Within this reporting framework the Commission will separately report on structural cases. In other words, if the Commission becomes aware of a national regulation that is in breach of EU law during the exercise of its control activity, it can start an inquiry and if necessary commence infringement proceedings.[71]

CONCLUSIONS

SOLVIT is a multi-level co-operation network that, since its inception, has definitely fostered the integration and better functioning of the internal market by contributing to the correct enforcement of EU law from the three standpoints that have been indicated above. All in all, those individual citizens and businesses that otherwise would not have had any legal protection have been provided with a mechanism which responds easily and quickly to an unlawful decision of a national authority that has infringed their European rights and liberties. Changes of attitude have been promoted among national authorities dealing with EU law and regulatory barriers have been removed after its intervention due to the introduction of amendments to national regulations. SOLVIT's main strengths are its user-centred, pragmatic and informal approach to problem-solving, facilitated through an online tool and the network structure that links administrations from different Member States. Despite SOLVIT's overall success, the documents adopted by the EU institutions to evaluate the network make it clear that problems remain and action should be taken to reinforce SOLVIT and promote its effectiveness. In line with these conclusions, the 'Recommendation' adopted in 2013 tries to provide solutions to remedy some of the shortcomings that have been identified, and tries to render SOLVIT more accessible by clarifying its mandate, its decision-making procedure, the role of the actors involved in the procedure, and so on. In reality, no substantial changes have been introduced. In this respect, it is worth noting that some SOLVIT Centres are of the opinion that in order to improve SOLVIT services, its mandate should be expressly extended to cases in which EU law has been misapplied by non-governmental bodies such as private companies or

[71] As a matter of fact, the Commission became aware of an internal market problem in Spain in relation to the recognition of the professional qualifications of Romanian nurses, as the Spanish authorities did not organize the required aptitude tests for them. The tests were subsequently introduced when the Commission addressed a letter to the Spanish authorities.

organizations.[72] The 'Recommendation' does not follow this suggestion. On the contrary, it confirms that the intervention of SOLVIT is limited to resolving disputes between individuals and national authorities for which it provides, as already mentioned, a specific definition. If SOLVIT's remit were extended to cover disputes between two private parties, this would be a major change in the activity and nature of the network, a change in relation to which there is of course plenty of room for discussion.

72 All in all, as already mentioned, SOLVIT Centres have accepted cases where the entity which allegedly acted in breach of EC law could not be considered a 'public authority'.

6. The effectiveness of transgovernmental networks: managing the practical application of European integration in the case of SOLVIT

Dorte Sindbjerg Martinsen and Mogens Hobolth

INTRODUCTION

This chapter aims to add to the discussion of new governance mechanisms to address and solve problems of misapplication of EU law. It draws on theory on transgovernmental networks from international relations studies and applies these to examine the practical application of, and compliance with, EU law.

Compliance with international agreements continues to be a challenge to international politics, and has increasingly received scholarly attention, not least within European Union studies. The 'governance dilemma' of a globalized world is still pertinent and international organizations continue to lack suitable instruments to monitor and ensure that states fulfil their international obligations.[1] If the agreements of international organizations are not complied with they are of little value. Therefore to inquire into states' compliance with the international agreements they have ratified is to inquire into the reach, regulatory strength and de facto impact of that international organization. The European Union is a prominent example of how important compliance is to the legitimacy and cohesiveness of an international organization. How to improve compliance and the practical application of EU rules is generally high on the European

[1] Burkard Eberlein and Abraham L Newman, 'Escaping the Intergovernmental Governance Dilemma? Incorporated Transgovernmental Networks in the European Union' (2008) *Governance* 25.

agenda. Scholarly research on international and regional integration within political science and law has advanced our knowledge considerably during the last decades. A growing number of studies have examined the extent to which EU Member States transpose binding decisions into national law on time and correctly as well as what may explain variation in transposition between the Member States.[2] However, we still know relatively little about compliance beyond the transposition of EU law.[3] For example, which instruments improve application of EU rules in practice? What compliance problems arise after transposition of EU law has taken place, that is, once an EU regulation applies in practice, and how common are these problems? Have new modes of governance developed to handle misapplication on the ground?

The EU constitutes the most legalized international organization in the world, able to judicially address and sanction non-compliance, and is exceedingly effective in doing so compared to other international organizations.[4] However, although the importance of management tools to improve compliance has been emphasized in international relations and European studies,[5] scholarly work tends to focus on central and decentralized enforcement mechanisms, that is, the infringement procedures monitored by the European Commission and private litigants and national courts bringing preliminary references to the European Court of Justice.[6]

---

[2] See, for example, Tanja A Börzel, Tobias Hofmann, Diana Panke and Carina Sprungk, 'Obstinate and Inefficient: Why Member States Do Not Comply with European Law' (2010) 43(11) *Comparative Political Studies* 1363; Markus Haverland and Marleen Romeijn, 'Do Member States Make European Policies Work? Analysing the EU Transposition Deficit' (2007) 85(3) *Public Administration* 757; Marcus Haverland, Bernard Steuenberg and Frans van Waarden, 'Sectors at Different Speeds: Analysing Transposition Deficits in the European Union' (2011) 49(2) *Journal of Common Market Studies* 265; Bernard Steuenberg and Dimiter Toshkov, 'Comparing Transposition in the 27 Member States of the EU: The Impact of Discretion and Legal Fit' (2009) 16(7) *Journal of European Public Policy* 951; Thomas König and Brooke Luetgert, 'Troubles with Transposition? Explaining Trends in Member-State Notification and the Delayed Transposition of EU Directives' (2009) *British Journal of Political Studies* 163.

[3] Esther Versluis, 'Even Rules, Uneven Practices: Opening the "Black Box" of EU Law in Action' (2007) 30(1) *West European Politics* 50.

[4] Jonas Tallberg, 'Paths to Compliance: Enforcement, Management and the European Union' (2002) 56(3) *International Organization* 609.

[5] Abram Chayes and Antonia Handler Chayes, 'On Compliance' (1993) 47(2) *International Organization* 175; Tallberg n 4; König and Luetgert n 2 167.

[6] Karen J Alter and Jeanette Vargas, 'Explaining Variation in the Use of European Litigation Strategies: European Community Law and British Gender Equality Policy' (2000) *Comparative Political Studies* 452; Karen Alter, *Establishing*

We know relatively little about concrete management instruments, how they work, how they have developed and whether they are effective means to improve compliance.

This chapter examines the role of transgovernmental networks (TGNs) in monitoring and overseeing the practical application of EU law, focusing on the SOLVIT network. TGNs differ from transnational networks by having government representatives as the actors instead of independent experts or representatives from interest organizations which are main actors in transnational networks.[7] The chapter enquires into the modus operandi of TGNs and the effectiveness of this new governance tool as a mode of enforcing EU law. It finds that TGNs have developed as important and effective monitoring instruments for the practical application of EU law, operating mainly in line with management logics. We define effective enforcement as the *problem-solving capacity* and *resolution speed* of the network in question. Problem-solving capacity concerns the ability of the network to identify, mediate and solve problems of misapplied EU law. Resolution speed concerns the time used to solve such problems. These dual elements of effective enforcement thus define effectiveness both in terms of the instrumental ability to enforce EU law as well as the timely aspect of it. The latter part of the definition is often disregarded, but is highly important if EU law is to work on the ground, for citizens and enterprises.

1. EFFECTUATING EUROPEAN INTEGRATION: THE STATE OF THE ART IN POLITICAL SCIENCE STUDIES

By virtue of extensive EU transposition and compliance studies, political scientists have developed a fairly good grasp of whether EU directives are transposed on time, but we have little scholarly insight into 'the EU law in action', that is, the practical application of EU rules.[8] Furthermore, our knowledge remains limited in relation to how national public administrations respond to and assume the obligations which make EU law work at all levels of society. Does the application of EU law function in practice when domestic authorities at the national, regional and local levels are to administer in accordance with supranational rules?

---

the Supremacy of European Law: The Making of an International Rule of Law in Europe (Oxford University Press 2001); Tallberg n 4.

7 For an analysis of transnational networks, see Versluis Ch 4 of this volume.

8 Esther Versluis, 'Even Rules, Uneven Practices: Opening the "Black Box" of EU Law in Action' (2007) 30(1) *West European Politics* 50.

Compared to other international organizations, the EU is seen to have developed fairly efficient enforcement procedures through which non-compliance is detected and pursued.[9] As a result, non-compliance is seen by some to be a temporal phenomenon.[10] Concerning the supranational enforcement practices, the vital role played by the European Commission and the Court of Justice of the European Union (CJEU) towards ensuring state compliance stand clear.[11] The role played by interest groups and national courts has also been emphasized as a key decentralized means of pushing for national compliance.[12] Tallberg has argued that this unique combination of central and decentralized enforcement mechanisms makes the EU very 'effective in combating detected violations'.[13]

However, the extent to which this model of 'dual enforcement' is able to detect and resolve the full scope of EU law violation is still open to critical examination. Central enforcement mechanisms have their shortcomings. The Commission lacks the resources and capacity to uncover and legally pursue the whole EU-wide spectre of non-compliance.[14] Furthermore, the decentralized strategies whereby non-compliance is challenged in national courts are no 'panacea' for the enforcement of EU law, as individuals acting as litigants often lack the necessary resources and time to carry out legal proceedings.[15] Finally, the EU is 'currently in a state of turmoil'[16] where both economic and legitimacy crises are likely to affect Member States' willingness and ability to comply with EU decisions.[17] The ability to enforce its rules and regulation is closely linked to the EU's credibility

---

9 However, see Chs 1 and 2 of this collection for a less positive view.

10 Tallberg n 4 614.

11 Tallberg n 4; Jonas Tallberg, *European Governance and Supranational Institutions: Making States Comply* (Routledge 2003).

12 Alter and Vargas n 6; Alter n 6; Lisa Jane Conant, *Justice contained: Law and Politics in the European Union* (Cornell University Press 2002); Tallberg n 4; Tallberg n 11; Marlene Wind, Dorte S Martinsen and Gabriel Pons Rotger, 'The Uneven Legal Push for Europe: Questioning Variation when National Courts go to Europe' (2009) *European Union Politics* 63; Reinhard Slepcevic, 'The Judicial Enforcement of EU Law through National Courts: Possibilities and Limits' (2009) 16(3) *Journal of European Public Policy* 378.

13 Tallberg n 4 610.

14 Börzel, Hofmann, Panke and Sprungk n 2 1374; Gerda Falkner and Miriam Hartlapp, 'Problems of Operationalization and Data in EU Compliance Research' (2009) 10(2) *European Union Politics* 281; and see Ch 2 of this volume.

15 See Ch 1 of this volume and Slepcevic n 12 391.

16 Gerda Falkner, 'The JCMS Annual Review Lecture. Is the European Union Losing its Credibility?' (2013) 51 *Journal of Common Market Studies* 13.

17 Although the Commission's statistics on centralized enforcement do not seem to betray any worsening compliance picture so far.

as a political system and as a system founded on the rule of law. According to Falkner, the EU is currently in need of restoring societal confidence that its commitments are 'real and binding'.[18]

1.1 The Practical Application of EU Law

We still know remarkably little about the *practical application* of EU rules, that is, how the rules work in practice and are applied 'out there' in order to regulate the daily lives and doings of citizens and enterprises. With some exceptions,[19] most studies dealing with implementation have examined the formal stage of transposition, also termed legal or judicial implementation, in which a directive is transposed into national legislation.[20] In these analyses, infringement proceedings and transposition records generally constitute the focus of research upon which conclusions are made on whether Member States are EU compliers.[21] However, the same scholars point out that infringements may not offer a representative sample of all of the violations of supranational obligations, but rather only the 'tip of the non-compliance iceberg'.[22] We are thus left to assume that there are many other incidents of misapplication beyond formal transposition than those detected and pursued by means of infringement proceedings.

Whereas *judicial implementation* is a process steered mainly by Member State governments and the core executive, correct *practical application* depends on the extent to which national public authorities at different levels of governance understand and act in accordance with the EU rule of

---

[18] Falkner n 16 14.

[19] Versluis n 8; Gerda Falkner, Miriam Hartlapp and Oliver Treib, 'Worlds of Compliance: Why Leading Approaches to European Union Implementation Are only "Sometimes-True Theories" (2007) 46(3) *European Journal of Political Research* 395; Slepcevic n 12.

[20] See, for example, Tanja A Börzel, 'Non-Compliance in the European Union: Pathology or Statistical Artifact?' (2001) 8(5) *Journal of European Public Policy* 803; Börzel, Hofmann, Panke and Sprungk n 2; Peter Bursens, 'Why Denmark and Belgium Have Different Implementation Records: On Transposition Laggards and Leaders in the EU' (2002) 25(2) *Scandinavian Political Studies* 173; Ellen Mastenbroek, 'Surviving the Deadline: The Transposition of EU Directives in the Netherlands' (2003) 4(4) *European Union Politics* 371; Haverland and Romeijn n 2; Steuenberg and Toshkov n 2; for overviews, see Ellen Mastenbroek, 'EU Compliance: Still a "Black Hole"?' (2005) 12(6) *Journal of European Public Policy* 1103; Oliver Treib, 'Implementing and Complying with EU Governance Outputs' (2008) 3(5) *Living Reviews in European Governance.*

[21] See Falkner and Hartlapp n 14 for a critical discussion of the data sources used.

[22] Börzel, Hofmann, Panke and Sprungk n 2 1374.

law. Correct practical implementation also depends on the extent to which the correctness of implementation is controlled. As noted by Falkner, there is no reason to think that EU law is generally obeyed. An effective law enforcement regime depends on 'basic pillars to work adequately: public administrations, labour inspectorates, court systems, media and civil society institutions that could act as whistleblowers and intermediate potential problems'.[23]

In order to address problems arising in the practical application of EU law, the EU has supplemented its coercive instruments of enforcement with cooperative means of management.[24] Side by side with the deterrent message of enforcement by sanctions, Member States are monitored by means of a more informal, softer managerial approach. This management approach implies dialogue and mutual trust.[25] The management approach recognizes that sometimes non-compliance is not the mere result of deliberate behaviour, that is, the Member State neglecting or ignoring to fulfil its EU obligations in a calculated manner. Instead, non-compliance can be caused by ambiguous treaty language, complex secondary legislation, as well as a lack of administrative capacity and/or transparency. Different solutions are therefore required:

> . . .the improvement of dispute resolution procedures goes to the problem of ambiguity; technical and financial assistance may help cure the capacity deficit; and transparency will make it likelier that, over time, national policy decisions are brought increasingly into line with agreed international standards.[26]

The management view introduces an important shift in the EU theoretical and empirical approach to compliance. It departs from a 'command and control' understanding of which instruments best solve problems of the misapplication of law. In order to improve compliance, the non-complier should be assisted to solve the problems – instead of sued and sanctioned. Dispute settlements by means of management are based on dialogue, trust, involvement, capacity building and transparency.[27] Problem-solving involves mediation of positions between all the involved

---

[23] Falkner n 16 22.

[24] Tallberg n 4; Tallberg n 11; Börzel, Hofmann, Panke and Sprungk n 2; Miriam Hartlapp, 'On Enforcement, Management and Persuasion: Different Logics of Implementation Policy in the EU and the ILO' (2007) 45(3) *Journal of Common Market Studies* 653.

[25] See also Ch 2 of this volume.

[26] Chayes and Chayes n 5.

[27] Ch 4 discusses these virtues in relation to transnational agencies as well, and in Ch 3 this would be considered a type of responsive regulation.

parties so that they come to terms with the mutual solution identified. In this way, the process of problem-solving aims to find a solution that appeases and works for all the involved parties. The dispute-solving mechanisms differ from legal proceedings in court where the court concludes on the 'correct' legal interpretation, which may ultimately please neither party. Transgovernmental networks constitute such fora for problem-solving, beyond traditional central and decentralized enforcement mechanisms.

2. TRANSGOVERNMENTAL NETWORKS AS A NEW MEANS OF EXECUTIVE GOVERNANCE

Political scientists recognize that transgovernmental networks have emerged as a constitutive part of European integration.[28] Whilst the importance of transgovernmental cooperation has long been accepted within the study of international relations, the scope and the policy areas covered by TGNs with the EU's infrastructure are currently found to have taken on 'completely new dimensions'.[29] A transgovernmental network consists of regular and purposive relations between government actors, dealing with cross-border policies and problems. The government actors represent the state but operate at levels below the heads of states. They act as sector-specific experts who together develop shared, standard operating practices, by means of regular and purposive action, focusing on sector-specific problems such as environmental sustainability, human rights, data protection, electricity, justice and home affairs.[30] Civil servants or 'regulators' are key actors in such networks, serving as the new diplomats of global governance.[31] When they interact with their foreign peers, they bring with them their domestic expertise and views, but are forced to exchange these views and present solutions on collective problems arising from transgovernmentalism in practice.

---

[28] Paul W Thurner and Martin Binder, 'European Union Transgovernmental Networks: The Emergence of a New Political Space beyond the Nation-State?' (2009) 48(1) *European Journal of Political Research* 80; Mogens Hobolth and Dorte S Martinsen, 'Transgovernmental Networks in the European Union: Improving Compliance Effectively?' (2013) 20(10) *Journal of European Public Policy* 1406.

[29] Thurner and Binder n 28 83.

[30] Anne-Marie Slaughter, *A New World Order* (Princeton University Press 2004); Thurner and Binder n 28; Eberlein and Newmann n 1.

[31] Slaughter n 30 63.

Transgovernmental networks serve as fora of sharing information, building capacity, developing experience and learning between the actors involved and thus rely on management, rather than enforcement, logics in the way they monitor disputes.[32] One of the concrete impacts that TGNs can have is to improve compliance with international rules.[33] Such transgovernmental enforcement networks are found to play a crucial role in the effectuation of international rules as they lower the transaction costs of enforcement. Although TGNs are accepted as an important and expanding form of governance, able to provide a fast and flexible alternative to the formal procedures of international organizations,[34] we know little about their actual modus operandi, less about their effect and what may condition effectiveness. Their effectiveness is often claimed, but not tested or systematically explored.[35] Can informal problem-solving mechanisms effectively monitor and oversee compliance problems of supranational governance? Can they monitor the practical application of EU law, and if so, do all units in a network function equally effectively? What may explain variations in effectiveness across the network? These questions will be examined below.

3. THE STUDY OF THE SOLVIT NETWORK: DATA, METHOD AND SCOPE

The transgovernmental network of SOLVIT is examined in this chapter. The SOLVIT network monitors the practical application of internal market law within the EU Member States as well as the three Member States of the European Economic Area (EEA); Norway, Lichtenstein and Iceland. SOLVIT was established in 2001[36] and handles complaints from citizens and businesses concerning the application of European law in cross-border cases. Conflicts are resolved via a dialogue between national SOLVIT centres, domestic authorities complained about and in some instances also the Commission. The network today processes a notable amount of cases and claims a high success rate in resolving

---

32 Anne-Marie Slaughter and Thomas N Hale, 'Transgovernmental Networks and Multi-Level Governance' in Henrik Enderlein, Sonja Wälti and Michael Zürn (eds.), *Handbook on Multi-Level Governance* (Edward Elgar 2010) 347.

33 Slaughter n 30 44.

34 Eberlein and Newmann n 1 27.

35 Eberlein and Newmann n 1 35.

36 European Commission, 'Recommendation on Principles for Using "SOLVIT": The Internal Market Problem Solving Network' COM (2001) 893.

disputes.[37] Although examining the single case of the internal market, SOLVIT mirrors a more general tendency in the European Union where regulatory networks are established to carry out key functions of executive governance.[38] Furthermore, the problems arising in practice when internal market law is to be applied essentially mirrors the challenges confronting national authorities, businesses and citizens when practising the rules of global governance.

In order to examine the work-mode and effectiveness of a transgovernmental network, we conducted an online survey enquiring into the characteristics and modes of the SOLVIT network. The survey was sent to all 30 national SOLVIT centres, that is, EU-27 as well as Iceland, Norway and Liechtenstein as part of the EEA.[39] The survey was carried out in the first half of 2011. It was presented as solely academic in its purpose. Most of the centres responded to our first enquiry. The centres that did not fill out the survey were subsequently contacted by e-mail and telephone. Over time, all of the centres answered and we thus managed to obtain a full response rate. In addition, data was provided to us by the European Commission in summer 2012 on the resolution rates of the individual SOLVIT centres, extracted from the Commission's database. This data is not publicly available but was provided by the Commission on our request on the basis of previously established contact.

The survey themes and questions were put together following close studies of the publicly available documents on SOLVIT together with explorative interviews with the national centres in the United Kingdom and Denmark. The explorative interviews were used to test our initial theoretical ideas and ensure that the questions would address the key

---

[37] European Commission, 'Background: Annual Reports' <http://ec.europa.eu/solvit/site/background/index_en.htm> accessed 3 September 2011; European Commission, '28th Annual Report on Monitoring the Application of EU Law' COM (2011) 588.

[38] TRESS (social security) and IMPEL (environment) regulatory networks are similar to this type of network in the way they also monitor and report on misapplication of European legislation (see www.tress-network.org and impel.eu). Also Eberlein and Newmann n 1 point to the increasing role of TGNs across policy areas in monitoring and overseeing the compliance with EU law.

[39] Mick P Couper, 'Web Surveys: A Review of Issues and Approaches' (2000) 64 *Public Opinion Quarterly* 464; Mick P Couper, Michael W Traugott and Mark Lamias, 'Web Survey Design and Administration' (2001) 65 *Public Opinion Quarterly* 230; David de Vaus, *Surveys in Social Research* (5th edn, Routledge 2001); for a critical discussion, see Ronald D Fricker and Mattihas Schonlau, 'Advantages and Disadvantages of Internet Research Surveys: Evidence from the Literature' (2002) 14(4) *Field Methods* 347.

dynamics of the network and appear understandable within its context.[40] The British and Danish SOLVIT centres also agreed to read through a draft of the survey and provided a final set of comments on our draft. Finally, we engaged in informal dialogue with the Commission on our project and questionnaire. We used this approach to ensure as fully as possible that the questions would be intelligible to the network participants. Towards the end of the survey, we also asked the participants if we might return with follow-up questions.

The survey consisted of 30 questions. The centres could mainly respond to them on a scale such as increased/decreased or strongly agree/strongly disagree. We thereby attempted to obtain answers that would be more easily summarized across all participating states. The key questions also included a text box for additional comments.

Our enquiry addressed three overall themes. The first was the *resources and relations* of the network. Here, we explored the amount of contact with other centres, other parts of the national public administration, the Commission and changes in the level of institutionalization over time. The second was the *case management process in practice*. This section explored the efficiency of the network, the role and monitoring of the Commission and reasons for misapplication. The third and final section examined the *values of the network*. Here, we asked questions concerning the network's source of legitimacy, the character of an ideal case solution and their orientation towards either national or European interests. The specific survey questions asked are stated alongside each illustration reporting on our findings. Apart from the survey data and explorative interviews, the analysis draws on relevant supplementary material, such as the Commission's annual reports on the network.

3.1 Informal Dispute Settlements in the EU: Presenting the SOLVIT Network

The European Commission officially proposed the establishment of the SOLVIT network in late 2001, enabling citizens or enterprises to submit complaints to nationally based centres concerning the misapplication of internal market rules.[41] The Council of Ministers endorsed the Commission's proposal shortly afterwards, and the network started

---

40 Couper n 39 475f.

41 European Commission, 'Communication from the Commission to the Council, the European Parliament, the Economic and Social Committee and the Committee of the Regions: Effective Problem Solving in the Internal Market ("SOLVIT")' COM (2001) 702.

handling cases in 2002.[42] The executive summary of the Commission's initial communication highlighted the purposes and means of the network. It was to provide effective problem-solving in relation to cross-border disputes in the sphere of the internal market by means of administrative dispute settlements, enhanced transparency and peer pressure. Specifically, the envisioned network was to be based on an online database where examined disputes could be registered and solutions reported on. Furthermore, it was to undertake preventive actions by seeking to remove the causes of recurring problems as well as to promote itself and target information to citizens and business.[43] The Commission proposed an alternative dispute settlement mechanism intended to offer speedier problem-solving than the formal setting of cases before the CJEU could offer. When the internal market does not appear to function in practice:

> . . . speedy redress needs to be available. Resolving such practical problems is critical to the credibility of the Internal Market in the eyes of citizens and economic operators, particularly small and medium-sized businesses. We know from experience, however, that resolving problems can take a long time [. . .] This prevents a lot of people from doing what they are entitled to by Community [Union] law. When this happens, confidence in the European Union is eroded.[44]

These original aims and means still represent today the core idea of SOLVIT as a network. As a network, SOLVIT appeals directly to EU citizens and businesses, offering them fast, practical solutions to disputes over the application of internal market rules.[45] All 27 Member States and Norway, Lichtenstein and Iceland have established a SOLVIT centre, based within the national central administration, in most cases within the ministry of economic or foreign affairs.[46]

The dispute settlement work-mode is quite unique. It is based on recurrent dialogues between citizens, companies, SOLVIT centres and the

---

[42] Council of the European Union, 'Internal Market Problem-Solving: Council Conclusions on the "SOLVIT" Network' 6503/02 (Presse 41 – G); European Commission n 37.

[43] COM (2001) 702.

[44] Ibid 3.

[45] European Commission, 'SOLVIT 2010 Report: Development and Performance of the SOLVIT Network' <http://ec.europa.eu/solvit/site/docs/solvit_2010_report_en.pdf> accessed 3 September 2011; European Commission, 'About SOLVIT' <http://ec.europa.eu/solvit/site/about/index_en.htm> accessed 3 September 2011.

[46] European Commission, 'National SOLVIT Centres' <http://ec.europa.eu/solvit/site/centres/index_en.htm> accessed 3 September 2011.

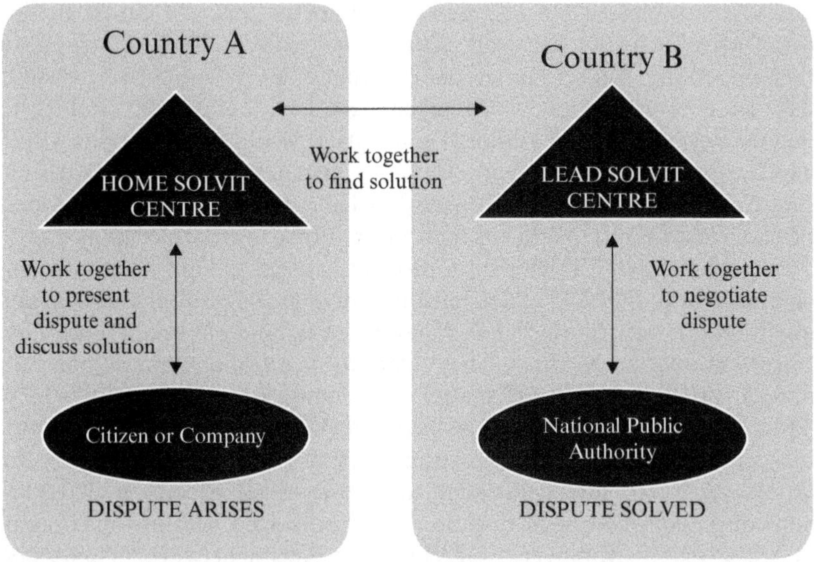

Figure 6.1 The organization and work process of the SOLVIT network

responsible national authorities. A complaint is first lodged to a 'home' centre; the centre with the same nationality as the complainer. If the home centre deems the case to be within the remit of the network and apparently involving a breach of EU legislation, the dispute is registered in the network and sent to the 'lead' centre. The 'lead' centre is located in the Member State where the problem occurred. Should it accept the case, it subsequently initiates dialogue with the national public authority complained about.[47] Within the Commission's internal market Directorate General (DG), a SOLVIT unit is responsible for supporting the network, for example by assisting with the use of the case management database, engaging in dialogue with the centres on cases and organizing events bringing all the actors together. The organization and work process of the network can be illustrated as shown in Figure 6.1.

Thus, problem-solving unfolds via several national and cross-national communication and justification processes whereby the application of supranational law is questioned and monitored primarily by national public administrations. The citizen or business needs to present and give reasons to the 'home' SOLVIT centre, which again is to clarify, present

[47] COM (2001) 702; European Commission n 45.

and give reasons on the disputed matter to the SOLVIT centre in the other Member State: the 'lead' centre. The 'lead' SOLVIT centre must then present the subject matter and breaches of EU law to the responsible national authority in its own Member State. Last, but certainly not least, the responsible national authority must give reasons and justify its ways, which again are reviewed and eventually critiqued by the two SOLVIT centres. As an outcome of the dispute settlement process, the cross-border problem may be solved and misapplication turned into correct application.

Since 2001, SOLVIT has been institutionalized around a set of main characteristics: SOLVIT cases have a *'cross-border' element*, such as the sale of goods across internal EU borders or the use of social security by European migrant workers. They relate to *practical application* and not judicial implementation. A matter must concern a situation in which national legislation is deemed in line with the European obligation but the problem arises in the post-transposition phase.[48] Furthermore, as an alternative to time-consuming and costly legal processes, SOLVIT aims at *speedy redress*. A dispute should be solved within a maximum of ten weeks.[49] Moreover, SOLVIT constitutes a network of *informal problem-solving* based on recurring dialogues addressing whether supranational law has been misapplied, questioned and monitored. Problems must be solved without legal proceedings. These characteristics make the SOLVIT network differ from traditional enforcement mechanisms and makes it possible to extend research beyond the conventional focus within compliance studies on the timely transposition of EU law.

Becoming a successful dispute settlement mechanism

Over the years, SOLVIT's workload has increased significantly. Figure 6.2 illustrates the major increase in the number of cases handled by the SOLVIT network. The statistics only include cases accepted by the network. Acceptance implies, as mentioned, that a submitted dispute has undergone 'pre-screening', where the home SOLVIT centre has assessed the case and found it involves a cross-border element, does not involve legislative changes, and agrees with the claimant that it appears likely that EU law has been misapplied.[50]

---

48 Most SOLVIT centres also take on so-called 'SOLVIT+' cases in which changes to the rules behind national implementation appear necessary (COM 2011d). When a SOLVIT+ case is dealt with, the problem-solving process will also address the institutional cause of misapplication, that is, incorrect judicial implementation.

49 COM (2001) 702; European Commission n 45.

50 European Commission n 45.

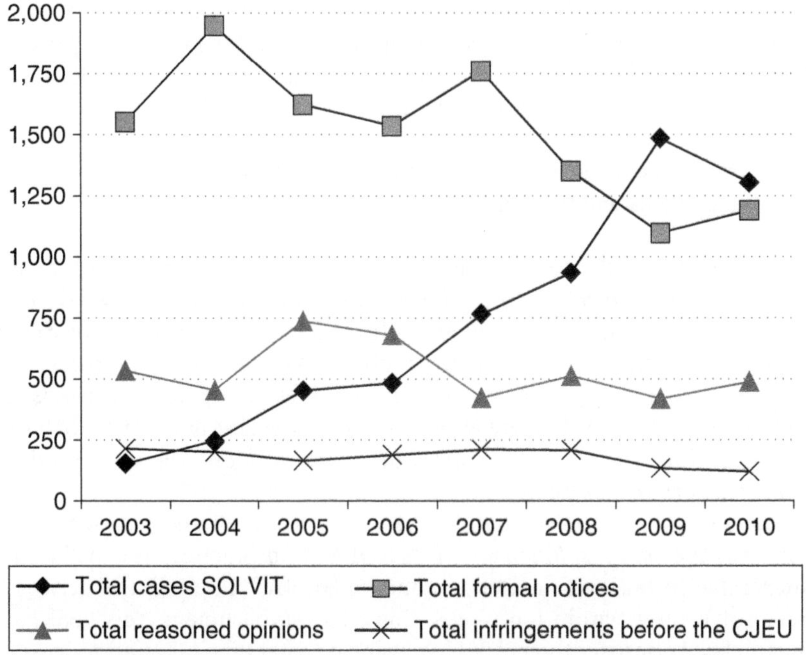

Note: SOLVIT cases and infringement procedures compared 2002–10. The data on infringement procedures are from the Commission's Secretariat General's annual reports on monitoring the application of Community law. The data on SOLVIT cases were provided by the Commission.

Figure 6.2 Total SOLVIT caseload compared to infringement procedures 2002–10

A case accepted by the SOLVIT regime thus implies that the dispute is regarded as substantial. The network receives a considerable number of other requests which are not accepted as SOLVIT cases and thus not registered. These include requests concerning purely national problems or require help and guidance on the EU only.[51]

In 2003, the network handled 154 cases; by 2010, the figure had grown to 1304. The request for and success of the informal dispute settlement mechanism stands out when comparing SOLVIT to the traditional formal EU public enforcement procedures. In comparison as part of the formal legal process of the infringement procedure, in 2010 the Commission sent

[51] European Commission n 37.

1,188 letters of formal notice to the Member States, issued 488 reasoned opinions and referred 120 cases to the CJEU in the same time period. Hence, compared to the much analysed formal infringement procedure, the SOLVIT workload is considerable.

3.2 The Effectiveness of Transgovernmental Networks in Dispute Settlements and the Role of the Commission

From the size of the caseload itself, it is clear that misapplication cases are brought to SOLVIT to a considerable extent. Nevertheless, we should still expect – especially from an enforcement perspective – informal dispute resolution to be of limited utility, as national authorities are likely to hinder a dispute mechanism which does not operate by means of 'command and control'. Here we examine effectiveness in accordance with our definition as *the resolution speed* of the network and the actual *ability of the network to resolve cases.*

The first proxy for estimating the effectiveness of the network thus concerns the *case resolution speed.* Is SOLVIT in practice an expeditious alternative to taking a matter to court? The official aim of the network is to solve cases within ten weeks. Since its establishment, this goal has overall been consistently met.[52] However, the total time taken to process a claim from its submission is somewhat higher. This is due to the ten-week deadline only applying from when a case has been accepted by a lead centre.[53] The home centre's preparation time and the time taken by the lead centre to consider whether to accept the case is therefore not included. In 2010, it took the centres on average five weeks to prepare a case; and one week to consider whether to accept a case from another centre.[54] The total case processing time is therefore roughly 16 weeks, that is, approximately four months. This is still a short period of time compared with other formal enforcement mechanisms, both public and private, and the network stands out as efficient in terms of prompt dispute resolution.

The second proxy for effectiveness is the *ability of the network to resolve cases.* Here, the Commission's statistics again provide a picture of a highly successful system.[55] The official aim of the network is a resolution rate of 80 per cent. This target has generally been achieved from 2002 onwards, although with some differences between the Member States. But what does

---

52 Ibid.
53 Ibid.
54 European Commission n 45.
55 European Commission n 37.

it mean that a case is resolved? In its 2010 Annual Report, the Commission notes that in practice 'resolved' can, mean two different things: a changed decision or a clarification.[56] The former entails the initial administrative act being altered following the intervention of SOLVIT, namely that misapplication is transformed into correct application. The latter means that the claimant ultimately only receives additional information clarifying the background and reasons behind the decision, but the decision is not changed. Both outcomes are important as to how national administrations adapt to EU governance in the sense that they engage national public authorities and claimants in a mode of reasoning structured in EU legal terms.[57] However, when the dispute is settled by means of a changed decision, this most directly substantiates the effectiveness and impact of the network, as it demonstrates the ability of the network to improve practical application.

The Commission states that 23 per cent of all cases in 2010 ended with a clarification, meaning that the rest of the cases solved led to altered decisions.[58] This suggests that the network is in fact able to generate alterations to decisions, that is, altering administrative acts. Figure 6.3 shows the SOLVIT centres' estimates of the proportion of their cases which ended in 2010 with a changed decision, according to our own survey data.

Sixteen of the SOLVIT centres report that complaints end with a changed decision in about a half to all cases. Nine indicate that changes are less common. Five centres answered 'do not know' or left the question blank. The figure thus shows that the network is generally able to convince national public authorities to alter their practices.

Figure 6.4 points out what the centre reports to be the preconditions for resolving cases.

We asked the centres to assess the importance of four aspects: good working relations with other public authorities, ministerial support, legal case analysis and political contestation. No ranking was requested. The responses substantiate that all factors have some importance – but not equally so. There is a clear trend in what aspects the centres 'agree' or 'strongly agree' with as important. Good working relations with other parts of the national administration together with sound legal case analysis stand out as very important. Several centres also stress the necessity of ministerial and political backing. This element was particularly emphasized by one centre in a supplementary comment:

---

56 European Commission n 45.
57 Hobolth and Martinsen n 28.
58 European Commission n 45 20.

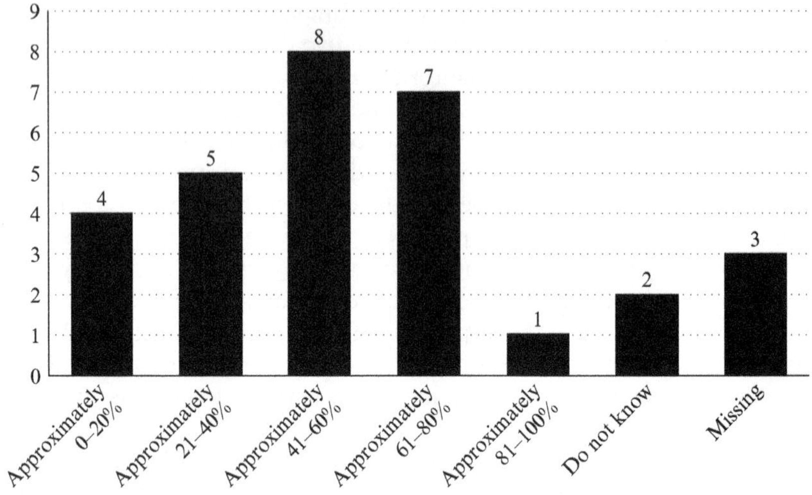

Note: We also asked the centres, as a control, to make a similar assessment of how many cases ended solely with a clarification. The answer to the two questions gave the same picture.

Source: SOLVIT survey 2011, Question 10, 'Of the SOLVIT cases handled as "lead" in 2010, what was the outcome?'

Figure 6.3 The SOLVIT centres' estimation of the proportion of cases in 2010 which ended with a change of the initial decision by the national public authority

> [. . .] unfortunately we do not feel support for SOLVIT cases from our superiors, especially for citizen cases [. . .] This is due to the fact that SOLVIT [. . .] is established at the Ministry of Industry and Trade so the attention from our hierarchy concentrates a lot on business cases but cases of ordinary citizens are not viewed that importantly. For example, social security cases which affect daily life and situations of European families [. . .] [are] not seen as something significant and we are almost discouraged to talk about them/advertise them, etc.[59]

The survey data thus highlight the importance of good working relations, legal analysis and to a large extent also ministerial backing. On the

[59] Source: SOLVIT Survey, 'Academic Survey of the SOLVIT Network' (2011). (Own web-survey submitted and replied to by all National SOLVIT Centres, Question 28, 'If you have any further comments regarding the topics covered in the survey please enter them here').

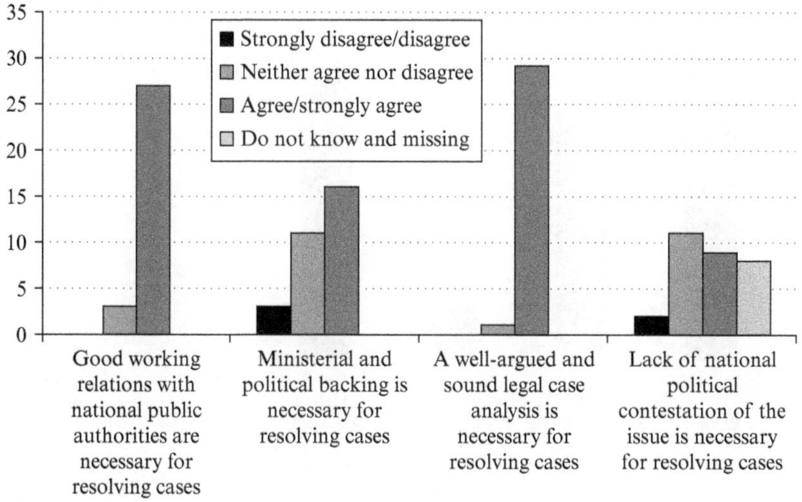

Note: The categories strongly disagree/agree and agree/strongly disagree have been combined. 'Do not know' and missing answers have also been joined together.

Source: SOLVIT survey 2011, Question 20, 'To what extent, if at all, do you agree with the following statements concerning the preconditions for resolving cases?'

Figure 6.4 The SOLVIT centres' estimation of the preconditions for resolving cases

other hand, overall, the centres do not find the extent to which an issue is politicized of high importance.

All in all, the official data presented by the Commission suggests that the network is an efficient problem-solving mechanism. Resolution speed is high compared to, for example, legal proceedings or formal infringement proceedings instigated by the Commission. Efficiency is also supported by the survey data collected for this analysis. Decentralized informal problem-solving is, in fact, able to address gaps between the transposition and practical application of EU legislation. We do see some differences in outcomes in that the end result may amount to a change in a decision or be solely a clarification. However, the vast majority of SOLVIT cases lead to a change in the original decision and, even in clarification cases, the work of the network promotes and strengthens the use of arguments framed in EU legal terms within national public authorities to justify the action they have taken.

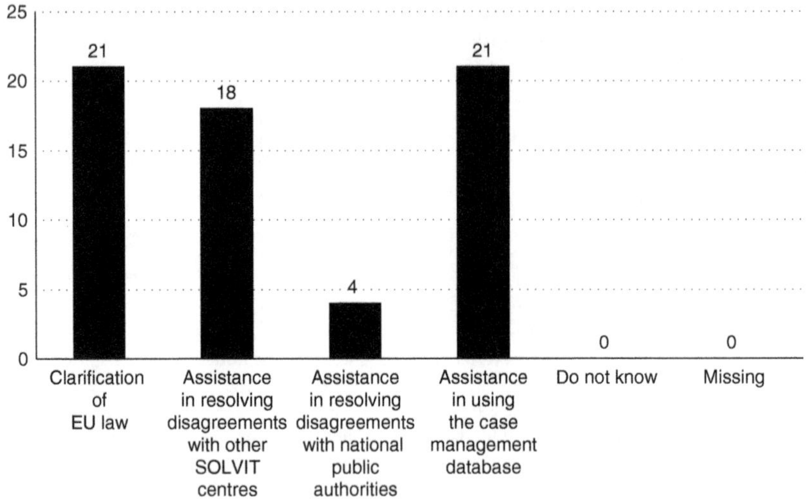

Note: The respondents were invited to tick as many of the stated reasons as relevant.

Source: SOLVIT survey 2011, Question 5, 'What is the purpose of the contact with the European Commission?'

Figure 6.5 The purpose of the contact with the Commission

The role of the Commission in informal dispute settlements

Our survey data provides new insights into the role of the Commission. The survey points out that most national SOLVIT centres have contact with the EU SOLVIT unit, that is, the Commission, on a regular basis. Some on an almost daily basis, others weekly, and others only a few times over the course of a month. In general, the European Commission is closely involved and consulted when the application of internal market rules is scrutinized.

Twelve centres are in contact with the Commission weekly or more; 18 a few times over the course of a month or year. The level of contact is thus high although varying, substantiating the central role of the Commission in the network. The involvement of the Commission proves essential for different purposes. When asked about the purposes of the contact, three different ways of assisting the centres stand out as central (see Figure 6.5).

The Commission assists the centres regarding the daily practices of the network. This includes giving advice on how to use the case management database, with understanding the legal content and meaning of EU law, as

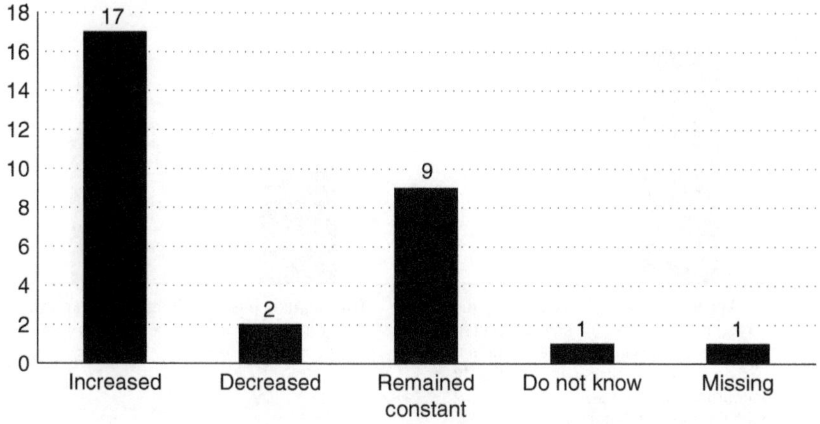

Source: SOLVIT survey 2011, Question 7, 'Since your SOLVIT centre was established, the amount of contact with the European Commission has in general . . .?'

Figure 6.6 Changes in the level of contact with the Commission

well as assisting with the solution of horizontal disagreements with other SOLVIT centres. However, the Commission does not appear to intervene very much when there are disagreements between SOLVIT centres and national public authorities within Member States. Thus, the Commission plays a role in the more technical matters of the network, and assumes a supervisory role in the network being continuously involved in the dispute settlements.

Moreover, for most SOLVIT centres, contact with the Commission has increased over the years, as the responses to the question in Figure 6.6 demonstrate.

Nevertheless, the continuous and increasing involvement of the Commission in the dispute settlement of the network does not tell us whether the Commission enjoys sufficient authority to have its opinions and interpretations taken into account when there is a conflict between the view of the Commission and that of the national authority. In the survey we inquired into the degree to which the Commission's view supersedes national views in the event of a conflict between the two. The result was unequivocal. Where a conflict arises, the supranational hierarchy is clear. If the preferred case solution of the national public authority is in conflict with the recommendations made by the Commission, the Commission's recommendations are followed (see Figure 6.7).

Thus, the Commission plays a central role in assisting and advising on

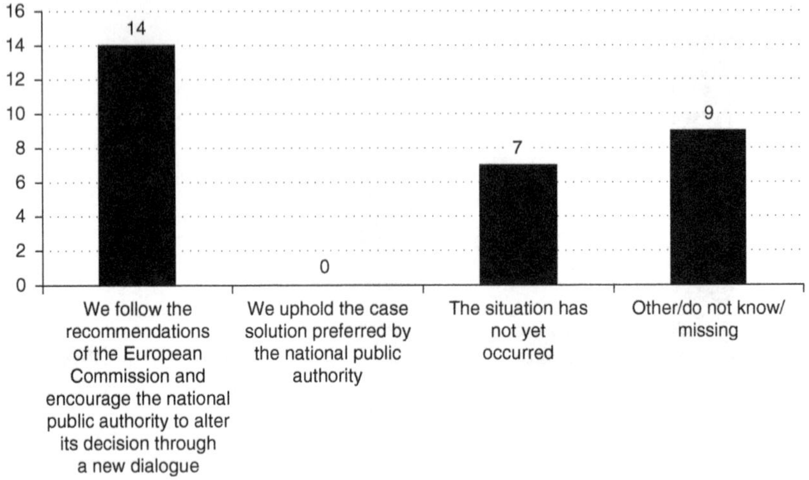

Source: SOLVIT Survey 2011, Question 17, 'If the European Commission recommends a case solution different from the one preferred by your national public authority, what do you do?'

Figure 6.7 The Commission's authority in the network

dispute settlements. Although the process of resolution appears horizontally organized between three entities, namely the individual or firm with a complaint, the relevant SOLVIT centres and the national public authority against which a complaint has been made, the Commission (vertically) shadows the dispute and masters the database, assists on the clarification of EU law, and has a final say when conflicts appear between national units. Although this form of alternative dispute settlement is not as coercive as traditional enforcement procedures, it operates in the shadow of supranational hierarchy.[60] If a conflict is unsolved or the solution does not appear to follow EU law, the Commission may decide to open an infringement procedure as the next step.[61] Against this background, informal dispute settlement stands out as an attractive alternative. This may in part explain the success of the transgovernmental network as a dispute

[60] Tanja A. Börzel, 'European Governance: Negotiation and Competition in the Shadow of Hierarchy' (2010) 48(2) *Journal of Common Market Studies* 191.

[61] See also European Commission, 'Commission Staff Working Document Setting Out the Approach for Assessing the Conformity of Solutions Proposed by the SOLVIT Network with Community Law' SEC (2004) 1159.

settlement mechanism. Although horizontal in structure, it has a vertical element of supranational supervision.

CONCLUSION

Our findings demonstrate that misapplication of EU law continues to occur on a regular basis even after the transposition of EU rules into national legislation. Despite considerable research being undertaken on the transposition of EU law, this does not necessarily tell us much about compliance *in practice*. Citizens and enterprises encounter daily barriers to exercising their rights and complying with the obligations formally provided by internal market law. Correct practical application depends on the extent to which national public authorities at different governance levels understand and are willing to act in accordance with EU legislation, and not simply on transposition of the EU rules into national law.

The findings of this empirical qualitative study demonstrate that the EU's enforcement-management system has added an important decentralized management dimension by means of transgovernmental networks. The findings thus point to transgovernmental networks such as SOLVIT as important and effective structures to address misapplication of EU law. The chapter has thus contributed to fill in the black hole of developing a better understanding of EU law in action. TGNs are effectively located in the core executives of the Member States, but reporting back to and taking advice from the Commission.[62] The Commission has quietly and discreetly rearmed in its battle against misapplication of EU law relating to the functioning of the internal market by Member States by focusing on compliance problems in the post-transposition stage. Alternative dispute settlement networks have developed and proven considerably effective as a mechanism of decentralized management practices ensuring EU compliance. The informal dispute resolution provided by a TGN such as SOLVIT provides a strong, supplementary means of enforcing EU law along with the two traditional public and private enforcement mechanisms. Whilst national courts are *decentralized private enforcement mechanisms*,[63] a transgovernmental network constitutes a *decentralized management mechanism* which may be remarkably effective and successful in solving problems of misapplication.

---

[62] On effectiveness and the importance of learning, see also Hobolth and Martinsen n 28.

[63] Slepcevic n 12.

In part, this success is explained by the fact that national public authorities become supervisors of national compliance whilst operating close to the units under 'surveillance'. The national SOLVIT centres are part of the national executives, located and financed there. At the same time, however, they are responsible for overseeing the conduct of their national counterparts; to question it, evaluate it, report on it and – eventually – take steps to ensure that it is in accordance with EU legislation. In this way, they become entrusted supervisors of EU law and key institutions in managing practical application, but in contrast to the national courts, do so in a manner more informed by trust, less by the threat of sanctions. They thus constitute an important part of the 'European executive space', monitoring EU law but located in the national administrations.[64]

Although horizontal in structure and operating by means of management, the transgovernmental SOLVIT network has an important vertical dimension. The Commission occupies a central role in assisting and advising dispute settlements. The Commission's involvement implies that, should the softer means of management not work, enforcement proceedings may be initiated. The continuous presence of the Commission means that supranational hierarchy shadows dispute resolution. In the shadow of supranational hierarchy, informal dispute settlements stand out as the attractive alternative. By creating a transgovernmental network of decentralized supervision through national public authorities, the Commission has taken another important step in boosting the enforcement-management machinery of the EU,[65] capable of detecting and resolving some of the disputes over the practical application of EU rule 'below the tip of the non-compliance iceberg'.[66]

64 Jarle Trondal, *An Emergent European Executive Order* (Oxford University Press 2010).
65 Tallberg at n 11.
66 Börzel noted at n 60.

7. Enforcing EU environmental policy effectively: international influences, current barriers and possible solutions

Mariolina Eliantonio

INTRODUCTION

The issue of the enforcement of EU environmental law has long been at the top of the EU enforcement agenda[1] because of the volume of EU environmental legislation[2] and the serious consequences for humans and nature alike in case of non-compliance. In its 2012 Communication 'Improving the delivery of benefits from EU environment measures: building confidence through better knowledge and responsiveness', the Commission notes that delayed or inadequate implementation of EU environmental legislation 'harms the environment and human health, generates regulatory uncertainty for industry and puts in question the level playing field of the Single Market'.[3] Furthermore, '[t]he long-term remediation costs – for example for clean-up of illegal waste sites and restoration of damaged habitats – can be much higher than the costs of prevention'.[4] The EU also confirmed in the context of its 2013–20 Environment Action Programme

---

[1] See e.g. Communication from the Commission to the European Parliament, the Council, the European Economic and Social Committee and the Committee of the Regions, 'Improving the delivery of benefits from EU environment measures: building confidence through better knowledge and responsiveness' COM(2012) 095 final, accessed 10 December 2015 at <http://eur-lex.europa.eu/legal-content/EN/TXT/?uri=CELEX:52012DC0095>.

[2] The Commission reports that the environmental acquis consists of more than 200 legal acts, accessed 8 December 2015 at <http://ec.europa.eu/environment/legal/law/>.

[3] Commission Communication on 'Improving the delivery of benefits from EU environment measures: building confidence through better knowledge and responsiveness' COM(2012) 095 final, n 1, 3.

[4] Ibid.

that implementation and enforcement of EU environmental law should be considered amongst the priority policy objectives for the EU.[5] In the area of environmental policy, the commitment to better and more effective enforcement of legislation also stems from another layer of governance. The EU is obliged by virtue of international law to ensure that the public has effective means to enforce EU environmental law, through, in particular, ensuring 'wide access to justice', as provided by the UN's Aarhus Convention.[6]

Despite the EU's policy commitments and international obligations, the state of enforcement of EU environmental law is far from satisfactory. The aim of this chapter is to shed some light on the current state of enforcement of EU environmental law and its effectiveness. For the purpose of this analysis, enforcement should be understood as encompassing a range of judicial or extra-judicial mechanisms aimed at ensuring compliance with EU (environmental) rules. The chapter will first focus on the shortcomings of the system of centralized enforcement of environmental law. Thereafter, the chapter will explore the decentralized enforcement system and contextualize this issue within the framework of the Aarhus Convention after having provided some background on the special characteristics of environmental law. As a set of rules often provided for the interest of no one and everyone at the same time, there are unique challenges for the effective enforcement of EU environmental law. The analysis will show how the (private) enforcement of EU environmental law before national courts, which is aimed at repairing the shortcomings of the system of centralized enforcement, also faces several obstacles. The second part of the contribution will focus on some new trends in the enforcement modalities adopted in the field of environmental law, analysing them in the framework of the debate on the 'new' modes of governance. The analysis will demonstrate how the move towards the use of enforcement tools which depart from the traditional command-and-control mechanisms may contribute to more effective enforcement of environmental law.

[5] Dec 1386/2013 of the European Parliament and of the Council on a General Union Environment Action Programme to 2020 'Living well, within the limits of our planet' [2013] OJ L354/171.

[6] United Nations Economic Commission for Europe, Convention on Access to Information, Public Participation in Decision-Making and Access to Justice in Environmental Matters, accessed 8 December 2015 at <http://www.unece.org/fileadmin/DAM/env/pp/documents/cep43e.pdf>.

1. CENTRALIZED ENFORCEMENT OF EU LAW IN THE CONTEXT OF ENVIRONMENTAL POLICY AND ITS LIMITATIONS

Over the past 30 years the EU has adopted a substantial and diverse range of environmental measures. Some legislation is sector specific covering water, air, nature, waste, noise and chemicals. Other measures are horizontal in nature and cut across all environmental sectors, for example, environmental impact assessments, access to environmental information, public participation in environmental decision-making and liability for environmental damage. The vast majority of these rules follow a typical command-and-control system in that they contain binding rules (very often in the form of directives) which provide judicially enforceable prohibitions. Furthermore, most environmental measures are implemented following the model of 'indirect administration',[7] whereby it is for Member State authorities to implement the EU measures in accordance with their national administrative framework subject to EU standards set out by the CJEU (principles of equivalence, effectiveness and effective judicial protection) and Article 47 of the Charter of Fundamental Rights of the European Union.[8]

The implementation of EU environmental law, that is to say the process of translating policy into action,[9] entails several stages, namely transposition into national law including the notification of the transposing measures to the Commission (phases which are necessary for directives only), the setting up of a legal and administrative framework for the proper application and enforcement of EU legislation (often referred to as the operationalization stage), its practical application to concrete cases and its enforcement.[10] All of these stages are to be overseen by the Commission fulfilling its role as 'guardian of the Treaties' in accordance with Article 17(1) TEU. The main enforcement mechanism available to the Commission in performing this function is set out in Article 258 TFEU, through which

---

[7] See further, Herwig C.H. Hofmann, Gerard C. Rowe and Alexander H. Türk, *Administrative Law and Policy of the European Union* (Oxford University Press 2011) 12 ff.

[8] Case 33/76 *Rewe* [1976] ECR 1989 and case C-45/76 *Comet* [1976] ECR 2043; C-432/05 *Unibet Ltd* [2007] ECR I-2271; case C-279/09 *DEB* [2010] ECR I-13849. For further discussion, see Chapter 1 in this volume.

[9] Susan M. Barret, 'Implementation Studies: Time for a Revival? Personal Reflections on 20 Years of Implementation Studies' (2004) Pub Adm 251.

[10] Koen Lenaerts and José Gutiérrez-Fons, 'The General System of EU Environmental Law Enforcement' (2011) YEL 3–4; Jan Jans, Sacha Prechal and Rob Widdershoven, *Europeanisation of Public Law* (Europa Law Publishing 2007) 13 ff.

the Commission has the right to open infringement procedures against a Member State for failing to comply with its environmental obligations and can eventually bring the non-compliant Member State before the CJEU.[11] The Commission is able to pursue Member State non-compliance with any Article 258 TFEU rulings of the CJEU through the imposition of financial sanctions as set out in Article 260 TFEU. Environmental law has played a prominent place in such proceedings with an environmental case being the first ever Article 260 TFEU proceeding started by the Commission.[12]

The pursuit of infringements for breach of environmental law under Article 258 TFEU is certainly at the top of the Commission's infringement list. In 2013, environment was once again the policy area where most infringement proceedings were initiated[13] reflecting a worrisome trend.[14] Specifically in the field of environmental law, the CJEU has accepted the Commission's argument that the subject matter of infringement proceedings may be 'systemic deficient administrative practices' thereby creating the concept of 'general and persistent breach' (GAP breach). This approach enables the Commission to speed up and render infringement proceedings more efficient because it enables the Commission to bundle recurrent and systemic breaches into one single procedure.[15] The significant improvement brought about by the GAP system lies thus in the effects of a GAP ruling vis-à-vis the 'regular' infringement proceedings. Whilst in a 'regular' infringement case, the Member State is obliged only to take the necessary measures to address the specific breaches at stake, the consequence of a GAP judgment is that the national authorities must rectify the specific infringements *and* correct the administrative practice in place so that subsequent infringements do not occur.[16]

---

[11] For more detailed analysis of the Commission's use of Article 258 TFEU in the enforcement of EU law, see Chapter 2 in this volume.

[12] C-387/97 *Commission v Greece* [2000] ECR I-5047.

[13] Report from the Commission, *31st Annual Report on Monitoring the Application of EU Law (2013)* COM(2014) 612 final, 12, accessed 10 December 2015 at <http://ec.europa.eu/atwork/applying-eu-law/docs/annual_report_31/com_2014_612_en.pdf>.

[14] Report from the Commission, *30th Annual Report on Monitoring the Application of EU Law (2012)* COM(2013) 726 final, accessed 8 December 2015 at <http://eur-lex.europa.eu/legal-content/EN/TXT/?uri=COM:2013:726:FIN 8 December 2015>.

[15] See case C-494/01 *Commission v Ireland* [2005] I-03331. See further on this point, Pål Wennerås, 'A New Dawn for Commission Enforcement under Articles 226 and 228 EC: General and Persistent (GAP) Infringements, Lump Sums and Penalty Payments' (2006) CMLRev 31.

[16] Ibid at 42–3.

Despite the Commission's efforts to monitor the implementation of EU environmental law and to pursue infringements, and despite the improvements brought about by the creation of the concept of 'general and persistent breach' in environmental matters, there are several shortcomings with this centralized model of enforcement which are well known, but can have particular resonance in the field of environmental policy. First, the Commission does not have the capacity to exercise a proper monitoring system when the application (rather than the transposition) of EU environmental legislation is concerned. Whereas the Commission is able to obtain precise information on the national measures adopted for the transposition of directives, the practical application of EU legislation has been referred to as 'exceedingly difficult to monitor and to evaluate'.[17] Extensive legal and political research has confirmed that the lack of direct investigative and oversight powers,[18] and overoptimistic reliance on Member States' self-reporting powers[19] and civil society complaint activities[20] renders the Commission incapable of detecting all instances of non-compliance with EU legislation.[21] This undoubtedly leaves several instances of non- or incorrect application of EU environmental law undetected. Second, if detected, infringement proceedings under Article 258 TFEU are initiated at the full discretion of the Commission. The CJEU has granted some leeway for the Commission in its case law when it comes to deciding whether or not[22] and when[23] to start infringement proceedings (and whether or not, and when, to refer a case to the Court).[24] When this discretion is viewed in combination with the Commission's shift

---

17 Jonas Tallberg, 'Paths to Compliance: Enforcement, Management, and the European Union' (2002) IO 624.

18 Brian Jack, 'Enforcing Member State Compliance with EU Environmental Law: A Critical Evaluation of the Use of Financial Penalties' (2011) JEL 76; Martin Hedemann-Robinson, *Enforcement of European Union Environmental Law: Legal Issues and Challenges* (Routledge 2007) 161–4.

19 Peter Van den Bossche, 'In Search of Remedies for Non-Compliance: The Experience of the European Community' (1996) MJ 389.

20 Tanja Börzel, 'Non-Compliance in the European Union: Pathology or Statistical Artefact?' (2001) JEPP 809–10.

21 See e.g. Gerda Falkner, Oliver Treib, Miriam Hartlapp and Simone Leiber, *Complying with Europe: EU Harmonization and Soft Law in the Member States* (Cambridge University Press 2005); Tanja Börzel, Tobias Hofmann, Diana Panke and Carina Sprungk, 'Obstinate and Inefficient: Why Member States Do Not Comply with European Law' (2010) Comp Pol Stud 1363–90.

22 Case 247/87 *Starfruit v Commission* [1989] ECR 291.

23 Case 7/68 *Commission v Italy* [1968] ECR 423, 428.

24 See e.g. case C-562/07 *Commission v Spain* [2009] ECR I-9553. The doctrine talks about the principle of selective enforcement. Hofmann, Rowe and Türk, *Administrative Law and Policy of the European Union*, n 7, 748.

towards a clear prioritization of certain types of infringements[25] (which, in the environmental field, entails pursuing 'only' serious breaches of EU environmental legislation in addition to non-communication of transposition measures and Article 260 TFEU cases),[26] serious questions about the effectiveness of the centralized mechanism for enforcement may be raised. Third, the effectiveness of infringement proceedings can be limited by the excessive length of the proceedings. This can be particularly problematic in this policy area as environmental damage cannot always be undone. In earlier research Hedemann-Robinson noted that on average the time between notification of the letter of formal notice to the defaulting Member State and the notification of the judgment of the CJEU amounts to six years.[27] The length of proceedings may be extended if there is a need to instigate second round infringement proceedings under Article 260 TFEU.[28] The lapse of time may therefore create environmental damage which may be impossible to repair. Interim measures play a 'relatively limited' (though increasingly relevant) role in relation to environmental infringement actions.[29]

---

[25] Communication from the Commission, 'A Europe of results: applying Community law' COM(2007) 502 final, accessed 10 December 2015 at <http://eur-lex.europa.eu/resource.html?uri=cellar:6fc1ad14-7018-485f-bceb-ab767b5c5927.0003.02/DOC_3&format=PDF>.

[26] Communication from the Commission to the European Parliament, the Council, the European Economic and Social Committee and the Committee of the Regions, 'Implementing European Community environmental law' COM(2008) 773 final, accessed 10 December 2015 at <http://eur-lex.europa.eu/legal-content/EN/TXT/PDF/?uri=CELEX:52008DC0773&from=EN>. See further on this point, Susanne Kingston, 'Mind the Gap: Difficulties in Enforcement and the Continuing Unfulfilled Promise of EU Environmental Law', in Susanne Kingston (Ed.), *European Perspectives on Environmental Law and Governance* (Routledge 2013) 149–50.

[27] Hedemann-Robinson, *Enforcement of European Union Environmental Law: Legal Issues and Challenges*, n 18, 168. The period prior to sending the formal notice has now been formalized in the EU Pilot and as a consequence the previously indeterminate time for Commission–Member State negotiations is now limited in most cases to 20 weeks, significantly speeding up the amount of time taken to process infringement cases, see Chapter 2 of this volume.

[28] Hedemann-Robinson has assessed that as at the end of 2006 the average length of second round proceedings under Article 228(2) EC (the predecessor to Article 260(2) TFEU) was approximately 13 years: see Martin Hedemann-Robinson, 'Article 228(2) EC and the Enforcement of EC Environmental Law: A Case of Environmental Justice Delayed and Denied? An Analysis of Recent Legal Developments' (2006) EELR 317. However, this has now been shortened considerably since the introduction of the Lisbon reforms which removes the requirement of the reasoned opinion stage under Article 260(2).

[29] Martin Hedemann-Robinson, 'Enforcement of EU Environmental Law and the Role of Interim Relief Measures' (2010) EEELR 204.

All in all, it can be concluded that the road to an effective centralized enforcement of EU environmental law is paved with several obstacles, linked to the limited investigative capacity of the Commission, its selective infringement policy and the duration of the infringement proceedings. As will be shown below, the decentralized enforcement system cannot, as of today, fully compensate for these shortcomings.

2. EFFECTIVE DECENTRALIZED ENFORCEMENT AND ACCOMMODATING THE DISTINCT NATURE OF EU ENVIRONMENTAL LAW

The shortcomings of the centralized enforcement system render it of utmost importance for the EU to be able to rely on private litigation before the national courts to effectively enforce EU environmental legislation.[30] This has long been emphasized by the Commission itself.[31] National courts, however, are only able to intervene and repair instances of non-compliance when cases are brought before them by litigants and when the violation of EU environmental law can be successfully pleaded before them. In cases involving the infringement of EU environmental law, this is far from self-evident. Environmental law embodies certain features which can restrict the avenues of enforcement available for litigants and can also impair effective control by national courts. Furthermore, there are limitations encumbent in national standing rules and the implementation of the Aarhus Convention as well as the requirements imposed by the EU doctrines of direct effect and state liability.

---

[30] Please note that EU environmental law can be violated also by EU institutions. In such cases, private applicants are entitled to bring annulment proceedings according to Article 263 TFEU. This topic falls outside the scope of this contribution. For an extensive overview of the shortcomings of annulment proceedings in environmental matters, see Mariolina Eliantonio, 'Towards an Ever Dirtier Europe? The Restrictive Standing of Environmental NGOs before the European Courts and the Aarhus Convention' (2011) CYELP 69.

[31] The reliance of the EU on decentralized enforcement before the national courts has long been recognized as a necessary part of its enforcement strategy. In a 1996 Communication, the Commission reflected openly for the first time on the limited role and impact that infringement proceedings could have in relation to the enforcement of EU environmental law. In this light, in the Communication, the Commission chose to emphasize that it should prioritize its focus on infringements of long-term strategic importance, namely non-communication and non-conformity cases. Communication from the Commission, 'Implementing environmental law' COM(1996) 500 final.

2.1. National Standing Rules and the Aarhus Convention: Securing 'Access to Justice'

The conception of the environment as a 'common good' and the rules aimed at protecting the environment, which provide for the interest of no one and everyone at the same time, have led to difficulties in enforcing EU environmental law before national courts. In 2011, the European Commission stated that '[e]ffective enforcement of EU law is of utmost importance for citizens and businesses alike' and that '[r]ights which cannot be enforced in practice are worthless. Where substantive EU rights are infringed, citizens and businesses must be able to enforce the rights granted to them by EU legislation.'[32]

However, the need to preserve and strive for the effective enforcement of EU law seems to presuppose the existence of a 'substantive EU right' which has been violated by the national authorities (or by private parties). This requirement is certainly not excluded in environmental matters,[33] but fulfilling it is problematic in this policy field due to the nature of environmental law itself. The vast majority of environmental measures (such as those contained in the Habitats Directive[34] and the Birds Directive)[35] protect interests of a diffuse nature rather than individual rights or interests. In general, such measures do not confer any rights on individuals but serve the collective public interest in the protection of biodiversity.[36] In such cases, according to the applicable national procedural rules, there is no one party who will have standing before a national court[37] as nobody

---

32 Commission Staff Working Document, 'Towards a Coherent European Approach to Collective Redress' SEC(2011) 173 final, 1, accessed 10 December 2015 at <http://ec.europa.eu/dgs/health_consumer/dgs_consultations/ca/docs/cr_consultation_paper_en.pdf>.

33 See e.g. on air quality, case C-237/07 *Janecek* [2008] ECR I-6221.

34 Dir 92/43 of 21 May 1992 on the conservation of natural habitats and of wild fauna and flora [1992] OJ L206/7.

35 Dir 2009/147 of the European Parliament and of the Council of 30 November 2009 on the conservation of wild birds [2010] OJ L20/7.

36 See further on this point, Chris Backes and Mariolina Eliantonio, 'Access to Courts for Environmental NGOs at European and National Level: What Improvements and What Room for Improvement since Maastricht?', in Maartje de Visser and Anne-Pieter van der Mei (Eds), *The Treaty on European Union 1993–2013: Reflections from Maastricht* (Intersentia 2013) 559–60.

37 That, is, excluding the rare cases of legal systems offering the possibility of an *actio popularis*, i.e. where anyone can bring a claim against the actions of public authorities without showing that his or her rights or interests have been violated. This possibility is very limited, and, as comparative research has shown, almost non-existent in environmental matters with some notable exceptions, such

can prove an infringement of his or her rights or interests by a public authority. In view of this characteristic of environmental law, the role of non-governmental organizations (NGOs) is of fundamental importance. It follows that the effectiveness of the enforcement of EU environmental law is highly dependent on the ability of environmental NGOs to bring claims for alleged violations of environmental provisions before national courts.[38]

The Aarhus Convention,[39] a UN Convention,[40] was drafted in order to enhance the possibilities for environmental NGOs to supplement the lack of interest or ability of citizens to bring environmental claims before national courts and enable them to take action against infringements of environmental law. The Convention is structured around three main pillars: access to information, public participation and access to justice in environmental matters. It binds not only the EU, but also the Member States when they are acting within the scope of application of EU law.[41] In assessing the effective enforcement of environmental law, it is necessary to focus on the access to justice pillar and its two key provisions: Article 9(2) provides that the contracting parties should ensure that concerned members of the public with a qualified interest[42] have access to a review

---

as the case of Portugal. See further, Mariolina Eliantonio, Chris Backes, C.H. van Rhee, Taru Spronken and Anna Berlee, *Standing Up for Your Right(s) in Europe* (Intersentia 2012) Section 4.6, 69–70, accessed 10 December 2015 at <http://www.europarl.europa.eu/committees/fr/studiesdownload.html?languageDocument=EN&file=75651>; Sophie Roussel and Olivier Fuchs, 'Accès Des Citoyens à La Justice et Organisations Juridictionnelles en Matière d'Environnement, Spécificités Nationales et Influences du Droit de l'union Européenne: Rapport General', 8, accessed 10 December 2015 at <http://www.aca-europe.eu/seminars/Bruxelles2012/Rapport_general.pdf>.

[38] That is, if one excludes the possibility of a public prosecutor, ombudsman or other public authority in charge of pursuing environmental violations in the public interest.

[39] See n 6.

[40] Specifically it was developed within the United Nations Economic Commission for Europe (UNECE).

[41] The Convention was adopted by the then European Community on 17 February 2005 by Dec 2005/370 on the conclusion, on behalf of the European Community, of the Convention on access to information, public participation in decision-making and access to justice in environmental matters [2005] OJ L124/1. It should also be added that, since all the Member States have ratified the Aarhus Convention, this international instrument is binding on them outside the scope of application of EU law as well. However, in such cases, the effect of the Convention within the legal order of the Member States is dependent upon their constitutional orders.

[42] That is, either (1) a sufficient interest or (2) maintaining impairment of a right (where the administrative procedural law of a state requires this as a precondition).

procedure to challenge the substantive and procedural legality of decisions concerning projects which can have a significant environmental impact; Article 9(3) imposes a general obligation on the signatories to provide wide access for the public to access review procedures to challenge the legality of all kinds of decisions affecting the environment.[43]

2.1.1. Article 9(2) Aarhus Convention

The EU has taken steps to align Member States' legislation with Article 9(2) through the enactment of Directive 2003/35/EC.[44] Like the Convention, the Directive proposes two models of access to justice and allows the Member States the option of choosing whether to grant standing for the 'public concerned' where an applicant can show the impairment of a right *or* when it is able to show a sufficient interest. For both these options, the Directive mandates that the national rules on standing must be consistent with the overall objective of giving the public concerned wide access to justice. To this end, any NGO promoting environmental interests and meeting any standing requirements under national law shall be deemed as capable of showing sufficient interest. Such organizations shall also be deemed to have rights capable of being impaired in a legal system that has opted for a rights-based approach. The freedom of Member States to choose a standing regime

---

[43] See further on Article 9 of the Aarhus Convention, Luc Lavrysen, 'The Aarhus Convention: Between Environmental Protection and Human Rights', in Paul Martens, Marc Bossuyt, Marie-Francoise Rigaux, Bernadette Renauld (Eds), *Liber amicorum Michel Melchior* (Anthemis 2010) 663; Jerzy Jendroska, 'Accès à la justice: remarque sur le statut juridique et le champ des obligations de la convention d'Aarhus dans le contexte de l'Union Européenne' (2009) RJE Special Issue 31; Thomas von Danwitz, 'Aarhus Konvention: Umweltinformation, Öffentlichkeitsbeteiligung, Zugang zu den Gerichten' (2004) *Neue Zeitschrift für Verwaltungsrecht* 272; Martin Hedemann-Robinson, 'EU Implementation of the Aarhus Convention's Third Pillar: Back to the Future over Access to Environmental Justice? Part 1' (2014) EEELR 102.

[44] Dir 2003/35/EC of the European Parliament and of the Council of 26 May 2003 providing for public participation in respect of the drawing up of certain plans and programmes relating to the environment and amending with regard to public participation and access to justice [2003] OJ L156/17. This Directive amended two other Directives. On this point, see Birgit Dette, 'The Aarhus Convention and Legislative Initiatives for its Implementation', in Thomas Ormond, Martin Führ and Regine Barth (Eds), *Liber amicorum Betty Gebers* (Lexxion 2006) 63. Further on the interplay between the Aarhus Convention and EU law, Jonas Ebbeson, 'Access to Justice at the National Level: Impact of the Aarhus Convention and European Union Law', in Marc Pallemaerts (Ed.), *The Aarhus Convention at Ten: Interactions and Tensions between Conventional International Law and EU Environmental Law* (Europa Law Publishing 2011) 247.

creating a more or less limited enforcement framework for NGOs in environmental matters is thus limited by the overarching requirement to ensure wide access to justice. However, Directive 2003/35 only applies to procedural rules concerning legal actions brought against projects which can have a *significant environmental impact*. It does not apply to all other environmental measures such as measures taken for the protection of an endangered species under the Habitats Directive or permits to discharge waste water.

The transposition of Article 9(2) of the Aarhus Convention through Directive 2003/35 has been in general rather smooth. Recent comparative research by legal scholars including this author has shown that these provisions have been correctly transposed in most of the Member States examined. In the majority of the nine EU legal systems surveyed, the legislation on access to justice was amended in order to adequately transpose the Directive or the existing law has been interpreted by the courts in such a way as to ensure compliance with the Aarhus Convention and Directive 2003/35.[45] However, there are also Member States in which the legislation and case law has not been changed because the Member States in question are convinced that their national law is already compliant. For some Member States such as France and Italy, the outcome of this assessment may be correct. For some other legal systems such as Poland, Germany and Belgium, it is either doubtful whether they currently meet the requirements of the Convention, or it is very likely that they do not.[46] Finally, some Member States are evidently in breach. Indeed, their national legislation has been declared by the CJEU to be in breach of Directive 2003/35 (and, therefore, indirectly, Article 9(2) of the Aarhus Convention). The most prominent example being Germany. In all cases where issues of non or incorrect implementation of the Directive have been referred to the CJEU,[47] the national legislation has been subsequently amended in order to comply with the EU requirements.[48]

---

45 See further Mariolina Eliantonio, Chris Backes, C.H. van Rhee, Taru Spronken and Anna Berlee, *Standing Up for Your Right(s) in Europe*, n 37, Sections 4.7.4 and 4.10.1; Sophie Roussel and Olivier Fuchs, 'Accès Des Citoyens à La Justice et Organisations Juridictionnelles en Matière d'Environnement, Spécificités Nationales et Influences du Droit de l'union Européenne: Rapport General', n 37, 16–17.

46 Ibid.

47 Case C-263/08 *Djurgården-Lilla Värtans Miljöskyddsförening v Stockholms kommun genom dess marknämnd* [2009] ECR I-9967. For a comment on this case, see Ainé Ryall, 'Comment to *Djurgården*' (2010) CMLRev 1511. Case C-115/09 *Bund für Umwelt und Naturschutz Deutschland, Landesverband Nordrhein-Westfalen eV v Bezirksregierung Arnsberg* [2001] ECR I-3673.

48 For Sweden see § 13, Chapter 6, Miljöbalk (1998:808) accessed 10 December 2015 at <http://www.notisum.se/rnp/sls/lag/19980808.HTM>. For Germany, see

2.1.2. Article 9(3) Aarhus Convention

A more general provision on access to justice covering all environmental matters, and not just those of significant impact, transposing the requirements of Article 9(3), is currently lacking. In 2003, the Commission presented a Proposal for a Directive of the European Parliament and of the Council on access to justice in environmental matters[49] which would give effect to Article 9(3) of the Convention. The Directive has not been adopted to date on the ground that 'Member States remained unconvinced that legislative action at EU level was needed to implement Article 9(3)'[50] and that the proposal was overly intrusive into the national judicial systems of the Member States.[51] Since 2012 the Commission has been preparing a new proposal for a directive which takes the legal situation in the Member States and the recent case law of the CJEU into account.[52]

Meanwhile, in the absence of EU harmonizing measures giving effect to Article 9(3), the CJEU has been required to determine whether Article 9(3) could be directly relied upon by individuals before national courts.[53] In its 2011 *VLK* case, a preliminary ruling submitted by a Slovakian court, the Court denied direct effect to this provision arguing that it was not sufficiently precise and unconditional. However, it added that national courts had a duty to interpret their national law in a way which is to the fullest

---

the ruling of the Higher Administrative Court of Muenster, 1 December 2011, 8 D 58/09 AK; and the ruling of the Higher Administrative Court of Mannheim, 20 July 2011, 10 S 2102/09. Legislative amendment: BGBl. I, 95. See further, Mariolina Eliantonio, 'Collective Redress in Environmental Matters in the EU: A Role Model or a "Problem Child"?' (2014) LIEI 257–73.

49 Proposal for a Directive of the European Parliament and of the Council on access to justice in environmental matters, COM(2003) 624 final.

50 European Commission, 'Explanatory Consultation Document', 2, accessed 10 December 2015 at <http://ec.europa.eu/environment/consultations/pdf/access.pdf>.

51 European Commission, 'Roadmap, Commission Initiative on Access to Justice in Environmental Matters at Member State Level in the Field of EU Environment Policy', 1, accessed 10 December at <http://ec.europa.eu/smart-regulation/impact/planned_ia/docs/2013_env_013_access_to_justice_en.pdf>.

52 The Commission has undertaken a number of studies: European Commission, 'The Aarhus Convention: 2012/2013 Access to Justice Studies', accessed 10 December 2015 at <http://ec.europa.eu/environment/aarhus/access_studies.htm>.

53 Case C-240/09 *Lesoochranárske zoskupenie VLK v Ministerstvo životného prostredia Slovenskej republiky* [2011] ECR I-1255. For a comment on this case, as well as the *Trianel* ruling discussed above, see Mariolina Eliantonio, 'Case C-240/09 *Lesoochranárske zoskupenie VLK v. Ministerstvo životného prostredia Slovenskej republiky*, Judgment of the Court of Justice (Grand Chamber) of 8 March 2011' (2012) CMLRev 767.

extent possible consistent with the objectives laid down in Article 9(3) of the Aarhus Convention. As a consequence of this ruling, the referring court, by way of consistent interpretation (or indirect effect), admitted the NGO as a party to the proceedings.[54] This approach has been followed by national courts in other Member States.[55] In general, this ruling implies that national courts are under the duty to test all the requirements for access to court for NGOs against Article 9(3) of the Aarhus Convention and, if necessary, allow claims by NGOs in environmental matters even where national rules on standing would not allow it. While this development can be considered as a positive step towards achieving compliance with the standards set by the Aarhus Convention and in improving the effective enforcement of EU environmental law, it cannot be overstated that it may also bring about a certain degree of uncertainty. Potentially, there could be wide differences in the assessments of the courts of 28 Member States as to whether their national procedural standards are in compliance with Article 9(3).

In the aftermath of the case law on Article 9(3) and the potential state of uncertainty it could bring about, the Commission is very keen on promoting a new legislative agenda. In the 2012 Communication, the Commission explicitly referred to the Court's case law and reminded national courts of their duty of consistent interpretation.[56] Furthermore, the Commission has launched a series of initiatives including a public consultation[57] in order to prepare the ground for a possible legislative initiative. In particular, a study conducted under the direction of Jan Darpö discussed four options which the Commission had brought forward to consider for future actions.[58] The first option would be to enact a directive on access to justice

---

[54] These cases can be found with numbers 3Sžp/49/2009, 3Sžp/50/2009, 3Sžp/48/2009 and 3Sžp/47/2009 on the website of the Supreme Court of the Slovak Republic, accessed 10 December 2015 at <http://www.supcourt.gov.sk/rozhodnutia>. The role of the doctrine of indirect effect in the private enforcement of EU law is discussed in more detail in Chapter 1 of this volume.

[55] For Germany, see the ruling of the Lower Administrative Court of Wiesbaden, 10 October 2011, 4 K 757/11 and the ruling of the Lower Administrative Court of Augsburg, 13 February 2013, Au 2 S 13.143. See for a Finnish case, the ruling of the Finnish Supreme Administrative Court n. 49/2011, accessed 10 December 2015 at <http://www.finlex.fi/fi/oikeus/kho/vuosikirjat/2011/201101351?search[type]=pika&search[pika]=2011%3A49>.

[56] Commission Communication on 'Improving the delivery of benefits from EU environment Measures: building confidence through better knowledge and responsiveness' COM(2012) 095 final, n 1, 9.

[57] Accessed 10 December 2015 at <http://ec.europa.eu/environment/aarhus/consultations.htm>.

[58] Jan Darpö, 'Effective Justice? Synthesis Report of the Study on the Implementation of Articles 9.3 and 9.4 of the Aarhus Convention in Seventeen

reflecting the legal regime of the Member States concerning NGO standing and the recent case law of the CJEU which essentially mirrors Directive 2003/35 with regard to Article 9(2). The second option was to reiterate the old proposal which had stalled in the Council since 2003.[59] Third, it proposed using soft law instruments to promote collaboration between national courts possibly supplemented by Commission guidelines explaining the significance and implications of the case law. Finally, it suggested using infringement proceedings as a tool to promote compliance with the requirements of the CJEU's case law.

It is argued that the study rightfully concluded that a legislative measure should be adopted. It deemed it the most effective way of achieving the aims set out in Article 9(3) and ensuring the effective enforcement of EU environmental law. In particular, the study considered that the 'soft law' option would leave national differences intact and would not provide any incentive for Member States to comply with CJEU case law. The infringement proceedings option would be too time and resource consuming and would not ensure the necessary uniformity. Furthermore, neither of these options are considered to guarantee a sufficient level of legal certainty and a level playing field for NGOs throughout the EU.[60] As a next step, the Commission has produced a roadmap document for the purposes of an impact assessment review.[61] The roadmap is subject to ongoing review and awaiting formal approval.[62]

Given the legal uncertainty generated by the lack of transposition of Article 9(3) and the unsuitability of the alternative mechanisms (i.e. the use of soft law for streamlining national procedural standards or infringement proceedings), it is certainly desirable to set common EU criteria for

---

of the Member States of the European Union' (2012) accessed 10 December 2015 at <http://ec.europa.eu/environment/aarhus/pdf/synthesis%20report%20on%20access%20to%20justice.pdf>. New link: <http://ec.europa.eu/environment/aarhus/pdf/synthesis%20report%20on%20access%20to%20justice.pdf>.

59 For the difference between these two options, see ibid, 24.

60 Ibid, 23. Please note that this preference also seems to be shared by those who participated in the public consultation launched by the Commission on this theme: <http://ec.europa.eu/yourvoice/ipm/forms/dispatch?userstate=DisplayPublishedResults&form=A2JUST> accessed 10 December 2015 (see in particular under question 12(c)).

61 European Commission, 'Roadmap, Commission Initiative on Access to Justice in Environmental Matters at Member State Level in the Field of EU Environment Policy', n 51.

62 See European Commission, Roadmaps 2014 <http://ec.europa.eu/smart-regulation/impact/planned_ia/roadmaps_2014_en.htm#ENV> accessed 10 December 2015.

NGO standing. Having different national procedural rules may create divergent results when national courts apply the same EU environmental provision endangering the effective enforcement of EU environmental law. Furthermore, the Commission indicates that the current state of uncertainty raises a number of further problems. First, there is a failure to maximize the benefits of environmental legislation and potential non-compliance with EU law. Second, this in turn may create market distortions of competition and a lack of legal certainty for investments. Finally, a growing number of complaints which are not resolved at national level will lead to complaints overwhelming the Commission who is seen as the final enforcer of EU law.[63]

The analysis carried out above shows that the effectiveness of decentralized enforcement of EU environmental law requires environmental NGOs to have access to court and to be able to engage in litigation. The possibility to do so has been enhanced by the EU ratification of the UN Aarhus Convention, but is undermined by the fact that it has not been fully transposed at the EU level. Whilst Article 9(2) has been generally well transposed, Article 9(3) has not been transposed yet, leaving national courts with the task of interpreting their standing rules in such a way as to ensure an effective enforcement of EU environmental law. The Commission is currently in the process of finalizing a proposal on a new directive on access to justice, the destiny of which remains uncertain.

2.2. Private Enforcement of EU Environmental Law: The Limitations of Direct Effect and State Liability

The nature of environmental law and its aim to protect diffuse (rather than individual) interests results in a lack of standing for individuals in a great number of cases where there is a breach and in the necessary reliance on environmental NGOs to promote the effective enforcement of EU environmental law. However, even when access to court is gained by individuals or associations, further constitutional hurdles present themselves.

The doctrine of direct effect gives individuals the possibility to enforce before national courts the rights granted to them by EU law.[64] However, most provisions of environmental law are not intended to confer rights on individuals and therefore an orthodox application of the notion of direct effect can bar private applicants from relying on EU environmental law

---

[63] European Commission, 'Roadmap, Commission Initiative on Access to Justice in Environmental Matters at Member State Level in the Field of EU Environment Policy', n 51, 3.

[64] Case 26/62 *van Gend en Loos* [1963] ECR-1.

before national courts.[65] However, some scholars have considered that direct effect should prescind from the existence of a right.[66] This interpretation is justified by the need to ensure an effective enforcement of EU law in light of the nature of environmental law and is to a certain extent supported by the CJEU's case law. In its *Kraaijeveld*[67] and *Linster*[68] judgments, the Court seems to have detached direct effect from the existence of a right and given individuals the possibility of enforcing legal duties enshrined in environmental provisions intended to benefit the public interest.[69] This allows a provision of EU law to be regarded as having direct effect if it is sufficiently precise and unconditional in its wording.[70] Such a development could certainly be seen as favouring the effective enforcement of EU environmental law since it seems to create, as some authors have suggested, a 'public interest effect' whereby individuals are allowed to rely on EU law provisions for the collective interest.[71] However, because many provisions in the environmental field impose only broad obligations on the national authorities, few norms in this area fulfil the precision and unconditionality criteria.[72] This often leaves applicants without the possibility of pleading the violation of EU environmental law before their national courts.

In addition, the nature of environmental law and its aim to protect diffuse interests may prove a hurdle for the purpose of state liability actions. As is well known, the first condition to be fulfilled by an individual seeking to hold a Member State liable in damages for the violation of EU law is that the relevant provision must be intended to confer rights on an individual.[73] This hurdle may prove insurmountable in many environmental cases. Accordingly, Prechal and Hancher have argued that:

---

[65] See further, Pål Wennerås, *The Enforcement of EC Environmental Law* (Oxford University Press 2007) 18.

[66] Sacha Prechal and Leigh Hancher, 'Individual Environmental Rights: Conceptual Pollution in EU Environmental Law?' (2012) YEEL 98.

[67] Case C-72/95 *Kraaijeveld* [1996] ECR I-5403.

[68] Case C-287/98 *Linster* [2000] ECR I-6917.

[69] Hedemann-Robinson, *Enforcement of European Union Environmental Law: Legal Issues and Challenges*, n 18, 241 ff.

[70] Jan H. Jans and Hans H.B. Vedder, *European Environmental Law* (3rd edition, Europa Law Publishing 2008) 170–71.

[71] Prechal and Hancher, n 66, 89.

[72] See e.g. the case C-236/92 *Comitato di Coordinamento per la Difesa della Cava and others v Regione Lombardia and others* [1994] ECR I-483 and the further discussion in Hedemann-Robinson, *Enforcement of European Union Environmental Law: Legal Issues and Challenges*, n 18, 225 ff.

[73] Joined cases C-46/93 and C-48/93 *Brasserie du Pêcheur SA v Bundesrepublik Deutschland and The Queen v Secretary of State for Transport, ex parte: Factortame Ltd and others* [1996] ECR I-1029.

> as long as liability and injunctions are linked to the issue of infringement of an individual right [. . .] these remedies will not necessarily work for directives which seek to protect general environmental interest, as for example in the field of habitat protection.[74]

There is some support in the case law of the Court that this rights-based approach to liability has been modified. In its *Wells*[75] judgment, the EU environmental provision at stake (concerning the environmental impact assessment procedure) clearly did not confer rights on individuals. In addition to granting direct effect, the CJEU also held that an individual may be entitled to monetary compensation in spite of the fact that the provision breached did not confer a right directly upon her. As this statement has only been made *obiter*, it is not yet clear whether this is a trend which signifies a change of approach on the part of the Court of Justice. It has been argued[76] that the lack of a clear stance on the possibility for individuals to claim compensation for breaches of EU environmental law has been remedied by the adoption of the Environmental Liability Directive which is aimed at preventing and repairing environmental damage.[77]

3. THE FUTURE OF ENFORCEMENT OF EU ENVIRONMENTAL LAW: NEW METHODS, NEW ACTORS . . . NEW TRENDS?

In light of the shortcomings of both centralized and decentralized enforcement systems to secure the effective enforcement of EU environmental law and policy, a range of new initiatives have emerged to complement these classic EU law enforcement mechanisms. This new strategy can be considered as an exemplification of 'new governance'[78] which is not solely typical

---

74 Prechal and Hancher, n 66, 108.

75 Case C-201/02 *Wells* [2004] ECR I-723.

76 Michael Dougan, *National Remedies before the Court of Justice: Issues of Harmonisation and Differentiation* (Hart, 2004) 45.

77 Dir 2004/35 of the European Parliament and the Council of 21 April 2004 on environmental liability with regard to the prevention and remedying of environmental damage [2004] OJ L143/56.

78 See further on this, Grainne de Búrca and Joanne Scott, *Law and New Governance in the EU and the US* (Hart Publishing 2006). Specifically on environmental law, see Ingmar von Homeyer, 'Emerging Experimentalism in EU Environmental Governance', in Charles F. Sabel and Jonathan Zeitlin (Eds), *Experimentalist Governance in the European Union: Towards a New Architecture* (Oxford University Press 2010) 121–50; Neil Gunningham, 'Environmental Law, Regulation and Governance: Shifting Architectures' (2009) JEL 179.

of environmental policy. Broadly speaking, three main features distinguish 'new governance' from traditional forms of EU law-making: first, its emphasis on flexibility over strict command-and-control methods and the use of soft law over binding legislation; second, its collaborative nature and the inclusion of a range of private and public actors in the decision-making process; third, its responsiveness and adaptive capacity, thanks to the importance attached to information and knowledge generation.[79]

Whilst binding rules imposing requirements for licences, setting standards for inspections and providing judicially enforceable prohibitions still constitute the backbone of the EU's 'enforcement style' in this particular policy area, it is the EU institutions themselves, and in particular the Commission, which have promoted the use of new governance tools aimed at assisting in the prevention of breaches by Member States.[80] In the following section, two examples of these 'new governance' initiatives will be discussed, namely the use of soft law and networked enforcement. Their usefulness towards a more effective enforcement of EU environmental law will be examined.

3.1. The Emergence of 'Soft Law' as an Enforcement Tool

Environmental law is certainly one of the EU policy fields which has seen a burgeoning use of soft law measures. Virtually every area of environmental law has seen the emergence of guidance documents, mostly authored by the Commission, and often in cooperation with Member States. The virtues and vices of soft law have been extensively elaborated elsewhere.[81] In the context of enforcement, guidance documents can play an important role in ensuring the effective and coherent implementation of EU measures.[82] By indicating how the Commission will make use of its

---

[79] Maria Lee, *EU Environmental Law, Governance and Decision-Making* (Hart 2014) 81.

[80] See, for instance, the Commission Communication on 'Implementing European Community environmental law' COM(2008) 773 final, n 26. In this Communication, the Commission advocated the need to use exchanges of information and expertise as a way to resolve implementation and enforcement issues.

[81] Linda Senden, 'Soft Post-Legislative Rulemaking: A Time for More Stringent Control' (2013) ELJ 57; Joanne Scott, 'In Legal Limbo: Post-Legislative Guidance as a Challenge for European Administrative Law' (2011) CLMRev 329; Ingmar von Homeyer, 'Emerging Experimentalism in EU Environmental Governance', n 78, 121–50; Joanne Scott and David M. Trubek, 'Mind the Gap: Law and New Approaches to Governance in the European Union' (2002) ELJ 1–18.

[82] Linda Senden, *Soft Law in European Community Law* (Hart 2004) 146–8, 151–2.

enforcement powers or interpret certain rules, Member States can adapt their own behaviour (or that of their national authorities) where necessary. Moreover, it has been argued that post-legislative guidance may have the function of 'reassuring' the national authorities that they are acting in compliance with the law, at least those that act in accordance with it.[83] Guidance documents may be useful in preventing infringement proceedings in the first place since national authorities may correct existing instances of non-compliance of their own motion, when, for example, infringements are not intentional.

From the perspective of the Commission, guidance documents may help the Commission substantiate a breach of an underlying norm. Specifically in the field of environmental policy, it has been shown that where legislative provisions are complex or open (in that they provide for vague standards such as the 'good water status' contained in the Water Framework Directive), guidance documents prove useful for the Commission in infringement proceedings since it is in these situations that conflicting interpretations of a norm are more likely to occur. Guidance documents which are agreed in a collaborative way by the Commission and Member States working together are particularly useful in infringement proceedings. When an understanding of a vague term is agreed upon, Member States are less likely to challenge these understandings in infringement proceedings.[84]

In the field of environmental law, two important examples of soft law are the Best Available Techniques Reference Documents (BREFs) adopted in the context of the Industrial Emissions Directive (IED)[85] and the Guidance Documents issued in the framework of the Water Framework Directive (WFD).[86] The BREFs[87] provide guidance on the application of the best available techniques for categories of industrial activities listed in Annex I

---

[83] See Scott, 'In Legal Limbo: Post-Legislative Guidance as a Challenge for European Administrative Law', n 81, 330, specifically in the area of environmental law.

[84] Emilia Korkea-aho, 'Watering Down the Court of Justice? The Dynamics between Network Implementation and Article 258 TFEU Litigation' (2014) ELJ 664–5.

[85] Dir 2010/75 of the European Parliament of 24 November 2010 on industrial emissions (integrated pollution prevention and control) [2010] OJ L334/17. Further on this, Maria Lee, *EU Environmental Law, Governance and Decision-Making*, n 79, 108.

[86] Dir 2000/60 of the European Parliament and of the Council of 23 October 2000 establishing a framework for Community action in the field of water policy [2000] OJ L327/1.

[87] All BREFs are retrievable online, on <http://eippcb.jrc.ec.europa.eu/reference/> accessed 10 December 2010.

to the IED and serve to fill in the vague requirement of having to apply the 'best available techniques' (BAT) when national authorities have to issue permits for the industrial activities covered by the Directive. The BREFs thus may be considered as serving the purposes of a better enforcement of EU environmental law by providing a 'framework' within which national authorities can be reassured that they are acting in conformity with EU law.

As an instrument containing open-ended concepts such as 'good water status',[88] the WFD requires subsequent specifications for the purpose of its implementation. To this end, several guidance documents have been elaborated with the aim of providing technical and scientific support for the Member States in the implementation of the WFD: 'They embody an impressive number of technical specifications, clarifications and recommendations on a variety of issues pertinent to implementation of the WFD'.[89] Once again, it can be argued that guidance documents lead to better enforcement of environmental law as they provide Member States with detailed information on how to act in accordance with the WFD and therefore avoid infringement proceedings.

As with all soft law measures, both the BREFs and the Guidance Documents issued under the WFD are not legally binding in the formal sense, but nevertheless can have important practical and legal effects.[90] Under the predecessor of the IED, namely the IPPC Directive, the BREFs constituted non-binding guidance only.[91] The BREFs themselves expressly stated that they do not set legally binding standards and are designed to give guidance information for industry, Member States and the public.[92] The non-binding nature of the BREFs was confirmed by the Court.[93] Nevertheless, the later IED enhanced the status of the BREFs

---

88 See Article 4, of Dir 2000/60, n 86.

89 Korkea-aho, 'Watering Down the Court of Justice? The Dynamics between Network Implementation and Article 258 TFEU Litigation', n 84, 656.

90 Senden, 'Soft Post-Legislative Rulemaking: A Time for More Stringent Control', n 81, 57; Scott, 'In Legal Limbo: Post-Legislative Guidance as a Challenge for European Administrative Law', n 81, 329.

91 It was indeed sufficient if Member States ensured that the competent authorities take account of 'the general principles [. . .] when they determine the conditions of the permit'. See Article 3(2) of Dir 2008/1 of the European Parliament and the Council of 15 January 2008 concerning integrated pollution prevention and control [2008] OJ L24/8.

92 See e.g. the BREF on the intensive rearing of poultry and pigs (version of 2003), n 87, 274.

93 Case C-473/07 *Association nationale pour la protection des eaux et rivières-TOS and Association OABA v Ministère de l'Ecologie, du Développement et de l'Aménagement durables* [2009] ECR I-319, para 30.

and made a specific part of the BREFs, the (BAT) conclusions, 'the reference' for the permitting framework, rather than one factor to be taken into consideration.[94] This means that the BAT conclusions now contain legally binding standards with which Member States need to adhere and from which derogations can be invoked only in limited circumstances.[95] The 28 Guidance Documents produced under the WFD are, on the other hand, still of non-binding force, but they constitute a powerful tool to give flesh to the vague notions of the WFD.

Whether guidance documents enhance the effective enforcement of EU environmental law is not an easy question to answer. Political scientists have acknowledged that 'in spite of strong normative assumptions regarding the alleged effectiveness of soft law forms of regulation to facilitate better regulation in heterogeneous environmental regimes, the actual capacity of novel regulatory approaches is rarely being addressed in a systematic way'.[96] There is thus a lack of empirical evidence as to the actual usefulness of guidance documents which should be tackled in future research. An empirical study conducted on the application of the IPPC Directive, the predecessor of the IED, in four countries has shown, for example, that the effectiveness of guidance documents is strongly dependent on a number of factors including the material and cognitive resources available in terms of the administrative capacity and knowledge and expertise on the functioning of the Directive by national authorities and business actors, mutual trust amongst the stakeholders involved and credible national and EU pressure.[97]

3.2. Networked Implementation and Enforcement

A second tool of 'new governance' which has found application in the environmental field is that of networks, both in the application and in the enforcement phases. Networks stress the collaborative nature of 'new governance' initiatives aimed at creating horizontal links between actors at different levels and/or different jurisdictions. As such governance networks may be described as structures of autonomous actors who are in

---

[94] Article 14(3) of Dir 2010/75, n 85. For a discussion on the new status of the BREFs under the IED Directive, see Maria Lee, *EU Environmental Law, Governance and Decision-Making*, n 79, 119 ff.

[95] See Article 15(3) and (4) of Directive 2010/75, n 85.

[96] Charalampos Koutalakis, Aron Buzogany and Tanja A. Börzel, 'When Soft Regulation Is Not Enough: The Integrated Pollution Prevention and Control Directive of the European Union' (2010) Regul Gov 331.

[97] Ibid, 339–40.

a relationship of interdependence and horizontal cooperation for the sake of achieving common public goals.[98] The literature on networks is vast and several attempts have been made at categorizing networks according to, for example, their membership, function and level of formality.[99] The Commission has showed itself very fond of 'network governance' and has in several official documents stressed the importance of networks for the implementation of EU law.[100] The added value of networks is expected to be manifold and has been elaborated on extensively before and need not be discussed in depth here.[101] Suffice to say that amongst the many advantages of this form of cooperation, networks are capable of bringing together knowledge and expertise that single actors may not possess.[102] Furthermore, they may enable learning experiences for networks participants.[103]

In the field of environmental law, again the WFD and the IED can be regarded as good examples of instruments which entail the creation of 'network-like' structures for the implementation of EU law. In the framework of the WFD, the Common Implementation Strategy (CIS) provides for a joint approach in the implementation of the WFD with networks of experts which include national and EU level authorities as well as experts and stakeholders. It is explicitly aimed at 'allow[ing], as far as possible, a coherent and harmonious implementation of the framework directive'.[104] For this purpose, the CIS has been responsible for 'clarify[ing] and develop[ing], where appropriate, supporting technical

---

98 E.g. Tanja Börzel and Karen Heard-Laureote, 'Networks, EU Multi-Level Governance: Concepts and Contributions' (2009) JPP 137.

99 See e.g. Eva Sørensen and Jacob Torfing, 'Governance Network Research: Towards a Second Generation', in Sørensen and Torfing (Eds), *Theories of Democratic Network Governance* (Palgrave-Macmillan 2007) 1–21.

100 See e.g. Commission of the European Communities, 'Report to the Council and to the European Parliament on cooperation between administrations for enforcement of internal market law: a progress report' COM(96) 20 final; European Commission, 'European Governance: A White Paper' COM(2001) 428 final.

101 For an overview, see Chapter 4 in this volume.

102 Eva Sørensen and Jacob Torfing, 'The Democratic Anchorage of Governance Networks' (2005) SPS 198–9.

103 James S. Mosher and David M. Trubek, 'Alternative Approaches to Governance in the EU: EU Social Policy and the European Employment Strategy' (2003) J Com Mar St 76–7.

104 'Common Implementation Strategy for the Water Framework Directive (2000/60/EC)', Strategic Document as agreed by the Water Directors under Swedish Presidency, 2 May 2001, 2, accessed 10 December 2015 at <http://ec.europa.eu/environment/water/water-framework/objectives/pdf/strategy.pdf>.

and scientific information to assist in the practical implementation of the Directive'[105] and it provides a forum for exchange of best practices and experiences in implementation. One of the most important tasks of CIS has been to develop the guidance documents mentioned above. Also, it seems to have been useful for the Commission for gathering information which has subsequently been used in infringement proceedings.[106]

In addition, the IED features an interesting system of cooperation linked to the so-called 'Seville process' aimed at identifying the 'best available techniques' standards. This process evolved initially outside the framework of the IPPC Directive, the predecessor to the IED. It has now been formalized under Article 13 of the IED. The Seville process is managed by the European IPPC Bureau, which carries out its work through Technical Working Groups (TWGs). These informal groups which comprise technical experts representing Member States, industries, environmental organizations and the Commission are set up by the Commission for the development and review of the BREFs mentioned above.[107] In addition to the exchange of information that takes place within the TWGs, the IED imposes an obligation on the Commission to establish and convene a 'Forum' which is to be composed of 'representatives of Member States, the industries concerned and non-governmental organizations promoting environmental protection'.[108] Its main task is to provide an opinion of the content of the BREFs proposed by the TWGs.[109] This form of collaborative governance has been regarded as providing 'crucial information and knowledge from a range of sources, and open[ing] up the possibility of shared problem-solving'.[110] The information sharing and problem-solving platform created by the Seville process may lead in turn to better application and enforcement of EU law. It allows national authorities to profit from each other's experiences with regards to compliance problems and to decide on mutually agreed solutions on how to tackle certain compliance failures uniformly.

Both of the network structures discussed above have the prime function of developing guidance documents which themselves are designed to help

---

105 Ibid.

106 Korkea-aho, 'Watering Down the Court of Justice? The Dynamics between Network Implementation and Article 258 TFEU Litigation', n 84, 662.

107 An interesting analysis of the BREF Documents drafting process was carried out by Bettina Lange, 'From Boundary Drawing to Transition Points: The Creation of Normativity under the IPPC Directive' (2002) ELJ 226–46.

108 Article 13(3) of the IED Directive.

109 Article 13(4) of the IED Directive.

110 Lee, *EU Environmental Law, Governance and Decision-Making*, n 79, 114.

implementation of EU environmental law. However, their virtues lie also in their very existence since they provide a forum for national authorities to exchange ideas, develop best practices and create a sense of mutual learning which may ultimately improve the implementation of environmental law. In other words, there may be fringe benefits for authorities participating in these networks next to the prime 'products' created by these networks.[111]

Finally, in the framework of environmental law, mention must be made of a network which is specifically aimed at tackling enforcement issues, the European Union Network for the Implementation and Enforcement of Environmental Law (IMPEL). Originally created in 1992 as an informal forum for the exchange of information and experience without any formal involvement on the part of the EU, IMPEL has become progressively more embedded in the EU institutional framework with a Secretariat located within the Commission's Directorate General for Environment.[112] The purpose of IMPEL is 'to create the necessary impetus in the [EU] to make progress on ensuring a more effective application of environmental legislation'.[113] It aims at achieving this purpose by, amongst others, promoting the exchange of information and experiences between environmental authorities on the implementation of EU environmental law; identifying and developing best practices; and producing guidance, tools and common standards. Recently it also started to act as the Commission's advisor on how environmental legislation may be drafted so as to be made easier to implement.[114]

Political science research suggests that it is in particular those networks that are perceived by the network participants themselves as allowing for informal cooperation that may be useful for supporting national administrations in the implementation of EU law. Networks facilitate mutual learning and mutual trust, promote conflict resolution and allow for resource sharing. As a result, they play an important role in improving the application and enforcement of EU law.[115]

---

[111] See further Chapter 4 of this volume.

[112] Maria Martens, 'Administrative Integration through the Back Door? The Role and Influence of the European Commission in Transgovernmental Networks within the Environmental Policy Field' (2008) J Europ Integration 644.

[113] See <http://impel.eu/about/history/> accessed 10 December 2015.

[114] Martens, 'Administrative Integration through the Back Door? The Role and Influence of the European Commission in Transgovernmental Networks within the Environmental Policy Field', n 112, 640–41. For some critical remarks on this latter role, see Hedemann-Robinson, *Enforcement of European Union Environmental Law: Legal Issues and Challenges*, n 18, 462–5.

[115] See Chapter 4 of this volume.

The role of IMPEL in the context of EU environmental law, is no exception.

CONCLUSION

The EU's 2013–20 Environmental Action Programme acknowledges the serious implementation gap which concerns EU environmental law[116] and stipulates that '[i]mproving the implementation of the Union environment acquis at Member State level will therefore be given top priority in the coming years'.[117] In order to do so the EU has pledged to ensure that by 2020 'the principle of effective legal protection for citizens and their organizations is facilitated' through making sure that national provisions on access to justice comply with the case law of the CJEU.[118] This chapter reveals that whilst the shortcomings of the infringement proceedings make reliance on the decentralized enforcement of EU law through national courts and NGOs a necessity for the EU, there are currently still several legal gaps and constitutional obstacles which natural and legal persons have to face at national level when enforcing violations of EU environmental law. First of all, the specific nature of environmental law and its protection of diffuse rather than individual interests demonstrates the crucial role played by NGOs in the enforcement of EU environmental law where individuals would not have the legal possibility or the interest to pursue legal proceedings. The need to ensure wide access to justice for citizens and such organizations in environmental matters is recognized at international level and is an obligation mandated by Articles 9(2) and (3) of the UN's Aarhus Convention. Overall, the transposition of Article 9(2) into the national laws of the Member States by virtue of Directive 2003/35 has been successful. Gaps in its implementation by the Member States have been corrected following several preliminary rulings of the CJEU. Nevertheless, a gap still remains as far as Article 9(3) is concerned. Political consensus could not be reached on the scope of transposition measures. This has left national legal conditions of access to courts throughout the EU intact (and potentially divergent). To some extent, the resulting uncertainties and inequalities have been remedied by the rulings of the CJEU which has imposed an

[116] Dec 1386/2013 of the European Parliament and of the Council of 20 November 2013 on a General Union Environment Action Programme to 2020 'Living well, within the limits of our planet', n 5, para 56.

[117] Ibid, para 57.

[118] Ibid, para 65(e) and (v).

important duty on the national courts to ensuring that the requirements of the Aarhus Convention are respected through the application of the principle of consistent interpretation. This chapter submits that the necessary legal certainty and level playing field can only be achieved through clear legislative intervention to harmonize national standing rules for NGOs' claims and by setting criteria which are to be applied EU-wide. The CJEU, using the preliminary reference mechanism, can then contribute to the interpretation of the relevant legislative provisions. However, it cannot be considered as a self-standing alternative to legislative intervention given the case-by-case nature of the intervention, and the necessary reliance on the national court's willingness to question their own national law.

Even when access to court is granted to natural and legal persons, a further obstacle lies in the ability of individuals to enforce EU law before national courts through the doctrines of direct effect and state liability. Whilst the case law of the CJEU has extended somewhat the possibility of relying on the direct effect of EU environmental norms in circumstances where the requirement of the conferral of a right by the infringed provision has not been met, the absence of rights in several EU environmental provisions is still a hurdle for individuals seeking to bring damages claims based on the principle of state liability.

The future of the enforcement of EU environmental law lies not just in typical command-and-control systems. New tools and new mechanisms based on non-binding measures, collaborative networks, and collecting and sharing information have gradually acquired greater prominence in the field of environmental law. This chapter has examined two examples of these 'new' modes of governance, namely guidance documents and networks, and has shown that they present several advantages for the effective enforcement of EU environmental law. The 2013–20 Environmental Action Programme demonstrates the priority that the EU attaches to information gathering and spreading, and cooperation between different administrative levels, with the IMPEL network being mentioned explicitly as a way to foster better implementation of EU environmental law.[119] The Commission seems therefore to show a preference for a combination of judicially enforceable rules (and the necessity to create an adequate judicial enforcement framework) with softer, more cooperative ways to achieve compliance with EU environmental law. Yet, whilst this chapter demonstrates that networks and guidance documents represent a promising addition to the more traditional instruments, further legal and political

119 Ibid, para 63.

academic attention should be devoted to exploring their actual effectiveness (and the conditions for their effectiveness) in order to promote a higher level of compliance with EU environmental law.

8. Enforcing EU consumer policy more effectively: a three-pronged approach

Pablo Cortés*

INTRODUCTION

Consumer expenditure is a key element of every economy; it accounts for more than half (56 per cent) of the European Union's total gross domestic product (GDP).[1] Increasingly, many elements of these consumer transactions are regulated by European Union (EU) consumer laws. The rationale of this regulation is underpinned by the economic view that a degree of consumer protection is required for the Internal Market to function effectively.[2] In a typical consumer transaction, consumers pay in advance and they are bound by the standard terms and conditions chosen by the business from which they have purchased their goods or services. This creates an inequality of power between the parties, which, if abused by the stronger party, would deter consumers from further economic activity with that business and could impact more generally on that economic sector. EU consumer policy provides consumers with legal safeguards encouraging them to participate in a regulated market where their reasonable expectations will be met.

The legal provisions regulating consumer policies are enshrined in the Treaty on the Functioning of the European Union (TFEU)[3] and in the

* Part of the research for this chapter was made possible by the support given by the European Commission Action Grant (EMEDEU Project – JUST/2013/JCIV/AG/4689) and a grant from the Nuffield Foundation. The usual disclaimers apply.

1 European Commission Communication, 'A European Consumer Agenda: Boosting Confidence and Growth' COM(2012) 225 final p 1.

2 Mark Armstrong, 'Interactions between Competition and Consumer Policy' (2008) 4(1) *Competition Policy International* 97–147.

3 See Articles 12, 114(3) and 169(1) TFEU.

EU Charter of Fundamental Rights[4] and require a high level of consumer protection in the implementation of EU policies. The EU legal corpus, commonly referred to as the consumer *acquis*, seeks to achieve this goal by removing national protectionist measures that hinder the free movement of goods and services in the Internal Market. This has emerged mainly through EU directives. Traditionally, a minimum level of harmonization was imposed on Member States, both in sector specific areas[5] and in directives affecting all consumer contracts.[6] Over the last decade, there has been a shift towards maximum harmonization,[7] and a preference for horizontal instruments that apply across all sectors.[8] A significant role has also been played by the Court of Justice of the European Union (CJEU) in the development of substantive consumer law since its seminal ruling in *Cassis de Dijon*.[9]

Effective enforcement of the consumer *acquis* is essential to guarantee a high level of consumer protection that in turn produces trust in the market on the part of consumers.[10] Furthermore, the more European consumers and businesses engage in cross-border transactions, particularly through the digital market, the greater the need for effective enforcement options to be developed that are suited to the demands of these new types of transactions. To be effective, enforcement mechanisms need to incorporate adequate procedures to investigate complaints so compliance with consumer law can be ensured.[11]

This chapter analyses the three prongs of the EU's enforcement policy towards EU consumer law and considers their effectiveness and limitations. The first prong refers to public enforcement and how it is carried out by multiple actors in addition to the European Commission (Commission)

---

4 See Article 38 of the Charter of Fundamental Rights of the European Union.

5 See e.g. Dir 2006/114 concerning misleading and comparative advertising [2006] OJ L376/21.

6 See e.g. Dir 93/13 on unfair terms in consumer contracts [1993] OJ L95/29.

7 See e.g. Dir 2005/29 concerning unfair business-to-consumer commercial practices in the internal market [2005] OJ L149/22.

8 See e.g. Dir 2011/83 on consumer rights [2011] OJ L304/64.

9 C-120/78 *Cassis de Dijon* [1979] ECR 649. See generally, Stephen Weatherill, *EU Consumer Law and Policy* (Edward Elgar, 2014).

10 European Commission Staff Working Paper, 'Impact Assessment Accompanying the Document of the Proposal for a Directive on Alternative Dispute Resolution for Consumer Disputes and the Proposal for a Regulation on Online Dispute Resolution for Consumer Disputes' SEC(2011) 1408 final p 5.

11 UK Department for Business Innovation & Skills, 'Enhancing Consumer Confidence Through Effective Enforcement' (March 2012) p 6.

under Article 258 TFEU;[12] the Member States, pan-European networks and consumer representative groups all have an important role in ensuring that businesses comply with consumer law. Yet, the role of the EU institutions and national enforcement bodies focus on deterrence and have limited powers and resources to deliver individual redress to consumers whose rights have been violated. Thus, the second prong of consumer enforcement is for consumers to obtain redress through private enforcement mechanisms through the courts.[13] In terms of consumers pursuing individual redress in court, high value claims are pursued through the ordinary civil procedures provided that the claimant can afford the cost of participating in the process, or through the small claims procedure if this is available.[14] At EU level there is an increasing interest in promoting the use of collective redress; where a large group of consumers have suffered a small economic loss as a result of the trader's same breach of consumer law. However, in reality, the majority of consumer complaints do not end up in court. This is because most consumers are discouraged from pursuing small and even medium value claims in a court setting. Research has found that 48 per cent of EU consumers will not go to court for levels under €200, while 8 per cent of consumers will never go to court regardless of the amount of their claim.[15] The third, and most recent prong, has been the push towards alternative dispute resolution (ADR) options including mediation and ombudsman schemes. Indeed, in practice, the majority of disputes based on breach of consumer rights are resolved either directly between the trader and the consumer, or increasingly with the assistance of an independent extrajudicial body, commonly referred to as an ADR scheme. It should be noted from the outset that consumer ADR (also known as CADR or CDR) is very different to traditional ADR methods used to resolve civil and commercial disputes. While traditional ADR is

---

[12] See European Commission, 'EU Law: Commission Acts to Ensure that European Legislation Is Fully and Properly Implemented' (29 September 2011) MEMO/11/646. Article 258 TFEU is discussed further in Chapter 2 of this volume.

[13] This route can be problematic for consumers as directives, the main legislative instrument adopted to enact consumer law, only have vertical direct effect and cannot be invoked horizontally in actions against other private parties: Weatherill, n 9, 292. See further discussion in Chapter 1 of this volume.

[14] Pablo Cortés, 'The European Small Claims Procedure and the Commission Proposal of 19 November 2013' In-Depth Analysis for the European Parliament JURI (February 2015). Available at http://www.europarl.europa.eu/RegData/etudes/STUD/2015/510003/IPOL_STU(2015)510003_EN.pdf (hereinafter, last accessed 8 December 2015).

[15] Eurobarometer No. 342. Available at http://ec.europa.eu/consumers/consumer_empowerment/docs/report_eurobarometer_342_en.pdf.

seen as an alternative to the court system, where parties may compare what they might get in court to what is being offered in a settlement,[16] consumer ADR often presents itself as the only pathway to find redress in a cost-effective and proportionate manner,[17] particularly for settling low-value cross-border disputes.[18] Accordingly, when consumers want to enforce their EU rights, this is increasingly being achieved through extra-judicial consumer redress mechanisms, leaving public enforcement and judicial enforcement through the courts as last resorts. Indeed, the cost of litigation is often higher than the amount at stake.[19]

The chapter is divided into three parts that correspond with these main prongs of the enforcement of consumer policy in the EU. Accordingly, Part 1 discusses how public authorities monitor and cooperate within the EU through pan-European Networks to ensure a higher level of compliance by traders. Part 2 analyses the main tools that consumers have to enforce their rights before the national courts. In so doing, this part examines two judicial instruments which despite having great potential have not yet delivered an effective redress option for the majority of EU consumers: the European Small Claims Procedure and collective redress. Part 3 focuses on consumer ADR schemes which are increasingly playing a crucially important role in the enforcement of EU consumer policy. More significantly, it evaluates the new European legal framework on consumer ADR which intends to increase the participation of consumers and traders in effective ADR schemes. The chapter concludes arguing that only a holistic approach, with consumer ADR at its core, and that sufficiently interconnects the three prongs will offer consumers an effective enforcement system that ensures a high level of consumer protection.

---

16 Michael Moffitt, 'Three Things to Be Against ("Settlement Not Included")' (2009) 78 *Fordham Law Review* 1203, 1207.

17 Christopher Hodges, Iris Benöhr, Naomi Creutzfeldt-Banda, 'Consumer-to-Business Dispute Resolution: The Power of CADR' (2012) 13 *ERA Forum* 199.

18 Richard Susskind, *Tomorrow's Lawyers: An Introduction to Your Future* (OUP, 2013), Chapter 10.

19 It should be clarified that in the field of EU competition law, public enforcement tends to be the norm, but private enforcement by consumers is under reform: see further Chapter 9 in this volume.

1. FIRST PRONG: PUBLIC ENFORCEMENT AND THE EMERGENCE OF A PAN-EU NETWORK ENFORCEMENT

1.1. Enforcement of Consumer Law by National Public Authorities

The majority of directives on consumer rights bestow on national public administrative bodies the role of monitoring compliance with the law. These public enforcement bodies then target breaches that affect large groups of consumers and can do so in a manner which is far more effective than consumers litigating on an individual basis. Public enforcement bodies, such as the Competition and Market Authority and Trading Standards in the UK, can correct civil breaches of consumer rights (e.g. when a trader is unaware of how to apply the law correctly), but also those arising from criminal activity, such as fraud or large pyramid schemes. Although they have wide enforcement powers, their resources are being reduced in this age of austerity. There is an increasing demand to offer more services with fewer resources, referred to by Susskind as 'the more-for-less challenge'.[20] The competence of public enforcement bodies and their remit is governed by national law. The effectiveness of their enforcement powers can be limited by national law which may allow them to prosecute traders who have breached consumer laws, but not go further and order traders to compensate consumers.[21]

1.2. The Emergence of Network Enforcement in EU Consumer Law and Policy

In the EU one of the main challenges to effective enforcement by national public authorities is the territorial limitation of their competence, which does not correspond with the economic liberalization of the Single Market.[22] Consequently, there is a growing need to build and enhance

---

20 Richard Susskind, n 18, 4–5.

21 Although it should be noted that these restrictions are being lifted in some jurisdictions: see e.g. in the UK, the Consumer Rights Act 2015, which provides enforcers with the ability to seek additional remedies, including compensation for affected consumers, when taking an action under the Injunctions Directive: Dir 2009/22 on injunctions for the protection of consumers' interests [2009] OJ L 11/30. See also The European Consumer Organisation (BEUC), 'Improving Enforcement Cooperation: BEUC Response to the Consultation on the Review of Consumer Protection Cooperation (CPC) Regulation' BEUC-X-2014-005 (3 February 2014) p 2.

22 Ibid 4.

existing cooperative enforcement structures that allow for more effective cooperation between national enforcement bodies and consumer associations; such cooperation will lead to a more effective tracking of market abuses that increasingly operate cross-border. In the context of EU consumer policy, the EU has set up a legal framework for promoting the Consumer Protection Cooperation Network (CPC Network) for national enforcement authorities and the European Consumer Centres Network (ECC-Net) which encompasses consumer organizations. The effectiveness of both these networks in ensuring compliance with EU consumer law will now be considered.[23]

CPC Network

The 2004 Consumer Protection Cooperation (CPC) Regulation[24] sets out the legal framework for the establishment of a pan-European network encompassing all of the national consumer authorities of the EU Member States and the European Economic Area (EEA) partner countries.[25] It also cooperates with a number of international organizations.[26] The CPC Network provides a mechanism for cooperation in the investigation of breaches of EU law that affect consumers in two or more EU Member States.[27] The goal of the CPC Network is to safeguard consumers' collective interests across the EU. This is mainly achieved by sharing information and enforcing consumer protection law across borders,[28] which in effect requires the use of the administrative resources of one country of the Network to favour the interest of consumers resident in another country. The CPC Regulation sets out the provisions which enable the Commission to coordinate the enforcement activities of the competent

23 See further discussions on network cooperation more generally and in other policy sectors in other chapters of this volume.

24 Reg 2006/2004 on Cooperation between National Authorities Responsible for the Enforcement of Consumer Protection Laws (CPC Regulation) [2004] OJ L 364. See also Dec 2007/76 setting out the details on the cooperation between national authorities responsible for the enforcement of consumer protection laws as regards mutual assistance [2007] OJ L32/192.

25 The EEA partner countries are Iceland, Liechtenstein and Norway.

26 Currently, the CPC Network cooperates closely with the following organizations: the International Consumer Protection and Enforcement Network (ICPEN), the Organisation for Economic Co-operation and Development (OECD), and the US Federal Trade Commission (FTC).

27 European Commission, 'Report on the Functioning of Regulation (EC) 2006/2004 on Cooperation Between National Authorities Responsible for the Enforcement of Consumer Protection Laws (CPC Regulation)' COM(2014) 439 Final p 1.

28 Article 8 of the CPC Regulation, n 24.

national authorities, especially when tackling a particular sector on an EU-wide basis. Recently, it has targeted app purchases, online games and car rentals.[29] The Commission is also developing guidelines to further facilitate enforcement and voluntary compliance by traders.[30]

One of the ways in which the CPC Network operates is through sweeps of websites,[31] whereby the national public authorities that form the network assess whether the websites investigated comply with the EU law. More than 3,000 websites operating in the EU have been screened to check their compliance with EU law.[32] A sweep in 2013 found that 382 out of 552 websites checked did not respect consumer law.[33] The lack of compliance was due to various problems, such as lack of mandatory information on the trader's indemnity, lack of information on how to complain, and the lack of opt-out options for price supplements. The sweep led to traders being requested to cease unfair commercial practices that breached EU law. Of these websites, 62 per cent voluntarily brought their business practices in line with the consumer law.[34] This type of enforcement action, which has been replicated with app purchases,[35] is effective because it leads to a high level of voluntary compliance.

A 2014 report by the Commission observed that there is still significant room for improvement within the CPC Network with a range of difficulties identified: the coordination framework established in the Regulation which is claimed to be too vague in setting out the obligations for national enforcement bodies to cooperate with their counterparts in other Member States;[36] the current alert system, which notifies all of the Network members, is inefficient because only the national enforcement bodies can use it, while the Commission and consumer organizations are not currently allowed to use it.[37] Furthermore, the competent national authorities

---

[29] Article 9 of the CPC Regulation, n 24. European Commission Report, n 27, 4.

[30] See e.g. http://ec.europa.eu/justice/consumer-marketing/rights-contracts/directive/index_en.htm.

[31] This is where a large number of websites are randomly selected and their level of compliance with the applicable law is checked: Article 9 of the CPC Regulation, n 24.

[32] European Commission Report, n 27, 2.

[33] European Commission, 'Co-ordinated Enforcement Action Leads to Greater Compliance with Consumer Rights on Travel Websites' IP/14/436 (14 April 2014).

[34] Ibid.

[35] European Commission Report, n 27, 2.

[36] Ibid 8.

[37] Ibid 9.

forming the CPC Network have very different forms of autonomy. While some are fully independent and autonomous, others are under the supervision of judicial or governmental authorities, requiring them to request permission before taking certain actions. This can obstruct cooperation amongst these national enforcement bodies.[38] Lastly, the Commission has noted that there is a need for a well-functioning pan-European IT platform to share enforcement expertise and infringements of consumer protection laws.[39] An effective platform would lead to better and quicker enforcement by enhancing the coordination action of public enforcers to target infringers of consumer laws.

ECC-Net

The ECC-Net was created in 2005 as a result of a merger between the network for the extrajudicial settlement of consumer disputes (EEJ-Net)[40] that advised on ADR schemes, and the European Consumer Information Centres (the Network of Euroguichets) that informed consumers about their legal rights. The budget for the ECC-Net is provided under the EU programme for consumer policy. The main objective of this network is to support the cooperation of Member States concerning information, advice and appeals in consumer protection matters. Alongside the ECC-Net is FIN-Net, which carries out the same role in the financial sector. The ECC-Net also cooperates with other European networks, namely SOLVIT[41] (Internal Market) and the European Judicial Network on civil and commercial matters. The ECC-Net is co-financed through grants by the EU (Directorate General Justice) and by each of the participating Member States, which are the 28 EU countries, as well as in Norway and Iceland. Each participating country has a point of contact and at least one office.[42] The aim of ECC-Net is to provide consumers entering into cross-border transactions with information about their rights and obligations, and it also helps them to resolve disputes as a result of these transactions without having to bring legal proceedings.

Each national European Consumer Centre (ECC) responds and advises consumers on their queries about cross-border transactions. Questions are often submitted via their website or by email. In the event of a complaint,

---

[38] Ibid 10.

[39] Ibid 13.

[40] The EEJ Network was created following a Council Resolution of 25 May 2000.

[41] Discussed further in Chapters 5 and 6 in this volume.

[42] The list of national contacts is available online at http://ec.europa.eu/consumers/ecc/contact_en.htm.

the ECC will help and support consumers in their contacts with the trader. The process starts by a consumer passing a complaint to its national ECC contact point, which, unless they think the complaint is manifestly unfounded, will liaise with their partner contact point at the other Member State, who in turn will contact the trader with the objective of reaching an amicable solution. If parties through their national ECC contact points cannot reach a settlement, then the consumer may be advised to take legal action or consider ADR options if these are available. According to the 2013 Annual Report the ECC-Net dealt with more than 80,000 consumer contacts for information which led to over 32,000 complaints.[43] The ECC-Net carries out an important role in the enforcement of consumer policy. This includes assisting consumers to resolve complaints, informing consumers about their rights and producing annual reports and ad hoc studies which inform regulators and public bodies on what regulatory changes may be necessary to facilitate compliance and improve enforcement options.

2. PRONG II: PRIVATE JUDICIAL ENFORCEMENT – INDIVIDUAL AND COLLECTIVE REDRESS

National courts are seen as the official guarantors of the rule of law as they can ensure the application of consumer law through injunctions[44] and through the criminal and civil court processes. For many consumer claims, however, the most effective mechanisms of private enforcement are the small claims procedure and collective actions. These judicial routes for individual redress are suited for the many consumer claims which tend to be of low value. Domestic consumer disputes can be resolved through these procedures when they are available under national law.[45] Enforcement is less effective when dealing with cross-border consumer claims. This section is limited to examining the effectiveness of these two judicial avenues to enforce EU consumer rights in *cross-border transactions which are of low value*. The resolution of such cases is becoming increasingly important for the development of a fully integrated Single Market. Accordingly, this section will examine the European Small Claims Procedure and the EU efforts to promote the use of collective redress.

---

[43] The European Consumer Centres Network 2013 Annual Report. Available at http://ec.europa.eu/consumers/ecc/docs/report_ecc-net_2013_en.pdf.

[44] In particular under Dir 2009/22 on injunctions for the protection of consumers' interests [2009] OJ L11/30.

[45] See e.g. Nanette Neuwahl and Said Hammamoun, *The European Small Claims Procedure and the Philosophy of Small Change* (Les Éditions Thémis, 2014).

2.1. The European Small Claims Procedure

Small claims procedures provide a middle ground between formal litigation and ADR and enable low-value disputes to be resolved before the courts using a less formal and expeditious judicial procedure.[46] The European Small Claims Procedure (ESCP) aims to increase access to justice for European litigants with cross-border claims.[47] The ESCP is designed to be an optional and informal court procedure that allows parties, without legal representation, to resolve cross-border low-value disputes of up to €2,000 (recently increased to €5,000) through a written and simplified civil procedure. Litigants can use standard forms for submitting a claim and a response, and judgments are enforceable across the EU without the need for a declaration of enforceability (i.e. exequatur).

In a 2013 review, the ESCP was considered to be more effective as an enforcement instrument than the alternative domestic procedures: on average the ESCP has reduced the cost of litigating cross-border cases by up to 40 per cent and reduced the duration of litigation from two years and five months, to five months only.[48] While it can be argued that this is a significant improvement, it is still considered to be too expensive and too long for many, if not the majority of low-value cross-border consumer claims.[49] As is argued in the next section of this chapter, most of these claims could be addressed in a more cost-effective manner through ADR processes. Indeed, the ESCP as an enforcement instrument has not been as effective as originally expected by the Commission. Indeed, thus far there has been very limited use of the ESCP – on average around 100 cases per Member State.

During the review process the Commission identified two main obstacles to the use of the ESCP. First, the lack of awareness about its existence; only 12 per cent of EU citizens seem to be aware of the ESCP, but

---

[46] Pablo Cortés, 'Does the Proposed European Procedure Enhance the Resolution of Small Claims?' (2008) 27(1) *Civil Justice Quarterly* 83–97.

[47] Reg 861/2007 establishing a European Small Claims Procedure (ESCP) [2007] OJ L199/1. The European e-Justice Portal is a single point of entry to all relevant information about the ESCP. Forms to be used in the European Small Claims Procedure can be accessed at https://e-justice.europa.eu/content_small_claims_forms-177-en.do and to find out which court has jurisdiction, see http://tinyurl.com/p2vmb78.

[48] European Commission, 'Report from the Commission to the European Parliament, the Council and the European Economic and Social Committee on the application of Regulation (EC) 861/2007 of the European Parliament and the Council establishing a European Small Claims Procedure' COM(2013) 795 final.

[49] Cortés, n 14.

more surprisingly, only half (53 per cent) of the judges and courts of the Member States are aware of the ESCP; and out of those courts that are aware, many are not fully informed about the ESCP.[50] The second obstacle identified by the Commission is the unpredictability of costs and duration in litigating small claims, where one-third of litigants use lawyers despite the fact that the procedure is designed for parties to participate without legal representation; also parties are often required to attend oral hearings even though this should only occur in exceptional circumstances.[51] A third obstacle, which has not been addressed by the Commission in its proposed amendments, are the difficulties that consumers face when they attempt to enforce judgments by a small claims court in other jurisdictions. This is unfortunate as the research findings on the effectiveness of the enforcement of judgments is unclear and requires further clarification.[52] The Commission based its decision not to introduce any new measures on a survey conducted by Eurobarometer which found that there were no difficulties in the enforcement of 97 per cent of judgments.[53] In contrast, in an independent report required by the Commission (the Deloitte report),[54] it was reported that in more than four out of ten cases (42 per cent) the claim was still ongoing, without clarifying for how long these cases have been open. It is suggested that a key question would be to assess the percentage of cases that were at the enforcement stage – that is, where the judgment has been issued in favour of the claimant, but the defendant has not yet complied with the court order. Another interpretation of these findings is that the ESCP is mainly used in commercial cases (between two businesses) where parties often have legal representation and, according to the conflict of law rules, are required to sue in the defendant's forum. Hence, the court enforcement of these cases is easier as they occur in the same jurisdiction as the judgment. By contrast, in consumer matters,

---

[50] European Commission, 'Impact Assessment of the Proposal for a Regulation of the European Small Claims Procedure' SWD (2013) 460, p 24.

[51] Ibid.

[52] Cortés, n 49.

[53] Of the respondents, 23 per cent said that the defendants complied voluntarily while 74 per cent obtained a successful enforcement order. See Eurobarometer 395 at p 35. Available at http://ec.europa.eu/public_opinion/archives/ebs/ebs_395_en.pdf.

[54] Deloitte, *Assessment of the Socio-Economic Impacts of the Policy Options for the Future of the European Small Claims Regulation* (European Commission, 2013). The Commission sub-contracted Deloitte to conduct a research study that examined practical difficulties in the use of the ESCP. The findings of this study formed the basis for proposed amendments made by the Commission during the review process of the ESCP Regulation.

often consumers are able to sue in their own jurisdictions, but they will have to enforce the judgment in the defendant's jurisdiction. Therefore, if consumers were using the ESCP, then they will surely have found great difficulties in seeking the enforcement of judgments in a different language and through a foreign enforcement procedure. This is why the ECC-Net and many other consumer bodies have observed in the past that that the main obstacle to the effectiveness of the ESCP is the enforcement of the court judgment.[55]

In order to assess the effectiveness of the enforcement process it would be necessary to gather new empirical data distinguishing between those ESCP users who find out about the process of enforcement (when, for instance, the enforcement takes place in the same jurisdiction of the court which issued the judgment, or when the applicant has hired a lawyer) to those cases where applicants do not seek enforcement because of the lack of information and resources. Moreover, Member States should facilitate details of how to contact lawyers who can assist applicants from other Member States during the enforcement process. There would also be important improvements made if the enforcement procedures in the Member States could be accessible online.[56]

The European Commission considered that there is a need to enhance the use of the ESCP without taking any substantive measures to facilitate the enforcement of judgments. To that end, in 2013 the Commission brought a proposal to amend the present Regulation and to increase the effectiveness of the ESCP in light of the obstacles identified by the Commission.[57] In doing so, it has also proposed to reform the European Order for Payment so that when a defence is submitted by the debtor, instead of the claim moving automatically from the European Order for Payment procedure to the national procedure, it will go to the ESCP if the claim falls within the scope of the ESCP. This is a welcome change for money claims as it offers a more cost-efficient enforcement process to creditors involved in cross-border claims. In addition, the Commission

---

55 ECC-Net, *European Small Claims Procedure Report* (2012) p 22. Available at http://webcache.googleusercontent.com/search?q=cache:9AxUs9UtHCIJ:www.konsument.gov.pl/en/uploads/427/small_claims_procedure_2012-pdf.html+&cd=1&hl=en&ct=clnk&gl=uk.

56 Cortés, n 49.

57 European Commission, 'Proposal for a Regulation of the European Parliament and of the Council amending Reg 861/2007 establishing a European Small Claims Procedure and Regulation (EC) 1896/2006 of the European Parliament and the Council creating a European Order for Payment Procedure' COM(2013) 794 final.

has proposed the following key amendments to make the ESCP more effective:

1. Lifting the financial limit from €2,000 to €10,000;
2. Expanding the definition of cross-border cases;
3. Requiring more use of electronic communication, especially for conducting oral hearings and taking the payment of court fees;
4. Setting a maximum limitation on court fees;
5. Limiting the translation of the enforcement form to the actual judgment;
6. Imposing information obligations on the Member States about the availability of the ESCP.

At this point the extent to which these changes would make the ESCP more accessible to European consumers is unclear, but expanding its scope, requiring electronic and distance means of communication and providing more information to consumers are all geared towards creating a more effective enforcement regime. Yet, court processes, no matter how informal they are, can never become the main means of consumer redress, and hence of consumer enforcement. It had already been noted by legal scholars that small claims procedures generally only benefit well-informed and articulate individuals.[58] As a result, a large portion of society, including vulnerable consumers, may not see a small claims process as an accessible redress option. Although there is insufficient empirical research available to evaluate the ESCP fully,[59] existing studies in the EU found that in most Member States the cost of ADR is lower than the cost of the small claims procedure.[60] Accordingly, in the consumer context, the Commission has acknowledged that there is a need to complement access to courts with more effective (i.e. faster and cheaper) and informal out-of-court redress options.[61]

---

[58] John Baldwin, *The Small Claims Procedure and the Consumer* (Office of Fair Trading, 1995); Fiona Cownie, Anthony Bradney and Mandy Burton, *English Legal System in Context* (5th edn, OUP, 2010) 208. Hodges et al argue that national SCP is not user-friendly and that they 'generally represent a failure of planning by those ministries of justice that did not provide a proper service or alternative to the courts'. See Christopher Hodges, Iris Benöhr and Naomi Creutzfeldt-Banda, *Consumer ADR in Europe* (Hart, 2012) 397.

[59] Xandra Kramer, 'Small Claim, Simple Recovery? The European Small Claims Procedure and Its Implementation in the Member States' (2011) 1 *ERA Forum* 119–34.

[60] Hodges et al, n 58, 385.

[61] European Commission Impact Assessment, n 10.

Despite that, the ESCP Regulation and the proposed amendments do not require claimants to consider the suitability of extrajudicial mechanisms before filing a claim, nor does the Regulation penalize those who are unreasonable in refusing to settle a claim. The synergy between the ESCP and ADR mechanisms would increase awareness, making the option of judicial redress a more valuable one. It is submitted that the ESCP should require parties to consider the suitability of using ADR for resolving a consumer dispute. Claim and response forms should include clear provisions requesting parties to consider the use of ADR before and during the ESCP. National court-annexed ADR schemes that operate through distance means of communication should be extended for cross-border claims. These schemes should cooperate with the ECC-Net and nationally certified ADR schemes in order to provide these services in English and in other major EU languages. Furthermore, when filing a claim, the claimant should indicate whether ADR was attempted, and if it was not attempted, then the claimant should explain the reasons for not considering ADR appropriate for that case. Parties could also be allowed to bring offers to settle throughout the whole procedure. But, for these offers to be fully effective they must be accompanied by cost incentives, that is, allowing the national courts to penalize parties who have been unreasonable in not accepting a settlement. Another incentive should be to facilitate the submission of these offers by enabling an online tool that would allow for ubiquitous access. The forthcoming EU Online Dispute Resolution Platform, discussed in Part 3 of this chapter, could be the right instrument to channel these offers to settle.

2.2. Collective Redress for Consumers in the EU

If a large group of consumers has been affected by the illegal activity of a trader, the abuse can be remedied by a collective or class action. This redress option, which is not popular in the EU but has a very strong tradition in the US, can also be an important tool in enforcing consumer policy.[62] Consumers with low-value disputes do not have the resources or the motivation to pursue litigation against a trader, unless they can join their similar claims into a single action with others. The European Commission describes collective redress in the following manner:

> Collective redress is a procedural mechanism that allows, for reasons of procedural economy and/or efficiency of enforcement, many similar legal

---

62 See further discussion in Chapter 9 of this volume.

> claims to be bundled into a single court action. Collective redress facilitates access to justice in particular in cases where the individual damage is so low that potential claimants would not think it worth pursuing an individual claim. It also strengthens the negotiating power of potential claimants and contributes to the efficient administration of justice, by avoiding numerous proceedings concerning claims resulting from the same infringement of law. Depending on the type of claim, collective redress can take the form of injunctive relief, where cessation of the unlawful practice is sought, or compensatory relief, aimed at obtaining compensation for damage suffered.[63]

Similarly, Cappelletti observes that collective and class actions break from traditional litigation in a number of ways, notably, by allowing standing to a claimant who has suffered a small fragment of the loss to sue on behalf of the other claimants.[64] This can be done on an opt-in or opt-out basis and it may require the court's approval for its operation.[65] The right to have standing may be extended in collective actions to a number of entities, such as consumer associations. Interestingly, Hodges notes that the origin of collective actions was not to improve access to justice, but to provide more cost-effective procedures for judges who were faced with the management of multiple similar claims.[66]

The European Parliament and the Commission are presently exploring ways of developing and encouraging judicial and extrajudicial collective redress for resolving small claims. Indeed, the term of 'collective redress' has been used as opposed to 'collective action' in order to encapsulate extrajudicial mechanisms, particularly voluntary models such as ombudsman schemes.[67] The EU appears resolute to avoid replicating the US model for class actions, which has been criticized for providing excessive

---

[63] European Commission Communication, 'Towards a Coherent European Approach to Collective Redress' COM(2013) 401 final para 1.2.

[64] Mauro Cappelletti, 'Alternative Dispute Resolution Processes within the Framework of the World-Wide Access-to-Justice Movement' (1993) 56 *Modern Law Review* 282–96, 285.

[65] The opt-in model requires each consumer affected by the same breach to agree expressly to join the collective action. By contrast, the opt-out model automatically includes all the consumers in the collective action unless a consumer expressly requests to be left out.

[66] Hodges provides the example of the Spanish scandal on contaminated oil which in 1981 caused the death of more than 1,100 Spanish people and the poisoning of over 60,000: Christopher Hodges, 'Collective Redress: A Breakthrough or a Damp Squib?' (2014) 37 *Journal of Consumer Policy* 67–89, 82.

[67] See the European Commission Communication, 'Towards a European Horizontal Framework for Collective Redress' COM(2013) 401 final and the Commission Recommendation 2013/396/EU of 11 June 2013 on common principles for injunctive and compensatory collective redress mechanisms in the Member

economic incentives to lawyers (with the counterpart of significantly lower recovery for consumers) and promoting unmeritorious claims that can even lead to 'blackmailing' defendants into settling cases. The European Commission has noted that punitive damages and pre-trial discovery procedures fuel class actions in the US into what they have termed a 'toxic cocktail' that should not be introduced in the EU.[68] Hodges rightly argues that the US model would not work in the EU because the US system relies on important economic incentives: namely, the US costs rule,[69] the widespread use of contingency fee agreements[70] and extended third party funding.[71]

In 2012 the European Parliament issued a Resolution supporting a horizontal framework of national procedural laws for collective actions to avoid fragmentation, while respecting the different legal traditions of the Member States.[72] The Parliament has been very clear that safeguards should be put in place to avoid the use of collective redress for unmeritorious claims.[73] Although the Commission supports a horizontal framework on consumer redress in its 2013 Recommendation, it states that it does not intend to harmonize Member States' national procedures, at least for the time being.[74] It is thus not clear yet whether the Commission will introduce a hard law instrument, like a directive or a regulation, as that will depend on how satisfactory the Commission considers the national legal frameworks to be.[75] The stated rationale for developing a

---

States concerning violations of rights granted under Union Law [2013] L 201/60 25–8.

[68] European Commission MEMO/08/741, p 4.

[69] In the US, claimants who lose a case do not have to pay the legal costs of the successful defendants.

[70] They are also known as damage-based agreements. This is when the legal costs of the claimant are agreed as part of the recovery made in the court judgment or in a settlement.

[71] This is where a third party funding company provides a litigant with the requisite finances to bring the litigation in exchange for a percentage of the settlement. See Christopher Hodges, 'Collective Redress in Europe: The New Model' (2010) 29(3) *Civil Justice Quarterly* 373.

[72] European Parliament Resolution of 2 February 2012 'Towards a Coherent European Approach to Collective Redress' 2011/2089(INI).

[73] Ibid 20.

[74] Commission Recommendation 2013/396/EU of 11 June 2013 on common principles for injunctive and compensatory collective redress mechanisms in the Member States concerning violations of rights granted under Union Law [2013] OJ L201/60. It must be noted that consumer rights is not the only area where collective actions may apply. See Recital (4) of the Commission Recommendation.

[75] See further Chapter 9 in this volume.

horizontal instrument is 'to avoid the risk of uncoordinated sectorial EU initiatives and to ensure the smoothest interface with national procedural rules'.[76] The Recommendation contains a series of common principles for collective redress mechanisms and requires Member States to introduce a generic collective action procedure within four years. At the time of writing only 17 Member States out of the 28 have such systems in place already.[77] There is no doubt that making collective redress more readily available will increase the enforcement avenues for many consumers who would otherwise not be able to enforce their rights.[78]

3. PRONG III: THE EMERGING EU LEGAL FRAMEWORK FOR EXTRAJUDICIAL REDRESS – ADR AND ODR

Consumer ADR is increasingly becoming the most important prong for consumer enforcement.[79] Unlike the courts, ADR is user-friendly (i.e. parties can use it without legal representation), fast and cost-effective.

---

[76] European Commission Communication, n 67, para. 4. Cf. Dir 2014/104 which introduces common procedural rules for damages claims in the field of EU competition law: Dir 2014/104 on certain rules governing actions for damages under national law for infringements of the competition law provisions of the Member States and of the European Union [2014] OJ L349/1.

[77] For the consultation process in the EU, see generally, http://ec.europa.eu/consumers/redress_cons/collective_redress_en.htm.

[78] The first day that the French collective action law entered into force (L. 423-17 of the French Consumer Act (*loi Hamon*) of 13 February 2014), a collective action was submitted in the French courts, *UFC-Que Choisir v Foncia*, for charging a monthly fee to tenants for sending the rent bills. See France 24 'UFC-Que Choisir vs Foncia: L'action de Groupe Loin de la "Class Action"' (1 October 2014). Available at http://www.france24.com/fr/20141001-ufc-que-choisir-foncia-action-groupe-class-action-difference-loi-hamon-proces-france-etats-unis-associations-justice/.

[79] It must be noted that chargebacks are also an important and complementary means of enforcement allowing consumers to obtain a refund for the payment of goods or services when unauthorized or fraudulent payment of a debit or credit card had taken place. Although, chargeback provides consumers with redress, it cannot be strictly classified as an ADR scheme because the payment is simply reversed back to the consumer where there have been fraudulent charges, non-delivery or non-conforming goods. Also, chargeback outcomes do not affect the validity of the contract which could be challenged in court. In the EU the chargeback system is regulated by two directives: Dir 2007/64 on payment services in the internal market [2007] OJ L319/1 and Dir 2008/48 on credit agreements for consumers [2008] OJ L133/66.

In some Member States, such as the UK, consumer ADR has already become the main route for consumer redress, processing many more consumer claims than national courts. This trend has been intensified by restrictions in legal aid for civil court matters and the increase in court fees. By way of example, in England and Wales there were under 30,000 small claims adjudicated by the courts in 2013, while consumer ADR schemes resolved over half a million consumer claims.[80] In some sectors, such as financial matters in the UK, ADR schemes have in effect replaced the courts as the main forum for providing consumer redress.[81] Yet, the availability of ADR is quite patchy, varying significantly across the EU Member States and the economic sectors. This is partly due to its organic growth at national level as a mechanism to deal with complaints more efficiently.

Consumer ADR is gradually being used to enforce consumer protection laws while resolving disputes arising from consumer transactions. The take-up of ADR schemes has been fuelled in recent years by various European and national laws that, on one hand, made the use of ADR compulsory in certain economic sectors (e.g. energy, financial services, and telecommunications) and, on the other hand, promoted high standards for consumer ADR schemes. Until recently, the Commission had only adopted soft law instruments,[82] which sought to encourage the use of consumer ADR schemes, but the real boost came in many Member States with the implementation of the Mediation Directive, which allows the imposition of mediation as a pre-condition to court litigation.[83] Despite its limited application to cross-border cases, many Member States (but not the UK) have decided to transpose its contents to domestic matters. The validity of this approach has been confirmed by the CJEU in the *Alassini*

---

[80] Christopher Hodges, Naomi Creutzfeldt and Sonia Macleod, 'Reforming the EU Consumer ADR Landscape: Implementation and its Issues' Third Oxford Consumer Conference Report (30–31 October 2014) p 7.

[81] Peter Cartwright, 'The Vulnerable Consumer of Financial Services: Law, Policy and Regulation' available at: http://www.nottingham.ac.uk/business/forum/documents/researchreports/paper78.pdf.

[82] Soft laws are rules that are not binding; like the UN model laws, they intend to provide guidelines to legislators setting standards of conduct while encouraging legal harmonization. See the Commission Recommendation 98/257/EC of 30 March 1998 on the principles applicable to the bodies responsible for out-of-court settlement of consumer disputes [1998] OJ L115/31 and the Commission Recommendation 2001/310/EC of 4 April 2001 on the principles for the out-of-court bodies involved in the consensual resolution of consumer disputes [2001] OJ L109/56. See also the European Commission Communication on 'Alternative Dispute Resolution for Consumer Disputes in the Single Market' COM(2011) 791.

[83] Article 5(2) of Dir 2008/52 on certain aspects of mediation in civil and commercial matters [2008] OJ L136/3.

case provided the ADR process meets a minimum number of safeguards and does not deny the parties access to the courts in the event of an unsuccessful mediation.[84]

3.1. The New Legal Framework for Consumer ADR

Despite the recent growth of consumer ADR, which in many Member States has surpassed the redress provided by courts and public enforcers, its effectiveness as a pillar for effective enforcement is well below its potential since only a very small percentage of European consumers currently benefit from its use. According to European surveys, only 3 per cent of European consumers who had a complaint unresolved by the trader brought the complaint to an ADR scheme.[85] Also, it has been reported that only 9 per cent of European traders have used an ADR scheme.[86] Furthermore, the Commission has estimated that if EU consumers can rely on well-functioning and transparent ADR for their disputes, both national and cross-border, they could save around €22.5 billion a year, corresponding to 0.19 per cent of EU GDP.[87]

With the aim of improving the enforcement avenues of consumer policies, the EU decided to bring new legislation based on Article 169 TFEU and in compliance with Article 38 of the Charter, namely the Directive on Alternative Dispute Resolution for Consumer Disputes (hereinafter the ADR Directive) and the Regulation on Online Dispute Resolution for Consumer Disputes (hereinafter the ODR Regulation).[88] The new legal framework aims to encourage the use and increase the availability of high quality ADR schemes. These ADR procedures will be accessible online which is commonly referred to as online dispute resolution (ODR). The EU has designed a legal framework which does not prescribe a procedure, but aims at ensuring a high standard of coordination and accessibility of

---

84 Namely it requires mandatory mediation to be cost-effective and that electronic means are not the only way in which the settlement procedure may be accessed where a party does not have access to technology: C-317/–320/08 *Alassini* [2010] ECR I-2213. Cf. Jim Davies and Erika Szyszczak, 'ADR: Effective Protection of Consumer Rights?' (2010) 35(5) *European Law Review* 695.

85 Flash Eurobarometer 300, 'Retailers' Attitudes Towards Cross-Border Trade and Consumer Protection' (March 2011) p 45. Available at http://ec.europa.eu/public_opinion/flash/fl_300_en.pdf.

86 Ibid 76.

87 See European Commission Impact Assessment, n 10, 5.

88 Dir 2013/11 on alternative dispute resolution for consumer disputes (ADR Directive) [2013] OJ L165/63 and Reg 524/2013 on online dispute resolution for consumer disputes (ODR Regulation) [2013] OJ L165/1.

ADR processes including those available online.[89] ADR schemes operating in the EU that would like to obtain certification as an ADR entity by their national authorities need to ensure that their scheme complies with six procedural principles: (i) expertise, independence and impartiality; (ii) transparency; (iii) effectiveness; (iv) fairness; (v) liberty; (vi) legality.[90] This will ensure that the enforcement process is effective and as a result deliver a high level of consumer protection.

By July 2015 all Member States must have complied with most of the requirements set in the ADR Directive. The Directive is accompanied by the ODR Regulation which mandates the Commission to establish a pan-European ODR platform that will become a single point of entry for resolving consumer complaints arising from e-commerce. The platform, expected to be fully operational in January 2016, will link complainants to nationally approved ADR schemes that resolve e-commerce disputes. It is argued that this restriction to e-commerce may be too restrictive. While an ODR platform seems the natural place to resolve e-commerce disputes, it is not clear why its scope has been restricted to these disputes, as there will be many other disputes that could benefit from this platform to channel the resolution. An explanation may be found in the need to narrow the scope to facilitate the design of complaint forms as well as to make the platform more manageable for the administrator. Hence, if the ODR platform becomes a useful instrument for resolving e-commerce disputes, it should in due course expand to other sectors covering all types of consumer disputes.

Yet, the mere availability of consumer ADR schemes, even outside the ODR platform, that comply with procedural standards will provide consumers with more effective enforcement options. The ADR Directive seeks this objective by imposing an obligation on the Member States to ensure the provision of ADR entities (i.e. ADR schemes that comply with the procedural standards set in the Directive) for all consumer complaints in all sectors (with the exception of health care services and public providers of higher education),[91] so consumers will have better redress

---

[89] Unlike the model ODR procedure that the UN Commission for International Trade Law (UNCITRAL Working Group III) is developing. See UNCITRAL Working Group III (Online Dispute Resolution) at http://www.uncitral.org/uncitral/commission/working_groups/3Online_Dispute_Resolution.html. See also, Pablo Cortés and Fernando Esteban de la Rosa, 'Building a Global Redress System for Low-Value Cross-Border Disputes' (2013) 62(2) *ICLQ* 407.

[90] Articles 6–11, ADR Directive, n 88.

[91] Article 2(2), ADR Directive, n 88. The reasons behind these exclusions are not entirely clear, but what is clear is that these economic sectors are mostly public

options against businesses without having to go to court. Its scope, in contrast with the European Small Claims Procedure, is very wide as it applies to all contractual disputes, domestic and cross-border, where a trader is established in the EU and a consumer is a resident of the Union.[92]

The ADR Directive describes ADR entities as adjudicative and consensual extrajudicial processes created on a durable basis. Under the new law traders will be legally obliged to inform consumers about the ADR schemes that are competent to deal with potential disputes. This means that traders must inform consumers when they have voluntarily adhered to an ADR scheme, and when the law requires them to do so, as is the case in certain sectors where ombudsmen have been created.[93] Participation by businesses in ADR will thus remain voluntary in most economic sectors,[94] but all traders, irrespective of whether they are obliged to or intend to use an ADR entity, must also provide information on paper or another durable medium about certified ADR entities that could handle the consumers' complaints. Moreover, online business must carry a link to the ODR platform.[95] Irrespectively of whether it is an e-commerce dispute, the ADR process must be accessible online and it must be free or low cost for the consumer.[96] Traders must inform consumers whether or not they intend to participate in the ADR process. This obligation was included because it is believed that it will encourage traders to refer disputes to ADR entities by forcing them to consider in every case whether ADR is appropriate.[97]

---

and already have their own redress schemes, so there may be no need to impose the obligation to provide ADR schemes under the conditions set by the Directive. See generally, Pablo Cortés, 'A New Regulatory Framework for Extra-Judicial Consumer Redress: Where We Are and How to Move Forward' (2015) 35(1) *Legal Studies* 114–41.

[92] Article 2(1) ADR Directive, ibid. It also excludes complaint handling mechanisms established by the trader, direct negotiation between the consumer and the trader, and judicial settlement.

[93] Article 13, ADR Directive, n 88.

[94] The list varies depending on the Member State. In the UK, the following regulated sectors make the provision of ADR mandatory: energy, estate agents, financial services, Higher Education, gambling, green deal (i.e. loans for energy saving measures for properties in Great Britain), legal services, pensions, postal services, property letting agents, and telecommunications.

[95] Article 14(1), ODR Regulation, n 88.

[96] Article 8, ADR Directive, n 88.

[97] UK Department for Business Innovation & Skills, 'Implementing the Alternative Dispute Resolution Directive and Online Dispute Resolution Regulation' (March 2014). Available at https://www.gov.uk/government/consultations/alternative-dispute-resolution-for-consumers.

Member States will be required to monitor compliance with these information obligations imposed on traders and the functioning of the ADR entities. The latter will be required to notify the public authorities of their rules and performance. In order to ensure compliance and effective enforcement, Member States will issue proportionate penalties to traders and withdraw the accreditation to ADR entities that do not comply with the information requirements or meet the criteria set in the national law that implements the Directive.[98] Certified ADR entities may only refuse to deal with consumer disputes on a limited number of grounds, such as those deemed frivolous or vexatious, when the consumer refused to contact the trader first, or when submitted after one year since the dispute arose.[99]

The ODR Regulation complements the ADR Directive by establishing an ODR platform that will facilitate the resolution of (both national and cross-border) consumer disputes within the EU related to online sales of goods and/or provision of services.[100] European consumers will be able to submit a standard complaint form in their own language, which will be forwarded to the trader in their own language. The interface of the platform will be a website that will act as a hub to deal with complaints where parties will be invited to agree on using an ADR process to settle their disputes. Currently, the main problem with the EU ODR platform is that it does not have a system of automatic referral to a sectorial mandatory ADR scheme if the business does not reply to the consumer's claim. Thus, the risk is that a consumer may be directed by the trader to the EU ODR platform and if the trader does not respond to the complaint then that complaint may be processed.[101] This risk would not occur if the consumer was directed directly to the mandatory ADR entity. It is therefore unfortunate that the Commission decided against a referral system as this restricts the effectiveness of the ODR platform.

Consumers (and also traders when the national law thus allows[102]) will

---

98 Article 22, ADR Directive, n 88.

99 Article 5(4), ADR Directive, ibid. Cf. Pablo Cortés, 'The Impact of EU Law in the Landscape of ADR in Italy, Spain and the UK: Time for Change or Missed Opportunity?' (2015) *ERA Forum* forthcoming.

100 Article 2, ODR Regulation, n 88.

101 Article 9(6) of the ODR Regulation states that the ODR platform will refer the claim to an ADR entity when parties have agreed; Article 9(8) states that if parties do not agree to an ADR entity, the claim will not be further processed; n 88.

102 The ODR Regulation allows for traders to bring complaints against consumers as long as the law of the country where the consumer is a resident allows for this. The Department for Business, Innovation and Skills has already expressed that the UK will not allow for this option, so complaints will only flow in one direction, from the consumer to the business. This seems to be the position

be able to submit complaints in the EU ODR platform free of charge and in their own language, but subsequently the ADR entities may charge a small fee and offer their services in a different language to that of the consumer.[103] A further challenge in the operation of the EU ODR platform is that it puts the onus on the consumers to provide the traders' email address. Providing the traders' correct email address can be tricky. Consumers may face difficulties in finding the correct email address as it may not be the one sent by the trader to confirm the transaction – if this proves to be an important hurdle, then the regulator might require traders to use the same email address, but it is acknowledged that this may be difficult to spot by the regulators unless they are flagged by consumer associations or the national ODR contact point.

Each Member State will establish one ODR contact point, which may be part of their national European Consumer Centres that belong to the ECC-Net, and each contact point will host at least two ODR advisors who will be available to provide parties with technical and language support.[104] The contact points will thus have the function of providing parties with information about the submission of the complaint and the available ADR processes. They will also inform parties about other means of redress in cases where the dispute cannot be resolved via the platform. For instance, they can advise consumers to pursue the claim through a sectorial mandatory ADR entity or the ESCP.

The final outcome must be reported back to the ODR platform.[105] The main role of the ODR platform is thus to increase awareness of ADR processes and to provide user-friendly ODR technology with the aim of making redress more accessible to consumers with e-commerce disputes. In so doing the platform is set to provide an electronic translation function supported by human intervention that will assist parties and

---

in most EU Member States because not only are many of these consumer ADR schemes financed by the State, but their procedures have been designed to address the power imbalances of the parties. Thus, those Member States that allow traders to bring complaints to consumers could change the dynamics in the operation of the ODR platform.

[103] ADR schemes will be certified by the national competent authorities if they comply with the criteria set out in the ADR Directive which requires them not to refuse cross-border complaints, but it does not oblige these certified ADR schemes to resolve the complaints in all the EU languages. This major obstacle is hoped to be overcome by using the EU ODR platform, which will be equipped with a translation tool and the assistance of ODR advisors recruited from the national European Consumer Centres.

[104] Article 7, ODR Regulation, n 88.

[105] Article 10(c), ODR Regulation, n 88.

ADR entities to exchange information. It remains to be seen how effective the new ODR platform will be in facilitating consumers with a user-friendly and accessible enforcement option, but there is little doubt that this is an ambitious step in the right direction. If successful, one can expect that it will incorporate the automatic referral to mandatory ADR entities as well as to expand its jurisdiction outside the e-commerce realm.

4. THE NEED FOR A HOLISTIC APPROACH TO CONSUMER ENFORCEMENT WITH ADR AT ITS CORE

With the goal of stimulating the Internal Market, the EU has adopted legislation that aims to overcome the obstacles that have impeded the growth of extrajudicial redress: namely, gaps in sectorial coverage, the absence of clear legal standards, and a lack of awareness by consumers. Online access to all certified ADR entities can impact positively on the level of awareness of an ADR landscape which is often patchy and difficult to navigate. The ADR Directive could represent a potential catalyst for real change in consumer redress. Accordingly, the implementation of the ADR Directive will be an opportunity to revise national schemes and it may lead to their rationalization, including the centralizing of its administration and oversight.[106] The new regulation of ADR is thus starting an institutionalization process which intends to improve the coordination and the quality of ADR processes, which may contribute to increase the effectiveness in the enforcement of consumer rights. Under the new rules, businesses will be required to notify consumers about ADR entities but in many cases they will not be compelled to participate in ADR. Therefore, the success of the new EU framework on consumer ADR will largely be dependent on how much of an opportunity both national governments and businesses will actually see the Directive providing.

When there are important gaps in its coverage of ADR, governments should consider making traders' adherence to ADR entities compulsory. For instance, airlines have notoriously refused to engage in meaningful independent ADR schemes, which led Germany to introduce sectorial legislation making it compulsory for airlines to participate in an ADR

---

[106] Christopher Hodges, 'Consumer Ombudsmen: Better Regulation and Dispute Resolution' (2015) *ERA Forum* 1–13.

scheme.[107] Likewise, the UK is contemplating a similar measure,[108] and the Commission has proposed to make it compulsory for delays and cancellation disputes across the EU.[109]

However, ADR entities have a limitation which is worth emphasizing. They normally deal with individual disputes. For example, if there is a train or a flight delay and the law states that all passengers are entitled to compensation, but only one consumer complains (first to the business, and then to the ADR entity), then it is likely that only that single consumer will receive compensation. The rest of the passengers will not be compensated even though they were equally entitled because they did not complain. Hence, effective enforcement cannot rely exclusively on consumer ADR schemes. Although the ADR Directive requires certified ADR entities to cooperate with national enforcement bodies,[110] as many ombudsman schemes in regulated sectors already do,[111] the ODR Regulation does not require such cooperation between the EU ODR platform and other enforcement bodies. This is a missed opportunity since the EU ODR platform will capture very useful information related to enforcement problems in the EU. It is therefore recommended that the EU ODR platform should incorporate clearly defined pathways that enable the coordination between the EU ODR platform (as well as the ADR entities operating within the platform) and the two other prongs of enforcement: public enforcement bodies and the courts. In other words, the EU ODR platform could be the best instrument not only for channelling e-commerce complaints to consumer ADR entities, but also to enable these two pathways to strengthen the effectiveness of consumer enforcement.

The first pathway should therefore be built to share information about complaints to national enforcement bodies and the CPC Network helping them to monitor problems with the enforcement of European consumer policy through recurring claims. The platform should be able to recognize when there is a pattern showing the lack of compliance with consumer rights as well as when there may be consumers who did not complain, but

---

[107] See the German Conciliation Body for Public Transport at https://soep-online.de/welcome.html.

[108] Civil Aviation Authority, 'Consumer Complaints Handling and ADR' CAP 1286 (15 April 2015).

[109] Article 16(a) of the Commission proposal amending Regulation 261/2004: COM(2013) 130 final.

[110] Article 17(1), ADR Directive, n 88.

[111] This is often the case in the regulated sector. For instance, the Financial Service Ombudsman in the UK often shares complaints data with the regulator and enforcement body, the Financial Conduct Authority.

who would be entitled to compensation. The second pathway should be to redirect consumers, when appropriate, to court processes, especially to the ESCP and collective redress options when these are available. In time, the ODR platform could also provide national courts with a simple and user-friendly case-management tool. Such tools could assist parties and courts to communicate online when processing consumer claims. Their design would need to be tailored in order to allow for the interoperability between national courts and the ODR platform. Although it is acknowledged that the design of such tools will be challenging, if successful it would bring the benefits associated with economies of scale. In doing so, it will also facilitate the communications amongst national courts and, as a result, it could deliver a more expeditious and accessible judicial redress when other more informal and cost-effective ADR options are unavailable.

The role of public enforcement through either private litigation or through national enforcement bodies remains very important since there will always be consumers who are unable to use ADR. In these cases only judicial enforcement (for instance, through collective action) and pressure from public bodies can ensure that vulnerable consumers do not miss out on receiving appropriate redress. There is indeed a correlation between the use of ADR and collective action. Hodges observes that one of the reasons why the class action procedure is not used frequently in some countries is due to their effective ADR infrastructure.[112] Indeed, the EU and US disparity on collective action reflects the different approaches on how to correct market failures; whereas the EU relies more on the roles of public enforcement authorities to take civil proceedings and criminal prosecutions against legal breaches affecting consumers (e.g. the Competition and Market Authority as the lead enforcers of the Unfair Terms Directive in the UK), US law provides individuals (i.e. consumers and lawyers) with tools (i.e. class actions) to stop market abuses and enforce consumer policies. This is notwithstanding that the US also has public enforcement bodies that monitor business compliance with consumer law (e.g. the Federal Trade Commission and equivalent state bodies), but the role and budget of these bodies are less significant than those of the EU counterparts.

Hodges notes that 'what seems to be occurring is a 'redress competition', between different options. If the collective action technique is not going to work much, then it will be necessary to cement the approaches based on regulatory and ADR techniques.'[113] Other reasons may be

---

[112] Hodges, n 66, 80–81.
[113] Ibid 84.

having well-resourced enforcement bodies, or having national rules on costs that disincentive mass litigation. Hence, there are significant disparities between the enforcement approaches of the 28 EU Member States as these are deeply rooted in their own redress cultures. While in some countries, such as in Germany, consumers often purchase insurance to cover their legal costs and have a quicker and cost-effective court system; in others, such as the UK, courts are increasingly seen as a last resort option as legal advice and representation is very expensive. As a result, consumers rely more heavily on ADR.

In terms of effective enforcement of consumer protection laws, a key concern is that increasingly using courts as a last resort and moving disputes from public enforcement and courts to ADR could, arguably, lead to an inadequate enforcement of European consumer rights as ADR will not always resolve disputes based on the parties' full legal entitlements under EU law. Indeed, most ADR entities operate consensual procedures (such as mediation techniques) that enable parties to reach amicable settlements. If these settlements are not properly monitored, they could lead parties with asymmetric powers (i.e. consumer and businesses) to reach settlements that do not reflect effective enforcement of EU consumer law. To put it bluntly, the experienced trader could put pressure on consumers to settle for less than what they would be entitled to (and thus with what would be recognized by a court of law or a public enforcement body). Such abuses could even compromise the rule of law, particularly when cloaked under confidentiality agreements. Hence, the more private ADR becomes, the greater the need for transparency and for developing an effective mechanism to evaluate its performance.

The ADR Directive attempts to counterbalance this risk by requiring a high level of transparency to certified ADR entities and imposing a supervisory role to the national competent authorities whose role is to ensure compliance by the certified ADR entities.[114] Importantly, these certified ADR entities have the obligation to cooperate with the national authorities entrusted with the enforcement of consumer law. In addition, the publication of annual activity statistics and biannual reports under the Directive should lead to a greater level of public scrutiny and accountability of ADR schemes. Moreover, the ODR platform will capture much information on consumer complaints and settlements which, if this big data is adequately processed, could be instrumental for the Commission and the Member States when designing legal responses to the market inability to ensure compliance with consumer protection laws. In this regard, Hodges argues

---

114 Article 19, ADR Directive, n 88.

that the link between ADR schemes and public regulatory schemes has the important function of collecting aggregated data on consumer disputes, which will lead to more effective cooperation with public enforcement bodies, as they will be able to identify market abuses and lack of compliance with consumer policies earlier.[115] These exchanges of information are hoped to have a knock-on effect in improving the coordination between public and private enforcement bodies. Hence, for instance, the ODR platform should identify rogue traders that break the law on a systematic basis and pass on this information to public enforcement bodies, so action can be taken promptly.[116] In addition, when specific economic sectors are not opting voluntarily into ADR entities, then mandatory adherence by law should be considered.

Greater access and accountability of ADR entities will, however, put greater pressure on public authorities which may not always be well resourced. Therefore, adequate public funds must be provided initially in order to ensure the appropriate monitoring of ADR entities, and it should then become self-financed by the fees paid by the traders participating in the ADR system (which, of course, are then passed on to the consumers). By contrast, if consumer ADR entities, which are becoming the main pillar of consumer enforcement, are inadequate, it will impact negatively on the trust that consumers have in these ADR entities, and in turn on the functioning of the Internal Market.

CONCLUDING REMARKS

In terms of consumer enforcement options the EU Commission noted that 'the current redress systems have their strengths and weaknesses and no single mechanism is ideal for all types of claims'.[117] This chapter has argued that the EU enforcement of consumer policy relies on three prongs – namely, the public enforcement authorities (and their pan-European Networks), judicial procedures tailored for consumer issues (particularly small claims procedures and collective action), and consumer ADR. While national enforcement bodies focus on deterrence and have limited powers to deliver individual redress, the courts are often not the best fora to addressing the vast majority of breaches of consumer disputes. Indeed, ADR is increasingly seen as the preferred option because it is

---

115 Hodges, n 106, 5.
116 Ibid 6.
117 European Commission, n 68, 3.

user-friendly, fast and cost-effective. In this vein, the EU and the Member States have begun shifting their policies, putting greater efforts in the promotion of out-of-court options by enacting legislation that promotes the use of nationally certified ADR entities, which can assist in ensuring better compliance with consumer protection laws while improving market regulation. The implementation of the Mediation Directive and the ADR Directive recognize that the judicial avenue should be seen as the last resort for resolving many consumer complaints. Yet, the participation of businesses in ADR remains voluntary in many economic sectors. Thus, only a holistic approach that effectively combines public and private enforcement options can guarantee a high level of consumer protection. It has been submitted that the ODR platform could be instrumental in providing this synergy if it enables coordination between consumer ADR entities (and not only those with competence to resolve e-commerce disputes) with the two other prongs of enforcement: the national enforcement bodies on one hand, and the judicial system on the other hand.

9. Effective private enforcement of EU competition law: an input and output legitimacy analysis of collective redress*

Carlo Petrucci

INTRODUCTION

Traditionally, infringements of EU competition law have been enforced through public enforcement carried out by the European Commission (Commission). Private enforcement through the national courts has been scarce.[1] In 2004, a radical modernization of the enforcement of EU competition law came into force.[2] The Commission would no longer be the main enforcer of the EU antitrust rules.[3] Enforcement would be decentralized so that the national competition authorities (NCAs) and national courts could play a fuller role. In view of the fact that the Commission and NCAs do not have limitless resources to investigate all breaches of EU competition law, the Commission has sought to encourage further private enforcement of competition law. The central focus of this policy is to facilitate the ability of

* Part of the research leading to these results has received funding from the European Research Council under the European Union's Seventh Framework Programme (FP/2007–2013)/ERC Grant Agreement n. 313642–LASI ('Law, science and interests in European policymaking'). The author wishes to thank Sara Drake for her assistance and comments on this chapter. Any mistakes remain solely mine.

1 Broadly speaking, private enforcement includes the ability of individuals to claim for injunctive relief, that is, bringing unlawful conduct to an end as well as damages. This chapter will focus on compensatory damages only.

2 Reg 1/2003 on the implementation of the rules on competition laid down in Articles 81 and 82 [now, 101 and 102 TFEU] of the Treaty [2003] OJ L1/1.

3 The term 'private enforcement of EU competition law' is specifically used to denote enforcement of Articles 101 and 102 TFEU and does not deal with merger control or state aid. These Treaty provisions are often referred to as the EU antitrust provisions.

individual litigants to bring claims for damages before national courts for losses suffered as a result of breaches of Articles 101 and/or 102 TFEU. From a pragmatic viewpoint, private enforcement means that private resources will be used in order to enforce competition law. A key difficulty with this approach is that infringements of competition law often result in a multitude of low-value losses. Individuals are deterred from making a claim as the litigation costs can be greater than the losses sustained. Collective redress[4] is seen as the answer to this problem since it allows the aggregation of a great number of claims into a single action. The rationale is that the grouping of a multitude of claims lowers the cost of the action which makes compensation of antitrust losses feasible and cost-effective both for individual claimants and for the civil justice system in general. In essence, an effective system of private enforcement requires effective rules on collective redress.

In 2013, the Commission adopted a Communication and a Recommendation on Collective Redress.[5] These non-binding measures complemented a new Damages Directive[6] and non-binding guidance on quantification of harm.[7] The goal of this chapter is to assess the effectiveness of these new EU rules on collective redress by adopting an original interdisciplinary approach. The analysis draws upon the political theory of input/output legitimacy combined with the legal notion of effectiveness. In particular, it asks whether the inputs provided by the European Parliament and various stakeholders throughout the policymaking process have improved or lessened the effectiveness of the rules on collective redress in the field of competition law. These two situations are referred to as the

---

[4] Many names may be used to designate the phenomenon of a plurality of claimants acting jointly in the same action against one or more defendants: collective actions, class actions, mass claims, and so on. Each name reveals a certain viewpoint on this type of litigation. This chapter uses the term 'collective redress' as this is the official name used in EU law, which generally refers to the aggregation of a great number of claimants to obtain redress for a prejudice suffered as a result of a breach of EU rights, including breach of competition law.

[5] Commission Recommendation 2013/396/EU of 11 June 2013 on common principles for injunctive and compensatory collective redress mechanisms in the Member States concerning violations of rights granted under Union Law [2013] OJ L201/60; and Commission Communication 'Towards a European Horizontal Framework for Collective Redress' COM(2013) 401 final. Hereinafter: Recommendation and Communication respectively.

[6] Dir 2014/104 on certain rules governing actions for damages under national law for infringements of the competition law provisions of the Member States and of the European Union [2014] OJ L349/1.

[7] Commission Communication, 'Quantifying Harm in Actions for Damages Based on Breaches of Article 101 or 102 of the Treaty on the Functioning of the European Union' [2013] OJ C167/19.

synergy and trade-off hypothesis respectively. However, the chapter goes beyond such a dichotomy and presents new insights into the relationship between legitimacy and effectiveness. The central idea is that for a policy to be effective, it needs to comply with some essential legal values without which the actors entrusted with its implementation may not regard it as legitimate. This is particularly the case with legal reforms which rely on enforcement before national courts. Such reforms must adapt to a pre-existing legal framework informed by longstanding legal values, the respect of which makes it more likely that the actors entrusted with their implementation (e.g. judges and lawyers) will apply the rules correctly, without undermining their scope or setting out restrictive interpretations. In other words, the legal community's acceptance of the legitimacy of legal reforms in relation to essential legal principles is one of the conditions for its proper implementation, thus making it more effective.

There are two reasons why the input/output legitimacy theory is appropriate for an analysis of the EU rules on collective redress. The first concerns the 'input' side: the policy on collective redress proposed by the Commission has been the subject of wide consultation involving a number of different actors including the European Parliament and numerous stakeholders. This has increased the democratic nature of the legislative process resulting in the adoption of the new rules. The second reason concerns the fact that 'output' legitimacy is assessed precisely in terms of the effectiveness of a policy to solve the problem for which it was promoted. The theory of input/output legitimacy does not offer a standard definition of effectiveness.[8] It refers to the general idea that a policy must deliver solutions capable of solving collective problems by investigating whether it is able to achieve the goal for which it was made. Put differently, it may be understood as formal or instrumental rationality which evaluates the adequacy of an action (e.g. a policy) to achieve an end (e.g. a desired state of affairs).[9] Given the vagueness of this concept of effectiveness, this chapter employs a more concrete concept of effectiveness, which refers to the enforcement of Union law before national courts.[10] Broadly speaking,

---

[8] For example, the word 'effectiveness' in the subject index of the Oxford Handbook of Political Science recurs only once, but no definition is given in the text. Robert E. Goodin (ed), *The Oxford Handbook of Political Science* (OUP 2009).

[9] For a description of instrumental rationality, see the entry: 'Instrumental Rationality' in the Stanford Encyclopaedia of Philosophy. <http://plato.stanford.edu/entries/rationality-instrumental/> accessed 25 May 2015.

[10] Takis Tridimas, *The General Principles of EU Law* (2nd ed, OUP 2006) 418. Other scholars have developed various meanings of the EU principle of

the EU's legal notion of effectiveness refers to the conferral on individuals of EU rights enforceable before national courts, which pursues two goals. First, individuals who suffer prejudice because of a breach of EU law may obtain a form of redress, for example, compensation. Second, actions based on EU rights exert pressure upon Member States or private parties to comply with EU law. Under this latter perspective, this type of effectiveness is consistent with the concept of deterrence: the prospect that an addressee of an EU legal duty is found responsible before the national court is an incentive to comply with EU law. Accordingly, for the purpose of this chapter, effectiveness refers to the capability of the EU rules on collective redress to facilitate individuals' redress, for the prejudices suffered as a result of breach of competition law, namely compensation and to promote compliance with Articles 101 and 102 TFEU.

From a methodological viewpoint, this chapter analyses four key legal rules which underpin a collective redress regime and tracks their development through the EU policy process. It will examine how the rules were framed in the original policy documents prepared by the Commission, namely the Green Paper 2005[11] and White Paper 2008[12] on damages actions for breach of the EC antitrust rules. It then summarizes the responses of the European Parliament and a sample of stakeholders' views of these two documents. This constitutes our 'input' legitimacy analysis. Next, the chapter demonstrates how the content of the rules has changed following the inputs of the European Parliament and stakeholders. This allows the extent to which such inputs have had an impact on the Commission's proposals to be identified. Finally, the chapter discusses whether the inputs have enhanced or decreased the effectiveness of these rules by taking into account the EU measures in which such rules are provided and the content of such rules in relation to their capability to promote compliance and facilitate antitrust victims' compensation. This amounts to our 'output' legitimacy analysis. As explained above, this assessment is made on the basis of the EU legal notion of effectiveness.

This chapter is structured as follows. Section 1 sets out the legal and

---

effectiveness. For an earlier contribution, see Francis Snyder, 'The Effectiveness of European Community Law: Institutions, Processes, Tools and Techniques' (1993) 56 *Michigan Law Review* 19; Michael Dougan, *National Remedies Before the Court of Justice: Issues of Harmonisation and Differentiation* (Hart 2004) 27 discussed in the Introduction of this volume.

[11] 'Green Paper on damages actions for breach of the EC antitrust rules' COM(2005) 672 final.

[12] 'White Paper on damages actions for breach of the EC antitrust rules' COM(2008) 165 final.

theoretical framework. First, it provides a legal overview of collective redress in the context of antitrust claims and the Commission's regulatory response. Secondly, it expounds the theory of input/output legitimacy and explains why it has been applied to collective redress. Section 2 is concerned with the empirical analysis. The aim is to discover the extent to which the European Parliament and stakeholders have had an impact on the rules on collective redress. To this end, it presents the four key rules selected on collective redress which were discussed by the European Parliament and stakeholders, and briefly illustrates their relevance to the system of collective redress. Secondly, it shows the views of two samples of stakeholders taken from two different stakeholders' consultations (2006 and 2008) and of the European Parliament on these four key rules. Thirdly, it analyses the views and how the Commission responded to them. Section 3 assesses the effectiveness of the new collective redress measures and discusses whether the European Parliament and stakeholders' inputs have made such rules more or less effective. Finally, the chapter will present new insights into the relationship between effectiveness and legitimacy.

1. THE LEGAL AND THEORETICAL FRAMEWORK

1.1. Regulating Collective Redress in the Context of EU Antitrust Law: The Legal and Policy Background

Regulation 1/2003[13] is the key provision governing the enforcement of competition law and sets out the legal framework for co-operation between the different actors involved in the enforcement of the EU antitrust rules. With regard to the role played by national courts, it states in its recitals that national courts play an essential part in applying the EU competition rules by awarding damages to the victims of infringements.[14] In an important legal development, Article 6 conferred on national courts the power to apply Articles 101 and 102 of the TFEU (previously 81 and 82 respectively) in their entirety in proceedings brought before them by private actors.[15] Unfortunately, Regulation 1/2003 did not provide any rules on the right to compensation of antitrust losses or on the procedural rules applicable before national courts to obtain such compensation.

---

[13] See n 2.

[14] Recital (7), ibid.

[15] This involved extending direct applicability in full to Article 101 TFEU and removing the Commission's monopoly on the application of Article 101(3) TFEU.

In fact, these two aspects were dealt with by the Court of Justice of the European Union (CJEU) in its *Courage* ruling[16] in which it had conferred upon individuals the EU right to claim damages for losses caused by a breach of the EU antitrust provisions directly before their national courts. The novelty of *Courage* was to fill a gap and establish a new EU remedy, namely the EU substantive right to compensation of damages (a remedy which would have previously been dependant on the national law of a Member State). However, the right was to be applied in accordance with the procedural law of the Member State in which proceedings were brought subject to the longstanding principles of equivalence and effectiveness.[17] Whilst the EU right to claim antitrust damages provided a new incentive for private parties to bring antitrust proceedings, it became apparent to the Commission that some Member States' procedural rules were inadequate to facilitate antitrust actions.[18] On this basis, the Commission embarked on a programme to harmonize some procedural and substantive rules applicable to antitrust actions before national courts with a view to providing a legal framework suited to the characteristics of antitrust litigation.

The Commission's proposed harmonization programme included rules on collective redress for compensation of antitrust damages. DG COMP first published its 2005 Green Paper[19] which was followed by its White Paper in 2008.[20] Importantly, at the same time, DG SANCO had started considering the remedy of collective redress for breach of EU law within its remit, in particular, for breach of EU consumer law. In 2009, DG SANCO had issued a Green Paper on consumer collective redress.[21] In

---

[16] Case C-453/99 *Courage* [2001] ECR I-6297.

[17] Ibid, para 29. See further, Sara Drake, 'Scope of *Courage* and the Principle of "Individual Liability" for Damages: Further Development of the Principle of Effective Judicial Protection' (2006) 31 EL Rev 841. Here the principle of effectiveness refers to the minimum standard that national procedural law must respect when it is relied on to enforce EU rights before national courts. The current formula, which was adopted in *Courage*, is that national law must not make the exercise of EU rights virtually impossible or excessively difficult: see Case C-312/93 *Peterbroeck* [1995] ECR I-4599. See further discussion in Chapter 1 of this volume.

[18] The first external report commissioned by the Commission on this matter was the Ashurst study: Denis Waelbroeck, Donald Slater and Gil Even-Shoshan (Ashurst), 'Study on the Conditions of Claims for Damages in Case of Infringement of EC Competition Rules: Comparative Report' (2004). <http://ec.europa.eu/competition/antitrust/actionsdamages/economic_clean_en.pdf> accessed: 22 April 2015.

[19] Green Paper, n 11, Option 25.

[20] White Paper, n 12, p 4.

[21] 'Green Paper on consumer collective redress' COM(2008) 794 final.

2009, a proposal for a Council Directive was drafted by DG COMP (and leaked) but withdrawn before being formally published. This withdrawal is thought to be in response to criticisms of the proposed Directive from the European Parliament which, inter alia,[22] had asked the Commission to refrain from presenting collective redress rules applicable solely in antitrust damages proceedings and to consider a horizontal approach instead whereby collective redress rules could be relied upon by individuals for an infringement of any type of EU law.[23] It is suggested that another reason for the withdrawal was tension over the most appropriate legal basis for a directive on damages actions. The 2008 White Paper had not specified a legal base. The leaked directive referred to Article 83 of the Treaty (EC) (now Article 103 TFEU), which does not involve the European Parliament in the law-making process. The European Parliament advocated that Article 95 EC (now Article 114 TFEU), the so-called harmonization clause, was the correct legal base. This provision provided for the co-decision (now ordinary legislative procedure) to be followed in which the European Parliament and Council are co-legislators.

In 2011, DG SANCO launched a public consultation on collective redress for the enforcement of any EU rights.[24] Once again, the European Parliament requested that a model of collective redress be advocated that would allow compensation for any type of scattered loss[25] regardless of the nature of violation of EU law.[26] The Commission respected the European Parliament's requests and did not introduce collective redress rules in the 2013 proposal for a directive on antitrust damages.[27] Rather, it released a Communication on a horizontal framework for collective redress[28] and a Recommendation on collective redress mechanisms concerning violations

---

[22] A copy of the leaked draft directive is on file with the author.

[23] European Parliament resolution of 26 March 2009 on the White Paper on damages actions for breach of the EC antitrust rules (2008/2154(INI)), point 5.

[24] Commission Staff Working Document, Public Consultation: 'Towards a Coherent European Approach to Collective Redress' SEC (2011) 173 final.

[25] Scattered losses refer to widespread losses affecting a great number of victims resulting from single unlawful conduct.

[26] European Parliament resolution of 2 February 2012 on 'Towards a Coherent European Approach to Collective Redress' (2011/2089(INI)), points 1 and 15.

[27] Commission, 'Proposal for a Directive of the European Parliament and of the Council on certain rules governing actions for damages under national law for infringements of the competition law provisions of the Member States and of the European Union' COM(2013) 404 final.

[28] Commission Communication, 'Towards a European Horizontal Framework for Collective Redress' COM(2013) 401 final.

of Union rights, which include breaches of competition law.[29] This chapter refers to the rules on collective redress, but the analysis focuses on their application in the field of competition law.

These 'soft law' measures set out a general approach to collective redress that Member States are asked to incorporate into their national law.[30] They provide broad principles regulating the standing accorded to entities entitled to bring a representative action, the verification of the admissibility of an action at the early stages of litigation, reimbursement of legal costs and funding, the opt-in principle, alternative dispute resolution and settlements, and the prohibition of punitive damages. By July 2017, the Commission will assess the Member States' experience of operating collective redress based on statistics collected by the Member States themselves[31] and then consider whether further measures should be taken.[32]

1.2. The Theoretical Framework for Assessment: Input and Output Legitimacy

In political theory, the word 'legitimacy' refers to the consent of the ruled over the political regime in which they live.[33] Input legitimacy relates to the decision-making process through which political decisions are made, in particular, by taking into account procedures that enable citizens or their representatives to express their views on the policy under discussion. It stresses the need to enhance the democratic credentials of the decision-making process by broadening and including a wide range of people and actors who are part of a community and are affected by the resulting decisions. The argument is that participation and opportunity to express personal views in the decision-making process create support for the resulting resolutions. The quality of the decisions also improves because the greater inclusiveness enables policymakers to take into account more evidence and information on the matter under discussion. In contrast, output legitimacy relates to the government's capability to deliver effec-

---

[29] Commission Recommendation on common principles for injunctive and compensatory collective redress mechanisms in the Member States concerning violations of rights granted under Union Law [2013] OJ L201/60.

[30] Communication, n 5, p 16.

[31] Recommendation, n 5, Article 41.

[32] Ibid.

[33] The literature on this topic is extensive. See, for example, Richard Bellamy, 'Democracy without Democracy? Can the EU's Democratic 'Outputs' Be Separated from the Democratic "Inputs" Provided by Competitive Parties and Majority Rule?' (2010) 17 *Journal of European Public Policy* 2.

tive solutions to collective problems. The people's consent arises from the effectiveness of the policy rather than the characteristics of the decision-making process. From this perspective, technical experts occupy a key role in guaranteeing the effectiveness of a certain policy. Because of their detailed knowledge into specific matters, experts are trusted in the analysis of the problem and/or in the exercise of delegated powers to make relevant decisions.

The debate on input and output legitimacy has resonance in the EU.[34] Due to the EU's institutional tasks, for many years the Commission's focus was on achieving output legitimacy.[35] However, with the increasing recognition of the democratic deficit of the EU, the focus of the EU institutions has now shifted towards enhancing the participatory quality of the EU decision-making process.[36] Opinions differ as to the extent to which input rather than output legitimacy is more desirable. Furthermore, it has been highlighted that whilst theoretical discussion on the input/output legitimacy is extensive, there is still little empirical research on whether input legitimacy results in better or worse policy outcomes, two situations that are referred to as the synergy and trade-off hypotheses.[37] As mentioned above, this chapter investigates whether the democratic inputs given by the European Parliament and stakeholders have resulted in more rather than less effective policy on collective redress.

2. THE EMPIRICAL ANALYSIS

There are a number of features of the policymaking process on collective redress which will be taken into account when assessing input legitimacy. First, previous EU competition law legislation based on Article 103 TFEU simply required consultation of the European Parliament. In contrast, the 2014 Damages Directive[38] was adopted on the basis of Article 103 TFEU *and* Article 114 TFEU and the ordinary legislative procedure was

---

34 Fritz Scharpf, *Governing in Europe: Effective and Democratic?* (OUP 1999).

35 Majone is an exponent of the need to focus on the effectiveness of policymaking. Giandomenico Majone, 'The Regulatory State and its Legitimacy Problems' (1999) 22 *West European Politics* 1.

36 Karl-Oskar Lindgren and Thomas Persson, 'Input and Output Legitimacy: Synergy or Trade-Off? Empirical Evidence from an EU Survey' (2010) 17 *Journal of European Public Policy* 449. Grace Skogstad, 'Legitimacy and/or Policy Effectiveness? Network Governance and GMO Regulation in the European Union' (2003) 10 *Journal of European Public Policy* 321.

37 Ibid, 450.

38 Dir 2014/104, n 7.

followed. Thus the input of the European Parliament has increased as it plays an equal role with the Council in the ordinary legislative procedure. No legislation can be adopted without its approval. Second, the Commission undertook extensive consultations with stakeholders on the broader issue of reforming the legal framework to encourage private enforcement of the EU's antitrust rules (four in total) and which received a large number of responses.[39] Public consultations are consistent with the idea of deliberative democracy and are designed to facilitate and widen people's participation in the decision-making process. Given the extent of the stakeholders' consultations and the involvement of the European Parliament, it is argued that there has been an enhanced democratic input.

In order to test the trade-off and synergy hypotheses, it is first necessary to understand whether the European Parliament and stakeholders had an impact on the EU (soft law) measures on collective redress. To do so, this section has selected four key rules, which play a pivotal role in a system of collective redress. Table 9.1 gives a chronological overview of the positions expressed by the European Parliament and stakeholders on these four rules and how the Commission responded to them at the different stages of the policy process. It starts from the options set out in the Commission's 2005 Green Paper. Next, it summarizes a sample of 20 stakeholders and the European Parliament's views. Subsequently, it illustrates how such rules were changed in the Commission's 2008 White Paper. Again, it presents a sample of 20 stakeholders[40] and European Parliament's views on the rules set out in the White Paper. It also presents the European Parliament's view on a DG SANCO Commission's policy document on horizontal approach to collective redress. Finally, it summarizes how the selected rules have been framed in the 2013 EU Communication and Recommendation on collective redress.

It should be noted that the Green Paper set out some general options

---

[39] A first consultation was made in 2006, in relation to the Green Paper. A second in 2008, in relation to the White Paper. The third consultation took place in 2011 on quantification of antitrust harm. These consultations were launched by DG COMP. The consultation documents and the stakeholders' contributions are available at: <http://ec.europa.eu/competition/antitrust/actionsdamages/documents.html> accessed 17 April 2015. The fourth, still in 2011, was on collective redress in general and was run by the then DG SANCO. The consultation document and the stakeholders' contributions are available at: <http://ec.europa.eu/dgs/health_food-safety/dgs_consultations/ca/collective_redress_consultation_en.htm> accessed 17 April 2015.

[40] This sample is different from the previous sample of stakeholders of the 2006 consultation since many stakeholders who participated in the 2006 consultation did not participate in the 2008 consultation and vice versa.

rather than precise legal rules. Such options were then discussed in the 2006 stakeholders' consultation. This means that it is difficult to accurately assess how the rules were modified following the stakeholders' inputs and the position taken by the European Parliament in a resolution of 2007. Nonetheless, in the 2008 White Paper the Commission proposed clearer rules which were discussed during the second stakeholders' consultation of 2008 and examined by the European Parliament in its resolutions of 2009 and 2012. In summary, the following are the documents on which the analysis is made:[41]

- 2005: Commission Green Paper on antitrust private enforcement;[42]
- 2006: First stakeholders' consultation on the Green Paper;[43]
- 2007: European Parliament resolution on the Green Paper;[44]
- 2008: Commission White Paper on antitrust private enforcement;[45]
- 2008: Second stakeholders' consultation on the White Paper;[46]
- 2009: European Parliament resolution on the White Paper;[47]
- 2012: European Parliament resolution on collective redress;[48]

---

[41] Throughout the policymaking process on private enforcement in the context of the EU antitrust rules, the Commission prepared two impact assessment reports. They have not been included in the analysis because they do not add to the Commission's position as expressed in the White Paper and proposed Damages Directive: Commission, 'Commission Staff Working Document, Accompanying document to the White Paper on damages actions for breach of antitrust rules: Impact Assessment' SEC (2008) 405 final (hereinafter: Impact Assessment Report on the White Paper (2008)); and Commission, 'Impact Assessment Report, Damages actions for breach of the EU antitrust rules accompanying the proposal for a Directive of the European Parliament and of the Council on certain rules governing actions for damages under national law for infringements of the competition law provisions of the Member States and of the European Union' COM(2013) 404 final (hereinafter: Impact Assessment Report on the Proposal for a Directive on damages actions (2013)).

[42] See n 11.

[43] <http://ec.europa.eu/competition/antitrust/actionsdamages/green_paper_comments.html> accessed 12 April 2015.

[44] European Parliament resolution of 25 April 2007 on the Green Paper on damages actions for breach of the EC antitrust rules (2006/2207(INI)).

[45] See n 12.

[46] <http://ec.europa.eu/competition/antitrust/actionsdamages/white_paper_comments.html> accessed 12 April 2015.

[47] European Parliament resolution of 26 March 2009 on the White Paper on damages actions for breach of the EC antitrust rules (2008/2154(INI)).

[48] European Parliament resolution of 2 February 2012 on 'Towards a Coherent European Approach to Collective Redress' (2011/2089(INI)).

– 2013: Commission Communication and Recommendation on collective redress;[49]

With regard to the stakeholders' consultations, a sample of 20 submissions for each consultation has been taken.[50] The samples include different categories of stakeholders such as businesses' associations, law firms,[51] consumers' associations, and think-tank groups. Some Member States and national authorities submitted their views too, but they have not been taken into account. The theory of input/output legitimacy considers the input of civil society, not of the Member States. In the context of the EU, the Member States may express their views through the Council.

Before proceeding, it is helpful to briefly outline the four rules selected and explain why they are important in an effective system of collective redress.

Standing of consumers' associations

This refers to the legal standing of consumers' associations to commence legal proceedings before a court on behalf of their members. Since breaches of antitrust often result in low-value losses, single consumers may not wish to make a claim as the litigation costs are greater than the loss. Consumers' associations are able to group a large number of victims and bring an action on their behalf. They may also have both the resources and the expertise to assess whether there are factual and legal grounds to make a claim. Accordingly, granting standing to consumers' associations enhances the effectiveness of collective redress by facilitating compensation of antitrust victims.

Funding of actions and cost allocation

Most of the Member States' legal systems adopt the so-called 'loser-pays' principle according to which the losing party has to pay the legal costs and

---

49 See n 5.

50 The exact figures of the total submissions are not available. The Impact Assessment Report on the White Paper (2008) indicates 150 submissions (at p 6). The Impact Assessment Report on the Proposal for a Directive on damages actions (2013) indicates 170 submissions (n 9, at p 6).

51 The Impact Assessment Report on the Proposal for a Directive on damages actions (2013) reports that law firms had similar views on some rules such as protection of corporate statements and disclosure of documents covered by legal privilege. However, apart from these aspects, their contributions differed either because of the different legal cultures or because they tended to represent claimants or defendants, at p 8. For the purposes of this chapter, it is not important to report such differences, rather, to summarize the overall stakeholders' positions in order to compare them with the adopted rules.

expenses. Changes to this rule were considered because the risk of paying such costs may discourage would-be claimants to make a claim even if it was substantiated by convincing evidence. The proposed shift of allocation of litigation costs consisted of imposing the payment of litigation costs upon the defendant, even in case of rejection of the claim. The fact that a claimant would not be responsible for such costs may encourage would-be claimants to make a claim as they would not bear the risk of an unsuccessful litigation outcome.

Choice between opt-in and opt-out model of collective redress

An opt-in regime provides that individual consumers must take explicit steps to join a collective action and become claimants; conversely, an opt-out system provides that a certain class of victims is automatically included in a collective action which has been commenced by other victims or their representatives. Here, individual victims retain the right to opt out and start proceedings on their own. An opt-out regime is controversial because it incorporates victims into a collective action without their consent; on the other hand it is very effective because by automatically aggregating all victims, if successful, the amount of compensation awarded will be higher than under the opt-in variant. This increases the deterrent effect of a collective action.

Punitive damages

The ordinary principle underpinning compensation is that of 'compensatory damages', which means that the compensation awarded must restore the claimant into the position they would have been in had the wrong not been committed. In the Commission's policy documents, the expression 'full compensation' is used to refer to this principle and reflects the Court's case law on remedies.[52] In contrast, 'punitive damages' refers to an award of compensation greater than the loss incurred. One of the reasons why the award of punitive damages for antitrust damages actions is considered is because the threat of compensatory damages may not be sufficient to deter undertakings from breaching competition law. In some instances the illegal gains are greater than the compensatory award. Furthermore, not all violations of competition law are discovered. As a result, it may still be beneficial for businesses to violate antitrust law. The imposition of punitive damages may offset both the gap between illegal gains and compensatory awards and the would-be violator's estimate that it may not be caught. Thus, punitive damages increase the deterrent effect of antitrust

---

[52] Case C-271/91 *Marshall v Southampton (No 2)* [1993] ECR I-4367.

Table 9.1 Actors' positions on four key rules

	Standing of consumer associations	Cost allocation	Opt-in/opt-out	Punitive damages
Commission's Green Paper (2005)	Conferral of standing for consumers' associations	Unsuccessful claimants will have to pay costs only if they acted in a manifestly unreasonable manner Courts' discretionary power to order at the beginning of a trial that the claimant not be exposed to any cost recovery even if the action were to be unsuccessful	Not explicitly discussed	Double damages for horizontal cartels. Such awards could be automatic, conditional or at the discretion of the court
Sample of stakeholders' view on Green Paper (2006)	Agreement with conferral of standing to consumers' associations: 15 Disagreement: 4 Position not declared: 1	Acceptance of Commission's proposal: 4 Rejection of Commission's proposal (maintenance of the loser-pays principle): 14 Position not declared: 2	Rejection of opt-out: 9 Preference for opt-out: 3 Position not declared: 8	Rejection of punitive damages: 14 Acceptance of punitive damages: 2 Position not declared: 4
European Parliament on Green Paper (Resolution 2007)	Agreement with Commission's proposal: yes (point 21) 'victims should be able voluntarily to bring collective actions,	Agreement with Commission's proposal (point 22) Judicial authorities should be able to take into account the different economic situation of	Implicitly rejected (point 21) 'victims should be able *voluntarily* to bring collective actions'	Payments awarded to complainants should be compensatory and should not exceed the actual damage (*damnum emergens*)

Table 9.1 continued

	Standing of consumer associations	Cost allocation	Opt-in/opt-out	Punitive damages
	either directly or via organisations whose statutes have this as their object'	the parties and, where appropriate, should make an assessment at the outset of proceedings	[The adverb 'voluntarily' suggests that victims must give their consent to join a collective action, which excludes their automatic inclusion as it occurs in the opt-out model]	and losses ('*lucrum cessans*') suffered, (point 17) Any proposed measure must fully respect the public policy of the Member States, in particular with regard to punitive damages (point 18)
Commission's White Paper (2008)	Conferral of standing to consumers' associations	Acceptance of the loser-pays principle, but granting national courts the power to derogate from this principle	Acceptance of the opt-in regime (ie: rejection of the opt-out system)	Full compensation, but the Commission held that punitive damages may be awarded according to national law
Sample of stakeholders' view on White Paper (2008)	Agreement with conferral of standing to consumers' association: 12 Disagreement: 6 Position not declared: 2	Agreement with Commission's proposal: 5 Disagreement: 10 Position not declared: 5	Rejection of opt-out: 13 Preference for opt-out: 1 Position not declared: 6	Rejection of punitive damages: 14 Acceptance of punitive damages: 1 Position not declared: 5

Table 9.1 (continued)

	Standing of consumer associations	Cost allocation	Opt-in/opt-out	Punitive damages
European Parliament on White Paper (Resolution 2009)	Agreement with Commission's proposal: yes (letter E and point 9)	Rules on allocation of costs should be determined by the Member States (point 20)	Agreement with Commission's proposal: opt-in regime (point 10)	Rejection of punitive damages (letter F)
European Parliament on collective redress in general (Resolution 2012)	Standing to consumers' associations	Member States should determine rules on allocation of costs, but preference for the maintenance of the loser-pays principle	Opt-in regime	Principle of full compensation (i.e. no punitive damages)
Final Commission's proposal (Commission's Communication and Recommendation 2013)	Standing to consumers' associations (point 4 of Recommendation and 3.3 of Communication)	Adoption of the loser-pays principle but possibility to rely on third parties' funding (point 13 of the Recommendation and 3.9 of the Communication)	Opt-in regime (point 21 of Recommendation and 3.4 of Communication)	Rejection of punitive damages (point 31 of the Recommendation and 3.1 of Communication)

litigation. In addition, the prospect for claimants to be awarded compensation greater than the incurred loss encourages them to make a claim.

The findings

The table shows that there are some clear differences between the Commission's initial proposals set out in the 2005 Green Paper and the final rules adopted in its 2013 Communication and Recommendation. The only exception seems to be the conferral of standing on consumers' associations. However, since the Commission, the European Parliament and stakeholders all agreed that such bodies should be given standing, it cannot be said that the European Parliament and stakeholders have improved rather than worsened the effectiveness of collective redress.

Although the Green Paper set out a range of options framed in general terms, stakeholders fully understood the issues at stake. For example, the possibility of adopting the opt-out system was not explicitly mentioned in the Green Paper, yet a great number of stakeholders expressed their opposition. Equally, with regard to the European Parliament, in a debate of 23 April 2007, some of its members voiced their concern about the adoption of some rules imported from the US class actions such as the opt-out regime. In response to such concern, the then Competition Commissioner, Neelie Kroes, declared: 'So let us be clear – and I repeat – US style opt-out class actions are *not* on the agenda and will not be on my agenda.'[53]

With regard to the first consultation (2006) and the first European Parliament resolution (2007), and bearing in mind that stakeholders' views have been inferred through a sample, it is interesting to note that the majority of stakeholders' views broadly coincided with the European Parliament. This is the case relating to the grant of standing to consumers' associations (or certain qualified bodies), the adoption of the principle of compensatory damages (with the corresponding exclusion of punitive damages), and the rejection of the opt-out regime. In contrast, a difference between stakeholders and the European Parliament emerged in relation to the funding of antitrust litigation and cost allocation: here the majority of stakeholders preferred to maintain the loser-pays principle, which is common in most EU legal systems, whereas the European Parliament seemed open to consideration of the Commission's proposal to grant national courts discretion to change the allocation of litigation costs.

The Commission articulated more clearly the rules on collective redress

---

[53] European Parliament Debate held on 23 April 2007. <http://www.europarl.europa.eu/sides/getDoc.do?pubRef=-//EP//TEXT+CRE+20070423+ITEM-023+DOC+XML+V0//EN&language=EN> accessed 23 April 2015.

in the White Paper (2008). In particular, it kept those rules on which there was consensus among stakeholders and the European Parliament (i.e. standing to consumers' associations) and dropped the proposal to introduce punitive damages for horizontal cartels, a measure that both stakeholders and the European Parliament had been opposed to. The choice of the opt-in regime was also made explicit. Finally, with regard to rules on allocation of litigation costs, the Commission expressly referred to the 'loser-pays' principle, however, it still maintained that national legal systems could adopt rules derogating from this principle.

In response to the White Paper, stakeholders confirmed their acceptance of the standing to consumers' associations and their opposition to punitive damages (only one out of the sample of 20 was in favour). In relation to the opt-in regime, more than half of the stakeholders were in favour of this regime, whereas 7 out of 20 did not take any stance. As for the rules on allocation of litigation costs, the majority of stakeholders were against the Commission's proposal to grant national courts the power to derogate from the 'loser-pays' principle. The European Parliament expressed its position on consumers' association standing, cost allocation, opt-in versus opt-out and punitive damages in the 2009 and 2012 resolutions, which were all in line with those of the stakeholders. Overall, the rules formulated by the Commission and contained in the 2013 Recommendation and Communication are consistent with the European Parliament and stakeholders' positions.

In summary. With regard to consumers' associations' standing to bring collective actions, the Commission adopted a balanced approach. On the one hand, it provides that representative entities may bring representative actions, on the other hand a number of safeguards have been provided to guarantee that such entities pursue the interests of their members. For example, representative entities should have a non-profit-making character and there must be a relationship between their main objective and the infringed rights for which collective actions are brought.[54] The loser-pays principle has been adopted[55] without the possibility for national courts to derogate from this principle. Perhaps in order to balance the lack of exception to this principle, the Commission provided that third parties may fund collective actions,[56] subject to some conditions aiming to prevent conflicts of interests between third party funders and claimants and to avoid third parties' undue influence over procedural decisions.

---

54 Recommendation, n 5, Article 4.

55 Article 13, ibid.

56 Article 14, ibid.

This solution represents a compromise. On the one hand, the adoption of the loser-pays principle may discourage would-be claimants to make a claim, thus reducing the effectiveness of collective redress. On the other hand, allowing third parties' funding may facilitate collective actions even if this is subject to certain safeguards aiming to avoid conflicts of interests. The opt-in system has been adopted although exceptions to this principle are allowed on the grounds of sound administration of justice.[57] With respect to punitive damages, the Commission took the view that they should be prohibited,[58] without providing any exceptions to this prohibition.[59]

3. OUTPUT LEGITIMACY: ASSESSING THE EFFECTIVENESS OF THE EU RULES ON COLLECTIVE REDRESS

In a political process characterized by a multiplicity of actors, it is difficult to identify the 'causes' and 'contributing factors' that result in a specific outcome. However, in the present case, it is plausible to say that stakeholders and the European Parliament had an impact on the final rules proposed by the Commission. Although the initial Commission's rules as set out in the Green Paper were formulated vaguely, the final ones contained in the 2013 Communication and Recommendation correspond fully with the views of the selected stakeholders and the European Parliament. In the testing of the trade-off and synergy hypotheses, it is submitted that the European Parliament and stakeholders have had an impact on two aspects that are relevant to the effectiveness of this policy: the type of legislative act adopted to enact collective redress rules and the content of these rules (as examined above).

3.1. Effectiveness and Soft Law

The first aspect concerns the Commission's choice to adopt the Communication and the Recommendation to express its policy on

---

57 Communication, n 5, point 3.4 and Recommendation, n 5, Article 21.

58 Article 31, ibid.

59 This prohibition seems at odds with the Court's ruling in Joined Cases C-295–298/04 *Manfredi* [2006] ECR I-6619 in which the Court established that awards of punitive damages are a matter of national law. Perhaps a way to reconcile these two positions is that Member States should not award punitive damages in collective redress cases.

collective redress and its overall strategy. Whilst stakeholders advocated a regulatory approach based on common principles rather than specific rules, they also stressed that such principles had to fit the different legal systems of the Member States and take into account the experience so far developed by the Member States.[60] The best way in which the Commission could put into effect this stakeholders' request was to adopt soft law, which can be adopted quickly given that it does not require the involvement of the Council or other EU institutions, and it is less intrusive in national legal orders, which means that Member States will enjoy more room to develop their system of collective redress. By July 2015 the Member States have to implement the principles contained in the soft law here discussed,[61] and by July 2017 the Commission will evaluate the Member States' implementation and their experience of collective redress.[62] If the Commission's evaluation on the effectiveness of non-binding EU measures on collective redress is negative, then further measures will be considered.[63]

The decision to adopt soft law measures can be praised because it confirms the Commission's commitment to developing evidence-based policies. Nevertheless, it also confirms the trade-off hypothesis since the democratic input of stakeholders has resulted in the adoption of arguably less effective legislative tools since soft law is not binding,[64] which means that Member States may not implement it.

3.2. Effectiveness of the Selected Collective Redress Rules

The second aspect where the input of the European Parliament and stakeholders has had an impact on the effectiveness of the EU's collective redress policy concerns the contents of three of the rules previously analysed (the loser-pays principle, the opt-in regime and punitive damages).[65] It is important to recall that the term effectiveness signifies the capability of collective redress rules to promote compliance with EU law and facilitate antitrust victims' compensation. With regard to the capability of these

---

60 Communication, n 5, at p 6.

61 Communication, n 5, point 38.

62 Communication, n 5, point 41.

63 Recommendation, n 5, Article 41.

64 Article 288 TFEU provides that recommendations shall have no binding force.

65 As explained above, with regard to standing of consumers' associations both the Commission and stakeholders agreed that this rule would be desirable. There was no difference between the original formulation of this rule in the Green Paper and the final formulation in the EU soft law on collective redress.

rules to facilitate victims' compensation, the adoption of the principles of full compensation and opt-in regimes is unlikely to hinder access to court. However, the adoption of the loser-pays principle may have a tangible effect as it discourages victims from making a claim given the costs of antitrust litigation. With respect to the capability of these rules to promote compliance with competition law, the new collective redress rules are unlikely to be effective due to the absence of punitive damages, particularly in horizontal cartels (the most harmful category of antitrust violation). The rejection of the opt-out regime is also a missed opportunity to maximize the effectiveness of the rules given that the automatic inclusion of a class of claimants would have increased the amount of compensation, thus exerting more pressure upon undertakings to comply with the competition law provisions. Arguably, the absence of these rules means that the deterrent effect of the rules on collective redress in relation to infringements of the antitrust rules has not been optimized. Finally, not allowing exceptions to the loser-pays principle has removed an incentive for would-be claimants to make a claim. Again, this lessens the deterrent effect of antitrust compensatory claims since the loser-pays principle is likely to result in fewer antitrust claimants. Accordingly, it may be argued that the trade-off hypothesis has been confirmed. The inputs of the European Parliament and stakeholders have reduced output legitimacy, the latter being measured in terms of how far the new rules achieve their goal of increasing compliance with the EU antitrust rules through private enforcement. However, as mentioned in the introduction, this chapter goes further than the traditional 'input/output' dichotomy. It argues that the accommodation of the submissions of the European Parliament and stakeholders allows a new dimension to the concept of legitimacy to be promulgated which has a positive impact on the effectiveness of the EU's policy on collective redress.

3.3. The Relationship between Effectiveness and Legitimacy in the Eyes of the Legal Community

On the basis of our analysis so far, if by effectiveness we mean the capacity of rules to make it easier for private parties to litigate and hence increase compliance with EU law by enhancing their deterrent effect, the democratic input of the actors concerned has undermined the effectiveness of the examined rules. However, as will be demonstrated below, our assessment varies if we consider that the deterrent approach is not the only lens through which we should view the effectiveness of the rules.

The availability of punitive damages, the opt-out system and shift of allocation of litigation costs all play a central role in the US system of class actions.[66] Yet, it is important to highlight that the US legal doctrine conceptualizes the opt-out system and punitive damages through the law and economics approach. For example, punitive damages are justified on the basis that they discount the probability that the wrongdoer may not be caught: the imposition of a compensatory award greater than the suffered losses is supposed to offset the wrongdoer's calculation that not all antitrust violations are detected and therefore he may escape liability.[67] In the EU, the law and economics approach was adopted by some experts who prepared a report on antitrust damages to assist the Commission in the formulation of effective private enforcement rules.[68]

However, the European Parliament rejected such a 'technocratic' approach based on the US experience because they believed it has created a system of incentives conducive to abusive litigation and limited benefits. The dubious effectiveness of the deterrence approach derives from the fact that it works under the traditional law and economics assumptions which hold that would-be violators have full information about the probability of being found liable and their decision-making process is fully rational (i.e. they pursue their self-interest and want to avoid the sanctions attached to the rule they are considering to breach). Clearly, this is an abstract and idealized model that rarely occurs in real-world situations.

This chapter advances a different reading of the policy process on collective redress in relation to legitimacy and effectiveness. The European Parliament and stakeholders' submissions show that they placed considerable importance on the legal traditions and values of the Member States.[69] Any new rules on collective redress introduced at the instigation of the EU

---

66 The literature on US class actions is extensive. For a general overview: Rand Institute for Civil Justice – Deborah R. Hensler, Bonnie Dombey-Moore, Beth Giddens, Jennifer Gross, Erik K. Moller, and Nicholas M. Pace, *Class Action Dilemmas: Pursuing Public Goals for Private Gain: Executive Summary* (RAND 1999) 1. <http://www.rand.org/pubs/monograph_reports/MR969z1.html> accessed 22 April 2015.

67 Mitchell Polinsky and Steven Shavell, 'Punitive Damages: An Economic Analysis' (1998) 111 Harv.L.Rev. 869, 921.

68 Andrea Renda, John Peysner, Alan J. Riley, Barry J. Rodger, Roger J. Van Den Bergh, Sonja Keske, Roberto Pardolesi, Enrico Leonardo Camilli, and Paolo Caprile, 'Making Antitrust Damages Actions More Effective in the EU: Welfare Impact and Potential Scenarios: Final Report' (2007) 281. <http://ec.europa.eu/competition/antitrust/actionsdamages/documents.html> accessed 22 April 2015.

69 See, for example, the intervention by the then MEP Antolín Sánchez Presedo during the debate on 23 April 2007 in the European Parliament on the Green Paper on damages actions, who stressed the need to respect legal traditions. <http://www.europarl.europa.eu/sides/getDoc.do?type=CRE&reference=20070423&secondRef=ITEM-023&language=EN&ring=A6-2007-0133> accessed 10 May 2015.

will not apply in a vacuum, but in domestic legal systems reflecting legal values and legal traditions. These may include, for example, the principle that compensation should restore the victim's status quo ante and not result in overcompensation, or that a claimant should give his or her consent to be part of a collective action. If the EU's collective redress rules had conflicted too sharply with the law and legal traditions of the Member States, they would not have been supported by the legal community (lawyers, judges, legal academics), the actors who will play a central role in judicial enforcement. Without such support, the legal community may interpret the rules in such a way as to avoid or minimize any conflicts with deeply held national values. As a result, the rules on collective redress may not be applied properly in practice, which would jeopardize their effectiveness.

Input and output legitimacy refer to the consensus over the way policy decisions are made and the effectiveness of such decisions. It is argued that consensus can also relate to the compatibility of new, supranational non-binding rules on collective redress with the legal system in which they will be expected to operate. There is a risk that putting in place rules that excessively alter the balance between claimants and defendants (e.g. the opt-out system) may result in greater effectiveness, but harm some important legal values contained in the Member States' procedural systems. To oversimplify, the means do not justify the end. The examined inputs sent the message that legal reforms should comply with certain essential legal values enshrined in the law of the Member States.[70] When new rules can be integrated in the national legal system in a fashion consistent with its legal values, those entrusted with the application of such rules (e.g. judges or lawyers) will regard them as legitimate. Without such a consensus, the legal community may put in place a conservative reaction undermining the new rules and thus their effectiveness.

CONCLUSIONS

It is generally accepted that an effective enforcement regime of the EU competition law rules requires a system of collective redress. This enables

[70] See, for example, the European Parliament, which stressed the need to take into account legal traditions and legal orders in the formulation of European rules on collective redress. European Parliament resolution of 2 February 2012 on 'Towards a Coherent European Approach to Collective Redress' (2011/2089(INI)) para 16. Respecting national legal traditions was recognized also by the Commission in its Impact Assessment Report on the Proposal for a Directive on damages actions (2013) p 28 and Recital 13 of the Recommendation.

consumers who have suffered low financial-value loss as a result of a breach of Articles 101 or 102 TFEU to gain compensation by amalgamating their claims. To this end, the Commission has introduced two non-binding instruments, a Communication on a horizontal framework for collective redress and a Recommendation on collective redress mechanisms concerning violations of Union rights. The goal of this chapter was to assess whether the European Parliament and stakeholders' inputs provided in the policy process have increased, rather than decreased (synergy and trade-off hypothesis) effectiveness. For the purposes of this chapter, effectiveness meant the capacity of these measures to promote compliance with Articles 101 and 102 TFEU and facilitate victims' compensation.

With regard to the empirical analysis, this chapter selected four key procedural rules essential for an operational collective redress regime and tracked their development from their initial formulation by the Commission in its 2005 Green Paper to how they have been finally framed in the 2013 Communication and Recommendation. The research shows that the substance of the final version of these rules is consistent with the European Parliament and stakeholders' positions. In the course of the policymaking process, the Commission modified such rules in line with such actors' positions.

With regard to the effectiveness of the collective redress regime, this is an *ex ante* assessment given that there is not yet empirical evidence on the working of this regime. Here, two conclusions may be drawn. First, the European Parliament and stakeholders' positions have induced the Commission to introduce soft law. Since soft law is not binding, there is the risk that the relevant rules will not be effective as Member States may simply not implement them. Second, with respect to the contents of these rules, it has been argued that, with the exception of the loser-pays principle, they will not facilitate victims' compensation. In addition, they are unlikely to promote compliance with Articles 101 and/or 102 TFEU since they will not increase the deterrent effect of collective actions. These considerations point to the confirmation of the trade-off hypothesis.

This chapter challenges this reading of the effectiveness of the new measures as capable of promoting compliance with EU competition law since it is based on deterrence theory which in turn rests on some questionable assumptions. It is argued that the system of collective redress which emerges from the soft law measures may not necessarily result in a loss of effectiveness. Rather, the European Parliament and stakeholders' contributions reminded the Commission of some essential legal values that should not be compromised when adopting new EU policies whose implementation relies on national courts. Respect for central legal principles is important to secure effective implementation because it makes it more likely that the EU policy will be implemented by the national legal community without putting in place restrictive interpretations that may undermine the policy goals underpinning collective redress. Ensuring the legal community's consensus arising from the fact that the EU policy is consistent with important legal values is also a type of legitimacy. Whilst the Commission may not have been able to pass collective redress rules consistent with a strong deterrent perspective, the democratic process in which these rules were debated has resulted in a greater consensus among the addressees of this policy. It is submitted that this is a precondition to ensuring that such rules will be properly applied, rendering them more effective.

10. A case of 'nested enforcement': Article 83(2) TFEU, compliance and the Area of Freedom, Security and Justice post-Lisbon*

Estella Baker

INTRODUCTION

Article 83(2) of the Treaty on the Functioning of the European Union (TFEU) was newly introduced into the treaties as part of the Lisbon reforms and falls within the Treaty's Area of Freedom, Security and Justice (AFSJ) Title, which covers the area of policy that was referred to in earlier versions of the treaties as 'Justice and Home Affairs' (JHA). Sometimes referred to as the 'annex competence', it shares common ground with Article 83(1) TFEU in that both paragraphs confer legislative competence upon the Union to establish minimum rules with respect to the definition of criminal offences and sanctions. In terms of their ethos, however, the two provisions are materially distinct.

Article 83(1) TFEU, which is not the focus of attention here, is addressed at combating serious forms of cross-border crime. It is therefore primarily intergovernmental in character in that it is designed to assist the Member States in overcoming the limitations of their individual criminal justice systems. By contrast, Article 83(2) TFEU is supranational in orientation; that is, it is focused on the Union's own interests, as it applies 'in an area which has been subject to harmonisation measures' and empowers the Union to require Member States to deploy criminal law measures if doing so 'proves essential to ensure the effective implementation of a Union policy'.

Article 83(2) TFEU has many interesting features but the one that is immediately pertinent is that it is wholly, and unavoidably, concerned

* I would like to thank Anthony Bottoms and Christopher Harding for their thoughtful comments on an earlier draft. The usual disclaimer applies.

with the facilitation of enforcement. Thus, while the preponderance of the literature on Article 83 TFEU discusses the significance of its companion provisions in terms of the evolving criminal law competence of the Union and its setting within the project to construct the Union as an AFSJ,[1] this chapter is different. It offers an original contribution that analyses Article 83(2) from the alternative perspective of enforcement. That does not mean, however, that either the broader criminal law context or the setting of Article 83(2) TFEU within the legal architecture of the AFSJ is irrelevant; on the contrary.

A second significant point with regard to Article 83(2) TFEU concerns the implied mechanism through which exercise of the competence is presumed to result in the desired empirical effect; that is, the effective implementation of the relevant policy. Once reflected upon, it becomes apparent that it is premised not upon the workings of a single dose of enforcement but upon a process that relies upon a series of episodes of enforcement, involving a range of actors, at multiple governmental levels. In other words, for applicable legislation to work, it must trigger a sequence of enforcement responses through which the Union's normative concern to combat behaviours that militate against effective implementation is transmitted to those who are tempted to engage in them and succeeds in persuading them otherwise. As the chapter will proceed to argue, regarded from this perspective, Article 83(2) TFEU can be conceived as describing an 'outer shell' that relies upon a vertical concept of 'nested enforcement', which lies implicitly within it, in order for the measures that are based upon it to achieve their desired impact. It can therefore be differentiated from the enforcement settings that are discussed in other contributions to the volume, which focus upon the horizontal, or lateral, strategy of 'networked enforcement'.[2]

Vital to the reasoning that supports this conceptual understanding is the literature in criminology that is directed at fashioning a theoretical understanding of legal compliance. Developed to a materially more sophisticated level than the literature on deterrence and compliance-based strategies that is associated with the generic regulatory sphere,[3] this intrinsically important body of work must have some bearing upon the issues

---

[1] See, for example, Petter Asp, *The Substantive Criminal Law Competence of the EU* (Jure Bokhandel 2012); André Klip, *European Criminal Law: An Integrative Approach* (2nd edn, Intersentia 2012); Valsamis Mitsilegas, *EU Criminal Law* (Hart 2009); Steve Peers, *Justice and Home Affairs Law* (3rd edn, OUP 2011); Helmut Satzger, *International and European Criminal Law* (Verlag C.H. Beck oHG 2012).

[2] See in particular Chapters 4 and 5 of this volume.

[3] See further Chapter 3 of this volume.

that are of central concern here. That supposition exposes but one of the reasons why the criminal law character of Article 83(2) TFEU is relevant to its analysis in terms of enforcement.

As for the link to the AFSJ, to appreciate it, it must first be recognized that the term has a status beyond that of the label that happens to be in vogue for the area of policy that began life as JHA. In its substantive guise, the AFSJ is presented in the post-Lisbon Treaty on European Union (TEU) as a major infrastructural benefit that the Union offers to its citizens[4] and which is (somehow) commensurate with the Union's fundamental values.[5] Underscoring the gravity of that commitment, the Union has been engaged in the AFSJ's construction for 15 years and had pledged to engage in a further five, although the pledge has not been followed up in the manner that was originally envisaged.[6] The real significance of the AFSJ, therefore, lies not in its deployment as a term of art in the treaties, but in its constitutional complexion.

Tying these observations back to Article 83(2) TFEU, a further matter to be addressed below is what implications might follow for the realization of the constitutional project from developing an understanding of this provision in terms of a model of nested enforcement. This applies in particular to its bearing upon efforts to forge a constitutional relationship between the Union and the legal and natural persons who inhabit it. Thus, it is not just through its analytical perspective that the chapter seeks to make a novel contribution to the literature, but through its interdisciplinary approach and attempt to set the issues at stake in this overarching constitutional context.

The discussion that follows is divided into three principal parts. Part 1 provides a brief introductory background to, and analysis of, Article 83 TFEU, focusing especially on Article 83(2) TFEU. Part 2 develops the thesis that Article 83(2) TFEU can be conceived as a system of nested

---

4 Article 3(2) TEU(L). This chapter adopts the convention of identifying different versions of the TEU through the use of a suffix that denotes the treaty that amended it. Thus: TEU(L) and TEU(A), referring respectively to the Treaties of Lisbon and Amsterdam.

5 Article 2 TEU(L).

6 European Council, 'Presidency Conclusions of the Tampere European Council on the Creation of the Area of Freedom, Security and Justice, 15 and 16 October' (1999) *Bulletin EU 10-1999*; European Council, 'The Hague Programme: Strengthening Freedom, Security and Justice in the European Union' [2005] OJ C53/01; European Council, 'The Stockholm Programme: An Open and Secure Europe Serving and Protecting Citizens' [2010] OJ C115/01; European Council, 'Conclusions of the European Council 26/27 June 2014' EUCO 79/14, Brussels, 27 June 2014.

enforcement. Part 3 then considers the broader implications in terms of the concept of compliance and the AFSJ. The conclusion then offers some comments on the significance of the thesis and its potential as a basis for further analysis and research.

1. CRIMINAL LAW AND ARTICLE 83 TFEU

This section examines the reasons why criminal law poses challenges for the pursuit of integration and then proceeds to analyse the terms of Article 83 TFEU.

1.1 Criminal Law as a Challenge for Integration

The criminal law field is particularly contentious territory when it comes to integration. Put succinctly, this is because of the fundamental conflict between Member States' pursuit of crime control and their continued subscription to the doctrine of national sovereignty. According to the logic of the former, they should overcome the limitations of their individual power and resources[7] by maximizing their exploitation of the collaborative environment of the Union to address the criminogenic consequences of integration and the generic phenomenon of cross-border crime.[8] The difficulty is, however, that, conceptually, the notion of criminal law is so intertwined with a number of core goods that are regarded as intimately associated with the notion of sovereign statehood.[9] Therefore, more acutely than in most policy spheres, conferral of criminal competence upon the Union carries with it an implicit question as to the ultimate constitutional settlement between the Union, its Member States and its citizens. The initiative of the AFSJ must be seen in this context, a matter that will be returned to in the concluding part of this chapter.

In terms of explaining the historical pattern of development of the

---

7 See further, David Garland, 'The Limits of the Sovereign State: Strategies of Crime Control in Contemporary Society' (1996) 36(4) *British Journal of Criminology* 445.

8 The Member States acted upon this even before the third pillar was founded. See further, Estella Baker and Christopher S Harding, 'From Past Imperfect to Future Perfect? A Longitudinal Study of the Third Pillar' (2009) 34(1) *European Law Review* 25.

9 Felt to differing degrees by the Member States: see further, Leonard FM Besselink, 'Sovereignty, Criminal Law and the New European Context' in Peter Alldridge and Chrisje Brandts (eds), *Personal Autonomy, the Private Sphere and the Criminal Law* (Hart 2001).

Union's criminal competence, the persistence of this politically uncomfortable tension has more power than any other factor. It is not, however, the issue of the moment as far as the present chapter is concerned. Rather, the task for now is to expand upon the proposition that criminal law is closely interrelated with a series of elementary constitutional goods.

It is hard to better the splendid summary of this idea that is contained in Advocate General Mazák's Opinion in the *Ship-Source Pollution* case.[10] He declared:

> In many respects, criminal law stands out from other areas of law. Availing itself of the most severe and most dissuasive tool of social control – punishments – it delineates the outer limits of acceptable behaviour and in that way protects the values held dearest by the community at large. As an expression essentially of the common will, criminal penalties reflect particular social disapproval and are in that respect of a qualitatively different nature as compared with other punishments such as administrative sanctions.
>
> Thus, more so than other fields of law, criminal law largely mirrors the particular cultural, moral, financial and other attitudes of a community and is especially sensitive to societal developments.[11]

And, to conclude the point, he added: 'the way in which this *ultimum remedium* of the law is used. . . indicates the social standards underpinning the community concerned and is therefore, in the last analysis, inherently related to the identity of that community.'[12]

What this passage captures so eloquently is the sense of an inextricable link between the collective values of a given community, which define and shape its identity, and the criminal law that it creates through which to declare those values and provide a basis for regulating behaviour in accordance with them.[13] Translated into more jurisprudential terms, criminal law thus represents a statement of 'positive morality'; that is, a statement of 'the morality actually accepted and shared by a given social group'.[14] This in turn has a bearing on its normative power because it therefore constitutes an assertion of how those individuals who are subject

---

[10] Case C-440/05 *Commission v Council (Ship-Source Pollution)* [2007] ECR I-9097.

[11] Ibid, Opinion of Advocate General Mazák, paras 67–8.

[12] Ibid, para 71.

[13] For discussion of this 'mirror thesis', see Brian Z Tamanah, *A General Jurisprudence of Law and Society* (OUP 2001).

[14] Anthony E Bottoms, 'Morality, Crime, Compliance and Public Policy' in Anthony E Bottoms and Michael Tonry (eds), *Ideology, Crime and Criminal Justice: A Symposium in Honour of Sir Leon Radzinowicz* (Willan 2002), 23–4, quoting Herbert LA Hart, *Law, Liberty and Morality* (OUP 1963) 20.

to it ought to behave. Subjects are intended to modify their behaviour in response to the principles and standards that the criminal law lays down.

The relevance to the present discussion of Advocate General Mazák's remarks and of the latter observations will be returned to in due course. Suffice it for now to note two things. First, the concepts of 'collective values', 'community', 'identity', 'positive morality' and normative regulation are all important constitutional building blocks. Second, there is a clear causal direction to the relationship that the Advocate General describes. For him, criminal law is an outcome from the formation of a community. The two do not develop in tandem; nor does the creation of criminal law play a part in the construction of a community. In the context of the Union, much may hang on the empirical validity of this directional assumption.

1.2 Analysis of Article 83 TFEU

Article 83 TFEU provides two legal bases in reliance upon which the Union may legislate by means of directive (only) to require Member States to criminalize and punish behaviour. Article 83(1) TFEU constitutes an updated equivalent of the former third pillar competence under Article 31 TEU(A), whereas Article 83(2) TFEU codifies and enlarges the controversial rulings of the CJEU in the *Environmental Crimes* and *Ship-Source Pollution* cases into a general principle.[15] They established that the Union already enjoyed some inherent supranational competence under the pre-Lisbon treaties to legislate to require the Member States to deploy criminal measures, at least in so far as such measures were essential to ensure the effectiveness of Union rules on environmental protection. Whether or not the environmental field was unique in that respect was never resolved and is almost certainly now a redundant question.

Reflecting these independent origins, the two provisions have materially different 'centres of gravity'. That is to say, while there is some conceptual overlap between them, they each have an analytically distinct focus and purpose. Table 10.1 shows this by separating out their core features.

Regarding the question of overlap, it is not hard to identify forms of behaviour that might be proscribed by means of Article 83(2) TFEU but which could justly be described as intrinsically wrong (*mala in se*) and not merely regulatory (*mala prohibita*). Behaviours that entail substantial

---

[15] Case C-176/03 *Commission v Council (Environmental Crimes)* [2005] ECR I-7879; Case C-440/05 *Commission v Council (Ship-Source Pollution)*, noted at n 10.

Table 10.1 Articles 83(1) and 83(2) TFEU compared

Core Features	Article 83(1)	Article 83(2)
Legislative competence	'minimum rules concerning the definition of criminal offences and sanctions in [specified] areas of particularly serious crime* with a cross-border dimension resulting from the nature or impact of such offences or from a special need to combat them on a common basis'	'minimum rules with regard to the definition of criminal offences and sanctions' in an 'area which has been subject to harmonisation measures', 'if the approximation of criminal laws and regulations of the Member States proves essential to ensure the effective implementation of a Union policy'
Principal target	Behaviour that is *mala in se*	Behaviour that is *mala prohibita*
Overriding penological goal	Punishment of 'real crime'	Compliance with Union policies
Dominant mode of governance	Intergovernmental	Supranational

Note: * For the time being the areas of crime are: 'terrorism, trafficking in human beings and sexual exploitation of women and children, illicit drug trafficking, illicit arms trafficking, money laundering, corruption, counterfeiting of means of payment, computer crime and organised crime.' (Article 83(1) TFEU provides that: 'On the basis of developments in crime, the Council may adopt a decision identifying other areas of crime that meet the criteria specified in this paragraph. It shall act unanimously after obtaining the consent of the European Parliament.')

damage to, or destruction of, the environment might be said to fall within this category, for example. Moreover, that this is the case might be said to afford a justification in principle for the fact that Article 83(2) TFEU confers a criminal competence upon the Union at all.[16] Nevertheless, that competence is constructed in a manner that is reminiscent of the concept of 'enforcement pyramids' which form part of the 'responsive regulation' approach.[17] That is to say, the legal criteria for its exercise mark it out as being designed for use as a last resort, when other tactics for securing

16 Such reasoning would reflect the famous harm principle, originating in the work of John Stuart Mill, that is the starting point for many discussions of criminalization.

17 Ian Ayres and John Braithwaite, *Responsive Regulation: Transcending the Deregulation Debate* (OUP 1992) discussed in Chapter 3 of this volume.

the 'effective implementation' of a relevant policy have, or would, fail. It is thus fundamentally regulatory in ethos and, considered in penological terms, is aimed at securing compliance with the policy to which a resulting legislative measure is linked. In that way, there is a further contrast with the behaviours that are targeted by Article 83(1) TFEU. Being *mala in se*, although the achievement of compliance of course remains relevant to them, the overriding penological objective is to punish perpetrators for their moral wrongdoing.

Overlap can also be detected with respect to the dominant modes of governance with which the two competences can be identified. Article 83(1) TFEU is identified as equating with intergovernmentalism on the basis that its foremost purpose is to enable the Member States to surmount the limitations of their individual crime control capabilities. Conversely, Article 83(2) TFEU is equated with supranationalism because of its role in promoting policies that are set at Union level. It is elementary, though, that the interests of the Member States and those of the Union are interdependent. Accordingly, the forms of crime that are the target of Article 83(1) TFEU can also be classed as damaging supranational interests of the Union because, for example, they amount to abuses of free movement or of the Single Market. Similarly, the Member States are primary stakeholders in the policies of the Union. Therefore, a failure to secure their effective implementation can be understood as detrimental, not only to its interests but to theirs as well.

Notwithstanding that the conceptual line between Articles 83(1) and 83(2) TFEU is not clean, that the two provisions display a clear distinction in their critical mass should be apparent. Further corroboration is supplied by a factor that is not covered by the table. Picking up on the earlier discussion of Advocate General Mazák's remarks in the *Ship-Source Pollution* case, another point of difference between Articles 83(1) and 83(2) TFEU lies in the direction of their respective normative (moral) messages. It follows from the distinction between their modes of governance that, in the case of Article 83(1) TFEU, it is 'bottom up' whereas, in the case of Article 83(2) TFEU, it purports to be 'top down' – the opposite to that hypothesized by the Advocate General. This observation is highly relevant to the matters that lie at the heart of the discussion that follows, as should become clear.

2. ARTICLE 83(2) TFEU AS A SYSTEM OF 'NESTED' ENFORCEMENT

To establish the thesis that Article 83(2) TFEU can be understood as a system of 'nested' (or 'multi-level') enforcement, it is first necessary to engage in further analysis of the provision itself before shifting the focus of attention to the scheme of enforcement and compliance that nestles within it.

2.1 Further Analysis of Article 83(2) TFEU

Set out in full, the material part of Article 83(2) TFEU reads as follows:

> If the approximation of criminal laws and regulations of the Member States proves essential to ensure the effective implementation of a Union policy in an area which has been subject to harmonisation measures, directives may establish minimum rules with regard to the definition of criminal offences and sanctions in the area concerned.

Taken simply on its face, this text begs more questions than it answers. For example, what does 'effective implementation' of a relevant policy mean? And what are the criteria for determining that it has been achieved? Assuming that conundrum can be resolved, and it can be shown that effective implementation has not been secured, what are the criteria for establishing that approximation is 'essential' to secure that goal? And what exactly is the scope of the Union's competence to legislate anyway? That is to say, what precisely are 'minimum rules' and how does this concept relate to that of 'the definition of criminal offences and sanctions'? In principle, these two elements sit in tension with one another because the more detail with which a definition is sketched out, the less 'minimum' a resulting rule is liable to be, and vice versa.[18]

Pertinent as these questions undoubtedly are, they are not for discussion at this juncture of the argument. Rather, the issue for attention is the mechanism through which the terms of Article 83(2) TFEU convey that measures based upon it are intended to realize their goal. Interpreting its wording from that perspective, the logic of its legitimate use as a legislative base entails the propositions that:

1. 'effective implementation' of a relevant Union policy is being (or may be?) inhibited through non-compliant conduct by natural and legal persons within the jurisdictions of the Member States; and
2. achievement of compliance by the offending parties requires intervention by the Member States in the form of deployment by them of criminal law.

---

[18] Estella Baker, 'Sanctions in European Criminal Law', Response to the follow-up paper to the third meeting of the European Commission's Expert Group on EU Criminal Policy, February 2014.

I: Union legislates to require Member States to criminalize behaviour when essential to ensure effective implementation of Union policy

⇩

II: Member States implement directive, thereby requiring natural and legal persons to adjust their behaviour or face conviction and punishment

⇩

III: Natural and legal persons within Member States comply with normative instruction enshrined in relevant criminal law (on pain of punishment if they do not)

⇩

Effective implementation of policy secured

Figure 10.1 The nested mechanism of Article 83(2) TFEU

Without going further, this hints at an underlying hypothesis which involves episodes of enforcement at more than one level in order to generate an empirically successful outcome: hence the notion that Article 83(2) TFEU relies upon a mechanism of 'nested enforcement'.

Figure 10.1 illustrates the model in the form that will be used to found the remainder of the discussion. It divides the mechanism into three stages: stage I, at which the Union legislates; stage II, at which the Member States implement the resulting directive; and stage III, at which natural and legal persons within their territories regulate their behaviour according to the norms that are prescribed by the implemented directive.

In its compression into just three stages it should be acknowledged that the model is analytically crude because, in reality, stage II does not constitute a single step. Rather, it is comprised of a series of steps through which the norms that form the subject of a relevant Union instrument are translated into national criminal laws and are then enforced in order to regulate the behaviour of individuals within a Member State's jurisdiction. For the model to be elaborated properly, these steps would need to be disaggregated and explicitly added in.[19] That task, though, is beyond the scope of the present chapter, not least for reasons that derive from the current constitutional settlement with respect to the handling of criminal law matters in the Union.

Article 83 TFEU specifies that the Union must legislate by means of

---

[19] A further complication would arise from the need to take account of the specific features of each criminal justice system within the Union, which would result in more than 28 variations.

directives. Thus, while resulting instruments provide the impetus for Member States to criminalize proscribed types of conduct, they 'leave to the national authorities the choice of form and methods'.[20] Furthermore, responsibility for enforcing the resulting criminal law falls to the national criminal justice authorities as well because the Union lacks apparatus of its own with which to do it. Together, these features mean that, once transposition has been completed, in a literal sense, the processes that occur at stage II are ones that concern the workings of enforcement in Member States' domestic arenas. The 'EU dimension' to what occurs is undeniable, a point that will be expanded upon immediately below. From the perspective of those on the receiving end, however, it is *domestic* criminal law that is in issue, and which is being implemented, enforced and its violations punished by the *domestic* criminal justice system. This latter observation will become relevant later on. For present purposes the salient point is that the effect of incorporating a comprehensive discussion of what is involved at stage II would be to introduce a preoccupation with the role of the Member States. That would divert attention away from one of the central issues that this chapter is seeking to explore; namely, the capacity of Article 83(2) TFEU to make a contribution to the development of a constitutional relationship between the Union and the legal and natural persons who inhabit it.

2.2 Enforcement and Compliance

In order to develop the argument further, it is now necessary to examine the concept of 'enforcement' as it is used at stages II and III of the model. This entails shifting the territory of the discussion away from EU law to that of criminological theory regarding the concept of compliance.

Reiterating what was said above, much of the work at stage II is conducted by Member States' criminal justice systems. However, thanks to the obligation of sincere cooperation, those workings are not without regard to Union law. Now found in Article 4(3) TEU(L), the obligation plays a role in ensuring, in the first place, that Member States are legally bound to implement directives accurately, completely and in a timely fashion. And, in the second, it means that those 'branches', 'organs' and 'emanations' of a Member State[21] that are charged with applying criminal laws which originate in Union law are bound into the

[20] Article 288 TFEU.

[21] Case C-188/89 *Foster v British Gas plc* [1990] ECR I-3313; Case C-282/10 *Dominguez* EU:C:2012:33.

constitutional structure of the Union.[22] Thus, when acting within the scope of the treaties, police and prosecution agencies, criminal courts, and the agencies and institutions that are responsible for implementing punishments are elevated in status from national (and sub-national) to Union actors. Thus, what goes on at stage II of the model is subject to the sophisticated regime that has developed to promote the effective enforcement of Union law.[23] The dynamics of what is entailed at stage III, however, are quite different. In order to establish the point, it is necessary to step back and contemplate what is meant by 'enforcement' in conceptual terms.

Enforcement is an idea that can be thought about, and deployed, in a number of interrelated but distinct ways. For example, it can be equated with implementation in the sense that given normative rules are in place and are being put into operation (enforced) to a requisite degree. It can also be used in an adjectival sense to describe the act of insisting upon implementation, as in the principal work of the police, the prosecution service and the criminal courts (among others); hence the generic term 'law enforcement authorities'. The institutionalization of these authorities, and their consequent high visibility, means that they tend to dominate attention when it comes to considering enforcement in a criminal law context. A different way of understanding what they do, however, is that they step in when other mechanisms that result in individuals' adherence to the norms that are promulgated by the criminal law have failed. Identifying, and understanding, what those mechanisms are, and how they operate, has become the focus of some critically important contemporary scholarship in the discipline of criminology.

Rather than 'enforcement', the concept with which criminologists are engaged, and thus the terminology that they use, is the cognate one of 'compliance'. This reflects a concern to explain why individuals obey the criminal law, thereby contributing to the moral and social order, as a complement to the extensive body of work which examines why they do not. On the face of it, the proposition that the resulting criminological theory has something to offer when it comes to analysing the affairs of the

---

[22] See also Estella Baker, 'Sentencing Guidelines and EU law' in Andrew J Ashworth and Julian V Roberts (eds), *Sentencing Guidelines: Exploring the English Model* (OUP 2013) 258–60. While Member States enjoy a substantial measure of discretion as to how these functions are discharged, it may be subject to review for compliance with Union law. See Case C-265/95 *Commission of the European Communities v France (French Farmers)* [1997] ECR I-6959, Opinion of Advocate General Lenz, para 69.

[23] See further discussion in Chapters 1 and 2 of this volume.

EU may seem a wild one. None the less, it is upon the basis of that claim that the remainder of the discussion now proceeds.

Three factors underpin the suggestion that it is salient. The first is that, at the level of the individual, the concepts of enforcement and compliance are symbiotically intertwined. That is to say, it can be asserted both that 'X complies with a given norm and, as a result, that norm is enforced' and 'a given norm is enforced and, as a result, X complies with it'. It follows that an understanding of compliance ought, in principle, to be of relevance to a discussion of effective enforcement because the two phenomena operate hand in hand. The second is that there is a direct connection between the broader setting of the criminological work, as being concerned with notions of moral and social order, and the issues of constitutional construction that are integral to the extract from Advocate General Mazák's Opinion in the *Ship-Source Pollution* case that was reproduced above. The third is that the theory holds great utility in terms of the nested mechanism within Article 83(2) TFEU because it deals with 'compliant behaviour from the point of view of the ordinary person, outlining the principal reasons why she or he might comply with the law'.[24] That means that it is directly pertinent in understanding the micro level processes that sit at stage III of the model.

Moving from the general to the particular, the specific contribution that has been singled out for discussion here is the highly regarded typology of legal compliance mechanisms that was published by Anthony Bottoms in its original version in 2002.[25] Rooted in a diverse body of empirical and theoretical work across the criminological and social science field, it is set within a broader discussion of the role of morality in the workings of criminal policy. As the latter reflects one of the core concerns of the current chapter, there is thus a double justification for choosing to focus upon it here. Having said that, it is all but inevitable that the heavily summarized account that now follows can do little more than provide a flavour of the potential relevance of this fundamentally important work to the issues in hand. Unsatisfactory as that is, it should be borne in mind that this is all that is being attempted for present purposes.

The typology is set out in Figure 10.2. Of its four principal mechanisms, it is normative compliance that is of principal relevance to the remainder of the discussion. However, it is appropriate briefly to explain what each

---

24 Anthony E Bottoms, noted at n 14, 29.

25 He is continuing to develop this work: 'Understanding the Mechanisms of Compliance', presentation to The European Probation Rules: Compliance, Trust and Lessons for European Governance, STREAM project seminar, De Montfort University, 17 April 2014.

A. Instrumental/prudential compliance
 1. Incentives
 2. Disincentives

B. Constraint-based compliance
 1. Physical constraints
  (a) Physical restrictions on individuals leading to compliance:
   (i) natural; (ii) imposed
  (b) Physical restrictions on accessibility of target, availability of means to commit crime, etc.
 2. Social-structural constraints

C. Normative compliance
 1. Acceptance of or belief in social norm
 2. Attachment leading to compliance
 3. Legitimacy

D. Compliance based on habit or routine

Source: Anthony E Bottoms, 'Morality, Crime, Compliance and Public Policy' in Anthony E Bottoms and Michael Tonry (eds), *Ideology, Crime and Criminal Justice: A Symposium in Honour of Sir Leon Radzinowicz* (Willan 2002), 30.

Figure 10.2 Bottoms' outline of the principal basic mechanisms underpinning legally compliant behaviour

entails before turning attention to the reasons for singling out normative compliance for special attention.

The first of the mechanisms, instrumental or prudential compliance, is strongly related to the concept of deterrence as it is 'based on rational calculations of self-interest'. Accordingly, behaviour that results from this form of compliance is shaped in the light of relevant incentives and disincentives.[26] The second mechanism, constraint-based compliance, occurs where some kind of barrier exists to offending. That barrier may be physical, arising from natural or imposed constraints on a potential offender, or from an individual's lack of means to commit the offence, or from measures that have been taken to protect the potential target.[27] Alternatively, the barrier may be 'based on social relationships and social structures' and thus social-structural in character.[28] Next is normative

[26] Anthony E Bottoms, noted at n 14, 29.
[27] Ibid, 29–30.
[28] Ibid, 30–31.

compliance. More voluntary in nature, its defining characteristic is that it 'relates to actors' responses to "a principle or standard. . . that reflects people's expectations of behaviour. . . and serves to regulate action and judgment"'.[29] Lastly, there is compliance based on habit or routine, which is straightforward to understand and is 'the most "automatic" of the four mechanisms of compliance'.[30]

For reasons that will become clear, Bottoms himself promotes normative compliance as occupying 'a pivotal position' within the framework.[31] At this initial stage, however, it is the fact that it is 'necessarily related to one or more social norms'[32] and thus sits 'centrally in the realm of morality, the realm of the "ought". . .'[33] which provides the justification for affording it privileged attention in what follows. There is a clear point of connection with matters of fundamental relevance to the present chapter. They include the normative function of the criminal law that is based upon Article 83(2) TFEU; its potential relationship with an evolving notion of pan-Union morality; and any attendant consequences for the business of constitutional construction.

Examining normative compliance in more detail then, it can be seen from Figure 10.2 that Bottoms further divides it into three sub-forms. The first covers the straightforward case where compliance arises from an individual's own acceptance or belief in the relevant social norm and therefore has a clear moral reason for abiding by it.[34] The second, attachment leading to compliance, occurs where an individual obeys, not because of her or his personal belief but because of her or his attachment (or social bond) to an individual, social group or institution with non-criminal values.[35] The third, compliance based on legitimacy, is 'based on a degree of moral assent to the right of the person in power to hold that power', that moral assent supplying the reason for 'obedience to the wishes of a recognised legal or social authority'.[36]

Pausing briefly to consider the relevance of this material to the case of the Union's exercise of legislative competence under Article 83(2)

---

[29] Ibid, 31, incorporating a reference to the definition of 'norm' that was contained in the *Longman Dictionary of the English Language* (Longman 1984).

[30] Ibid, 31.

[31] Ibid, 33 (footnotes omitted).

[32] Ibid, 31.

[33] Ibid.

[34] Ibid, 33.

[35] Ibid, 34–5.

[36] Ibid, 36. An understanding of normative compliance might yield insights that are of use in the further study and development of 'smart regulation': see the discussion in Chapter 3 of this volume.

TFEU, some interim observations can be made. Regarding the first two sub-forms, it can be inferred that, the more that relevant Union-inspired norms are in keeping with the existing moral values of its population or those of social groups or institutions to which there is a high degree of attachment within and/or across Member States, the greater the chances of securing compliance with them. Conversely, if relevant norms contradict, or undermine, those inherent values, then it might be hypothesized that their institution in legislation will foment defiance.[37]

It can also be inferred that, if Article 83(2) TFEU is to prove capable in empirical terms of acting as a catalyst for the development of 'top down' Union-wide morality, then it is not through either of the first two sub-mechanisms that this is liable to be achieved. Regard to them implies that the values that are enshrined in relevant legislation should be in harmony with those that are already extant (rather in line with Advocate General Mazák's reasoning). They are therefore unsuited as mechanisms through which to establish fresh moral fabric with which to bind a community together. That means in turn that, if Article 83(2) TFEU is to be deployed to foster top down morality, then this must be on the basis of achieving compliance through respect for the legitimacy of the Union and its laws. Given the precarious standing of the Union's legitimacy and, more so, that of its extended reach into criminal law matters (exacerbated now that competence is transferring from an intergovernmental to a supranational basis),[38] the odds on success do not look promising. Moreover, difficulties with legitimacy are not the only obstacle to the fulfilment of the community-building potential of Article 83(2) TFEU as will become clear below.

Returning to Bottoms' discussion, he proceeds to make some broader points that highlight the potential importance of his framework to the task of policymaking. He starts by emphasizing that the different forms of compliance are not mutually exclusive, but are 'interconnected'.[39] 'Interconnectedness' has two dimensions, but only one, 'interactional

---

[37] Some corroboration for this view can be found, for example, in the circumstances that led to the litigation in Case C-265/95 *Commission v France (French Farmers)* noted at n 22.

[38] Hence the special arrangements that surround its treatment, which include the 'emergency brake': Articles 82(3) and 83(3) TFEU; the Commission shares the right of initiative with the Member States: Article 76 TFEU; and the lower threshold of reasoned opinions from national parliaments needed to trigger a review of draft legislation for compliance with subsidiarity: Protocol (No.2) on the application of the principles of subsidiarity and proportionality, Article 7(2).

[39] Anthony E Bottoms, noted at n 14, 31.

interconnectedness', is relevant here. This is the idea that, in a given setting, 'one mechanism of compliance might. . ., be specifically influenced by another of the mechanisms of compliance (or by factors closely associated with it)'.[40] Normative compliance, he suggests, makes an especially important contribution because it is 'probably. . . the [mechanism] that in practice interacts with the other mechanisms the most frequently and with the greatest practical effects'.[41] It is this consideration which underpins his description of it (normative compliance) as occupying 'a pivotal position'.[42]

Bottoms suggests that those engaged in the discussion of crime policy have failed to pay sufficient attention to the concept of interactional interconnectedness, tending to contemplate specific types of compliance in isolation from one another.[43] This is an observation that may be of relevance to other settings that are discussed in this volume. In terms of his own discussion, he suggests that the oversight should be rectified, particularly as it concerns normative compliance, because the effect of doing so should be to yield benefits by way of improving crime reduction.[44] Although he was not concerned with crime control at the initiation of the EU, these benefits are of course of material interest to policymakers at the level of the Union. After all, the formal purpose of Article 83(2) TFEU is 'to ensure the effective implementation of a Union policy in an area which has been subject to harmonisation measures' by tackling the non-compliant conduct of natural and legal persons within the Member States. Therefore, his proposal that interactional interconnectedness should be taken more seriously in policy development should be of as much interest to the Union's policymakers as to their counterparts at national and sub-national level. So too should certain of his further remarks.

Starting with his observations on the nature of morality, he points out that it is 'always practised within a specific social context' and that its standards 'can change'.[45] It is vital that policymakers recognize this fluid character when designing normative policies. If such policies are not sufficiently sensitive to what he calls the 'normative understandings' of the society to which they will apply, there is a 'serious risk' that they will be regarded as irrelevant by their target audience. Furthermore, he suggests that this is true 'not only for the substance of moral prohibitions, but also

---

40 Ibid, 31–2.
41 Ibid, 33 (footnote omitted).
42 Ibid.
43 Ibid.
44 Ibid, 42.
45 Ibid.

for the form in which they are couched and the reasons that are proffered as to why they should be obeyed'.[46]

To illustrate the point, he refers to some of the social transformations that have occurred in Western societies in recent decades, such as the declines of patriarchy and of social deference, and changes in the status and complexion of respect for religious belief.[47] Such fundamental shifts indicate the need 'to develop and consolidate. . . a new positive morality for our times'.[48] Although he does not mention it, one such transformation that might be regarded as feeding into this alleged need is the establishment, and continued evolution, of the EU.[49] There is thus a point of connection here between the constitutional goods that are the subject of what Bottoms has to say and the remarks of Advocate General Mazák. This will be taken up below.

There is also a second point in Bottoms' remarks that is worth noting. Unexpectedly perhaps, it relates to a concern that he articulates about the proliferation of technical and managerialist approaches to tackling crime (electronic monitoring, CCTV, risk offending scores and so on).[50] Empirical evaluations of such approaches have established that they can have positive effects. None the less, he suggests that there is a potential downside to the tendency to privilege investment in such techniques over that in other types of approach. This is because doing so obviates consideration of the moral realm, and thus the normative dimension to compliance, the pivotal role of which he has sought to establish.[51]

Union competence has yet to arrive at a point where it could insist that Member States adopt the sorts of approaches that Bottoms is concerned about. Nevertheless, there is a germ here of an idea that may be relevant when it comes to the adoption of legislation that is based on Article 83(2) TFEU. Rather than its being in relation to specific crime control interventions that such disregard for the moral realm may occur (the Bottoms case), the spectre in the Union context is that directives will be crafted in a manner that does so. That is to say, the Union legislator may adopt a style of drafting that puts a premium upon technocratic considerations, and which is uninformed by 'normative understandings' of the pan-Union

---

46 Ibid.

47 Ibid.

48 Ibid, 43.

49 For signs of resistance to this idea, see the House of Commons debate on EU Criminal Policy, 25 January 2012, HC Hansard cols 308–30.

50 Anthony E Bottoms, noted at n 14, 44.

51 Ibid, 44–5.

society to which the resulting instruments will in due course apply.[52] Or, in similar vein, legislation might be drafted in a manner that squeezes out the scope for Member States to accommodate the normative understandings of their particular societies. Indeed, from the vantage point that is offered by Bottoms' work, it might even be ventured that a precise part of the purpose of legislating by directive, so that 'the choice of form and methods' is left to national authorities,[53] is to ensure that this scope is left in. Were such features of legislative design to occur, it would be consistent with Bottoms' argument to expect the resulting instruments to prove less effective when it comes to individual compliance than would be the case if regard for the normative dimension was factored into their construction.

This last observation raises the more general question of how an appreciation of the theoretical framework that has just been discussed might be harnessed in the context of Article 83(2) TFEU, and what the implications of doing so might be. These are the topics for exploration in the next section.

3. ARTICLE 83(2) TFEU, COMPLIANCE AND THE AFSJ

Bearing in mind the parameters of the chapter, two interrelated issues arise. The first is how compliance theory might inform the Union's development of its approach to the exercise of competence under Article 83(2) TFEU. The second is how the theory (and any associated legislative approach) might be relevant to the constitutional vision of the Union as an AFSJ. They will now be examined in turn.

3.1 A Compliance-Informed Approach to Article 83(2) TFEU

Earlier in the chapter it was suggested that two propositions underpin the legitimate use of Article 83(2) TFEU as a legislative base. They were that:

---

52 A possible example is the draft provisions which would introduce mandatory minimum sanctions that the Commission has included in several recent proposals for directives. See, for instance, European Commission, 'Proposal for a Directive of the European Parliament and of the Council on the Fight against Fraud to the Union's Financial Interests by Means of Criminal Law' COM(2012) 363 final, Brussels, 11 July 2012, draft Article 8. So far, none of these provisions has survived the adoption process.

53 Article 288 TFEU.

1. 'effective implementation' of a relevant Union policy is being (or may be?) inhibited through non-compliant conduct by natural and legal persons within the jurisdictions of the Member States; and
2. achievement of compliance by the offending parties requires intervention by the Member States in the form of deployment by them of criminal law.

Returning to them now, on the assumption that Member States introduce and implement the relevant criminal laws, it will be seen that, logically, they rest upon a third proposition. That proposition is that 'effective implementation', a macro level outcome, is an aggregate product of multiple episodes of individual, micro level, compliance.

It was established above that, currently, the Union cannot intervene directly to criminalize individuals' non-compliant conduct under its own primary law by creating what might be termed 'federal Union offences'. By virtue of the current treaty settlement, the Union is therefore too remote a regulatory agent meaningfully to be able to address relevant detrimental behaviour at the individual micro level. At first sight, this means that little purchase upon the Union's criminal competence is gained by bringing this third proposition into relief. One of the ways in which Bottoms' work is of value, however, is that it enables the proposition to be modified, resulting in a version that has a natural synergy with the manner in which the Union's competence to legislate is constructed. Thus, rather than couching the issue in terms of individual acts, the same fundamental idea can be expressed instead in terms of effective implementation being a product of multiple episodes of the successful workings of the *mechanisms* of compliance. The attraction of this is that it effects a neat shift in focus from the role of individual actors to that of the social processes that operate to influence their behaviour. These latter the Union does enjoy some competence to do something about; specifically in the context of Article 83(2) TFEU, Member States' deployment of criminal laws and regulations, and associated sanctions.

A second point of value in Bottoms' discussion concerns the issue of choice in relation to policymaking. Both explicitly and implicitly, it is apparent from what he says that those seeking to promote compliance might elect to focus upon a particular compliance mechanism in isolation, or opt instead to harness more than one in an attempt to exploit their interactional interconnectedness.[54] This is an interesting perspective from

---

[54] An implication is that different selections might generate a similar compliance outcome and vice versa. If substantiated empirically, this insight might be of

which to view Article 83(2) TFEU because it implies that the concept of 'effective implementation' and determination of whether approximation has been 'prove[d] essential' might be seen in its light. That is to say, a decision to legislate on the basis of Article 83(2) TFEU constitutes a decision to deploy a mechanism that is preponderantly (but not exclusively) normative in kind. Whether it can be proven to be 'essential' to do it is a matter that might be evaluated in terms of an overall assessment of the compliance mechanisms that are, or might be, utilized in order to achieve a given policy's implementation, and the potential role of criminal law in their mix.

Likewise, the question of whether implementation is effective or not might be judged in a similar fashion. As a concept, 'effectiveness' has an ethereal quality that makes it resistant to measurement; but evaluating it by means of an audit of compliance mechanisms might prove productive in rendering it susceptible to such treatment.[55] That is not to suggest that the implementation of this approach would be straightforward from a practical point of view. Figuring out whether there was a genuine need to fortify the infrastructure of compliance mechanisms in respect of a particular Union policy by legislating to require the use of criminal law would require careful analysis. Moreover, the need to confront the tricky issue of how to handle differential internal regimes as between Member States and attendant concerns about so-called 'forum shopping' by offenders would remain.[56] Thus, to do full justice to this idea would take considerably more space than is available here. Before turning attention to the

---

material use in the prospective design of Union legislation. There would appear to be a natural synergy between compliance as an outcome and the inherent nature of directives. Furthermore, an understanding of the workings of compliance should encourage more technically informed decisions regarding those matters that require specification at Union level and those that are better left to the Member States. It is not a foregone conclusion, however, that Article 83(2) TFEU confers the necessary competence to permit the development of this informed approach.

[55] The most obvious alternative is to formulate a judgement on the basis of criminal statistics. There is a rich criminological literature which deals with the reasons why such data should be treated with caution, including the argument that what they actually provide is a measure of law enforcement activity; not crime. Adoption of the audit approach that is being suggested here would avoid the need to deal with this and other difficulties to which reliance upon criminal statistics give rise.

[56] It is hard to find robust evidence through which to assess how great a practical problem forum shopping presents. As for combating relative weaknesses in some Member States' enforcement regimes, a preferable response might be to develop an approach based on their purported breach of Article 4(3) TEU(L). This would build on the long-standing rulings in Case 68/88 *Commission v Greece*

AFSJ, however, it is important to add some further, clarifying remarks concerning the criteria upon which a conclusion that approximation had 'prove[d] essential' would rest.

Disregarding its grander constitutional dimension, the function of Advocate General Mazák's remarks in the *Ship-Source Pollution* case was to highlight the 'specialness' of criminal law. For the reasons that he spelt out, criminal law does not constitute merely one method among many through which compliance mechanisms can be put into operation.[57] With its overtures of compulsion and social censure, and its reinforcement through the imposition of state punishment; that is, its normative characteristics, it has a far greater significance than that. Therefore, and this is anything but a novel point, it should be used sparingly, and with care.

These are valid considerations in the context of a decision to legislate on the basis of Article 83(2) TFEU. Thus, 'proving' approximation to be 'essential' should not depend simply upon the absence of criminal law as an element in the matrix of enforcement measures that was attached to a given Union policy. Rather, that absence might operate as a threshold for triggering consideration of a decision to legislate. For it then to be proved that approximation was 'essential', the normative contribution that requiring criminal measures might make to securing effective implementation would have to be assessed in the light of other material factors, especially those that support restraint. In particular, these would surely include the fundamental principles of Union law (most notably, proportionality, subsidiarity and respect for fundamental rights), together with the constitutional principles to which the Member States subscribe when it comes to criminalization.[58] It is arguable too that conscious consideration should be given to the potential for the introduction by the Union legislator of criminalization requirements to interfere adversely with enforcement regimes in the Member States that are already functional.[59] In the

(Greek Maize) [1989] ECR 2965 and Case C-265/95 *Commission v France (French Farmers)*, noted at n 22.

57 See also the 'enforcement pyramid': Ian Ayres and John Braithwaite, noted at n 17.

58 For relevant discussion, see further: European Commission, 'Towards an EU Criminal Policy: Ensuring the Effective Implementation of EU Policies through Criminal Law' COM(2011) 573 final, Brussels, 20 September 2011.

59 This again raises the issue that different 'normative understandings' may exist within the Member States, which the Union must somehow accommodate. There is also a further matter that requires conscious resolution. When evaluating whether the 'effective implementation of a Union policy' has been ensured, what is the relevant governmental level at which the evaluation should be conducted? Should the assessment be conducted at the level of the Union itself, or at the level

light of this type of broader assessment it might well be concluded that the legal case for exercising competence under Article 83(2) TFEU was not made out, implying a need to invest in alternative, non-criminal modes of enforcement instead.

Usefully, the reference to applicable constitutional principles returns attention to the setting of Article 83(2) TFEU within the infrastructural framework of the AFSJ.

3.2 Article 83(2) TFEU and the Constitutional Vision of the Union as an AFSJ

At an earlier point in the discussion it was suggested that Article 83(2) TFEU is predominantly supranational in ethos in that the competence that it affords is designed to secure the implementation of Union policies. Accordingly, its normative function was identified as being to establish Union-wide social norms, and therefore to contribute to the shaping of a pan-Union 'top down' morality. As a contrast to that vision, the discussion has referred to Advocate General Mazák's characterization of criminal law in the *Ship-Source Pollution* case. One of its notable features is that it portrays criminal law as developing from the moral values of the community to which it applies; not the other way round. It thus captures an understanding of criminal law as being a statement of 'bottom up' morality; an understanding that is therefore at odds with the internal moral logic of Article 83(2) TFEU.

Notwithstanding the Advocate General's view, there is no reason in principle why the two conceptions should not each be borne out in practice, so that their manifestations coexist side by side, particularly in a complex social setting such as that of the Union. Regarded from the perspective of the AFSJ, however, what is significant is whether or not Article 83(2) TFEU has the normative capacity that has been ascribed to it. This is because the answer has implications for the further question of whether there is some legitimate expectation that, reciprocally attached to its role in fashioning top down morality, it is capable of having some 'bottom up', community-building effect. In other words, does Article 83(2) TFEU involve a complete reversal in generative direction of the relationship between criminal law, morality and community from that which was painted by Advocate General Mazák? If the AFSJ is to be regarded as a constitutional project that is constitutive of the bond between the Union and its citizens, and, more pertinently, one that

---

of each of the Member States? The answer has clear implications for the conditions under which intervention by means of Article 83(2) TFEU is legally justified.

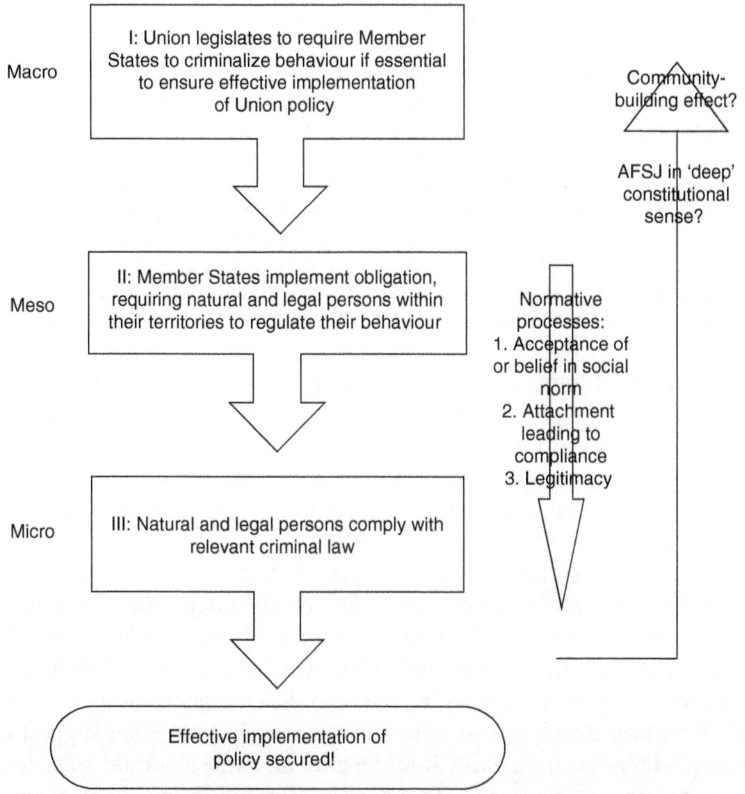

Figure 10.3 Article 83(2) TFEU as a constitutional mechanism

is capable of realization, then it matters that the answer to this question is 'yes'. Figure 10.3 attempts to illustrate the question schematically.

Looking to the literature, there is material which corroborates the view that such a thing is possible, in both theoretical and empirical terms. For example, in his jurisprudential discussion of criminal law and morality, Neil MacCormick notes that:

> Some. . . argue that it is the fact that some people violate the law and expose themselves to punishment that helps to build and sustain a kind of social solidarity. The punishment of the guilty reinforces the collective virtue of the innocent, at any rate of those whose wrongdoings have not (yet) been exposed.[60]

---

[60] Neil MacCormick, *Institutions of Law: An Essay in Legal Theory* (OUP 2007), 211–12, omitting his footnote which refers to the work of Emile Durkheim.

And he goes on to assert that:

> What is wrong about committing crimes is that it involves some wilful form of behaviour that violates the conditions of civil peace. . . In feudal kingdoms, each lord up to and including the king as highest lord of all lords had their own 'peace', their own domain in which maintaining the peace was their special concern. . . It seems not too fanciful to think that the evolution of modern states out of feudal kingdoms depersonalized the peace, so that we are left with the idea of 'breach of the peace' as a matter of common concern, not layered into different bits of peace. Peace, to the extent that the state's institutions succeed in securing it without infringing the fundamental right to and interest in personal liberty, is the common asset of, and common ground of, civil society.[61]

The Union's Member States can hardly be described as 'feudal', but none the less it is possible to perceive some measure of analogy with the processes that are underway towards building a common 'peace', or Union-wide concept of public order,[62] across its territories. In fact, it might well be argued that these latter notions are precisely integral to the ambition to fashion the Union as an AFSJ.

Putting MacCormick's remarks together, there is at least a basis for embarking upon an argument that the social and political commodity of 'community' can result from the operation of criminal law. And there are fragments in Bottoms' discussion too which concern this relationship. Rather than as a linear process, he refers to the emergence of society (community) and the development of its social norms in terms that suggest that he regards them as organically interdependent. This, it should be noted, is not necessarily inconsistent with what is occurring in the current context of the Union. Furthermore, he cites examples from the anthropological literature that lend support to his perspective,[63] thus fortifying a substantially theoretical account with empirically based content.

Relevantly, he then goes on to say:

> while it seems obviously true that in an organic, rural society the rules (including the prohibitions) of a given social group will be based on its evolving social norms, that is not necessarily the case in a more differentiated society. Here, rather than prohibitions arising out of positive morality, they may on occasion not reflect positive morality at all, but rather may be imposed by those in power

---

[61] Ibid, 216–17.

[62] See Case C-137/09 *Marc Michel Josemans v Burgemeester van Maastricht* [2010] ECR I-13019, Opinion of Advocate General Bot, paras 117–23; Case C-145/09 *Land Baden-Württemberg v Panagiotis Tsakouridis* [2010] ECR I-11979, Opinion of Advocate General Bot, para 95.

[63] Anthony E Bottoms, noted at n 14, 25.

> in the hope of securing obedience through deterrent calculation. Even in such a case, however, sometimes (though not always) the fact of prohibition, and citizens' evolving response to it, can influence the development of a new strand of positive morality.[64]

This, clearly, is a recognition of the potential for criminal laws to have the 'top down' moral effect that has been identified here with the legislative base in Article 83(2) TFEU. Furthermore, in similarly helpful vein, he continues slightly further on:

> rules or laws, once they are in force, are responded to by citizens (both those who obey and those who do not). . . . [T]he distinctive feature of rule-related behaviour is that 'the actor. . . knows that the rule exists, and must be conformed to for normal social relations to be sustained'.[65]

The notion that rule-related behaviour entails an understanding in actors of the impact of their conduct upon 'normal social relations' captures something of the idea that such behaviour is conducive to a sense of participation in the community to which the rules apply. On the face of it, therefore, there is material here from which it might seem feasible to derive a proposition that, in aggregate, individuals' acts of conscious conformity have a community-building effect of the type that is desirable if Article 83(2) TFEU is to realize its mooted constitution-building potential. That deduction, however, should not be drawn too hastily because there is an implicit, unexplored issue in what Bottoms has to say that is highly problematic when it comes to criminal law regulation by the EU.

The source of the trouble is the quote with which he concludes the latter statement; that is, the part that concerns the actor's knowledge. It is axiomatic that actors cannot regulate their behaviour by reference to rules of which they are oblivious. Therefore, it is not that aspect that requires attention, but the subsequent limb that relates to the setting of the knowledge, and associated decision-making, in the context of 'normal social relations'. For the overall scheme of thought to work, a great deal hangs on what this latter concept means.

The assumption appears to be that actors identify the rules in question as forming part of the normative expectations of the specific society or social group, the 'normal relations' of which they seek through their behaviour to sustain. In the context of Bottoms' discussion there was no

---

64 Ibid.

65 Ibid, 25–6, quoting Meyer Fortes, *Rules and the Emergence of Society*, Royal Anthropological Institute of Great Britain and Ireland Occasional Paper no.39 (Royal Anthropological Institute 1983) 40.

need to dwell on this, let alone to query it, because he was addressing the workings of compliance in the setting of nation-states, the UK in particular. In what remains the standard situation in such settings, where criminal laws are wholly internally instigated, there is no question of there being a mismatch between the source of the rules and the social context in relation to which an actor makes decisions about conformity. The assumption, though, does not hold good when it comes to criminal law measures that originate in Article 83(2) TFEU (or other Union law).

In their instance, the true authorship of relevant rules is not transparent, but, as noted above, it is obscured by the fact that the Union must rely upon the Member States to implement and enforce its normative requirements. That means that the Union's macro level normative message is channelled via the meso level of the Member States to individual micro level actors within their respective territories. As a result, the author of the message appears to those actors to be the Member State itself. Unless they are blessed with special knowledge, actors are therefore liable to infer that it is the national (or sub-national) environment to which their decisions about conformity are relevant because they cannot detect that the message originated at the level of the Union.[66]

The link with the Union being lost, it follows that so too is the capacity for conformity consciously to nourish a collective sense of pan-Union community. In short, any such aspiration on the part of the Union is frustrated by the mismatch between the message and the immediate messenger. Accordingly, there is an inbuilt structural obstruction to the potential for Article 83(2) TFEU to achieve its optimum constitutionalizing effect with respect to realization of the AFSJ. Conversely, and by the same token, in so far as measures based on Article 83(2) TFEU generate any community-building effect, that effect will be manifested at the meso level of the Member States. Whether or not the existence and implementation of relevant rules actually does that will be contingent upon the extent to which the measures concerned are either sympathetic, or antagonistic, to the normative understandings within the Member State concerned.[67] The implications for the prospective development of constitutional bonds

---

66 This analysis draws upon Ortwin Renn, 'Risk Communication and the Social Amplification of Risk' and Ortwin Renn and Debra Levine, 'Credibility and Trust in Risk Communication' both in Roger E Kasperson and Pieter Jan M Stallen (eds), *Communicating Risks to the Public* (Kluwer 1991).

67 See the point made previously about the circumstances that led to the litigation in Case C-265/95 *Commission v France (French Farmers)* noted at n 22.

between the Union, its Member States and the subjects of Member States' criminal laws are profound.

CONCLUSION

This chapter has been centrally concerned with the 'annex competence' that was newly conferred upon the Union by Article 83(2) TFEU as part of the Lisbon reforms. Providing, as it does, a legislative base in reliance upon which the Union may require the Member States to 'establish minimum rules with regard to the definition of criminal offences and sanctions', the conventional approach in the literature is to analyse this provision in terms of the Union's progressive acquisition of criminal competence. By contrast, the approach here has been to focus upon the instrumental purpose of the provision in securing the 'effective enforcement' of Union policies to which it is applicable. Seen through that lens, it has been argued that Article 83(2) TFEU can be understood in terms of a system of 'nested enforcement', which involves a vertical series of actors, at multiple governmental levels.

In the course of substantiating that view, the chapter has been particularly concerned with the mechanisms through which natural and legal persons are, or might be, induced to behave in a manner that complies with the norms that are set by means of measures that are based on Article 83(2) TFEU. To illuminate these, the discussion has drawn heavily upon the typology of legal compliance mechanisms that Anthony Bottoms has developed in the disciplinary field of criminology. As part of that work, Bottoms has argued that the mechanisms of normative compliance are pivotal. The discussion here has tried to build upon this proposition in order to address the two more detailed goals of the chapter. The first of these has been to explore the potential relevance of Bottoms' thesis to the development of a principled approach to the exercise of legislative competence based on Article 83(2) TFEU and, in particular, one that strives to accommodate the 'normative understandings' of those who will be subject to the resulting criminal laws. The second has been to link the analysis to a broader set of constitutional questions that concern the relevance of Article 83(2) TFEU in facilitating the emergence of a pan-Union positive morality and of a pan-Union community, and the cohesion of the Union as an AFSJ.

Notwithstanding that dealing with these issues has entailed some complex analysis, the chapter has provided little more than a sketch of the way in which an understanding of compliance might yield insights that are of value in enhancing effective enforcement in the context of the EU.

In addition to exploring its potential application to other enforcement contexts under the treaties, a further question that merits examination is whether and how the compliance framework might be harnessed in understanding the behaviour of aggregate actors, such as legal persons and the Member States. Regarded from this perspective, the chapter marks the start of an intellectual enquiry, rather than its completion.

11. The effective enforcement of economic governance in the European Union: brave new world or a false dawn?

Ryan Murphy

INTRODUCTION

At the risk of being trite, though no less true for it, it is said that the economic crisis revealed systemic weaknesses in the systems of financial and economic governance in the European Union and, in particular, exposed the ineffective enforcement of the 'rules'. The crisis provided a catalyst for change and an (almost inescapable) *opportunity* to reform not only the 'rules' but also how those rules are to be enforced.[1] The purpose of this chapter is to discuss critically the effectiveness of selected aspects of the new and revised system of enforcement of the rules of economic and financial governance in the European Union.

It is easy to forget, if one applies an overly legalistic analysis to the new systems described below, the element of danger that exists in the difference between the design of the legal regime and its operation in practice.[2] That difference has been brought into even sharper focus by the economic crisis. Although there were problems, pre-crisis, with the *legal framework* for economic governance, there were even greater problems in engendering the required *political will* to make the rules work. In this way it is important not to only judge the rules or structures in considering whether the new legal framework is 'stronger' or more effective than they once were. Throughout the chapter reference will be made to elements of

[1] This echoes the sentiments of John F Kennedy when, in Indianapolis in April 1959, he said that: 'when written in Chinese the word crisis is composed of two characters. One represents danger and the other represents opportunity.'

[2] This is a problem also suffered by some political scientists; see Chapter 2 of this volume.

the new system that are likely to be subject to the same dangers of political apathy, on the one hand, and political interference on the other. While the expressions of political commitment of some of the Member States should, based on past and present behaviour, be subject to a healthy dose of scepticism there is equally strong political rhetoric coming from the newly formed Juncker Commission. The introductory remarks by one of the Vice-Presidents of the Commission – Dombrovskis – confirm that should poor progress be made:

> [T]he reinforced rules [of economic governance] should be applied – both in terms of the Excessive Deficit Procedure and the Macroeconomic Imbalances Procedure. But it is not just our formal authority but the power of our argument that should convince all the decision-makers to do the right thing in our common interest. What happens in one Member State affects others.[3]

Whether the sentiment behind these comments is any more achievable or realistic than those expressed by the Member States will be assessed throughout this chapter.

In terms of structure, and as the entire architecture of economic governance has changed and continues to change, it would be impossible for this chapter to deal with every development in the economic and financial fields. The focus therefore will be on those changes that either introduced wholly new frameworks or that sought to deal explicitly with problems of poor enforcement under the 'old' system. The opening section will briefly consider the context and impetus for change as well as some of the principles that will inform the assessment as to whether the new processes are effective. To this end, the bulk of the chapter will consider: the Excessive Deficit Procedure (EDP); the Macro-Economic Imbalance Procedure (MIP); the Treaty on Stability, Coordination and Governance in the Economic and Monetary Union; the 'Two Pack' legislation; the conditionality of financial assistance; and the agencification of aspects of financial law. The concluding section will attempt to draw out common themes and emerging trends in the enforcement structures of this policy area.

The short-, medium- and long-term impacts of the crisis are self-evident. As well as strengthening existing methods of enforcement and introducing new mechanisms for ensuring compliance, there has been a more general review of the *framework* for economic governance and

---

[3] Speech by Vice-President Dombrovskis of the Commission (28 November 2014): http://europa.eu/rapid/press-release_SPEECH-14-2240_en.htm?locale=en accessed on 1 March 2015.

micro-prudential regulation and supervision. There is a real opportunity to 'do things differently'. This has centred on the introduction of a new European Semester.[4] This calendar of events for economic policy coordination acts as a form of enhanced monitoring and surveillance and can result in the triggering of more specific enforcement powers.[5] This increased concretization and formalization of policy coordination has the principle of enhanced and early compliance at its heart. This means that effective enforcement was not only the driver for change but also its key objective.

What is clear, even from these introductory comments, is that there has been significant innovation in the framework of enforcement in the area of economic governance. This chapter makes a novel contribution to the scholarship by bringing together the innovations from different aspects of economic governance (such as the EDP or the MIP) and analysing their collective and individual effectiveness. The contribution avoids the danger of looking at surface synergies that will inevitably be found within different aspects of a single policy area (even one as broad as economic governance) and instead attempts to evaluate whether the general trends are equally appropriate or effective within concrete situations. This leads to a multi-faceted and rich analysis of both broad level trends in enforcement in this area and of the effectiveness of those trends in achieving compliance in very particular situations (such as dealing with the existence of excessive deficits or of macro-economic imbalances).

The whole system has moved to one that is staged, ratcheted and dynamic both in process and in outcome. This has the *potential* to be more effective in terms of ensuring compliance through incentives *and* deterrence-based sanctions. In this regard, it is a mixed approach. Whether this is more effective in *reality* will depend largely upon the extent to which the political hurdles of the old systems have been overcome. While political will to embrace the new framework was strong in the immediate aftermath of the crisis, there are already indications that political interference remains a problem for economic governance. A framework that *looked* more robust and credible in the shadow of the financial crisis is now demonstrating weakness as the dawn of political change looms on the horizon. Thus, one of the central questions that pervades the analysis in this chapter is the extent to which the innovations in the *legal framework* are fundamentally

---

4 See http://ec.europa.eu/economy_finance/economic_governance/the_european_semester/index_en.htm accessed on 1 March 2015.

5 The link at n 4 also includes an informative diagram explaining the various stages of the European Semester.

flawed due to the still heavy reliance on non-legal (i.e. political) influence (or, for the cynical, interference).

As well as being staged and ratcheted, the new governance framework is typified by differentiated enforcement between the eurozone and non-eurozone members with different process and sanctions applying. This philosophy of differentiation affects most of the new processes discussed in this chapter and marks a further shift and innovation in enforcement practice in this area. It underlies a truth not often discussed in the context of traditional centralized enforcement based on Article 258, namely that different situations may need not only different approaches but a wider variety of sanctions that are not dominated by terminal fines.

1. UNDERSTANDING ENFORCEMENT IN ECONOMIC GOVERNANCE

Before exploring the detail of the new enforcement regimes, it would seem sensible to devote some space to discussing the notion of enforcement as it applies to economic governance. As other chapters of this edited work have explored, there are a multitude of understandings of the concept of enforcement that vary according to the subject matter being discussed. What constitutes *effective* enforcement may depend on the analytical (and discipline specific) framework used by a particular writer. For example, what may seem of crucial importance to a lawyer may not coincide with that which is viewed as important by a political scientist or economist. Moreover, even *within* a discipline there may be a different theoretical understanding of the purpose of enforcement and how we judge its effectiveness.

As a legal academic operating within the very technical dual worlds of macro- and micro-economic governance and prudential supervision, there are three key characteristics of a system that suggest enforcement is effective. The first is that enforcement should begin before a substantive breach of the rules has occurred, inasmuch as it should be preventative as well as curative. Changing excessive deficits and correcting macro-economic imbalances in a national economy is not something that can be solved in great haste, and so monitoring and preventing them from arising is an important part of the enforcement process. Second, where a breach is detected, compliance should follow swiftly. In this regard, the costs of non-compliance should quickly escalate in order to negate any advantage gained by the lack of compliance. Third, confidence and trust in the rules and in the processes of securing compliance – from the markets, the institutional actors, the Member States and citizens – ought to be maintained as a priority.

The first two (prevention and swift compliance) are mainstays of any legal analysis of enforcement.[6] Indeed, some writers suggest that the primary purpose of enforcement should be to reduce the benefits of free riding by Member States who will inevitably choose to breach when the conditions are correct.[7] Nonetheless, it is the third factor that has particular prominence within the discourse around a system of financial and economic governance. This concept of 'confidence' extends beyond any argument based solely on legal certainty, important though that is, and can be linked to the very efficacy of the policy area. As will be demonstrated below, a failure in the confidence of the market in the *robustness* of the enforcement regime for economic governance can lead to misallocation of economic risk and could be said to have contributed significantly to the ineffectiveness of the enforcement regime.

In this way a discussion of enforcement of economic governance and micro-prudential regulation within the EU should avoid the tendency that lawyers have to focus on 'hard' law and a primarily rules-based system.[8] The financial crisis, discussed below, has led to arguments for a resurgence of 'hard law' without recognition of the previous failure of the hard law mechanisms, with its command and control ideology, that were already in place. What should instead prevail is a greater mix of enforcement strategies, involving both soft and hard law approaches and a broader range of institutions. This would align the enforcement strategy towards a more mixed regulatory approach.[9] In order to ensure the confidence of the markets, the institutional actors should embrace a flexible and inclusive approach to enforcement that relies less on traditional centralized and decentralized enforcement paradigms. This would allow, for example, the markets to act in a more concerted way to correct non-compliance, in tandem with the more formal, centralized enforcement processes.

---

6 See generally, Marise Cremona, 'Introduction' in Marise Cremona (ed), *Compliance and the Enforcement of EU Law* (OUP 2012).

7 Lisa Conant, 'Compliance and what EU Member States Make of It' in Marise Cremona (ed), *Compliance and the Enforcement of EU Law* (OUP 2012) 6.

8 Kenneth Armstrong, 'The New Governance of EU Fiscal Discipline' (2013) 38 ELRev 601, 603.

9 See, for example, discussion by Helen Xanthaki, 'European Union Legislative Quality after the Lisbon Treaty: The Challenges of Smart Regulation' (2014) 35 SLRev 66.

2. INNOVATIONS IN ECONOMIC GOVERNANCE

The following sub-sections will explore the major developments in the enforcement of economic governance that came about as a result of the economic crisis. These are technically challenging and complex areas of law and an attempt will be made to locate each development within the overall framework of economic governance. This done, the sub-sections will explore what these developments add to our understanding of enforcement in the EU and an evaluation will be made of their effectiveness. The analysis will look at the phased, staged and differentiated approach taken to enforcement under the Stability and Growth Pact; the Macro-Economic Imbalance Procedure; the Treaty on Stability, Coordination and Governance; and the 'Two Pack' legislation on greater budgetary coordination in the eurozone.

2.1 Stability and Growth Pact and Enforcement of the Excessive Deficit Procedure

The Stability and Growth Pact (SGP) is a central feature of economic governance and has been the subject of constant reform since its inception in the 1990s, with changes in the mid-2000s and, more recently, in late 2011. The SGP was intended to coincide with the introduction of the single currency and was designed to promote budgetary responsibility and fiscal discipline. The economic crisis exposed the SGP as structurally flawed and, most importantly for the purposes of this chapter, that enforcement was piecemeal and wholly ineffective for the larger, more influential, Member States.[10] This sub-section is not intended to be an exhaustive examination of the SGP[11] but, after a brief explanation of the system, focus will be on the reforms that came into force on 13 December 2011 and their impact on effective enforcement.

The Member States have to commit to the following criteria under the SGP: government deficits should be no more than 3 per cent of GDP; public debt should not exceed 60 per cent of GDP; and achievement of a medium-term budgetary objective (MTO). Before 2005, this MTO was common amongst Member States and required a balanced budget over

[10] Koen Lenaerts, 'EMU and the EU's Constitutional Framework' (2014) 39 ELRev 753, 755.

[11] For such a review of the pre-2011 system, see Fabian Amtenbrink and Jakob De Haan, 'Reforming the Stability and Growth Pact' (2006) 31 ELRev 402.

a complete business cycle. Following on from 2005,[12] the MTO is now tailored more specifically to the individual Member States.

A Member State who, as a result of not abiding by these rules, had an excessive deficit could be placed under the corrective arm of the SGP – the Excessive Deficit Procedure (EDP). In this way, the operation of the SGP, and particularly the corrective arm, had strong elements of command and control type enforcement with rigid rules enforced from above. Before the 2005 reforms to the MTO, the command and control structures were even stronger as the system applied uniform and inflexible rules. Having said this, the monitoring of the preventative arm led to a hybrid approach with the system relying heavily on peer pressure between the Member States. This leads to the interesting mixed approach of non-legal methods of enforcement (such as peer pressure) being used to support the more formal legal regime. Even where the legal regime is clear and based on objective measures (as the EDP undoubtedly was, and still is) effective enforcement often requires non-legal enforcement practices to be developed outside of that legal regime.

The ineffectiveness of the EDP has long been recognized by academics[13] and the institutions of the EU.[14] This flowed partly from the structure of the SGP which was unable to predict some of the economic imbalances (e.g. problems in the property markets of some Member States or the amount of private debt in the national economies) and this is further discussed below. More than this, the rules that were there (particularly on the ratio of public debt to GDP) were not enforced rigorously. As was recently noted by the Director of the European Department of the International Monetary Fund (IMF), 'the incentives for compliance with the fiscal targets were weak and ineffectually enforced'.[15]

By early 2003 it was clear that a number of Member States, including

---

[12] Council Regulation (EC) 1055/2005 amending Regulation (EC) 1466/97 on the strengthening of the surveillance of budgetary positions and the surveillance and coordination of economic policies [2005] OJ L174/1 and Council Regulation (EC) 1056/2005 amending Regulation (EC) 1467/97 on speeding up and clarifying the implementation of the excessive deficit procedure [2005] OJ L174/5.

[13] For example, Amtenbrink n 11 and Andrew Scott, 'Does Economic Union Require a Fiscal Union?' in Niamh Nic Shuibhne and Laurence Gormley (eds), *From Single Market to Economic Union: Essays in Memory of John A Usher* (OUP 2012) 39–42.

[14] http://europa.eu/rapid/press-release_MEMO-14-2180_en.htm accessed on 1 March 2015.

[15] Reza Moghadam, 'Lessons from the Crisis Response for the Way Forward' (2014), http://www.imf.org/external/np/speeches/2014/061014.htm accessed on 1 March 2015.

France, Germany and Italy, had excessive deficits as measured against the criteria above. The real flaw in the corrective arm of the system became evident when the Commission tried to place Germany and France under the EDP.[16] The Council led by the larger states (including Germany and France) refused to ratify/approve the Commission's recommendation. As endorsement of the Commission recommendation required a qualified majority of Member States, it was fairly easy for a Member State (particularly a large and influential Member State) to gain a blocking majority. As a result, both Member States were able to avoid the sanctions and enforcement processes under the corrective arm of the EDP. The reforms of the process in 2005 exacerbated and accentuated the concerns over the EDP, as it was perceived that Member States were able to 'change the rules' to avoid enforcement.

Even the pressure of the recommendation being publicly known was not enough to ensure that the corrective arm of the SGP was invoked. It could be argued that in these circumstances the Commission's attempt to 'name and shame' the offending Member States was an indication of desperation and frustration. This desperation stems from the fact that the formal legal regime had failed from the outset inasmuch as the Commission was helpless to compel the Council to invoke the corrective arm of the SGP against France or Germany. This ineffectiveness was compounded by the fact that the Commission is precluded from bringing enforcement proceedings under Article 258 for Member State (in)action in relation to excessive deficits.[17] While weakness in the EDP did not *cause* the economic crisis, it contributed to the lack of preparedness to deal with the outcome of the same.

More importantly it could be argued that the lack of proper enforcement by the EU contributed to the market not taking the risks of excessive deficits as seriously as it could have done.[18] In matters of fiscal policy, the market can help to ensure compliance with EU rules through the way in which it lends to Member States. Or, to put it differently, the market wields a rather sharp stick in the form of control over the major supply of funding for government borrowing. Where a Member State is acting in a fiscally irresponsible way then the market may view it as at a higher risk of default and raise interest rates on lending and so curb the accumulation

---

[16] See Sideek Seyad, 'A Critical Evaluation of the Revised and Enlarged European Stability and Growth Pact' (2012) 27 JIBLR 202, 204–6.

[17] Article 126(10) TFEU.

[18] That is not to say that the market is blameless as it was, of itself, rather short-sighted as to the potential long-term risks and sustainability of public spending in some Member States.

of public debt and reduce any budget deficit.[19] However if, as was the case in the build-up to the crisis, the EU is perceived not to take the dangers of excessive deficit seriously by its ineffective attitude towards the EDP, then the market is less likely to take other indicators of risk (such as the potential for strict adherence to the 'no bail out' provision[20]) as seriously. The markets (correctly as it transpires) did not judge it a serious risk that a Member State would not be supported by the other states in the event of the former's economy failing.[21] This was, in turn, a contributing factor to the moral hazard[22] that arose during, and exacerbated the impact of, the crisis. This moral hazard was evident on two levels. First, financial institutions lent to Member States within the eurozone with high levels of public debt on the assumption that the risk would be borne by the EU (or more particularly the eurozone) as a whole.[23] Second, certain national governments were able to run unsustainable excessive deficits in the knowledge that enforcement of the EDP was unlikely. In this way, and what is most important for the purposes of this chapter, the failure of the market to act as a quasi-regulator is, at least in part, attributable to the failure of the EU to properly address the excessive deficits of its members.

In the wake of the financial crisis, political will was garnered to partially reform the EDP and to try to alleviate some of the problems associated with its enforcement, particularly for those Member States forming the eurozone. This reform was achieved through the so-called 'Six Pack' of legislative instruments. The Six Pack consists of five regulations and a single directive.[24] Much of the focus of the Six Pack was on strengthening

---

[19] European Union Committee, *The Future of Economic Governance in the EU* (HL 2010–11, 124–I) para 158.

[20] Article 125 TFEU.

[21] For more on the concept of 'moral hazard' and on the tension between the 'no bailout out' provision and the financial support given to Greece, see Phoebus Athanassiou, 'Of Past Measures and Future Plans for Europe's Exit from the Sovereign Debt Crisis: What Is Legally Possible (and What Is Not)' (2011) 36 ELRev 558, 560.

[22] By moral hazard here we mean that a risk-based decision is calculated by one person/institution in the knowledge that the negative consequences of that risk will be borne by another person/institution in case of the risk being realized.

[23] For more on this, see Tobias Troger, 'The Single Supervisory Mechanism: Panacea or Quack Banking Regulation? Preliminary Assessment of the New Regime for the Prudential Supervision of Banks with ECB Involvement' (2014) 15 *European Business Organization Law Review* 449, 460–62.

[24] Council Regulation (EU) 1173/2011 on the effective enforcement of budgetary surveillance in the euro area [2011] OJ L306/1; Council Regulation (EU) 1174/2011 on enforcement measures to correct excessive macroeconomic imbalances in the euro area [2011] OJ L306/8; Council Regulation (EU) 1175/2011

the SGP and, in particular, the enforcement of the EDP for eurozone countries. This took the form of procedural reforms and changes to available sanctions.

New sanctions were introduced for eurozone members who are under the EDP. Should a eurozone member fail to take action to address the warnings/recommendations given by the Commission[25] then the Council can require a deposit from that Member State on a further recommendation of the Commission.[26] The deposit will be *interest bearing* and of up to 0.2 per cent of GDP.[27] If the Council subsequently find that there is an excessive deficit, that deposit can be turned into a *non-interest bearing* deposit by a further Council decision.[28] If the Member State is still found not to have taken action to effectively respond to that decision then the Council can turn the deposit into a fine.[29] This new system of sanctions is intended to complement the enhanced monitoring and reporting that already exists under the SGP.

On the procedural front, regular qualified majority voting for the SGP has been largely replaced in key areas of decision-making by a new 'reverse qualified majority' voting (rQMV).[30] This means that a decision under the EDP will now be adopted *unless* enough Member States vote to block it. This may seem like a small change but its significance to enforcement should not be underplayed. This move makes the enforcement of the EDP rules, at least in theory, more automatic.[31] This lessens the likelihood of a Member State managing to escape from scrutiny and the formal process of excessive deficits. More than just making the process more automated,

---

amending Council Regulation (EC) No 1466/97 on the strengthening of the surveillance of budgetary positions and the surveillance and coordination of economic policies [2011] OJ L306/12; Council Regulation (EU) 1176/2011 on the prevention and correction of macroeconomic imbalances [2011] OJ L306/25; Council Regulation (EU) 1177/2011 amending Regulation (EC) No 1467/97 on speeding up and clarifying the implementation of the excessive deficit procedure [2011] OJ L306/33; Council Directive 2011/85/EU on requirements for budgetary frameworks of the Member States [2011] OJ L306/41.

25 As established by a Council decision under Article 126(9) TFEU.

26 Article 126(11) TFEU.

27 Council Regulation (EU) 1173/2011 on the effective enforcement of budgetary surveillance in the euro area [2011] OJ L306/1 Article 4.

28 Regulation 1173/2011 n 24, Article 5.

29 Ibid Article 6.

30 Ibid Articles 4(2), 5(2) and 6(2).

31 Greater automaticity was one of the criteria for a successful enforcement regime, as indicated by the IMF in 2014: Reza Moghadam, 'Lessons from the Crisis Response for the Way Forward' (2014), http://www.imf.org/external/np/speeches/2014/061014.htm accessed on 1 March 2015.

it also marks a significant shift in political impetus for more effective enforcement. The use of this new form of rQMV will take place for the earlier sanction stages (interest and non-interest bearing deposits) but the decision as to whether a Member State *has* an excessive deficit is still taken by regular qualified majority voting (QMV). This demonstrates the limits of political will in this area with the most serious sanction remaining under the same political constraints as before.

There are a number of general points about developments in enforcement that can be drawn out of the description and analysis above. Arguably the most important development is the move towards a system of early and *staged* enforcement. The traditional centralized enforcement system – as typified by Commission proceedings under Articles 258 and 260 TFEU – has terminal sanctions levied after a long and arduous procedure. The reformed EDP allows sanctions, albeit mild sanctions, to be imposed at a much earlier part of the process than was previously possible.[32] The sanctions also develop over time as non-compliance continues, from an interest bearing deposit to a non-interest bearing deposit to a fine. By staging not only the timing of the sanctions but also their severity, the EU has significantly reformed the enforcement regime of the EDP, as it applies to the eurozone. This more dynamic and ratcheted system has the *potential* to be more effective and dissuasive than its predecessor because of rQMV. It should be noted that many of the eurozone states that had excessive deficits during the height of the crisis have now been moved out of the corrective arm of the SGP. As of June 2014, 11 Member States remain under the EDP and, of these, only two (Cyprus and Greece) are eurozone countries. This is a significant reduction on the 24 Member States who were under the EDP in 2011, shortly after the height of the crisis. The extent to which the reforms noted in this section, as opposed to domestic pressures and recovering economies, played a part in this correction is uncertain. However, the Commission certainly attributes, in its Economic Governance Review, the success of reducing average fiscal deficits of Member States at least in part to the reformed system of economic governance.[33] The new system of *sanctions* has yet to be used and so its effectiveness will be judged in time.

There are mixed signs as to whether the *political* hurdles to the effective enforcement of the EDP have been successfully overcome by the recent reforms. The use of reverse majority voting certainly indicates an appetite

---

[32] See also Ch 3 on responsive regulation in this context.

[33] Commission, 'Economic governance review' (Communication) COM(2014) 905 final, 3–6.

to reduce the political influence of individual Member States, but the key decisions are still taken by the Council on the recommendation of the Commission. By vesting responsibility for each stage of the process with the Council, it is possible that some of the old problems relating to enforcement will resurface.[34] In this regard, '[t]he central role attributed to the Council adversely affects the credibility of the procedure'.[35] It is also important to note that the Member States have allowed rQMV for the less serious sanctions (the deposits) but the imposition of the intensifying of fines and the *finding* of an excessive deficit[36] is still reliant on 'regular' QMV. Moreover, and unlike under Article 258 TFEU proceedings, there is no prospect of the CJEU becoming involved. This accentuates the political nature of the EDP process and removes the pressure of negotiations 'in the shadow of court proceedings'[37] as are present under Article 258 enforcement proceedings.[38]

In many ways this area of policy is still dominated by a centralized 'command and control' enforcement ideology, with some minor experimentation and innovation at the fringes. There are still (theoretically) hard rules that stem from, and are enforced, centrally. This is perhaps sensible and to be expected, given that the causes of an excessive deficit often lie at a policy-setting level. Thus, what may *appear* to be modest tinkering with the system is actually quite significant given the practical constraints under which this policy area operates. Any innovation is constrained not only by political will but also by the limits placed by the legal framework. In this instance, improvement to the enforcement of the EDP takes place within the confines of Article 126(1)–(14) TFEU which limits not only the decision-making process (mainly to the Council) but also the types of sanctions that can be imposed for breach of the EDP. As a result, while the *process* for finding and remedying excessive deficits has been improved, it is still heavily reliant on political will for the effectiveness of the reformed system to be achieved. The new framework has gone as far as it is possible to go without further reform to the Treaty, which seems unlikely at present.

---

[34] Although others have noted that this also means that decision-making for imposing quite harsh sanctions is legitimized by the involvement of the Council. See European Union Committee, *The Future of Economic Governance in the EU* (HL 2010–12, 124-I) para 100.

[35] Roland Bieber and Francesco Maiani, 'Enhancing Centralized Enforcement of EU Law: Pandora's Toolbox?' (2014) 51 CMLRev 1057, 1070.

[36] Armstrong n 8, 611–12.

[37] Ibid, 613.

[38] A point also taken up by Bieber and Maiani n 35, 1066.

As well as creating a staged approach to enforcement, the reforms above also make further distinction between the eurozone and non-eurozone members. This differentiated philosophy on enforcement further expands on the 2005 reform of the SGP, which introduced country-specific MTOs. This may seem perfectly sensible given that the crisis demonstrated the threat of contagion within the eurozone; however, it also marks a shift to differentiated enforcement. This shift, although it is still very much in the framework of command and control enforcement, nonetheless shows significant attempts at innovation.

In addition to reforming the EDP, the EU has also passed other measures and proposed new methods for tackling the structural weaknesses of economic governance exposed by the financial crisis. The next subsection will discuss another of these developments – the Macro-Economic Imbalance Procedure. The parallels between the different processes and how this links to the broader lessons to be learned for the effective enforcement of the rules relating to economic governance will be explored later in the chapter.

2.2 Macro-Economic Imbalance Procedure

A further wholly new procedure was added as part of the Six Pack to the economic governance rules in 2011. Regulations 1174/2011[39] and 1176/2011[40] create the framework for the Macro-Economic Imbalance Procedure (MIP).[41] The new procedure was deemed necessary in order to monitor more closely the economic environment within each of the Member States.[42] This was because the EDP had proved an inadequate barometer for some of the economic conditions that contributed to the severity of the financial crisis. For example, the rules of the Stability and Growth Pact (SGP) focus heavily on *public* debt and *government* deficits. Even if the Excessive Deficit Procedure (EDP) had been more effectively enforced, some of the imbalances (such as private debt and unsustainable property markets) within the Member States' economies would still have exacerbated economic problems during the crisis. Control of levels of private debt and the property market within domestic economies is largely outside of the EU's direct control and competence in any case.

---

39 Regulation (EU) 1174/2011 on enforcement measures to correct excessive macroeconomic imbalances in the euro area [2011] OJ L306/8.

40 Regulation (EU) 1176/2011 on the prevention and correction of macroeconomic imbalances [2011] OJ L306/25.

41 The Regulations are based on Article 121(6) and Article 121(2) TFEU.

42 See Armstrong n 8 for further discussion.

The new imbalance procedure (MIP) is intended to deal with this issue and provide an early warning system where parts of a Member State's economy – measured on a scoreboard of 11 indicators – are unbalanced.[43] The 11 indicators relate to the following areas: current account balance as a percentage of GDP, fluctuations in the real effective exchange rates (REER), changes in nominal unit labour cost, net international investment position, private sector debt, private sector credit flow, export market share, public sector debt, house price changes, unemployment rates and financial liabilities in the financial sector. Some of these are related to potential *external* imbalances (such as the current account balance and REER) and others to *internal* imbalances (such as the private sector debt or house prices).

The scoreboard for these indicators then forms the basis of an annual Alert Mechanism Report. This will then be followed, if the Commission deems it necessary, by an in-depth review.[44] If an imbalance is found then this in turn will lead to 'recommendations' to the Member State about rebalancing their economy.[45] Depending on the severity of any imbalances found, the Commission will issue the recommendation on the basis of the preventative or corrective arm of the procedure. If the imbalance is deemed to be excessive, the Member State will be required to produce an action plan to correct the imbalances and this will be approved by the Commission and Council acting jointly.[46] This demonstrates elements of collaborative governance (as between the EU institutions and as between the EU and the Member States) and is part of the more fluid processes that precede the sanctions that may follow.

If the Member State fails to follow its plan, or the corrective action plan is not deemed to be sufficient, then this may trigger various enforcement powers. The Commission will continue to monitor the situation and the reports prepared by the Member State. The sanctions under the corrective arm of the MIP are applied only to the eurozone countries. In this way, there are strong similarities between the MIP and the EDP discussed above. Much like the EDP, the sanctions include a staged approach. Under the MIP, there are only two stages of non-compliance to the corrective process, as opposed to the three stages under the EDP. The first failure to comply with the corrective action necessary will lead to the requirement

---

43 Regulation 1176/2011 n 40, Article 4.

44 Ibid Article 5.

45 Ibid Article 6.

46 Ibid Articles 7 and 8.

of an interest bearing deposit, whereas a second failure would lead to the conversion of that deposit into a fine.[47]

While the staged *sanctions* aspect of the MIP is shorter, the lead-up to the finding of an *excessive* imbalance is much longer than the finding of an excessive deficit. There are five categories under the MIP before the Excessive Imbalance Procedure is utilized in the sixth category. Of the 26 Member States subject to the framework on imbalances:[48] 10 States have no imbalance (Category 1),[49] 6 have imbalances that require monitoring and policy action (Category 2),[50] 2 have imbalances that require monitoring and *decisive* action (Category 3),[51] 3 have imbalances that require *specific* monitoring and decisive policy action (Category 4)[52] and 5 have excessive imbalances that require specific monitoring and decisive policy action (Category 5).[53] There are currently no Member States in the final category, which is that the Member State has excessive imbalances which require decisive policy action and the launching of the Excessive Imbalance Procedure (Category 6).[54]

The MIP suffers from a number of problems that will likely impact on whether enforcement of its rules are effective in the long term.[55] Most importantly, the scoreboard for assessing the potential for excessive imbalance makes use of a very wide range of indicators, none of which is determinative in assessing whether a Member State has an excessive imbalance. As such, and in sharp contrast to the very specific 'rules' of the EDP,

---

47 Regulation 1174/2011 n 39, Article 3(1) for the deposit and Article 3(2) (a)–(b).

48 Greece and Cyprus are not included as they are subject to a different legal framework, due to them currently being part of macro-economic adjustment programmes. The data from this section is drawn from here: European Commission, http://ec.europa.eu/economy_finance/economic_governance/macroeconomic_imbalance_procedure/index_en.htm accessed on 1 March 2015.

49 Austria, Czech Republic, Denmark, Estonia, Latvia, Lithuania, Luxembourg, Malta, Poland and Slovakia.

50 Belgium, Finland, Romania, Sweden, the Netherlands and the United Kingdom.

51 Germany and Hungary.

52 Ireland, Slovenia and Spain.

53 Bulgaria, Croatia, France, Italy and Portugal.

54 This data can be found at European Commission, http://ec.europa.eu/economy_finance/economic_governance/macroeconomic_imbalance_procedure/index_en.htm accessed on 1 March 2015, which also gives an in-depth report for each of the Member States in categories 2–6.

55 The enforcement regime of macroeconomic policy is also said to lack legitimacy as it is questionable whether the EU has competence to do what it is doing – see Bieber and Maiani n 35, 1071.

the Commission must form a more nuanced judgement as to whether it should make a recommendation that a particular Member State should be classified as having an excessive imbalance requiring opening of the MIP. This enhanced flexibility, as to whether the imbalance exists and whether it is *excessive*, leaves the Commission open to greater political influence and the Council in a stronger position to reject a Commission recommendation.[56] In many ways the discretion of the Commission will be central to the effectiveness of enforcement and the level of discretion present in the MIP system suggests that some of the well-known problems of centralized enforcement under Articles 258–60 TFEU will also be present in the system designed to deal with excessive imbalances.[57]

Similarly, whereas the SGP has criteria (debt and deficit) over which the Member State governments have direct control, the same cannot always be said of the scoreboard indicators of the MIP. The direct control that a government can have over house prices and private debt (MIP indicators) is more limited than over things like government borrowing (EDP criterion). That is not to say that government policy *cannot* influence these things but that influence is both less direct and less tangible. A change of interest rates, for example, can and probably will, impact on the property market and private debt levels. However, this has two important limitations, particularly for the states in the eurozone.

Primarily, some states have less control over individual monetary policy by virtue of their membership of the eurozone and so their toolbox for remedying an excessive imbalance may be more limited. For example, the key interest rates for the eurozone are set by the Governing Council of the European Central Bank (ECB), rather than by the individual central banks of the Member States, and this is an important form of monetary policy control.[58] This means that the use of interest rates to indirectly control market rates on domestic or commercial loans and deposits is unavailable (on an individual level) to the eurozone members. Also, the degree of policy control over some of these measures by all Member States is much less direct and may take a greater time to feed through to changes in the imbalances. Thus even though changes to the interest rate set by the central banks which are not part of the eurozone, or the ECB for eurozone members, on lending to commercial banks will increase the costs of private borrowing, and so would tend to reduce the amount of private debt in an

---

56 The political reality is noted by the House of Lords n 34, para 158.

57 See Smith, Ch 2 of this volume.

58 Article 12(1) Statute of the European System of Central Banks and the European Central Bank.

economy, which may take time to filter through to the market.[59] Taking the further example of the Spanish property market at the height of the financial crisis, it would have required quite significant policy measures to reduce the imbalances and these (on the upswing) would have been countercyclical and politically sensitive. In summary, determining the presence and affecting the reduction of excessive imbalances is more difficult than the control of excessive deficits under the EDP. It is, it could be argued, unfair for the enforcement regime to take too hard a line on the presence of an excessive imbalance for this reason. This may help to explain the broader categories of imbalance that exist under the MIP.

More importantly, a holistic judgment as to whether an *excessive* imbalance exists (which adopts a broader approach and does not simply apply the indicators in a mechanical way) will undermine the effectiveness of the *hard* rules and sanctions. This will mean that the soft law aspects (enhanced monitoring and guidance) will take a more central position under the MIP. It is perhaps for this reason that (as the Commission notes[60]) the sanctions are imposed not for the imbalance itself but for the failure to engage with the process (e.g. by putting forward an inadequate corrective plan on multiple occasions).

In summary, there are some commonalities between enforcement of the EDP and the MIP, as would be expected due to them covering seemingly similar issues. The phased and staged approach to the process, the use of rQMV and the introduction of new forms of sanction (deposits) mark the largest synergies between the systems. However, these surface synergies do mask some significant differences between the EDP and MIP that may affect their effectiveness in practice.

On the legal framework, under the MIP there is a progression directly from interest bearing deposits to fines without the interim step of converting the deposit to one that is non-interest bearing. This means that the advantages of a fully phased system present under the EDP are not realized under the MIP and this creates a more politically charged 'jump' between sanctions. Moreover, the complexity and number of categories of imbalance and the less concrete and less controllable indicators of an excessive deficit adds significant doubt as to the effectiveness of the system. The non-mechanical application of the indicators (to be contrasted with

---

[59] The reverse is also true in that Member States are limited in how far they can force private lenders to make domestic and commercial loans. Indeed, a low national/nominal interest rate may be an incentive to encourage lending but it is no guarantee that such lending will become more readily available.

[60] http://europa.eu/rapid/press-release_MEMO-14-2180_en.htm accessed on 1 March 2015.

the debt and deficit requirements under the EDP) also provides additional room for political negotiation between the Commission and the Member States. This, in itself, may be an effective way of securing *compliance* with the rules but this will be in the shadow of the formal system of enforcement through sanctions. The former is only truly effective when the latter is suitably dissuasive.

A final but important note should be made in relation to the role of market participants in the MIP, as opposed to the EDP. Under the latter, the markets have the ability (though in an indirect way) of curbing excessive deficits through the interest rates it sets on government lending. Although this failed under the old system of EDP,[61] as described above, there is hope that the lessons learned from the crisis will make this aspect (market participant enforcement) more effective in the future. This is not necessarily because of the substantive changes to the EDP but rather because of the experience the market has had of the current financial crisis. If we consider the MIP on the other hand, the market does not play the same active role as 'enforcer'.[62] Indeed, the lack of the market as a brake on irresponsible macro-economic policy means that there is a need for greater caution in how the EU enforces the MIP as it does not have the backstop of more direct enforcement by market participants. This also further evidences that what, at first glance, appear to be similar legal frameworks (the EDP and MIP) for enforcement may have different enforcement practices at play *outside* of that formal framework.

As well as the new Union frameworks on excessive deficits and imbalances, some of the Member States have sought to go further and have attempted to bolster the SGP by agreeing to an international treaty on further coordination of economic governance. The next sub-section will deal with this novel use of an international treaty to further what are essentially EU law objectives.

2.3 Treaty on Stability, Coordination and Governance in the Economic and Monetary Union (Fiscal Compact Treaty)

In 2012, the Member States sought to improve the robustness of the Stability and Growth Pact (SGP) through the creation of a new treaty: the Treaty on Stability, Coordination and Governance in the Economic

---

[61] Largely because the markets, as it transpired correctly, did not believe the Treaty guarantees of 'no bailout', which were designed to deal with the problem of moral hazard.

[62] House of Lords n 34, para 158.

and Monetary Union (TSCG).[63] This Treaty has also come to be known as the 'Fiscal Compact Treaty'. This Treaty is of particular interest because it was ratified outside of the EU framework and remains an international agreement rather than an EU treaty. The eurozone members are bound by the Treaty and other Member States may choose to ratify it. Two Member States, the UK and the Czech Republic, did not ratify the Treaty at all and a number of other Member States are signed up to only parts of it. Although it could be argued that this places the discussion outside of the remit of this edited work, the links between the TSCG and the EU are so close as to make discussion, in terms of enforcement, useful, if not essential. It is also to be borne in mind that the final provision of the TSCG contains a requirement for the Member States to 'work towards' incorporating this Fiscal Pact into the main EU framework and so the innovations here may end up as part of mainstream EU law in the future.[64]

The TSCG requires a number of things from the Member States but space, and considerations of relevance, preclude a more detailed examination of *all* of its provisions.[65] For the purposes of this chapter, the TSCG introduces a new, stricter regime of ensuring compliance with the SGP for those Member States who are signatories. First, and almost as a preparatory step, the Member States must ensure as a matter of national law that there is an automatic mechanism for national budgets to be brought into balance or surplus where they deviate from the SGP.[66] These measures are to be monitored by an independent body.[67] The rules surrounding a balanced budget should be implemented 'through provisions of binding force and permanent character, preferably constitutional'[68] in nature. Failure to comply with this requirement can lead to fines of 0.1 per cent of GDP being levied per year of non-compliance.[69]

---

63 This is also known as the 'Fiscal Pact'.

64 Article 16 of the TSCG reads as follows: 'Within five years, at most, of the date of entry into force of this Treaty, on the basis of an assessment of the experience with its implementation, the necessary steps shall be taken, in accordance with the Treaty on the European Union and the Treaty on the Functioning of the European Union, with the aim of incorporating the substance of this Treaty into the legal framework of the European Union.' This would mean that the Treaty's provisions should be incorporated by the end of 2018.

65 For such an analysis, see Paul Craig, 'The Stability, Coordination and Governance Treaty: Principle, Politics and Pragmatism' (2012) 37 ELRev 231.

66 Article 3(1) TSCG.

67 Ibid Article 3(2).

68 Ibid.

69 Ibid Article 8(2).

Failure to comply with the broader requirements of the TSCG[70] can lead to the offending Member State being brought before the CJEU by one of the other Member States who have ratified the Treaty.[71] The CJEU then has powers, to be exercised in a way consistent with its powers under Article 260 TFEU, to impose lump sums or periodic payments, with the latter being restricted to 0.1 per cent of GDP.[72] A major limitation to this form of enforcement is that proceedings may only be brought before the Court by one of the contracting members and not by the Commission. This, due to the highly politicized nature of such an action, is likely to severely limit the effectiveness of such enforcement. In some ways this could be seen to be a matter of enhanced peer pressure with the *potential* for an action dissuading Member States from breaching their obligations. However, a partial comparison could be drawn with the power of a Member State under Article 259 TFEU to bring another Member State before the CJEU for breach of EU law. Article 259 TFEU has been rarely invoked due largely to the political capital that would be lost through such an action.[73] This is, of course, only a partial comparison due to the very fact that the Commission cannot bring an action under the TSCG and so, if a Member State is unwilling, any breach will go unaddressed. This is a significant limitation on the effectiveness of the new regime.

The political tension underlying an Article 259 TFEU action is heightened when considering an action under the TSCG. This is again linked to the requirement to implement the Treaty through national law of a permanent and potentially (and even preferably!) constitutional nature. To bring an enforcement action under Article 8 of the TSCG is not only to suggest that international law obligations have been broken but also that a Member State has potentially breached its own constitutional rules. This would be a highly significant move on the part of a contracting state and, it is suggested, unlikely to be a regular occurrence. The monitoring and reporting by national authorities and annual reports by the Commission would appear to be a form of enforcement reliant as much on peer pressure as hard powers. In this way, although enforcement tools are potentially serious, they are still heavily reliant on political expediency and this again threatens to undermine the effectiveness of the new system of governance.

70 The requirement to have a balanced budget – defined by reference to the medium-term budgetary objective and the structural deficit of the Member State.

71 Article 8(1) TSCG.

72 Ibid Article 8(2).

73 For a rare example of such an action, see Case C-145/04 *Spain v United Kingdom* [2006] ECR I-7917. See Paul Craig and Grainne De Burca, *EU Law: Text, Cases and Materials* (5th edn, OUP 2011) 432.

As well as this flawed form of enforcement, the automatic correcting mechanism implemented into national law is intended to add an element of decentralized enforcement. By decentralized we mean that the measures are enforced by a national authority, rather than directly by an EU institution. The detail of how this mechanism is to operate is a matter for national law to decide. As an aside, it has also been suggested by Armstrong that the reference to the Treaty being incorporated as binding rules of national law, preferably of a constitutional nature, gives rise to the potential for national courts to also be involved in the enforcement of the TSCG.[74] It is not yet clear *how* such an action would end up before a constitutional court but the Treaty's preference for the rules to be incorporated into national law by constitutional means at least makes such an action theoretically possible.

The above reveals (at the least) a dual approach to enforcement with the fines imposed by the CJEU serving as a blunt form of compliance control. More significantly, the requirement for a self-correcting mechanism, enshrined in national (constitutional) law is an attempt to innovate with enforcement and regularize compliance, albeit with international treaty obligations rather than EU law in the strictest sense, within the framework of domestic law. The involvement of national courts would be a welcome development that could potentially legitimize action to enforce the tightened fiscal rules, something sadly lacking more generally in the Excessive Deficit Procedure and the Macro-Economic Imbalance Procedure discussed previously.

2.4 'Two Pack'

In 2011, in an attempt to further bolster and strengthen the objectives of the Stability and Growth Pact (SGP), the Commission brought forward proposals for increased coordination and surveillance of financial and budgetary stability within the eurozone. These proposals were eventually passed into law by a package of two regulations (so-called 'Two Pack')[75] that came into force in mid-2013. This complements the 'Six Pack' described earlier in the chapter.

---

74 Armstrong n 8, 604–5.

75 Regulation (EU) 472/2013 on the strengthening of economic and budgetary surveillance of Member States in the euro area experiencing or threatened with serious difficulties with respect to their financial stability [2013] OJ L140/1 and Regulation (EU) 473/2013 on common provisions for monitoring and assessing draft budgetary plans and ensuring the correction of excessive deficit of the Member States in the euro area [2013] OJ L140/11.

With a legal basis of Article 136 TFEU, and applying only to euro members, the new monitoring processes under the Two Pack are intended to coincide with and form a part of the new European Semester. One of the two regulations establishes a system of budgetary planning review, while the other is intended to apply only to those eurozone members who are experiencing 'serious difficulties'[76] with their financial stability.

The major innovation under the Two Pack is the requirement for national governments to submit, by mid-October of every year, a 'draft budgetary plan' to the Commission. The draft budgetary plan is not a draft budget but rather a document that details certain information about the budget including: key expenditure on health, education and employment; the targeted budget balance; and projections for expenditure and revenue as a proportion of GDP.[77] There is an overriding requirement, in Article 3 of Regulation 473/2013, that the budgetary procedures of the Member States are 'consistent with', amongst other things, any recommendations issued in the context of the SGP.

The mechanism for monitoring and potentially enforcing the new system of draft budgetary plans can be found within Article 7 of the second Regulation. The Commission is required to give an opinion on each of the draft budgetary plans in a timely manner.[78] If the Commission is of the view that a particular plan risks 'serious non-compliance' with obligations under the SGP then it can request a revised budgetary plan to be submitted.[79] It is important to note that although the Commission can *request* a revised budgetary plan, it cannot *require* the Member State to revise the plan or the budget underlying it. This, in practice, creates a severe limitation on the enforcement powers of the Commission in this area. Due to the sensitivity surrounding national budgets, a power of compulsion would have proved too controversial. As of January 2015, no national authority has been asked to revise its draft budgetary plan in accordance with Article 7 of the Regulation.[80] At first blush this may give the appearance that the new mechanisms under the Two Pack are acting as an effective preventative enforcement tool. Indeed, Vice-President Katainen of the Commission goes so far as to say that the fact that the Commission has not had to issue an opinion requiring a revised plan is

---

[76] Those that are subject to a negative judgment under the Excessive Imbalance Procedure or that are in receipt of a financial assistance package.

[77] Regulation (EU) 473/2013 n 75, Article 6(3).

[78] Ibid Article 7(1).

[79] Ibid Article 7(2).

[80] http://europa.eu/rapid/press-release_MEMO-14-2226_en.htm accessed on 1 March 2015.

'good news and it shows that our economic governance is working and having an impact'.[81]

The position is, however, clouded by the strongly political nature of the processes. To take one example, in the run-up to the deadline for submission of draft budgetary plans at the end of October 2014, the Commission had to enter into 'consultations' with Italy, Finland, France and Austria to clarify some concerns over the draft plans.[82] This eventually led to a finding that there were no cases of 'particularly serious non-compliance' amongst the draft budget plans of the 16 Member States required to submit such plans.[83] The Vice-President went even further so as to suggest that 'Member States have responded constructively to our concerns'.[84] This rhetoric of compliance and constructive dialogue does not appear to be present at all levels within the EU. Prompted in part by the Commission consultations, senior politicians in France took an extremely confrontational tone when considering the prospect of the Commission issuing an adverse opinion on France's draft budgetary plan. The French Prime Minister, for example, stated that '[n]othing can lead to. . . demands for France to review its budget. That's not the way it happens. France should be respected. It's a big country.'[85] Despite the fact that France is seeking a further extension to the already extended date of 2015[86] in order to correct its excessive deficit, the Commission still did not require a redrafted budget plan. This demonstrates that some of the political hurdles present elsewhere have transferred over into the operation of the new 'Two Pack' provisions. The political nature of the system established by the Two Pack was also revealed, in a rather direct way, by comments from the Irish Finance Minister in November 2014. He stated that Ireland would

---

[81] http://europa.eu/rapid/press-release_STATEMENT-14-344_en.htm accessed on 1 March 2015.

[82] http://europa.eu/rapid/press-release_STATEMENT-14-344_en.htm accessed on 1 March 2015.

[83] Greece and Cyprus are still covered by macroeconomic adjustment programmes and, as a result, do not need to submit draft budget plans.

[84] http://europa.eu/rapid/press-release_STATEMENT-14-344_en.htm accessed on 1 March 2015.

[85] Paul Taylor, 'France Does the Splits on EU Economic Governance' (2014), http://www.reuters.com/article/2014/10/22/us-eu-france-analysis-idUSKCN0IB0ZC20141022 accessed on 1 March 2015.

[86] France already being given, in 2013, an extension of two years to bring its excessive deficit under control. See the country-specific recommendation of France for 2014 published only three months before the French Prime Minister's comments: Council Recommendation of 8 July 2014 on the National Reform Programme 2014 of France and Delivering a Council Opinion on the Stability Programme of France, 2014 [2014] OJ C247/09, para 10.

not support financial sanctions against France in the event of an adverse opinion because 'France was always first up to support Ireland'[87] during Irish attempts to negotiate on its bailout. This demonstrates the naked political influences that underpin even the new regime.

The above analysis of the contemporary political environment suggests a number of things in relation to the effective enforcement of economic governance as implemented through the Two Pack. First, the system will only function effectively, and there will only be high levels of compliance, while there is political will for it to be so. There is a real danger that as we get further away from the events of the last economic crisis the political honeymoon of consensus is entering its final stages. New leaders are taking office who were not involved in the negotiation of the new processes and who are facing real anti-austerity challenges within their own political orders. The Greek election of anti-austerity party Syriza in January 2015 aptly demonstrates this point. Unfortunately, the system developed under the Two Pack has the same systemic problems for its credibility that impacted on the effectiveness of the old Excessive Deficit Procedure (EDP) and the Macro-Economic Imbalance Procedure (MIP). Second, the enforcement powers of the Commission are weak in this area. The institution plays a coordinating role but the lack of compulsion in a request to review a draft budgetary plan means that the Commission is reliant on its powers of political persuasion and on the political pressure that would follow from the request to review a budgetary plan. The recent decision not to reject France's 2015 draft budgetary plan, despite the latter's proposals falling far short of promised deficit reduction plans, suggests that the Commission's will is not as strong as it needs to be in order to properly enforce the new economic governance framework.

In summary, the over-reliance on political solutions and the lack of a rigorous or staged sanctions system is likely to fundamentally undermine the effective enforcement of the new rules of the Two Pack. The legal framework is structurally unsound for building sustainable credibility. A system that looked more robust and credible in the shadow of the financial crisis is now showing its cracks as a new dawn of political change looms on the horizon.

---

[87] Padraic Halpin, 'Ireland Says It Would Not Back Budget Sanctions against France' (2014), http://uk.reuters.com/article/2014/11/28/uk-eu-budget-ireland-france-idUKKCN0JC1RI20141128?mod=related accessed on 1 March 2015.

3. CONDITIONALITY ON THE PROVISION OF FINANCIAL ASSISTANCE

The devastation caused by the economic and financial crisis left entire Member States in need of financial assistance to prevent governments being left unable to service their debts.[88] At the risk of oversimplifying the issue, this financial assistance came primarily in the form of low interest loans provided by the IMF and the EU. The EU used the crisis as an opportunity to improve the compliance of these states with certain aspects of EU law and to require of those states certain reforms of their financial systems. This section will briefly explore two developments in the use of conditionality and how they fit into the broader themes of enforcement of economic governance. Again, this is not intended to be an exhaustive review of the use of conditionality but to consider its effectiveness as an enforcement mechanism.[89]

Perhaps most notably, in terms of the effectiveness of conditionality as a mechanism of compliance, the EU used the financial assistance provided to Portugal to ensure compliance with the EU rules governing the free movement of capital and freedom of establishment. Prior to 2011, Portugal had been subject to two enforcement actions for its use of 'golden share'[90] schemes that were incompatible with the Treaty rules on capital and establishment. One case concerned EDP[91] (an energy company) and the other Portugal Telecom[92] (a telecoms company) but the outcome in both was an adverse judgment from the CJEU. Despite these enforcement proceedings, Portugal had maintained its golden shares in the named companies. However, the financial crisis meant that Portugal had to acquire some 78 billion euros in financial assistance from the EU and, as part of that package, the Portuguese Government made an announcement in July 2011 that it would be withdrawing the golden share schemes that applied to both companies.[93] This was a condition of the financial assistance package.

---

[88] Most notably Greece, Ireland and Portugal.

[89] See Gunnar Beck, 'The Court of Justice, Legal Reasoning, and the Pringle Case: Law as the Continuation of Politics by Other Means' (2014) 39 ELRev 234.

[90] Walter Ringe, 'Company Law and Free Movement of Capital' (2010) 69 CLJ 378.

[91] Case C-543/08 *Commission v Portugal* [2010] ECR I-11241.

[92] Case C-171/08 *Commission v Portugal* [2010] ECR I-6817.

[93] Reference to the announcement can be found in a news article by Reuters: Andrei Khalip, 'Portugal Scraps Golden Shares in Utilities' (2011), http://www.reuters.com/article/2011/07/05/portugal-goldenshares-idUSLDE76414L20110705 accessed on 1 March 2015.

What is particularly interesting about the use of conditionality in this regard was that it proved to be much more effective in ensuring compliance with the Treaty than the traditional methods of enforcement under Articles 258–60 TFEU. Moreover, the nature of golden share schemes was such that the role of the *individual* in decentralized (private) enforcement was severely limited and, as a result, their direct participation through actions taken in the national courts was virtually non-existent.[94] Coordinated action by the Commission, in the form of enforcement proceedings, had brought about only limited success and progress was slow in eradicating non-compliant systems of corporate governance (such as demonstrated by the 'golden share' cases). Even the involvement of the Court (under Article 260 TFEU) had not brought about the necessary reform. Although, particularly by lawyers, political solutions are often dismissed as less effective than legal process, this is an example of where political process was able to achieve outcomes that were proving difficult for the legal system to deal with.

The second example, and one that was still developing at the time of writing, comes from another state that required financial assistance in the aftermath of the financial crisis. Greece's predicament was even less favourable and the bailout package is estimated to be around 300 billion euros.[95] As with Portugal, the Greek bailout was hedged-in with conditions relating to structural reforms and deficit reduction plans. Although deeply unpopular the austerity package of Greece seemed, at least in the short term, to be effective in ensuring a certain level of compliance both with aspects of EU law and with the structural reforms of the Greek economy. However, it is also important to note that *political* events in Greece in early 2015 have cast a shadow over the *long-term* effectiveness of conditionality as a mechanism for ensuring compliance. Due to the political and flexible nature of the conditional loans, the current Greek government is attempting to 'renegotiate' its loan agreements and change the conditions attached to the package of financial assistance. Whether that negotiation will be successful remains to be seen, but, if it is, this will undermine the effectiveness of conditionality as a means of promoting the effective enforcement of EU law.

It should be noted that conditionality has, as was seen with Portugal, the potential to promote compliance particularly in the short term. The Portuguese situation demonstrates that conditionality is best used for the

---

[94] Case C-463/04 *Federconsumatori v Commune di Milano* [2007] ECR I-10419.

[95] Including 50 billion euros of Greek Government bonds held by European Central Bank.

achievement of narrowly defined and suitably circumscribed objectives. Otherwise, as the Greek situation demonstrates, longer-term objectives can be compromised by changes in political thought and leadership.

4. MICRO-PRUDENTIAL REGULATION AND THE INCREASED AGENCIFICATION OF EU LAW AND ITS ENFORCEMENT

Established by Regulation 1095/2010,[96] the European Securities and Markets Agency (ESMA) is one of a suite of new regulatory authorities – the others being the European Insurance and Occupational Pensions Authority (EIOPA) and the European Banking Authority (EBA) – created as part of the reconstruction of the European financial sector after the economic crisis. Collectively, these bodies are known as the European Supervisory Authorities (ESAs). ESMA is tasked with, amongst other things, ensuring investor protection through regulating the securities market. ESMA has regulatory and supervisory functions. These powers are extensive and varied. This section will focus on the innovative aspects of its enforcement powers in the context of its supervisory role, as opposed to its ability to regulate and authorize national credit rating agencies.[97] Of the three ESAs, ESMA has been selected due to the fact that it has more extensive enforcement powers than the other authorities.[98]

The European Securities and Markets Agency has powers to develop guidelines and recommendations for national authorities. These national authorities must enforce EU law in the first instance. This is what could be deemed network enforcement as it is decentralized but guided by a central (EU) agency. Although these guidelines are instruments of so-called 'soft law' (i.e. they are not legally binding), those addressed must make every effort to comply with them and must explain any non-compliance.[99] This 'comply or explain' approach can be an effective form of enforcement in

---

[96] Regulation (EU) 1095/2010 establishing a European Supervisory Authority (European Securities and Markets Authority), amending Decision No 716/2009/EC and repealing Commission Decision 2009/77/EC [2010] OJ L331/84.

[97] This would be more concerned with enforcement of EU law *against* individuals.

[98] For detailed examination see, for example, Takis Tridimas, 'Financial Supervision and Agency Power: Reflections on ESMA' in Niamh Nic Shuibhne and Laurence Gormley (eds), *From Single Market to Economic Union: Essays in Memory of John A Usher* (OUP 2012).

[99] Regulation (EU) 1095/2010 n 96, Article 16(3).

itself as it requires outliers to identify themselves and they are therefore brought to the attention of the regulators. For this reason, and because of the fear of corrective action, the underlying ideology bears some hallmarks of command and control enforcement. In this sense the powers of ESMA are unusual as they are soft law within a hard framework. They promote the idea of complying with strict rules even though those rules are not formally enforceable. Tridimas, however, suggests that this focus on soft law (when mixed with the hard law powers discussed below) may lead to problems of 'accountability and legal certainty'.[100] While this is undoubtedly true, it may be more effective than an approach based on only soft or hard law. This is particularly true where the hard law regime is so susceptible to political interference. Indeed, this area of law with its myriad of institutions and enforcement strategies appears to be embracing a new ethos of a mixed regulatory response. This is an important shift from being overly reliant on hard or soft law approaches towards a more hybrid system.

Most importantly, for the purposes of this chapter, ESMA has unusual powers designed at ensuring the full enforcement of micro-prudential rules. Article 17 of the ESMA Regulation lays down a four-stage process for enforcement by ESMA where a national competent authority fails to apply EU law.[101] The first stage is investigatory, prompted either by a complaint or of its own motion. Within two months, the second stage is activated and ESMA can give a 'recommendation' to the national competent authority relating to the action necessary to bring the breach to an end. If there is still no resolution within a month, the third stage will involve the Commission exercising its discretion to issue a formal opinion requiring action on the part of the national competent authority. Finally, and in the absence of compliance with the Commission opinion, ESMA may intervene directly and address market participants in the place of the national competent authority.[102] In addition to these powers, ESMA can also take emergency action (under Article 18 of the ESMA Regulation) and act to settle disagreements between national competent authorities (Article 19 of the ESMA Regulation).

The powers under Article 17 have some similarity to the processes under the Excessive Deficit Procedure (EDP) and Macro-Economic Imbalance Procedure (MIP) in the sense that the process is staged and escalating.

---

[100] Tridimas n 98, 71–2.

[101] Regulation (EU) 1095/2010 n 96, Article 17. This process is exhaustively explored by Tridimas n 98, 72–8.

[102] An engaging commentary on the implications of Article 17 can be found in Tridimas n 98, at 72–5.

However, the important difference is that ESMA can, as a last resort, step in and intervene directly by taking the place of the national competent authority where the latter fails to address its own breach of EU law. Even if this power is scarcely used, it marks an important innovation with almost a guarantee that a breach can be brought to an end. By substituting its own action for the (in)action of the national competent authority, ESMA has powers that extend beyond those common under centralized enforcement. As Marjosola convincingly argues, even if the direct supervisory powers are not used, their mere presence can add incentives for national authorities to comply.[103]

As an important procedural safeguard, none of the powers described above affect the Commission's right to bring more traditional enforcement proceedings under Article 258 TFEU.[104] It has been argued that the Commission has been afforded a large margin of discretion in furthering or undermining the new regulatory powers of ESMA.[105] As well as being able to continue an action against ESMA's wishes, the Commission is also able to stop the process where ESMA wishes to continue. This complicates the process and may impact on the effectiveness of any effort at enforcement by ESMA as it is operating within the shadow of the Commission's powers. There is also an emergency brake, executable by the Council, where action by ESMA would 'impinge on the fiscal responsibilities of the Member States'.[106] This furthers the trend, identified in the sections on MIP and EDP, of increased involvement of a variety of institutions in the decision-making process. This, when coupled with the potential involvement of the CJEU,[107] demonstrates that the inter-institutional balance is particularly important in this area but the presence of the emergency brake exercised by the Council, on relatively vague criteria, may limit the potential effectiveness of ESMA's powers.

The novel and interesting powers of ESMA are constrained not only by the legal framework of the European Supervisory Authorities (ESAs) but also by the important *Meroni*[108] principles that govern delegation of

---

103 Heikki Marjosola, 'Regulating Financial Markets under Uncertainty: The EU Approach' (2014) 39 ELRev 338, 346.

104 Regulation (EU) 1095/2010 n 96, Article 17(4).

105 Carmine Di Noia and Matteo Gargantini, 'Unleashing the European Securities and Markets Authority: Governance and Accountability after the ECJ Decision on the Short Selling Regulation (Case C-270/12)' (2014) 15 *European Business Organization Law Review* 25–7.

106 Regulation (EU) 1095/2010 n 96, Article 38.

107 Ibid Articles 61, 69 and 72.

108 Cases 9/56 and 10/56 *Meroni v High Authority* [1957] ECR 133.

powers to agencies within the EU.[109] *Meroni* requires that there be no delegation of core functions or of powers to make legally binding measures of general application.[110] This is important not only for ESMA but for all agencies to come in the future. If the new powers of ESMA are to act as a blueprint or foundation for new innovative enforcement powers in the future then it is important that the powers are framed in a way that is consistent with past CJEU decisions. Given the proliferation of agencies – a phenomenon known as agencification[111] – this model of enforcement may spread to other policy areas.[112]

The enforcement powers of ESMA are undoubtedly important and wide-ranging. However as well as the procedural hurdles to be satisfied, the agency also faces significant problems of legitimacy.[113] This will mean that its actions will be scrutinized not only by market participants[114] caught by its supervisory role but also by some Member States. This is evidenced clearly by the challenge of the UK to the competence of ESMA to regulate short selling, an allegedly abusive practice[115] involving the sale of securities before they are owned in the hope that the price will fall in the interim.[116] The UK launched an action for annulment against the use of Article 28 of the Short Selling Regulation[117] which permitted ESMA to require those with short positions to disclose them to a national competent authority or to prohibit a natural or legal person from entering into a short sale situation. The UK alleged that the powers granted exceed the *Meroni* limitations on delegation of an institution's power to an agency and that the power to compel national competent authorities to comply

---

109 For commentary on *Meroni*, see Herwig Hofmann and Alessandro Morini, 'Constitutional Aspects of the Pluralisation of the EU Executive Through "Agencification"' (2012) 37 ELRev 419, 423.

110 Tridimas n 98, 60–62.

111 Hofmann n 109, 435 suggests it could be the 'high water mark of delegation'.

112 Niamh Moloney, 'Resetting the Location of Regulatory and Supervisory Control over EU Financial Markets: Lessons from Five Years On' (2013) 62 *International Comparative Law Quarterly* 955, 963–4.

113 Ibid 964.

114 Which can now take the form of an action for annulment under Article 263 TFEU.

115 For a balanced argument on the economic advantages and disadvantages of short selling, see Jennifer Payne, 'The Regulation of Short Selling and its Reform in Europe' (2012) 13 *European Business Organization Law Review* 413.

116 Case C-270/12 *UK v Council and European Parliament* EU:C:2014:18 judgment of 22 January 2014, nyr.

117 Regulation (EU) 236/2012 on short selling and certain aspects of credit default swaps [2012] OJ L86/1.

with Article 28 was founded on the incorrect legal base.[118] Although the competence argument held weight with Advocate General Jääskinen,[119] the CJEU decisively held that the measure did not breach the *Meroni* principles and that the legal basis was legitimate.[120] The CJEU rejected the opportunity to reconsider the 'fitness for purpose' of *Meroni* in the modern context of not only increased agencification but also the increased accountability of such agencies.

The short selling case is important as it demonstrates clearly the limits within which ESMA's enforcement powers are exercised. There is true innovation in the powers granted to ESMA but these are hamstrung if not by the limitations placed on its actions by *Meroni* then by the shaky legal basis for its establishment and the establishment of its powers. As Advocate General Jääskinen noted, the case law on agency 'needs to be re-positioned into the contemporary fabric of EU constitutional law'.[121] Until the Court recognizes that the new challenges faced by the Union may require a reconsideration of the limits of delegation to agencies, the enforcement powers of ESMA may be undermined by questions over its *sustained* legitimacy and the legitimacy of its decisions.

Another case has also recently considered the limits to and accountability of ESMA for its decisions. The close involvement of *market participants* in the work of ESMA, and in ensuring the latter's role in enforcement, was made clear in a recent decision of the Joint Appeal Board of the ESA.[122] The appellant (Investor Protection Europe (IPE)) sought to force ESMA to take action to address alleged breaches of EU law by a national competent authority.[123] The applicant (IPE) did this in the hope of furthering the objective of 'building. . . a common Union supervisory culture and consistent supervisory practices, as well as ensuring uniform procedures and consistent approaches throughout the Union'.[124] The case centred on ESMA's 'decision' to refuse to take action to deal with alleged omissions by the competent authorities who had in turn not pursued breaches of EU law by market participants.

---

118 Article 114 TFEU.

119 Who suggested that the measure should be annulled for lack of competence but not on the basis of the *Meroni* decision at *UK v Council* n 116, paras 54–9.

120 Ibid para 100–18 on legal base and paras 41–55 on *Meroni*.

121 Ibid para 60 (AG Jääskinen).

122 Ref BoA 2014/05 *IPE v ESMA* decision of 10 November 2014, the ESA Board of Appeal: http://www.esma.europa.eu/system/files/boa_2014_05_decision_ipe_sprl_vs_esma_2.pdf accessed on 1 March 2015.

123 Commission de Surveillance du Secteur Financie of Luxembourg.

124 *IPE v ESMA* n 122, para 18, citing Article 29 Regulation 236/2012.

The Appeal Board was keen to assert its own jurisdiction from the outset and, despite the similar wording between Article 60[125] of the ESMA Regulation (which provides for an appeal) and Article 263 TFEU on judicial review of EU action, gave a surprisingly wide definition to the admissibility criteria for an appeal.[126] The Board noted that an 'appeal' is a very different procedure to a judicial review under Article 263 TFEU and, indeed, an enforcement action under Article 258 TFEU. The impact of this is that market participants will have greater opportunity to challenge ESMA for a failure to act than is possible for other forms of EU (in) action.[127] This has the potential to improve the enforcement of the micro-prudential rules quite significantly, as aggrieved market participants can potentially challenge inaction by the national competent authority through ESMA and by forcing it to exercise its supervisory role.

By involving the market participants more directly, there is the scope for decentralized enforcement to play a role where centralized enforcement has failed. Unlike individual actions before the national courts (such as in direct effect or state liability claims) individual claims under the ESMA structure become *part* of the centralized enforcement schema. By broadening the scope of challenge, the ESA Appeal Board has potentially rid the ESMA scheme of some of the problems of almost unchallengeable executive discretion associated with Article 258 and 263 proceedings. This would appear a more sophisticated form of regulation with a myriad of institutions involved at different stages.

To consider enforcement in the whole under the ESMA scheme, it is important to look to the interconnected methods of enforcement. As will be seen each failure of an institution will activate powers of another to remedy: the national competent authority is first charged with remedying breaches of EU law as against market participants, using the framework provided by ESMA (decentralized enforcement). Next ESMA can recommend ways in which the national competent authority could bring an end to the breach (*light touch delegated* centralized enforcement – even, potentially, network enforcement). Should this fail ESMA can intervene (with Commission approval) and directly address market participants, with the proviso that the Council may prevent such action (*delegated* cen-

---

125 Article 60 reads as follows: 'Any natural or legal person, including competent authorities, may appeal against a decision of the. . . which is addressed to that person, or against a decision which, although in the form of a decision addressed to another person, is of direct and individual concern to that person.'

126 *IPE v ESMA* n 122, para 38. This would seem to run counter to some arguments previously put forward by academics, see Tridimas n 98, 81.

127 Ibid para 39.

tralized enforcement). Individuals can also challenge ESMA's failure to act before the Appeal Board (indirect decentralized enforcement). Finally, individuals can appeal to the CJEU (judicial enforcement).

The above creates a network of enforcement opportunities, escalating from recommendations from ESMA to local enforcement by the national competent authorities all the way up to centralized judicial intervention, with various parts subject to Commission endorsement. The presence and *involvement* of market participants, national authorities, EU agencies, the Commission, the Council and the Court adds legitimacy and real stakeholder engagement to the process that extends beyond a command and control paradigm.[128] As Marjosola notes, the use of command and control forms of enforcement are 'ill-suited for complex and dynamic environments such as financial markets'.[129] These rely much more heavily on the cooperation between the regulator and the regulated as found within systems that embrace network enforcement. The implication of this is that command and control type measures may be *more* suited to areas such as the EDP and less suited to others. This is reinforced by the engagement of multiple actors and institutions in achieving full compliance.[130]

CONCLUSION

Economic governance and micro-prudential supervision are areas that are characterized by detailed, technical rules and an almost impenetrable number of acronyms. It is easy, therefore, to lose sight of the broader patterns of enforcement that underpin those detailed rules. The crisis has given the policymakers an opportunity to take stock and to develop new methods of working. It also provided an opportunity for academics to take a step back and to reconsider the principles that underpin enforcement in this area. This chapter has examined a number of disparate areas including: the Excessive Deficit Procedure (EDP), the Macro-Economic Imbalance Procedure (MIP), the Treaty on Stability, Coordination and Governance (TSCG), the 'Two Pack' and the work of the European Securities and Markets Authority (ESMA). In some cases, such as between the EDP and the MIP there are strong synergies in both subject

---

128 Although the increased number of actors does add additional complexity that may undermine the effectiveness of the process.

129 Marjosola n 103, 342.

130 The national competent authorities, market participants, ESMA, the Commission, the Court and the Council are all involved – to a greater or lesser extent – in the process of the various enforcement powers. See Noia n 105, 12.

matter and approach. In other areas, such as between the mechanisms under the Stability and Growth Pact (SGP) and ESMA, the differences are more noticeable. Nonetheless there are certain themes that appear to be emerging in the post-crisis era, the most important being differentiation and a move towards a mixed regulatory (and enforcement) approach. The effectiveness of this shift will be subject to a large degree, as it always was in this policy area, to the political will of the Member States to play by and enforce the rules.

Due in part to the greater integration of their financial systems, the new regulatory landscape draws a very clear distinction between the eurozone and non-eurozone countries. This is the start of a differentiated enforcement strategy with breach of the 'rules' having different consequences for different groups of Member States. When we look more closely at the overarching framework that applies to *all* Member States then there is emerging evidence of differentiated enforcement there as well. For example, the medium-term objectives under the EDP and the in-depth country reviews under the MIP allow for differences in approach to surveillance and monitoring. As such, we can trace differentiated enforcement in two ways. Firstly, in relation to the *soft(er)* law mechanisms characterized by monitoring, there is differentiation for all. Secondly, in relation to the *hard(er)* law mechanisms characterized by sanctions, there is differentiation between the eurozone and non-eurozone members. We have not yet reached the stage of fully differentiated enforcement, but the new framework takes significant steps in this direction.[131]

The second central theme to have emerged, which is linked to the concept of differentiation, is the increase in the regulatory mix. This relates not only to the mix of hard and soft law but also to the mix of actors involved in the process *and* the more staged approach to the sanctions aspect of enforcement. As mentioned earlier in this work, what at first looks like a sharp move in the direction of 'hard law' in this area in terms of the proliferation of sanctions should not be misconstrued as a step back to a 'command and control' type approach or a step away from 'soft law'. We should move beyond this dichotomy between hard and soft powers which is perhaps becoming an outdated model for legal academics to apply. What in fact is happening is a move towards a regulatory mix of hard and soft powers that is more consistent with a 'smart regulation'

---

[131] As Conant n 7 has noted, some states have a 'compliance culture' which may require a different approach to breach than those who are happier to make a simple cost/benefit analysis of (non-)compliance. This may mean that further differentiation is necessary to achieve full effectiveness.

agenda that has been advocated by others, even pre-dating the financial crisis.[132]

The increase in inclusion of automatically triggered sanctions may prove to be the most effective way of improving compliance. Perhaps the more important development, which underlies the hardening of powers relating to sanctions and the greater automaticity, is a greater *political will* amongst the Member States to achieve more effective enforcement. The effectiveness of the new framework will, in part at least, remain reliant on the political will of the Member States to use and enforce them. There are already countervailing indications in this regard. For example, the rumblings from the French and Greek governments suggest the reforms to the fiscal scrutiny and the use of conditionality may be of only limited effectiveness in ensuring compliance.

In closing it could be seen that the analysis contained within this chapter has revealed something of a gap between the strength of the legal framework and the political reality of its realization. On the one hand there has been a great deal of experimentation and innovation in enforcement strategies and a dramatic increase in the number of instruments for economic governance and micro-prudential supervision. However, the principles underlying much of the reform are based on principles that have, in the past, proved to be fatally flawed for political reasons. Innovation in regulation is to be welcomed but only when it achieves the effective enforcement of the rules. Otherwise we risk repeating mistakes of the past. At a time of existential crisis as to the future of the eurozone and broader European project, the new rules relating to economic governance need to have credibility and authority amongst the Member States, market participants and EU citizens.

---

[132] See in particular, Robert Baldwin, 'Is Better Regulation Smarter Regulation?' [2005] PL 485, 502.

Conclusions: assembling the jigsaw of effective enforcement – multiple strategies, multiple gaps?

Melanie Smith and Sara Drake

The contributions to this edited collection tackle discreet areas of law and policy, although it is clear that such enforcement mechanisms, strategies and techniques do not operate in isolation but rather make up a complex web of enforcement activities that have evolved from, and in order to complement, the original dual track system. The non-linear, organic development of the various enforcement regimes have not followed an enforcement master plan, and the ad hoc design leaves enforcement regimes vulnerable to claims of conflict, failure, overlap and ineffectiveness. The Commission and, to some extent, the Court of Justice sit at the centre of this complicated jigsaw puzzle, but these are not the only actors of importance when it comes to delivering EU law and policies on the ground. Whilst most enforcement studies focus largely either on the Commission and its litigation role under Article 258 TFEU, or on the Member States' role qua Member States' transposition of EU law, it is clear that both these approaches offer only very limited insights into any understanding of the *effective* enforcement of EU law and policy.

This short collection demonstrates that beyond the Commission and Court, many other actors have an increasingly important role to play. Other EU institutions such as the Council of Ministers, the European Council, the European Ombudsman and the European Parliament all have an interest in the effective enforcement of EU law.[1] Networks and agencies, both governmental and professional in nature, are also heavily involved in the space between the decision to adopt EU norms and their realization in practice. Businesses and other stakeholders, as regulatees and regulators, are also crucial to the enforcement process. Finally,

[1] Chiefly in the areas of economic and monetary governance and how the Commission exercises its discretion under Article 258 TFEU, but also in a panoply of other areas, including their role in designing enforcement regimes which deliver.

civil society, NGOs and the individual, as citizen, end user, beneficiary and regulatee, also have a strong interest in binding Member States to promises made at the EU level of governance. Moreover, not all of these different actors share the same objectives in relation to enforcement of norms: quite often, a conflict may arise between regulatory values (getting it done, output legitimacy) and transparency, certainty and participation (constitutional values). Indeed at times entrenched positions regarding which of these imperatives are superior, or a lack of understanding that such norms can be complementary as opposed to conflicting, also inhibit forward momentum in the search for better enforcement regimes. Such conflicts need to be taken into account when assessing the relative effectiveness of each enforcement approach, and importantly, made explicit in research agendas. The question of whose vision of effective enforcement we are adopting, and why we think this perspective is most appropriate, should be clearly framed, ideally with multiple actors and perspectives being included in any one assessment of effectiveness.

Mapping the various actors, mechanisms, processes, strategies and behaviours that have proliferated throughout the EU with the aim of achieving effective enforcement of EU law and policy is an enormous research task in and of itself. Understanding the development of these enforcement activities, and how they fit into the overall puzzle of delivering EU policies and rights, is an essential starting point in assessing their relative effectiveness. Only when we have an understanding of this bigger enforcement picture, and how each of the enforcement activities interlock (or conflict) and contribute to the whole (or undermine it), does knowledge of detailed and isolated elements of enforcement become meaningful. It is in the assemblage of this bigger picture that the various disciplines must work together in order to construct meaningful research questions in relation to enforcement of EU law.

In Chapter 3, van der Heijden maps the evolution of regulatory scholarship as it has developed from command and control, self regulation and enforced self regulation, responsive regulation, networked enforcement and so on. It is apparent that EU enforcement regimes have sometimes drawn inspiration from these various developments (explicitly or implicitly) although without keeping the faith with each successive development's *raison d'être*. Each iteration of new enforcement techniques seems to be manipulated in order to inhabit the peculiarly Brussels way of doing things. Hence, notions of responsive regulation are turned on their head, and smart regulation and networked enforcement take on very different meanings. Even this gap between academic language and bureaucratic practice can skew discourses on effective enforcement.

What has emerged from the chapters is a fundamental (regulatory) shift in all policy areas from reliance on the command and control view with its focus on deterrence to an embracement of additional instruments, mechanisms and actors to promote compliance. Actions brought by the Commission under Article 258 TFEU or private litigation through the national courts are increasingly seen as a measure of last resort. A general consensus seems to emanate from the chapters that this 'mix and match' approach is the best way of achieving effective enforcement.[2] The concept of effective enforcement necessitates hybridity in regulatory strategy, regulatory instruments and actors involved in the process. Furthermore, with this broader focus on compliance, enforcement is also about *ex ante* processes (institutional and policy design, impact assessment) with multiple stages and a range of instruments and actors and not just about *ex post* monitoring, redress or sanction. Whilst many of the authors see this hybridity as an essential step in the drive for effective enforcement, there is a call for more interconnectedness[3] between the different strategies, with Smith and Cortés calling, for example, for patterns of infringements to inform policy makers in the policy cycle.[4]

It appears that the Commission is still the predominant actor when it comes to the enforcement of EU law and policy, but its task as 'guardian of the Treaties' is multi-faceted and far broader than that of simply enforcing the law via Article 258 TFEU. It will determine the overall enforcement strategy and mix of regulatory approaches across the entire policy cycle, and is driving the institutionalization of the new pattern of compliance and enforcement. It plays an important supervisory or coordinating role in the networks. The empirical chapters on networks reveal distinctions between the different types of networks and policy areas. The effectiveness of such regimes can depend on the extent of the Commission's presence or absence within the network. In contrast, some chapters argue that the effectiveness

---

[2] See, for example, the European Commission's proposal for a General Data Protection Regulation (to replace Directive 95/46/EC) which envisages a mixed enforcement strategy based upon network enforcement through National Data Protection Authorities (NDA) combined with private enforcement through the national courts, an EU agency (European Data Protection Board) and the ability of the national supervisory authorities to impose significant fines: Proposal for a Regulation of the European Parliament and of the Council on the protection of individuals with regard to the processing of personal data and on the free movement of such data (General Data Protection Regulation) COM (2012) 11 final.

[3] See Chapter 10 by Estella Baker, referring to criminologist Anthony E Bottoms.

[4] See the European Commission's Better Regulation Agenda: Communication from the Commission to the European Parliament, the Council, the Economic and Social Committee and the Committee of the Regions COM (2015) 215 final.

of the policy seems to decrease in policy areas where the Commission and Court (or access to court) are excluded (Eliantonio, Murphy). The Commission is accompanied in its task by national administrations, agencies (Murphy) and ombudsmen (Cortés). In many policy areas, there has been a proliferation of soft law to complement or even as a precursor to hard law (Eliantonio, Petrucci). The chapters also reveal other key factors for successful normative compliance such as the scope for mutual learning and trust, peer pressure and conditionality.

All the contributions appear to agree that the different enforcement regimes require efforts to bring along other connected actors in order for the regimes to be effective. This might take the form of direct involvement in the design of the regime (the Commission and Member State in legislating), mutual trust (Article 258 TFEU, criminal law, economic and monetary governance), perceptions of ownership and beneficial involvement (networks) and ultimately a way to successfully operate within the system (citizens, businesses, stakeholders and other EU institutions). All of these actors, however, require differing inducements in order to 'buy in' to the system of enforcement under examination, whether it is a sense of mission (Commission), preservation of sovereignty and a level playing field (Member State), or concrete benefits in the form of expertise, money, fair competition or access to justice (stakeholders, networks, citizens, businesses). These differing motivations for engaging in the enforcement regime, explicitly addressed in the chapter by Polak and Versluis, are often ignored in the framing of research questions on enforcement, but they directly affect whether or not the regime will be successful. The importance of socialization (a constructivist approach) is highlighted in relation to networks and by Baker in the chapter on AFSJ.

Most striking is the chorus of calls for the chosen regulatory system to adhere to the values shared by those who are either required to comply with the law or enforce it. In many chapters, a link has been suggested between (regulatory) effectiveness and legitimacy. For Drake, Petrucci and Baker, legitimacy seems to be pivotal. In the realm of private enforcement, Drake argues that the Court has taken some time, but now seems to have found the outer limits of the legitimacy of its policy and its doctrines. New constitutional provisions in the Treaty of Lisbon and the Charter of Fundamental Rights give it the opportunity to make this legitimacy more visible and align it with the regulatory goal of effective compliance with EU law. Where the EU now has clear competence to adopt criminal law to promote the effective implementation of EU law under Article 83(2) TFEU, Baker draws attention to the challenge in gaining legitimacy (and consequently effective compliance) across the EU where the criminal law is imposed top down rather than bottom up. She draws attention to the legitimacy problems of using enforcement as a justification of competence expansion (eg, between immigration, Schengen and criminal law) and warns of the danger of focusing too much on developing technocratic rules rather than creating a positive morality which individuals want, or feel societal pressure, to comply with. Likewise, Petrucci warns of the need for key actors in the enforcement process to consider the rules legitimate for their effective operation, although does not contend with the potential problem of capture by vested interests in designing a truly legitimate enforcement regime.

In order to ensure that the normative rules reflect such values in some policy areas softer frameworks are being developed with the aim of facilitating a more 'bottom up' acceptance of norms (Petrucci, Cortés). Both the Commission's strategy on collective redress and ADR revolve around adherence to common principles, rather than hard law. Some of the empirical chapters make important contributions in revealing the factors which render these new enforcement mechanisms more effective (Martinsen and Hobolth, Polak and Versluis), at least in the perception of those actors within the networks. A culture of informality seems imperative to ensure that networks operate efficiently and effectively, regardless of whether there is informality in terms of organization. It is clear that further empirical research is needed, particularly given the Commission's preference for network enforcement as a regulatory enforcement strategy.[5]

These commonalities demonstrate the importance of adopting an interdisciplinary and cross-disciplinary dialogue in order to answer the questions posed at the outset. It can allow for a more systematic evaluation to be made (Drake, Smith), act as a springboard for policy development in new areas of competence (Baker) and can prevent false premises or conceptual leaps being made (Smith). This is neatly demonstrated in the two chapters on SOLVIT: both concerned with the same mechanism, but which present SOLVIT in completely different lights. Martinsen and Hobolth study SOLVIT from an essentially top-down and horizontal perspective, concentrating on the perceptions of the SOLVIT centre's staff in relation to effective enforcement, whereas in contrast, Lottini examines the system from three different perspectives, using particular complaints to highlight the very distinct role played by different SOLVIT centres in different EU Member States.

There are also clearly some contradictions in evidence. For example, the use of softer governance methods bring problems of their own, with a

[5] See, for example, the Commission's proposal for a General Data Protection Regulation (to replace Directive 95/46/EC) n 2.

lack of uniformity in their implementation across the Member States, and the consequent temptation to ignore soft law initiatives as mere suggestions is perilous for the attainment of EU policy goals. There appear to be some contradictions between a desire for uniformity, that is a single rule set uniformly enforced (Eliantonio, Murphy), and the idea that discretion is crucial to the effective operation of some regimes. The mix and match approach favoured by some scholars (van der Heijden, Cortés, Drake) and in evidence in many enforcement regimes (Smith, Eliantonio, Cortés, Petrucci) is redolent with discretionary choices, which work against other imperatives such as predictability and transparency. Similarly, not all the enforcement regimes prioritize legitimacy as a primary driver of effectiveness. Indeed under Article 258 TFEU the Commission regards the absence of values such as transparency and participation as imperative to achieving effective enforcement, instead championing secret negotiations and mutual trust as prerequisites for effective compliance.

The tendency for lawyers to single-mindedly call for recourse to even more law in the face of ineffective enforcement regimes, and the tendency for regulatory scholars to ignore the subtleties of what happens behind the legal framework at the institutional level in framing the potential responses by those regulatees on the ground, compounded by studies on one type of enforcement (transposition) through the lens of international relations, creates gaps in understanding and false premises in the construction of research questions. The constant re-peddling of received wisdom regarding, for instance, what we understand about the universe of compliance, or using the numbers of cases referred to the Court of Justice under Article 267 TFEU from the different Member States as an indicator of an effective private enforcement system, or how effective the EU law system is compared with the non-comparable international law regimes are often the starting point of many studies into the new methods regarding enforcement of EU law. But these assumptions are not well founded and as a consequence pivotal gaps and conflicts in research findings emerge. Crossing these disciplinary divides requires greater normative understanding between researchers, greater knowledge of other disciplines and their research findings and even greater patience in constructing a common discourse to enable innovative methodology to research effective enforcement. Construction of silos of expertise without communication is counter-productive.

Research into effective enforcement of EU law and policy must move beyond examination of the governing legal framework, although this remains a vital starting point. Understanding why the law has developed in the way that it has, the resulting conflicts, failures and successes as a result of this overarching context, and the way in which actors manipulate or circumvent the governing legal framework are all necessary prerequisites to understanding the behaviour of other actors further along the enforcement chain. What happens when law fails, or when it fails to materialize, are crucial questions to be considered in the study of effective enforcement.

As the reach of policies has become ever more complex, and spread deeper and wider across many spheres of everyday areas of life, the gap widens between those setting the rules and those who implement them or who are the subject of them. Different strategies have been adopted across different policy spheres and between different legislative norms within the same policy field in order to bridge this gap, travelling the spectrum from hard law and sanctions to self-regulation, enforced self-regulation, responsive regulation and so on. The EU abounds with numerous enforcement strategies, from hard law to soft, from centralized litigation to individual litigation, from ADR to ODR, to agencies and networks (governmental and professional).

This collection raises a key question: are these the only tools in the toolbox? Are there other strategies or methods that could be adopted to guarantee effective compliance with EU law? If so, how do we make these methods work better? There is a tendency on the part of the EU policymakers to stick to the same enforcement methods without fully questioning whether they truly deliver. Granting new EU rights to individuals is politically attractive (eg, Commission proposals for data protection rights[6]), but this is often based on the assumption that private enforcement through the courts is an effective avenue for redress. In many policy areas, this is arguably illusory.[7] At some point, the EU institutions and Member States need to bite the bullet and put private enforcement on a stronger footing by addressing its inadequacies. Soft law is often seen an alternative to hard law for various reasons, yet the effectiveness of this method is unproven. Networked enforcement may be the favoured tool in the toolbox, but the sheer variety of networks operating in different contexts and with distinct functions makes it difficult to identify the factors that make it effective; there is no one size fits all. In a Union which has law at its heart, law can so often fail. So why resolve to introduce more (hard) law at times of crisis? It is clear for us that this edited collection is only the start of a new research agenda. There is a need for EU scholars to strike out further, to engage

---

[6] See Commission Proposal for new data protection rules which grants individuals rights and gives them the right to take a company processing their data unlawfully to court in their own Member State: Commission Memo, 'Stronger data protection rules for Europe', 15 June 2015, MEMO/15/5170.

[7] See further Chapters 7, 8 and 9 in this volume.

with other disciplines (eg, sociology, psychology, criminology) to find new ideas and understandings of why actors comply with the law, why actors chose to cooperate on a cross-border basis and what, for example, triggers individuals to enforce their rights through litigation or ADR. In this complex and increasingly sophisticated multi-level legal order, the challenge of ensuring that EU law and policy is effectively enforced continues.

Index